Promoting and Managing International Investment

This book provides an overview of international investment policy and policy-making, drawing upon perspectives from law, economics, international business, and political science.

International investment is a complex phenomenon with significant effects worldwide. Developing effective policies and strategies to attract investment in sufficient quantities and marshal it to contribute to sustainable development is a critical challenge for governments at all levels. This book's interdisciplinary approach provides fresh insights into the mix of policy options available to governments seeking investment to support their country's (or region's) development. As well as identifying ways to effectively design, implement, and assess policies to attract foreign investment, it explores how to manage foreign investment's effects. Various dimensions of international investment policy are discussed, including benefits and costs (economic, environmental, social, and political) of foreign investment, the significance of global value chains, state-owned enterprises and sovereign wealth funds, and the role of tax policy, investment promotion, and policy advocacy, location branding, investment treaties, and national security considerations.

Through its contributions to a new interdisciplinary understanding of international investment policy-making, this book will benefit students and scholars working in areas such as international business, international economic law, international economics, development economics, international development, and international political economy as well as being a valuable resource for policy-makers.

J Anthony VanDuzer is a Professor and Hyman Soloway Chair in Business and Trade Law at the University of Ottawa, Faculty of Law in the Common Law Section, as well as an Adjunct Research Professor at the Carleton University's Norman Paterson School of International Affairs. Previously, he was Vice Dean of Research at the University of Ottawa. He has also taught at the Queen's University International Studies Centre in England, the Westfälische Wilhelms-Universität in Germany, and the University of Waikato in New Zealand. He was a Member of the Academic Advisory Council to Canada's Deputy Minister for International Trade from 2002 to 2006. Professor VanDuzer has written widely on investment and trade in services issues and participated in technical assistance projects in these areas in transition and developing economies around the world. His most recent book on investment law is J Anthony VanDuzer, Penelope Simons, and Graham Mayeda, *Integrating Sustainable Development into International Investment Agreements: A Guide for Developing Country Negotiators* (Commonwealth Secretariat, 2013).

Patrick Leblond is CN – Paul M. Tellier Chair on Business and Public Policy and Associate Professor in the Graduate School of Public and International Affairs at the University of Ottawa. He is also Senior Fellow at the Centre for International Governance Innovation (CIGI), Research Associate at CIRANO, and Affiliated Professor of International Business at HEC Montréal. Dr Leblond is an expert on economic governance and policy with a particular focus on Canada, North America, and Europe. He has published extensively on financial and monetary integration, banking regulation, international trade, and business–government relations. He is the co-editor, with Demosthenes Ioannou and Arne Niemann, of *European Integration in Times of Crisis: Theoretical Perspectives* (Routledge, 2016). Prior to moving to Ottawa, he taught international business at HEC Montréal and was director of the Réseau économie internationale (REI) at the Centre d'études et de recherches internationales de l'Université de Montréal (CERIUM). Before embarking on his academic career, he worked in accounting and auditing for Ernst & Young as well as in corporate finance and strategy consulting for Arthur Andersen & Co and SECOR Consulting.

Routledge Research in International Economic Law

Defences in International Investment Law
Francis Botchway

WTO Trade Remedies in International Law
Their Role and Place in a Fragmented International Legal System
Roberto Soprano

International Challenges in Investment Law and Arbitration
Edited by Mesut Akbaba and Giancarlo Capurro

Trade Facilitation in the Multilateral Trading System
Genesis, Course and Accord
Hao Wu

Asian Perspectives on International Investment Law
Edited by Junji Nakagawa

Cost and EU Public Procurement Law
Life-Cycle Costing for Sustainability
Edited by Marta Andhov, Roberto Caranta and Anja Wiesbrock

Promoting and Managing International Investment
Towards an Integrated Policy Approach
Edited by J Anthony VanDuzer and Patrick Leblond

Preferential Trade Agreements and International Law
Graeme Baber

International Investment Law and Gender Equality
Stabilization Clauses and Foreign Investment
Sangwani Patrick Ng'ambi and Kangwa-Musole George Chisanga

For more information about this series, please visit https://www.routledge.com/
Routledge-Research-in-International-Economic-Law/book-series/INTECONLAW

Promoting and Managing International Investment
Towards an Integrated Policy Approach

Edited by
J Anthony VanDuzer
and Patrick Leblond

LONDON AND NEW YORK

First published 2020
by Routledge
2 Park Square, Milton Park, Abingdon, Oxon OX14 4RN

and by Routledge
605 Third Avenue, New York, NY 10017

Routledge is an imprint of the Taylor & Francis Group, an informa business

First issued in paperback 2021

© 2020 selection and editorial matter, J Anthony VanDuzer and Patrick Leblond; individual chapters, the contributors

The right of J Anthony VanDuzer and Patrick Leblond to be identified as the authors of the editorial material, and of the authors for their individual chapters, has been asserted in accordance with sections 77 and 78 of the Copyright, Designs and Patents Act 1988.

All rights reserved. No part of this book may be reprinted or reproduced or utilised in any form or by any electronic, mechanical, or other means, now known or hereafter invented, including photocopying and recording, or in any information storage or retrieval system, without permission in writing from the publishers.

Trademark notice: Product or corporate names may be trademarks or registered trademarks, and are used only for identification and explanation without intent to infringe.

Publisher's Note
The publisher has gone to great lengths to ensure the quality of this reprint but points out that some imperfections in the original copies may be apparent.

British Library Cataloguing-in-Publication Data
A catalogue record for this book is available from the British Library

Library of Congress Cataloging-in-Publication Data
Names: VanDuzer, J. Anthony (John Anthony), 1958- editor. | Leblond, Patrick, editor.
Title: Promoting and managing international investment : towards an integrated policy approach / edited by J Anthony VanDuzer and Patrick Leblond.
Description: Abingdon, Oxon ; New York, NY : Routledge, 2020. | Series: Routledge research in international economic law | Includes bibliographical references and index.
Identifiers: LCCN 2019055741 (print) | LCCN 2019055742 (ebook) | ISBN 9780367181840 (hardback) | ISBN 9780429059957 (ebook)
Subjects: LCSH: Investments, Foreign–Law and legislation. | Investments, Foreign (International law) | Investments, Foreign.
Classification: LCC K3830 .P757 2020 (print) | LCC K3830 (ebook) | DDC 332.67/3–dc23
LC record available at https://lccn.loc.gov/2019055741
LC ebook record available at https://lccn.loc.gov/2019055742

ISBN 13: 978-0-367-18184-0 (hbk)
ISBN 13: 978-0-429-05995-7 (ebk)
ISBN 13: 978-1-03-223834-0 (pbk)

DOI: 10.4324/9780429059957

Typeset in Galliard
by Swales & Willis, Exeter, Devon, UK

Printed in the United Kingdom
by Henry Ling Limited

Contents

Acknowledgements	ix
List of acronyms	x
Notes on contributors	xiii

**1 Introduction to international investment policy
and rationale for an interdisciplinary approach**   1
J ANTHONY VANDUZER, PATRICK LEBLOND, AND STEPHEN GELB

PART I
International investment's changing context   29

2 Trade and foreign direct investment in the 21st century   31
ARI VAN ASSCHE

3 Actors, institutions, and policy in host countries   51
KRISTA NADAKAVUKAREN SCHEFER

**4 State-owned enterprises and sovereign wealth funds:
An economic assessment**   74
STEVEN GLOBERMAN, PHILLIP HENSYEL, AND DANIEL SHAPIRO

PART II
Promoting international investment   97

**5 The economics of foreign direct investment
and international investment agreements**   99
EUGENE BEAULIEU AND KELLY O'NEILL

viii *Contents*

6 Attracting foreign direct investment: Location branding and marketing 117
LEILA HAMZAOUI-ESSOUSSI, NICOLAS PAPADOPOULOS, AND ALIA EL BANNA

7 FDI policy advocacy and investor targeting 138
MATTHEW DURBAN

8 Tax competition as an investment promotion tool 160
ALLISON CHRISTIANS AND MARCO GAROFALO

PART III
Managing international investment 181

9 National security and the political economy of international investment policy 183
PATRICK LEBLOND AND SÉBASTIEN LABRECQUE

10 International investment agreements 200
LUKAS VANHONNAEKER

11 Investor–state dispute settlement 223
J ANTHONY VANDUZER AND PATRICK DUMBERRY

12 Social and environmental issues in foreign direct investment: A legal and policy perspective 247
LORENZO COTULA

PART IV
Conclusion 269

13 Moving beyond disciplinary silos: Towards an integrated approach to international investment policy 271
J ANTHONY VANDUZER, PATRICK LEBLOND, AND STEPHEN GELB

Index 283

Acknowledgements

This project has had a very long development process and we are very grateful to all the contributors for their patience. The idea for a book that would provide a foundation for the interdisciplinary study of international investment was developed by Tony VanDuzer and Stephen Gelb, then at the World Trade Institute (WTI) at the University of Bern, during 2013 and 2014.

The first versions of many of the papers for the book were presented in the spring of 2015 at a workshop in Ottawa jointly sponsored by the University of Ottawa's Faculty of Law and the WTI with additional funding from the Social Sciences and Humanities Research Council of Canada (Connections Grant), the Centre for International Governance Innovation, and the University of Ottawa's Office of the Vice-President Research. The organizers would also like to acknowledge the letters of support provided by Foreign Affairs, Trade and Development Canada (now Global Affairs Canada), the International Development Research Centre, and Export Development Canada. We are very thankful for all this encouragement and support, without which this project could not have been completed. In addition to the contributing authors, we would like to acknowledge the important contributions at the workshop from the following people who added significantly to the development of this book: Roberto Echandi, Saul Estrin, Oonagh Fitzgerald, Howard Mann, and David Schneiderman.

Finally, we are very grateful for the help of Clare Flatman and Najib Khan, the research assistants who performed countless tasks in connection with the development of the project and the organization and delivery of the workshop. We also want to thank Zunaira Asif for her assistance with preparing the book's proposal to publishers. Finally, we want to thank Kristianne Anor and Amelia Arsenault for their invaluable assistance with the preparation of the book's final manuscript.

J Anthony VanDuzer and Patrick Leblond
Ottawa, October 2019

Acronyms

ADR	Alternative dispute resolution
ASR	Articles on state responsibility
BIT	Bilateral investment treaty
BKPM	Indonesia's Badan Koordinasi Peranaman Modal
CAD	Computer-aided design
CAFTA	Central American Free Trade Agreement
CBD	Convention on Biological Diversity
CEDAW	Convention on the Elimination of All Forms of Discrimination Against Women
CETA	Comprehensive Economic and Trade Agreement
CFIUS	Committee on Foreign Investment in the United States
CSR	Corporate social responsibility
DFI	Development finance institutions
FSC	Foreign sales company
EFIC	Export Finance and Insurance Corporation
ELAW	Environmental Law Alliance Worldwide
ESIA	Environmental and social impact assessments
FCN	Freedom of commerce and navigation treaties
FDI	Foreign direct investment
FET	Fair and equitable treatment
FIPA	Foreign investment promotion and protection agreement
FIRB	Foreign Investment Review Board
FPIC	Free, prior and informed consent
FPS	Full protection and security provisions
FTA	Free trade agreement
ECOFIN	European Union's Economic and Financial Affairs Council
GATS	General Agreement on Trade in Services
GATT	General Agreement on Tariffs and Trade
GVC	Global value chains
ICESCR	International Covenant on Economic, Social and Cultural Rights
ICJ	International Court of Justice
ICSID	International Center for the Settlement of Investment Disputes
ICT	Information and communication technology

IFC	International Finance Corporation
IIA	International investment agreement
IJV	International joint venture
ILO	International Labour Organization
IPA	Investment promotion agency
ISA	Investor–state arbitration
ISDS	Investor–state dispute settlement
KADIN	Kamar Dagang dan Industri Indonesia
M&A	Merger and acquisition
MFN	Most-favoured-nation
MIGA	Multilateral Investment Guarantee Agency
MNC	Multinational corporation
MNE	Multinational enterprises
MOE	Mode of entry
NAFTA	North American Free Trade Agreement
NCP	National contact points
NGO	Non-governmental organisation
NT	National treatment
OECD	Organisation for Economic Co-operation and Development
OLI	Ownership, location and internationalization framework
PCA	Permanent Court of Arbitration
PCI	Product-country image
PLN	Perusahaan Listrik Negara
PWC	PricewaterhouseCoopers
RAL	Regional autonomy law
REC	Resource-extracting company
RET	Emissions reduction target
ROA	Return-on-assets
ROE	Return-on-equity
ROS	Return-on-sales
RSPO	Roundtable on sustainable palm oil
SADC BIT	South African Development Community Bilateral Investment Treaty
SCM	Subsidies and Countervailing Measures Agreement
SDG	Sustainable Development Goals
SEZ	Special economic zones
SME	Small-medium enterprise
SOE	State-owned enterprises
SOMNE	State-owned multi-national enterprise
SWF	Sovereign wealth funds
TFEU	Treaty on the Functioning of the European Union
TiVA	Trade in value added
TRIMS	Agreement on Trade-related Investment Measures
UDHR	Universal Declaration of Human Rights
UNCITRAL	United Nations Commission on International Trade Law
UNCTAD	United Nations Conference on Trade and Development

UKTI	UK Trade & Development
USMCA	US–Mexico–Canada-Agreement
VGGT	Voluntary guidelines on the responsible governance of tenure of land, fisheries
WTO	World Trade Organization

Contributors

Eugene Beaulieu is Professor in the Department of Economics at the University of Calgary. He is also Program Director, International Economics at the University of Calgary's School of Public Policy.

Lorenzo Cotula is Principal Researcher in Law and Sustainable Development and Team Leader of the Legal Tools Team, Natural Resources Group, at the International Institute for Environment and Development (IIED). He is also Visiting Professor at Strathclyde Law School.

Allison Christians is Associate Dean (Research) and H. Heward Stikeman Chair in the Law of Taxation at McGill University's Faculty of Law.

Patrick Dumberry is Associate Professor at the University of Ottawa's Faculty of Law (Civil Law Section).

Matthew Durban is the Australian Government's Senior Trade & Investment Commissioner for India managing offices and staff in Mumbai, Bengaluru, Hyderabad and Kolkata.

Alia El Banna is Senior Lecturer in Marketing and Head, Centre for International Business and Marketing Research at the University of Bedfordshire.

Marco Garofalo is an associate in Quinn Emanuel's Paris office.

Stephen Gelb is Senior Research Fellow at the Overseas Development Institute in London, where he leads the work on private sector development.

Steven Globerman was formerly the Kaiser Professor of International Business and Director of the Center for International Business at Western Washington University. He is currently Emeritus Professor at Western Washington University and Senior Fellow at the Fraser Institute.

Leila Hamzaoui-Essoussi is Associate Professor of marketing in the Telfer School of Management at the University of Ottawa.

Phillip Hensyel is Lead Economic Analyst for Cascade Natural Gas Corporation in Washington and Oregon.

xiv *Contributors*

Sébastien Labrecque is Research and Public Affairs Coordinator at CPA Canada.

Patrick Leblond is CN – Paul M Tellier Chair on Business and Public Policy and Associate Professor in the Graduate School of Public and International Affairs at the University of Ottawa. He is also Senior Fellow at the Centre for International Governance Innovation, Research Associate at CIRANO, and Affiliated Professor of International Business at HEC Montréal.

Krista Nadakavukaren Schefer is SNF Research Professor of International Law at the University of Basel. She is also Visiting Professor at the World Trade Institute of the University of Bern.

Kelly O'Neill is Analyst, Regulatory Economics and Costing, at Canadian Pacific.

Nicolas Papadopoulos is Chancellor's Professor of Marketing and International Business at the Sprott School of Business of Carleton University in Ottawa.

Daniel Shapiro is Professor of Global Business Strategy at the Beedie School of Business at Simon Fraser University in Vancouver. He currently serves as co-editor of *Multinational Business Review*.

Ari Van Assche is Professor of International Business and holds a Professorship in International Business Policy at HEC Montréal. He is Deputy Editor of the *Journal of International Business Policy* and a Research Fellow at the Institute for Research on Public Policy (IRPP) and the Centre for Interuniversity Research and Analysis of Organizations (CIRANO) in Montréal.

J Anthony VanDuzer is a Professor and Hyman Soloway Chair in Business and Trade Law at the University of Ottawa's Faculty of Law (Common Law Section), as well as an Adjunct Research Professor at the Carleton University's Norman Paterson School of International Affairs.

Lukas Vanhonnaeker is a Post-Doctoral Fellow at McGill University's Faculty of Law.

1 Introduction to international investment policy and rationale for an interdisciplinary approach

J Anthony VanDuzer, Patrick Leblond, and Stephen Gelb

1. Introduction

International investment is a complex phenomenon with significant effects worldwide. It affects jobs, innovation, and productivity as well as communities and the environment. Developing effective policies and strategies to attract foreign investment in sufficient quantities and marshal it to contribute to sustainable development is a critical challenge for governments at all levels.

To help policy-makers take on this challenge, it is essential to understand international investment activity and investor decision-making. To effectively design, implement, and assess policies to attract foreign investment as well as to manage their effects, policy-makers must understand the variables that affect the feasibility, appropriateness and success of particular policy approaches in specific contexts. Our focus in this book is to develop a more integrated approach to studying international investment policy-making. We conceive of international investment policy-making as involving an interconnected set of issues related to policy choices about attracting foreign investment and how to deal with its effects, both positive and negative. This approach implies that we also need to analyse the process of policy formation, which means considering the actors (and their preferences) and the institutions that influence it. The goal is not to prescribe any particular policy, but rather to begin to flesh out the elements of an integrated framework for thinking about investment policy. As such, it aims to provide present and future policy-makers with a clear and more comprehensive understanding of international investment policy issues in order to ultimately improve decision-making.

Developing a more integrated approach to international investment policy-making requires combining the perspectives offered by different disciplines, if we understand a discipline as a system of thinking that is internally coherent in terms of the choice of objects of analysis, assumptions about their behaviour, and theories and propositions derived from these assumptions.[1] Despite its

---

1 Christian De Cock and Damian Doherty, 'Management as an Academic Discipline?' in Adrian Wilkinson, Steven J Armstrong, and Michael Lounsbury (eds), *The Oxford Handbook of Management* (Oxford University Press 2017) 461–480.

significance, international investment is largely examined in a partial and incomplete way by researchers working in different disciplines. Economics, management, law, and political science have approached the analysis of international investment activity independently of each other with distinct assumptions, theories, and propositions. Each emphasizes different aspects of the phenomenon, often those more amenable to explanation and analysis from within the discipline. Even at the level of how to define the subject matter of enquiry, disciplines diverge. As a result, the understanding of investment within each discipline is incomplete, both in terms of the questions asked and the conclusions reached.

Examples of how disciplinary silos limit our understanding of international investment are easily identified. International business scholarship has focused on understanding the contextual elements that inform management decision-making in multinational enterprises. It has considered the significance in this regard of domestic property rights and political risk in host countries, but has largely ignored the impact of international investment treaties and other international institutions, subjects that have been substantially addressed in law and political science research.[2] Legal scholars studying international investment have focused narrowly on investment treaties and their interpretation without regard to the work of international business scholars and economists on how investors make decisions, the factors on which they base their decisions, the impact of foreign investment in host states, or how decisions and impacts vary according to the nature of investments and investors. Most legal scholarship on international investment has even ignored other areas of legal research like international trade, taxation, and domestic law and institutions.

If we are to understand investor decision-making and provide the necessary underpinnings for effective state policies on promoting and managing international investment, we must study the topic in a manner that integrates legal, economic, political, and business factors as they operate in different local or national circumstances. The scope and depth of research in one discipline can be expanded and enriched by insights and perspectives from other disciplines. Assumptions and theoretical conclusions – regarding the behaviour of investors and states (and state actors) as well as the roles played by domestic and international institutions that characterize one discipline – need to be tested and informed by the application of understanding and research methods from other disciplines.

Admittedly, the suggestion that there would be benefits to an interdisciplinary approach to understanding foreign investment is not new. In 1989, economist John Dunning called for a shift in international business research to include more work from other disciplines – including law, political science, and management – to respond to the increasing difficulty of understanding how

---

2 Srividya Jandhyala and Robert J Weiner, '*Institutions sans frontières:* International Agreements and Foreign Investment' (2014) 45 *Journal of International Business Studies* 649.

Introduction to international investment policy   3

international businesses behave.[3] Nevertheless, despite international economic activity becoming ever more complex, relatively little has been done to develop an interdisciplinary understanding of investment in international business research.[4] In recent years, there have been renewed expressions of the need for greater interdisciplinary understanding of investment policies and processes, including by UNCTAD, the OECD, and the World Bank.[5] Yet, almost all research and policy analysis on investment still proceeds from only one disciplinary perspective.[6] Investment experts, whether in academia or public agencies, are often remarkably unfamiliar with the conceptual tools, issues addressed, and insights produced in disciplines other than their own.

This volume represents a modest attempt to contribute to the development of an interdisciplinary approach to international investment, through chapters that look at key themes in each of the four disciplines that have the most well-developed analysis of international investment: law, economics, international business, and political science. We acknowledge that, for the most part, each paper is written from its own disciplinary perspective with the occasional nod to other disciplines. In that sense, most of the book is multidisciplinary rather than interdisciplinary.[7] As such, it reflects the challenge that interdisciplinary research represents.[8] To address this challenge, we develop in the conclusion, based on the contributions in this volume, an agenda for further interdisciplinary research on international investment. With this agenda, we hope to encourage and facilitate future work toward a more integrated approach to studying international investment and the policies that govern it so that policy-makers can make more informed decisions. It is our hope that

---

3 John H Dunning, 'The Study of International Business: A Plea for a More Interdisciplinary Approach' (1989) 20 *Journal of International Business Studies* 411, 423–424.

4 John Cantwell and Mary Y Brannen, 'Positioning JIBS as an Interdisciplinary Journal' (2011) 42 *Journal of International Business Studies* 1.

5 UNCTAD, 'The Global Academic Policy Research Network for Investment for Development' (2014); OECD, 'FDI Qualities Toolkit: Investment for Inclusive and Sustainable Growth. Progress Report III' (OECD 2019); World Bank, *Maximizing Potential Benefits of FDI for Competitiveness and Sustainable Development: World Bank Group Report on Investment Policy & Promotion Diagnostics and Tools* (World Bank Group 2017).

6 To help remedy this situation, the Academy of International Business created the *Journal of International Business Policy* in 2018 to study from a multidisciplinary perspective the interaction between international business enterprises and governments, NGOs, and supranational organizations.

7 On the meaning of interdisciplinarity, see David Roth-Istigkeit, 'The Blinkered Discipline? – Martti Koskenniemi and Interdisciplinary Approaches to International Law' (2017) 9 *International Theory* 1.

8 There are strong institutional barriers within academic institutions that impede interdisciplinary cooperation: Joseph LC Cheng, Witold J Henisz, Kendall Roth, and Anand Swaminathan, 'Advancing Interdisciplinary Research in the Field of International Business: Prospects, Issues and Challenges' (2009) 40 *Journal of International Business Studies* 1070; Dunning (n 3) 422–426.

4   *J Anthony VanDuzer et al.*

improved decision-making will ultimately ensure that international investment contributes to sustainable development.

This introductory chapter seeks to set the stage for moving toward an interdisciplinary (or integrated) approach by comparing law, economics, international business, and political science across five variables: (i) the scope of the discipline's study of international investment, (ii) the values that inform research on international investment within the discipline, (iii) its characterization of, and assumptions about, foreign investors and their investment decisions, (iv) its characterization of host countries, and (v) its assessment of the impact of foreign investment within a host economy.[9] This comparative characterization's goals are three-fold. First, we aim to provide a broader and more systematic introduction to each discipline than is contained in any of the individual chapters. Second, we locate the individual chapters in the context of their respective disciplines. Finally, our initial comparative analysis illustrates areas of commonality and difference in broad strokes.

2. Economics

2.1 Scope

Around 1960, economists began to ask why multinational enterprises (MNEs) existed and why they engaged in FDI.[10] The focus for many years was generally limited to what Van Assche calls a 'national production paradigm', where the starting point is that firms produce goods solely within one country and export to foreign markets.[11] The narrow question for economists was in what circumstances would a firm set up a production facility in a foreign country to sell its goods there instead of exporting.

In seeking to answer this question, economists focused on identifying when foreign investment would be more cost-effective than exporting. Benefits of foreign production, such as avoiding border tariffs on imports and lower production costs, had to outweigh losing the benefit of increased domestic production in the firm's home market to serve the export market in terms of cost reductions from producing at a higher scale.[12]

---

9 This approach was inspired by a similar effort to understand administrative action using an interdisciplinary approach: David Rosenblum, 'Administrative Theory and the Separation of Powers' (1983) 43 *Public Administration Review* 219.

10 This shift is often attributed to Stephen Hymer, *The International Operations of National Firms: A Study of Direct Foreign Investment* (Cambridge University Press 1960, republished MIT Press 1976). See John H Dunning and Alan M Rugman, 'The Influence of Hymer's Dissertation on the Theory of Foreign Direct Investment' (1985) 75 *American Economics Review* 228.

11 See Ari Van Assche 'Trade and foreign direct investment in the 21st century', Chapter 2 in this volume.

12 Hymer (n 10).

Introduction to international investment policy 5

This kind of analysis, however, did not explain why a business would engage in FDI, such as by establishing a subsidiary in a country to produce and sell its goods, instead of licensing a third party to produce its goods for that market. The answer was provided by transaction-cost analysis. Beginning with Coase, economists recognized the role of transaction costs in decisions about whether a business would carry on particular activities within the firm or buy them from third parties.[13] Coase's fundamental insight was that where costs of contracting for activities become too high a firm chooses to perform those activities internally instead. In relation to foreign investment, the transaction costs of licensing production can explain why firms engage in FDI instead of contracting for foreign production.[14] Licensing costs include monitoring licensing contracts with third parties to ensure they are complied with and maintaining control over the firm's information and know-how once these intangible assets are disclosed to the other party to the licensing contract.

In the 1970s, two approaches to the economic study of investment began to emerge. Some economists focused on the decisions and strategies of firms, including, in particular, whether to internalize the production of goods based on ever more sophisticated transaction-cost analysis. They established international business as a separate discipline from economics. The international business discipline is discussed in the next section. Other economists who were interested in trade adapted trade theories to explain the existence of FDI, its location, and the internalization of production and services. In doing so, they adapted formal new trade theory tools developed in the 1970s and early 1980s.[15] This approach tended to focus on the impact of country characteristics on trade and the location of economic activity.[16]

New trade theory-based approaches also focused on firms as having distinct characteristics. This led economists to distinguish vertical and horizontal FDI. Horizontal FDI fits the national production paradigm discussed above. Instead of exporting, businesses establish production operations in a new market to sell their goods and services in that market based on an assessment of the costs of exporting (e.g. tariffs imposed by importing countries) less the cost savings that would be associated with producing for export at a larger plant in the home market (when compared to costs of operating a new, likely smaller, plant in the host country) and administrative and coordination costs associated with operating in a foreign market (e.g. communication costs between the parent company in the home market and the host-country subsidiary).

---

13 Ronald H Coase, 'The Nature of the Firm' (1937) 4 *Economica* 386.

14 Peter J Buckley and Mark C Casson, *The Future of Multinational Enterprise* (McMillan 1976).

15 e.g. Paul Krugman, 'Scale Economies, Product Differentiation, and the Pattern of Trade' (1980) 70 *American Economics Review* 950.

16 The theory of comparative advantage is the leading example of this approach, see Ari Van Assche, 'From the Editor: Steering a Policy Turn in International Business – Opportunities and Challenges' (2018) 1 *Journal of International Business Policy* 117, 119.

6 *J Anthony VanDuzer et al.*

Where FDI is vertical, a firm allocates a stage in its productive process to a different country. Vertical FDI's existence is linked to differences in access to production inputs (sometimes called factor endowments) and their costs in different countries. A country attracts FDI for a stage of production where it has a comparative advantage in the factor endowments related to that stage.

The most recent shift in the scope of economic enquiry is that economists no longer think of production as a single activity but rather a series of tasks that must be performed to produce a good. Global value chains (GVCs) allocate or fragment the production process to subsidiaries and third-party suppliers around the globe based on discrete locational advantages. MNEs produce intermediate inputs and final goods in the countries and places where they can be done most efficiently before selling them to world markets.[17] The supply of intermediate goods and services by one unit of an MNE to another constitutes intra-firm trade.[18] Vertical FDI is one way that MNEs build GVCs. Economists have begun to emphasize the interconnection between international trade and FDI through GVCs.[19] Changes in the global economy have driven this shift in perspective. The OECD estimates that GVCs account for 80 percent of global trade.[20]

Economists use rigorous empirical analysis, usually based on regression models, to test the predictions of their theoretical analysis, such as whether increases in trade costs or scale effects can explain FDI flows. In terms of the effects of FDI on the host economies where it occurs, economists similarly engage in both theoretical and empirical analysis, as discussed below.

2.2 *Values*

The economics approach to FDI reflects core values common to most economic analysis, especially efficiency.[21] Improvements to efficiency in the operation of firms and markets are understood to contribute to social welfare. In competitive markets, the point where supply and demand intersect (described by economists as equilibrium) is optimally efficient in terms of resource allocation; any deviation from this point reflects social welfare-reducing inefficiencies. The free market is crucial to efficiency. This theoretical result leads to the view that free trade is the optimal policy when it comes to the buying and selling of goods and services across borders, a conclusion that has wider support among

---

17 Eugene Beaulieu and Kelly O'Neill, 'The economics of foreign direct investment and international investment agreements', Chapter 5 in this volume.

18 Van Assche (n 16) 121.

19 Beaulieu and O'Neill (n 17); Van Assche (n 11).

20 OECD-WTO-UNCTAD, *Implications of Global Value Chains for Trade, Investment, Development and Jobs* (OECD, WTO, UNCTAD 2013) 23.

21 The values are inherent in general equilibrium models widely used in economic analysis: Laurence Boland, *Equilibrium Models in Economics: Purposes and Critical Limitations* (Oxford University Press 2017).

economists than any other policy conclusion.[22] In the international investment context, the related policy conclusion is that markets should be open to foreign investment with limited state intervention. Market intervention by the state is only appropriate where there is a market failure, meaning that the market does not operate as it should for some reason, such as anti-competitive behaviour by foreign investors.

Economists' conclusions typically depend on strong assumptions. For example, some traditional economic models assume the following: (i) the market is perfectly competitive in the sense that no firm has market power allowing it to influence the price of goods, which means that firms are price-takers whether they are buyers or sellers; (ii) firms are rational profit maximizers; (iii) firms make their decisions to buy and sell with full information regarding product, market conditions, and prices.[23] Economists recognize that these kinds of assumptions lack realism; however, their use reflects an emphasis on the normative value of efficiency as a goal, as well as two key methodological values of economists: theoretical coherence and mathematical rigour.[24]

2.3 Characterization of investors

In much of economic analysis, individual firm characteristics are only taken into account in a limited way. Traditionally, firms were treated as identical rational profit maximizers responding to a given cost structure by making appropriate decisions regarding their relative use of production inputs.[25] In more recent analysis, firms are sometimes distinguished by their productivity. Foreign firms and domestic firms in the host market are often not differentiated from each other. The nationality of a firm (or a firm's multinationality) makes no difference to its behaviour or its cost structure. There is often no consideration of whether a foreign firm faces distinctive circumstances that may affect its competitive position, such as additional costs of operating in the foreign market. As a consequence, 'international economic research has had relatively little to say about the wide variety of business strategies and structures that internationalizing firms adopt, and why this matters for policy'.[26]

---

22 Alan S Blinder, 'The Free Trade Paradox: The Bad Politics of a Good Idea' *Foreign Affairs* (January/February 2019) <www.foreignaffairs.com/articles/2018-12-11/free-trade-para dox> accessed 2 April 2019.

23 Jonathan Schefer, *The Assumptions Economists Make* (Belknap 2012).

24 David W Katzner, 'In Defense of Formalization in Economics' (1991) 3 *Methodus* 17. But see Donald Gilles, 'Can Mathematics Be Used Successfully in Economics?' in Edward Fullbrook (ed), *A Guide to What's Wrong with Economics* (Anthem Press 2005) 187.

25 Van Assche (n 16) 120.

26 ibid 119.

8 J Anthony VanDuzer et al.

2.4 Host-state characteristics

Often, economists view host states as no different from home states, in the sense that there are no institutional differences that affect foreign and domestic firms differently or that affect foreign firms differently than in their home markets. Any such differences are somehow captured in factor markets and related costs. The nature of the host state is not an issue of interest. As noted above, the state is ideally a minimal presence, allowing markets to operate. The state's role is to provide the conditions for markets to operate efficiently: property rights, contract enforcement, and public infrastructure, as well as input factors like education and capital markets.[27] The state does not act to protect domestic interests against foreign investors – it is not considered 'political' or 'nationalistic' in that sense.

That is not to say that host-state characteristics do not matter. For economists, the location of economic activity depends on country-specific characteristics. Under the theory of comparative advantage, for example, a country should engage in the production and export of goods and services in which it has a comparative advantage and import goods and services in sectors where it does not.[28] Recent work that takes into account firm heterogeneity has meant more of a role for the state. For example, state policy can encourage shifting resources from low productivity domestic firms operating in a host state to higher productivity foreign ones by creating conditions attractive to foreign investors.[29]

2.5 Impact of foreign investment in host state

In economic theory, the impact of FDI in the host economy could be positive on the basis that it leads to transfers of technology and other resources into the host-country economy, thereby contributing to improved productivity, and provides more competition to local firms, thereby increasing competitiveness of all firms in the host-country market and lowering prices. Local firms may benefit by gaining access to knowledge and other forms of technology brought into the country by foreign firms and connections to the international market place. But these gains may be offset where foreign firms crowd out domestic firms, leading to job losses and other negative consequences.[30]

The impact of FDI in particular host states is thus an empirical question, though the scope of enquiry is relatively narrow. Empirical research investigates the effects of FDI by looking at the productivity of foreign firms and their

---

27 World Bank, *World Development Report 2002: Building Institutions for Markets* (Oxford University Press 2002).

28 ibid.

29 e.g. Davin Chor, 'Subsidies for FDI: Implications from a Model with Heterogeneous Firms' (2009) 78 *Journal of International Economics* 113, cited in Van Assche (n 16) 121.

30 The theoretical effects and empirical evidence are summarized by Beaulieu and O'Neill (n 17).

impact on domestic competitors. Economists have also studied the effects of FDI on employment and product variety, as well as on suppliers to foreign-invested firms and their customers.[31] There seems to be a consensus that FDI is necessary but not sufficient for growth and development.[32] Local institutions and other local factors also play a role in determining the effects of foreign investment.[33]

The focus of economic scholarship has been on the impact of foreign investment on states rather than firms. One important consequence is that economic analysis has played a significant role in policy-making on international investment, compared to International Business, which has instead focused its attention on MNEs, as discussed below.[34]

3. International business

3.1 Scope

The origins of the international business discipline are described above.[35] It developed in dialogue with management theorists and focuses on the MNE as a distinct form of business enterprise that operates across borders in countries with different political, legal, and social institutions as well as market characteristics and cultures.[36] It is concerned with MNEs' internal organization, decision-making, and interactions with institutions and stakeholders in their home and host economies.[37]

International business scholarship initially developed from Hymer's early insight that, as a result of being foreign, MNEs experience additional costs as compared with local firms in the host economy – the 'liability of foreignness', which implies that the MNE must have some advantage or asset relative to domestically-owned firms to be able to operate successfully in the host economy. Dunning's 'OLI paradigm' is used by most international business scholars to explain the nature of those advantages and, as a result, decisions by firms regarding whether to engage in FDI.[38] 'O' stands for

---

31 ibid.

32 ibid, noting that spillovers are hard to measure and the evidence on spillover effects is mixed.

33 Eduardo R Borensztein, José R De Gregorio, and Jongwha Lee, 'How Does Foreign Direct Investment Affect Economic Growth?' (1998) 45 *Journal of International Economics* 115.

34 Van Assche (n 16), citing Daniel Hirschman and Elizabeth P Berman, 'Do Economists Make Policies? On the Political Effects of Economics' (2014) 12 *Socio-Economic Review* 77.

35 Dunning describes a longer history (Dunning 1989 (n 3)).

36 David J Teece, 'A Dynamic Capabilities-based Entrepreneurial Theory of the Multinational Enterprise' (2014) 9 *Journal International Business Studies* 29; John Dunning and Sarianna Lundan, *Multinational Enterprises in the Global Economy* (2nd edn, Edward Elgar 2008).

37 ibid Dunning and Lundan.

38 John H Dunning, 'The Eclectic Paradigm as an Envelope for Economic and Business Theories of MNE Activity' (2000) 9 *International Business Review* 163; John Cantwell and Rajnessh Narula, 'Revisiting the Eclectic Paradigm New Developments and Current Issues' in John Cantwell and Rajnessh Narula (ed), *International Business and the Eclectic Paradigm Developing the OLI Framework* (Routledge 2003).

10   *J Anthony VanDuzer et al.*

a firm's *ownership* of unique intangible assets, including but not limited to intellectual property, that give it a competitive advantage when operating in a host-country market. 'L' stands for advantages existing in a particular *location*, including access to both physical assets, like natural resources, and created assets, like a skilled work force or intellectual property, as well as other attributes, such as low-cost labour and market size. Finally, 'I' refers to *internalization* advantages, meaning those benefits that arise from an MNE exploiting its ownership advantages internally in a particular location, rather than contracting with local firms. The basic proposition arising out of the OLI framework is that firms will only engage in FDI when they have sufficient ownership advantages and it is most efficient to exploit them within the firm in a foreign market that offers locational advantages.

In this so-called 'eclectic paradigm', the nature of the OLI factors, and how they interact, is different for each firm and the context in which they operate. For this purpose, the context includes the characteristics of a firm's home country or region and of the country or region in which they seek to invest, as well as their own characteristics, including the industry in which they operate and the nature of their activities. Significantly, the way in which the paradigm applies also depends on the firm's objectives and the strategies it employs to achieve those objectives. By considering the OLI paradigm's elements in light of these contextual factors, international business scholars develop hypotheses regarding how, why, and where FDI occurs and which firms are likely to do it so that they can be analysed (and tested) empirically.

The analysis of the interaction between the three factors in the OLI paradigm is not consistently well developed in international business scholarship. Researchers often focus primarily on one factor. For example, some scholars have focused on the internalization of transaction costs and how they are managed with a view to explaining what activities will be carried on internally,[39] while others have focused on cultural factors in business decision-making[40] Dunning characterizes the OLI paradigm as a common analytical framework that is an 'envelope' capable of accommodating a wide range of theoretical approaches that, in his view, are complementary.[41] Indeed, he argues that 'any comprehensive explanation of the existence and growth of the contemporary MNE must almost inevitably be judiciously pluralistic'.[42]

---

39   David J Teece, 'A Dynamic Capabilities-based Entrepreneurial Theory of the Multinational Enterprise' (2014) 9 *Journal of International Business Studies* 29; Oliver Williamson 'The Modern Corporation: Origins, Evolution, Attributes' (1981) *Journal Economics Literature* 1537.

40   Cantwell and Brannen (n 4) 2.

41   John H Dunning, 'The Eclectic Paradigm as an Envelope for Economic and Business Theories of MNE Activity' (2000) 9 *International Business Review* 166.

42   ibid. See also John Cantwell (ed), *The Eclectic Paradigm: A Framework for Synthesizing and Comparing Theories of International Business from Different Disciplines or Perspectives* (Palgrave Macmillan 2015).

Introduction to international investment policy 11

In early international business scholarship many aspects of MNE heterogeneity were not accounted for. More recently, some international business scholars have broadened the discipline's scope to incorporate dynamic interactions. For example, a number of scholars have sought to examine the impact of FDI on MNEs and their evolution, and the response of MNEs to domestic reactions to their investment from local competitors (e.g. when the latter combine their operations through mergers to increase their market power in relation to MNEs).[43] Teece has argued for moving beyond the traditional approach of internalization scholars, which assumes that markets exist even if they function imperfectly, to acknowledge that in the global economy a firm's success may depend on creating markets for new or existing products, such as by influencing demand from consumers.[44] These kinds of approaches recognize better the heterogeneity of MNEs as well as the diverse institutional, cultural, and linguistic contexts of the home and host countries in which they operate.[45]

3.2 Values

International business is preoccupied with understanding how MNEs behave and, in particular, the determinants of their success. In this sense, international business is largely descriptive rather than normative, unlike economics. Most scholarship views MNEs as more efficient and innovative than domestic businesses, but acknowledges that positive effects of MNE activities can be more than offset by negative ones. In particular, where MNE advantages include substantial market power or even monopolies, their activities may be welfare reducing.[46] State intervention may be needed to attract and obtain local benefits from MNE investment. The role of national and other governments is to adopt policies to attract foreign investment and encourage re-investment. Often, the focus, as with economists, is on the state providing the rudiments for markets to function efficiently, such as secure property rights. State intervention is also justified to address market imperfections, such as the failure of market participants to pay for the costs of their behaviour or information problems that increase transaction uncertainty and costs.[47] But international business scholarship is not limited to and often not focused on markets and ensuring that they work.

---

43 e.g. John H Dunning, 'The Geographical Sources of Competitiveness of Firms: Some Results of a New Survey' (1996) 5 *Transnational Corporations* 1.

44 Teece (n 39) 12.

45 ibid 24, 25. Mats Forsgren, *Theories of the Multinational Firm: A Multidimensional Creature in the Global Economy* (3rd edn, Elgar 2017).

46 Dunning and Lundan (n 36) 637. Effective competition law and requirements related to corporate social responsibility may be needed to address anti-competitive behaviour and its consequences.

47 Peter J Buckley, 'Towards a Theoretically-based FDI Policy' (2018) 2 *Journal of International Business Policy* 184, 185.

12   J Anthony VanDuzer et al.

Illuminating optimal government policy options has not been the discipline's focus. The prescriptive goal of most international business scholarship is to explain how MNEs can improve firm performance given their distinctive advantages and their costs.[48] Whether this is a good thing or a bad thing for the countries in which they operate or what policy options could be adopted to encourage investment and benefit from it have not been a particular focus of most international business scholarship, until recently.[49]

In terms of methodological values, international business is open to a wide range of research methodologies and theoretical approaches. It tests theories using comparative analysis and case studies as well as conventional empirical economic research techniques, like regression analysis.

3.3 Characteristics of investors

MNEs' nature, management, and how they structure themselves to operate in multiple distinctive environments are the key focus of international business. Recently, state-owned enterprises have been a particular focus.[50] By contrast, until recently, economics has tended not to incorporate much firm heterogeneity into its models and so has had much less to say on firm strategy and other issues internal to the firm. As well, international business acknowledges that MNEs can be networks that carry on some of their activities within a single firm while others are contracted for. The relationships that MNEs have with other firms in carrying out their activities is a subject for enquiry. By contrast, economists tend to look at firms as single entities.[51]

3.4 Host-state characteristics

Because of their focus on locational advantages, international business scholars view states as a complex of public institutions with distinctive characteristics. These institutions support, to varying degrees, the establishment and regulation of markets for goods, services, and production inputs. Public institutions affect

---

48 Brouthers, Brouthers, and Werner suggest that the OLI paradigm has a normative dimension in that it can be shown that firms that make entry mode choices based on the paradigm are more successful (Lance Brouthers, Keith Brouthers, and Steve Werner 'Is Dunning's Eclectic Framework Descriptive or Normative?' (1999) 30 *Journal of International Business Studies* 831).

49 Sariana Lundan, 'From the Editor: Engaging International Business Scholars with Public Policy Issues' (2018) 1 *Journal of International Business Policy* 1; Van Assche (n 16); Van Assche (n 11); and Steven Globerman, Phillip Hensyel, and Daniel Shapiro 'State-owned enterprises and sovereign wealth funds: An economic assessment', Chapter 4 in this volume, are examples of International Business scholarship that focus on policy issues.

50 ibid Globerman, Hensyel, and Shapiro.

51 Van Assche (n 16) 121–122; Peter J Buckley, *The Global Factory: Networked Multinational Enterprises in the Modern Global Economy* (Elgar 2018).

a range of local determinants of locational advantage, including infrastructure provision, contract and property rights enforcement, the skill level of the local workforce, its capacity for innovative work, taxation, and macroeconomic management (e.g. exchange rate and inflation policy).[52] In short, host state as well as home-state heterogeneity is an essential feature of international business's analysis of MNE decision-making related to investment.

Much international business scholarship treats state characteristics as fixed; however, recently, dynamic considerations such as policy changes to enable, facilitate, and even steer MNE investment have been addressed, including international investment treaties.[53]

Two chapters in this volume focus on specific host-state investment policies. Durban's chapter uses case studies of investment promotion authorities in Australia and Indonesia to analyse the role of such authorities in promoting investment, including through their involvement in the policy-making process.[54] Hamzaoui-Essoussi, Papadopoulos, and El Banna draw on marketing scholarship to explain the nature of MNE location choice emphasizing emotional factors and, in that context, discuss location-branding strategies.[55]

3.5 Impact of FDI in host state

Until very recently, international business scholars have tended not to focus whether the behaviour of firms is good or bad for the countries in which they operate. Their overwhelming interest has been in what Van Assche calls the 'private perspective', meaning firm performance.[56]

In general, the impact of international investment in host states is assumed to be positive. MNEs are thought to supplement domestic sources of investment and enhance competition in local markets, lowering prices and forcing all market players to become more efficient. MNEs bring their ownership advantages along with their investments and these can spill over into the local economy through the transfer of technology and in other ways.[57] More recent work has shown that outward FDI can have substantial benefits for firms, including those associated

---

52 Dunning and Lundan (n 36).

53 e.g. Guttorm Schjelderup and Frank Stähler, 'Investor State Dispute Settlement and Multi-national Firm Behavior' (2017) Discussion Papers 2017/4, Norwegian School of Economics, Department of Business and Management Science.

54 Matthew Durban, 'FDI policy advocacy and investor targeting', Chapter 7 in this volume.

55 Leila Hamzaoui-Essoussi, Nicolas Papadopoulos, and Alia El Banna, 'Attracting foreign direct investment: Location branding and marketing', Chapter 6 in this volume.

56 Van Assche (n 16), 118.

57 Beaulieu and O'Neill (n 17). See also Gordon Hansen, 'Should Countries Promote Foreign Investment' (United Nations 2001) UNCTAD/Center for International Development, Harvard University G-24 Discussion Paper No 9 <http://unctad.org/en/docs/pogdsmdpbg24d9.en.pdf> accessed 13 May 2019.

14   *J Anthony VanDuzer et al.*

with the scale of operations, enhanced efficiency, and backwards knowledge transfer. These benefits to firms may have positive spillovers in their home states.[58] The particular effects of FDI on a host state, however, depend on the characteristics of the state, including, in particular, its institutions, as discussed above, and to what extent they contribute to a state's ability to absorb the benefits of FDI.

4. Law

4.1 Scope

The study of international investment law has been limited largely to understanding the legal effects of the almost 3,000 bilateral investment treaties (BITs) and more than 350 preferential trade and other treaties with investment provisions (together referred to as international investment agreements (IIAs)) that girdle the globe and their interpretation by investor–state arbitration tribunals.[59] Most scholarship has focused on developing descriptive and critical analyses of (i) the scope of state obligations to protect foreign investors in IIAs as determined by the decisions of investor–state tribunals in individual cases and (ii) the investor–state arbitration process itself. The chapters in this volume by Vanhonnaeker on IIA protections and by VanDuzer and Dumberry on investor–state dispute settlement are representative in this regard.[60]

Much recent scholarship has been concerned with the extent to which investor protection provisions in IIAs threaten the ability of states to act in the public interest, including to achieve non-economic policy goals like protecting health, the environment, and human and labour rights.[61] A wide variety of proposals have been made to reform IIAs to better protect state flexibility to address public concerns without breaching their treaty obligations.[62] Similarly, the transparency, fairness, and efficiency of investor–state arbitration as well as the independence of arbitrators have been the subject of scholarly concern and proposals for reform.[63]

---

58 Simona Iammarino, 'FDI and Regional Development Policy' (2018) 1 *Journal of International Business Studies* 157, 161.

59 At 31 December 2017, UNCTAD, *Recent Developments in the International Investment Regime*, IIA Issues Note, no 1 (United Nations 2018) 2.

60 Lukas Vanhonnaeker, 'International investment agreements', Chapter 10 in this volume; J Anthony VanDuzer and Patrick Dumberry, 'Investor–state dispute settlement', Chapter 11 in this volume.

61 e.g. Marie-Claire Cordonier Segger, Markus Gehring, and Andrew Newcombe (eds), *Sustainable Development in World Investment Law* (Wolters Kluwer 2011).

62 Vanhonnaeker (n 60).

63 ibid; VanDuzer and Dumberry (n 60).

Introduction to international investment policy   15

In the last few years, there has been some work by legal scholars enquiring into the political economy of IIA making[64] as well as the economics of treaty provisions and the effects of investment treaties.[65] In terms of effects, by far the greatest concern of lawyers, as well as political scientists and economists, has been to investigate to what extent signing an IIA actually promotes foreign investment into party states. The empirical literature on this question includes regression analysis of investment flow data as well as qualitative work using surveys.[66] The effects of foreign investment on host-state economies, however, have largely been ignored by investment law scholars. Other lawyers with an interest in development have considered investment as an aspect of their work, but this kind of analysis has seldom been integrated into investment law scholarship.[67] Cotula's chapter for this volume is an exception in that regard; he investigates the social and environmental impacts of foreign investment.[68]

Surprisingly little attention has been paid by investment law scholars to other legal rules and institutions affecting investment and its effects, though this is starting to change. For example, while tax treatment of foreign investment and international tax treaties allocating tax jurisdiction between countries can affect investment decision-making, investment scholars rarely consider tax issues. Tax issues are addressed in their own specialized legal literature, as demonstrated by Christians and Garofolo's chapter in this volume, which looks at how countries use their tax systems to compete for foreign investment and how international rules could discipline such competition.[69]

Similarly, international trade law and its study have tended to evolve separately from investment law. The modern multilateral trading system began

---

64 e.g. Lauge Poulsen, 'Politics of Investment Treaty Arbitration' in Tom Schultz and Federico Ortino (eds), *Oxford Handbook of International Arbitration* (Oxford University Press forthcoming); 'Part II: The Politics of International Investment Treaty Making' in Tomer Broude, Marc Busch, and Ameila Porges (eds), *The Politics of International Economic Law* (Cambridge University Press 2011).

65 e.g. Jonathan Bonnitcha, *Substantive Protection under Investment Treaties: A Legal and Economic Analysis* (Cambridge University Press 2014); Olivier De Schutter, Johan Swinnen, and Jan Wouters (eds), *Foreign Direct Investment and Human Development: The Law and Economics of International Investment Agreements* (Routledge 2013).

66 Beaulieu and O'Neill (n 17); Jason Webb Yackee, 'Do Bilateral Investment Treaties Promote Foreign Direct Investment? Some Hints from Alternative Evidence' (2010) 51 *Virginia Journal of International Law* 397.

67 e.g. David M Trubek and Alvaro Santos (eds), *The New Law and Economic Development: A Critical Appraisal* (Cambridge University Press 2006), where the editors describe law and development as a discipline at the intersection of law, economics, and institutions (4).

68 Lorenzo Cotula, 'Social and environmental issues in foreign direct investment: A legal and policy perspective', Chapter 12 in this volume.

69 Allison Christians and Marco Garofalo, 'Tax competition as an investment promotion tool', Chapter 8 in this volume. A rare example of cross over is Julien Chaisse, *International Investment Law and Taxation: From Coexistence to Cooperation*, (2016) E15 Working Paper 24 <http://e15initiative.org/publications/international-investment-law-taxation-coexistence-cooperation/> accessed 16 August 2019.

16 *J Anthony VanDuzer et al.*

with the 1947 General Agreement on Tariffs and Trade.[70] A more ambitious project to establish an International Trade Organization administering rules that included investment was not successful.[71] As a result, investment rules have developed, for the most part, in IIAs between two or more countries. To this day, there are no multilateral rules on investment comparable to those found in IIAs. Legal scholars have tended not to deal with both trade and investment law, despite the complex interplay between trade and investment activity as illustrated by the discussion of global value chains in Van Assche's chapter for this volume and the fact that trade and investment share some common principles, like prohibiting nationality-based discrimination.[72] A few legal scholars have begun to break down this separation between trade and investment scholarship.[73]

Another area curiously ignored by most international investment law scholars is domestic law.[74] Domestic sources of investment law are canvassed by Nadakavukaren Shefer in her chapter for this volume.[75] Her chapter is also distinguished from most investment law scholarship because it provides a broader characterization of international investment law, including some trade law rules as well as soft law instruments and engages in an enquiry into the nature of legal rules and the processes through which they are formed. Adopting some aspects of this approach, Cotula examines the role of international law, domestic law, and international soft law standards in relation to areas of law not considered by international investment law scholars: environmental impact assessments for investments as well as land and labour rights.[76]

4.2 *Values*

The legal analysis of international investment has been mainly concerned with the extent to which investment treaties can contribute to enhancing certainty and predictability in state behaviour in relation to foreign investors. In part, this is to be achieved by obligations ensuring that foreign investors are treated in accordance with basic standards of fairness, including freedom

---

70 General Agreement on Tariffs and Trade (1947) 55 UNTS 194.

71 Final Act of the United Nations Conference on Trade and Employment (the Havana Charter) (1948) E/CONF.2/78.

72 Van Assche (n 11); Nicholas Dimascio and Joost Pauwelyn, 'Non-Discrimination in Trade and Investment Treaties: Worlds Apart or Two Sides of the Same Coin?' (2008) 102 *American Journal of International Law* 48.

73 e.g. Jurgen Kurtz, *The WTO and International Investment Law: Converging Systems* (Cambridge University Press 2016).

74 There are some exceptions, e.g. Jeswald Salacuse, *The Three Laws of International Investment: National, Contractual, and International Frameworks for Foreign Capital* (Oxford University Press 2013).

75 Krista Nadakavukaren Schefer, 'Actors, institutions, and policy in host countries', Chapter 3 in this volume.

76 Cotula (n 68).

Introduction to international investment policy 17

from discrimination and procedural due process.[77] Certainty and predictability are also to be achieved by extending treaty protection to all forms of property rights, including intellectual property rights, which are included in most treaty definitions of what constitutes a protected investment.[78] In addition to investor protection standards, the IIA regime seeks to achieve these objectives by permitting treaty standards to be enforced through investor–state arbitration. In this process, disputes are resolved through legal adjudication by an independent arbitration tribunal rather than political bargaining between states. IIA advocates seek to capture all of these values by asserting that investment treaties promote the rule of law.[79]

Most legal analysis assumes that IIA commitments encourage investment and that investment contribute to sustainable development. Typically, however, there is no enquiry into the extent to which treaty commitments are needed to provide better protection for investors than domestic rules in particular countries and so encourage investment.[80] Part of the reason for this decontextualized stance is that most IIAs were negotiated at the behest of developed countries seeking to obtain protection for their investors in developing countries, where concerns about the rule of law and the weakness of local institutions were endemic.[81] Until recently, few legal scholars have taken into account the variations in local conditions in host states as relevant to the need for and effect of international investment treaty obligations. Instead, there has been an emphasis on the need for consistent obligations regardless of the context.[82] Some legal scholars have sought to justify this approach on the basis that investment treaty standards are simply international norms of good governance that all countries should adhere to.[83]

Legal scholars have begun to analyse the compatibility of the international investment regime with other international legal norms, including obligations related to the protection of international human rights, labour rights, and the environment,[84] including the impact of international investment rules on

---

77 UNCTAD, *World Investment Report 2003: FDI Policies for Development: National and International Perspectives* (UNCTAD 2003) 91.

78 UNCTAD, *Scope and Definition: A Sequel* (United Nations 2011) 114.

79 e.g. Christoph Schreuer, 'Do We Need Investment Arbitration' (2014) 1 *Transnational Dispute Management* <www.transnational-dispute-management.com> accessed 8 August 2019.

80 There are some exceptions, e.g. Amanda Perry-Kessaris (ed), *Socio-Legal Approaches to International Economic Law: Text, Context, Subtext* (Routledge 2014).

81 Vanhonnaeker (n 60).

82 Wolfgang Alschner, 'Locked in Language: Historical Sociology and the Path Dependency of Investment Treaty Design' in Moshe Hirsch and Andrew Lang (eds), *Research Handbook on the Sociology of International Law* (Elgar 2018).

83 Benedict Kingsbury and Stephan Schill, 'Investor–State Arbitration as Governance: Fair and Equitable Treatment, Proportionality and the Emerging Global Administrative Law' in Albert Jan van den Berg (ed), *50 Years of the New York Convention, ICAA Congress Series 5* (Kluwer Law International 2009) 5–68.

84 e.g. Lorenzo Cotula, *Human Rights, Natural Resource and Investment Law in a Globalised World: Shades of Grey in the Shadow of the Law* (Routledge, 2012).

18 J Anthony VanDuzer et al.

the freedom of states to act to achieve particular policy goals, like sustainable development.[85]

Investor–state arbitration rules are informed by related but distinct legal values that derive from international commercial arbitration.[86] In international commercial arbitration, disputes are resolved by an expert panel appointed by the parties in an expeditious and, generally, confidential manner.[87] Often the dispute's practical resolution is more important than clear and convincing legal reasoning or consistency with prior decisions.[88] There is a strong emphasis on the process being efficient and the result final.[89] Arbitration awards are, generally, not subject to appeal and may be readily enforced worldwide, unlike domestic court judgements.[90]

Increasingly, however, many academics argue that other legal values need to be reflected in investor–state arbitration. Because many investor–state cases involve challenges to public acts of governments as opposed to commercial disputes, investor–state arbitration needs to meet higher standards for democratic accountability, including enhanced transparency and participation rights for affected interests, even if the cost is reduced efficiency.[91] These procedural requirements are beginning to emerge in some investor–state arbitration rules. As well, some argue that the investor–state dispute settlement process needs to incorporate some of the same guarantees of independence for decision-makers that characterize domestic judicial systems. Instead of being appointed and paid by the parties, decision-makers should be permanently appointed, independently funded, and precluded from engaging in outside activities to avoid conflicts of interest and concerns about bias.[92] Finally, in the interest of ensuring that standards are clear and predictable for investors and states, a degree of consistency across cases is required.

4.3 Characterization of investors

The legal analysis of IIAs and investor–state arbitration does not consider investors' individual characteristics or their investment objectives. All investors

---

85 e.g. Cordonier Segger, Gehring, and Newcombe (n 61).

86 Jan Paulsson, 'Arbitration without Privity' (1995) 10 *ICSID Review – FILJ* 232, 232–234; Cristoph Schreuer, *The ICSID Convention: A Commentary* (Cambridge University Press 2001) 233.

87 Joshua Karton, 'The Arbitral Role in Contractual Interpretation' (2015) 6 *Journal of International Dispute Settlement* 4; Alan Redfern and Martin Hunter, *Law and Practice of International Commercial Arbitration* (4th edn, Sweet & Maxwell 2004).

88 ibid Karton; ibid Redfern and Hunter 382–383.

89 ibid Redfern and Hunter 23, 406.

90 ibid 23, 430–431, 437.

91 VanDuzer and Dumberry (n 60); Gus van Harten, 'Judicial supervision of NAFTA Chapter 11 Arbitration: Public or Private Law' (2005) 21 *Arbitration International* 493.

92 ibid VanDuzer and Dumberry; Gus van Harten, 'Investment Treaty Arbitration, Procedural Fairness, and the Rule of Law' in Stephan Schill (ed), *International Investment Law and Comparative Public Law* (Oxford University Press 2010) 627, 643–655.

with a treaty-prescribed connection of nationality to a party state are protected in relation to their investments in another party state.[93] As well, all investors are assumed to be motivated to invest by the degree to which investment treaty protections and the corresponding values of certainty, predictability, and fairness are guaranteed. No enquiry is made regarding the relative importance of investment protections for particular kinds of investors or the form of their investments. 'Investment' is typically defined very broadly to include 'every kind of asset'.[94] In most treaties, no distinction is made, for example, between portfolio investors, like bondholders, and the operators of a mine, despite the very different exposure of these two categories of investors to political risk and the corresponding need for investor treaty protection against state action. There is no consideration of the scale of investors or the sector in which they operate.[95] This decontextualized approach is entirely at odds with the preoccupation of international business scholarship with the factors affecting MNEs' investment decisions.

Legal analysis is also informed by an assumption that foreign investors need protections that are distinct from those available to domestic investors. Foreigners are typically assumed to be uniquely vulnerable to host-state action because of their lack of familiarity with how things are done locally and their lack of access to local political decision-makers.[96] Again, typically, no distinction is made between types of investors or investments regarding their relative vulnerability.[97] This assumption has begun to be challenged.[98]

4.4 Host-state characterization

Legal scholars tend to treat all host states as actors with obligations without distinction based on their particular characteristics. The single pervasive assumption about host states is that domestic remedies for foreign investors complaining about host-state action are likely to be ineffective and need to be supplemented by the substantive protections in IIAs.[99] Local courts and administrative proceedings are presumed to be incapable of providing relief from

---

93 Vanhonnaeker (n 60).

94 ibid.

95 Some recent scholarship addresses this problem, e.g. Jandhyala and Weiner (n 2) investigate the petroleum industry and consider the significance of firm size and state ownership.

96 Edwin Borchard, *The Diplomatic Protection of Citizens Abroad or the Law of International Claims* (The Banks Law Publishing Co 1915) 43.

97 One exception is Liesbeth Colen, Miet Maertens, and Johan Swinnen, 'Determinants of Foreign Direct Investment Flows to Developing Countries: The Role of International Investment Agreements' in De Schutter, Swinnen, and Wouters (n 65) 116, 143.

98 e.g. David Schneiderman, 'Investing in Democracy? Political Process and International Investment Law' (2010) 60 *University of Toronto Law Journal* 909.

99 UNCTAD (n 78) 114–118.

20 J Anthony VanDuzer et al.

host-state actions because they do not meet basic requirements of the rule of law: they are corrupt, ineffective, or lack independence from the state.[100]

Traditionally, these assumptions have been relied on with little, if any, enquiry into the actual nature and effectiveness of local institutions in particular states party to an IIA. Increasingly, however, legal scholars are challenging these assumptions.[101] For example, some have doubted the need for investor–state arbitration in a future trade and investment agreement between the European Union and the United States, where both parties have strong protection for investors in their local laws and effective dispute resolution institutions.[102]

4.5 Impact in host state

As noted, IIA commitments are frequently characterized as conducive to enhancing the rule of law in host states for foreign investors and it is often argued that there will be spillover benefits in the form of improvements to the rule of law for all market-place participants.[103] It is also assumed that such commitments will lead to increased inward investment.[104] As noted, some lawyers, as well as some economists and political scientists, have tried to verify this effect empirically using aggregate investment flow data. In their review of empirical studies of the effects of IIAs on FDI flows in this volume, Beaulieu and O'Neill conclude that

> signing an IIA can attract FDI when the host country has characteristics that are attractive to foreign investors. Countries will not attract FDI by signing an IIA if they have low productivity, weak institutions and rule of law, high political risk, and are small economies far away from, and lacking connections with the source country.[105]

Despite the weak evidence of an investment inducing effect, few legal scholars have addressed how investment may be more effectively promoted in IIAs.

---

100 Schreuer (n 86).

101 e.g. Broude, Busch, and Porges (n 64); Bonnitcha (n 65).

102 Lauge Poulsen, Jonathan Bonnitcha, and Jason Yackee, *Transatlantic Investment Treaty Protection*, (2015) Paper No 3 in the CEPS-CTR Project on 'TTIP in the Balance' and CEPS Special Report No 102 <www.ceps.eu/system/files/SR102_ISDS.pdf> accessed 16 August 2019.

103 e.g. Schreuer (n 86).

104 Karl P Sauvant and Lisa E Sachs, 'BITs, DTTs, and FDI Flows: An Overview' in Karl P Sauvant and Lisa E Sachs (eds), *The Effect of Treaties on Foreign Direct Investment: Bilateral Investment Treaties, Double Taxation Treaties and Investment Flows* (Oxford University Press 2009) xxvi–lxii.

105 Beaulieu and O'Neill (n 17).

Introduction to international investment policy   21

As noted, some legal scholars have become concerned about the impact of investor protection provisions on the flexibility of states to act to help protect the environment, human and labour rights, and other social goals. They are also increasingly focusing their attention on the relationship between treaty protection and investment-led sustainable development.[106] The text of IIAs pays little attention to these kinds of impacts, however.[107]

As mentioned above, Cotula's chapter in this volume is an example of recent work departing from the traditionally narrow approach of legal scholars. He locates foreign investment in a much broader legal context, investigating its social and environmental impacts in relation to three areas: impact assessments, land rights, and labour rights. His chapter forces the reader to think beyond the binary conception of the investment relationship as one between the investor and the host state. He characterizes investment as a multi-actor phenomenon with wide ranging social, environmental, and economic effects and draws out implications for the development and content of national and international policies, given effect through law as well as non-binding soft law instruments, like guidelines, to protect affected interests.

5. Political science

5.1 Scope

In general terms, the political analysis of international economic policy is concerned with both the domestic and international factors that affect policy choices, taking into account the complex and dynamic ways in which they interact. In trying to understand a particular issue of international economic policy in a country (or region), political scientists identify the local social and economic interests affected by a policy or change in policy, what information those interests have, how they are organized, and how they engage with local institutions that aggregate and translate policy preferences into policy outcomes. They also enquire into how states interact at the international level, including through international institutions, and how these international interactions influence domestic interests, information, institutions, and, ultimately, policy.[108] Typically, theoretical hypotheses are developed and then tested empirically using

---

106 VanDuzer and Dumberry (n 60).

107 J Anthony VanDuzer, 'Sustainable Development Provisions in International Trade Treaties: What Lessons for International Investment Agreements?' in Markus Krajewski and Steffan Hindelang (eds), *Shifting Paradigms in International Investment Law: More Balanced, Less Isolated, Diversified Approaches* (Oxford University Press 2016) 142–176.

108 Jeffrey Frieden and Lisa Martin, 'International Political Economy: Global and Domestic Interactions' in Ira Katznelson and Helen V Milner (eds), *Political Science: The State of the Discipline* (WW Norton 2003). Domestic and international interactions have been characterized as two-level games by Robert Putnam, 'Diplomacy and Domestic Politics: The Logic of Two-Level Games' (1988) 42 *International Organization* 427.

22   J Anthony VanDuzer et al.

both quantitative and qualitative methods.[109] While this kind of approach has been used extensively in relation to international trade, political scientists have paid much less attention to international investment to date.[110]

Recent political science scholarship has focused on domestic investment policy. In particular, as discussed by Leblond and Labrecque in this volume, political scientists have investigated why some developing countries are open to investment by theorizing about the impact of inward FDI on policy preferences of social groups in particular countries and testing those theories empirically.[111] For example, political science scholars have studied the political consequences of labour market effects associated with MNE investment. Some have explained openness to MNE investment among higher-skilled workers on the basis of evidence that MNEs tend to hire more skilled workers than local firms and pay them higher wages.[112] Political scientists have also looked at how the political process in a country affects the impact of group preferences on political outcomes. For example, Pandya has shown that labour's policy preferences are likely to have a more significant impact on government policy-makers in democracies where policy-makers are more accountable to citizens.[113] Other studies have examined the link between state openness to investment and internal economic conditions. For example, openness to foreign investment may be a response to the needs of local businesses for foreign capital where local capital markets are inadequate.[114] Unlike work on the politics of international trade, however, not much research has been done on how social and attitudinal factors affect policy preferences on investment, though some work has been done on concerns about national security related to foreign investments as an influence on policy.[115]

There has been little work by political scientists to explain particular policy choices, though some studies have tried to explain the use of financial incentives to attract foreign investment.[116] Finally, some political scientists have studied

---

109 Hypotheses may also be based on work in other disciplines, most notably economics. ibid Frieden and Martin 140.

110 ibid 146. The same view is expressed in John Ravenhill, 'International Political Economy' in Christian Reus-Smit and Duncan Snidal (eds), *The Oxford Handbook of International Relations* (Oxford University Press 2008) 539–557.

111 Patrick Leblond and Sébastien Labrecque, 'National security and the political economy of international investment policy', Chapter 9 in this volume.

112 See Van Assche (n 11).

113 Sonal Pandya, 'Political Economy of Foreign Direct Investment: Globalized Production in the Twenty-first Century' (2016) 19 *Annual Review of Political Science* 455, 459.

114 Joshua Aizenman, 'Opposition to FDI and Financial Shocks' (2005) 77 *Journal of Development Economics* 467.

115 e.g. Leblond and Labrecque (n 111); Globerman, Hensyel, and Shapiro (n 49); Pandya (n 113) 458.

116 ibid Pandya 460 citing two studies of subsidy use: Nathan Jensen, Edmund Malesky, Mariana Medina, and Ugur Ozdemir, 'Pass the Bucks: Credit, Blame, and the Global Competition for Investment' (2014) 58 *International Studies Quarterly* 433; and Quan Li, 'Democracy, Autocracy, and Tax Incentives to Foreign Direct Investors: A Cross-national Analysis' (2006) 68 *Journal of Politics* 62.

FDI's effects on domestic political conditions other than investment policy, such as democratization, governance, human rights, and income equality.[117]

Over the past decade and a half, however, political scientists have focused much of their attention on decisions by countries, especially developing countries, to adopt a particular policy in relation to foreign investment: IIAs.[118] Explanations are wide ranging. The conventional argument has been that countries sign IIAs to attract investment and that this motivation has been encouraged by competition for investment among similarly-situated developing countries.[119] As discussed above, political scientists, as well as economists and lawyers, have investigated the presumed link between signing an IIA and attracting inward FDI.[120] Partly because the evidence is conflicting, a few political scientists have suggested alternative explanations. Some suggest that developed countries use their political and economic power to get developing countries to sign IIAs to protect their own investors.[121] Others suggest that developing countries are interested in signing BITs with developed countries because it increases the likelihood that they will subsequently negotiate an FTA.[122] Some work shows that once a state has defended an investor–state claim under one BIT its interest in signing more BITs declines.[123]

While most political science research on IIAs focuses on developing countries, a few studies have looked at developed countries, especially the US. Some have suggested that the US signs IIAs not just to protect US investors but also to achieve other political goals. One study, for example, argues that the US chooses to negotiate BITs with particular developing countries based on their political importance to the US and to secure their support on unrelated foreign policy initiatives at the United Nations.[124]

Another focus of political science research on international investment has been the impact of domestic political factors on the attractiveness of particular locations to foreign investors. This work, which complements that of international business scholars on MNE decision-making, examines both how political risk is relevant to MNE decisions and how host-country characteristics shape political risk. Both are directly relevant to policy choices about how to attract investment.

---

117 ibid Pandya 457; De Schutter, Swinnen, and Wouters (n 65).

118 ibid Pandya 460 describing this as the most studied issue related to FDI promotion.

119 e.g. Zachary Elkins, Andrew Guzman, and Beth Simmons, 'Competing for Capital: The Diffusion of Bilateral Investment Treaties 1960–2000' (2006) 60 *International Organization* 811.

120 Beaulieu and O'Neill (n 17); Pandya (n 113) 464.

121 e.g. Todd Allee and Clint Peinhardt, 'Evaluating Three Explanations for the Design of Bilateral Investment Treaties' (2014) 66 *World Politics* 47.

122 Jennifer Tobin and Marc Busch, 'A BIT is Better Than a Lot: Bilateral Investment Treaties and Preferential Trade Agreements' (2010) 62 *World Politics* 1.

123 Lauge Poulsen and Emma Aisbett 'When the Claim Hits: Bilateral Investment Treaties and Bounded Rational Learning' (2013) 66 *World Politics* 273.

124 Adam Chilton, 'The Political Motivations of the US Bilateral Investment Treaty Program' (2016) 23 *Review of International Political Economy* 614.

24 *J Anthony VanDuzer et al.*

An aspect of this branch of political science research is the relevance of domestic institutions to political risk and MNE investment location choice. At the level of national political regimes, research has sought to explain, for example, why democracies receive more inward investment.[125] Research has also explored how specific institutional features attract investment. Factors like the strong property rights and contract enforcement, the rule of law, and the judiciary have been found to be attractive to investors.[126] Similarly, policy stability has been found to be an important consideration for investors. Some research has studied variations in political risk and MNE response across sectors. For example, foreign investment in particular sectors in a host state has been explained on the basis that investment in those sectors is complementary to the business activities of supporters of the party in power in that state and so political risk in that sector is reduced.[127]

As noted above, there is an extensive and growing literature on the extent to which signing IIAs addresses the problem of political risk and, in that way, encourages inward FDI. Until very recently, this literature was only concerned with impacts on aggregate investment flows rather than particular types of investors.[128] A few studies have looked at the impact of investor–state arbitration claims on firms' perceptions of political risk, finding that countries that have been the subject of claims attract less investment, and the effect is more pronounced if they lose.[129]

5.2 *Values*

It is difficult to articulate a single set of values that informs political science research on investment. Most research in the discipline purports to be descriptive rather than normative.[130]

Nevertheless, most of the work in the past 20 years on international investment reflects an implicit consensus among political scientists that FDI has positive effects on welfare and growth in the host economy.[131] As with the other disciplines, much of the literature assumes that FDI is encouraged by political stability, policy stability, and predictability, especially regarding property rights protection, as well as an open regime providing market access for goods, services, and capital flows. To the extent these can be 'locked in' by IIAs, in the sense that they credibly commit host states to economically liberal policies, international investment will be further encouraged and, in

---

125 Pandya (n 113) 462–463; Leblond and Labrecque (n 111) also review this literature.

126 Joseph L Staats and Glen Biglaiser 'Foreign Direct Investment in Latin America: The Importance of Judicial Strength and Rule of Law' (2012) 56 *International Studies Quarterly* 193.

127 Pablo Pinto, *Partisan Investment in the Global Economy* (Cambridge University Press 2013).

128 Jandhyala and Weiner (n 2).

129 Todd Allee and Clint Peinhardt 'Contingent Credibility: The Impact of Investment Treaty Violations on Foreign Direct Investment' (2011) 65 *International Organization* 401.

130 Frieden and Martin (n 108) describe international political economy as 'positivist' (118).

131 Pandya (n 113).

Introduction to international investment policy 25

turn, will stimulate more growth. In identifying domestic interests at stake, political scientists' focus has been primarily on economic interests.[132]

The distributive effects of FDI, the impact on local competitors to MNEs, and the constraints on state sovereignty are acknowledged by many political scientists in their work on investment, although there is no consensus on the nature or relative importance of these effects.[133] Some argue that FDI can have negative effects on domestic political conditions, such as democratization, governance, human rights, and income equality. One specific concern is that limits imposed by IIAs on internal sovereignty – including by chilling host states' regulatory initiatives for fear that affected foreign investors will make investor–state arbitration claims against the host state – restrict not only the host government's freedom of action in terms of public policy, but also its legitimacy and accountability to its citizenry.[134] Contemporary political science literature appears little concerned about the legitimacy of MNEs in host states.

5.3 Characterization of investors

Some political science scholarship acknowledges that people and firms are differentiated and have multiple, sometimes conflicting interests, and that particular interests will be more strongly implicated than others in specific situations. But research on investor interests is not very developed.[135] Most political science research focuses only on what political factors will attract foreign investors, without much attention to investor characteristics. Little attention has been paid to foreign investors' actions in host states and their effect on investment policy.[136] Some work has been done on trade policy preferences of foreign investors. For example, foreign investors that rely on imported inputs in their production in a host-state support free trade in those inputs. By contrast, foreign investors that produce goods in the host state for sale only in the host state are likely to want protection from import competition.[137] The impact of MNEs on host-state investment policy, however, has not been thoroughly investigated.[138]

---

132 Frieden and Martin (n 108) 126; Leblond and Labrecque (n 111).

133 Stephen Kobrin, 'Sovereignty@Bay: Globalization, Multinational Enterprise, and the International Political System' in Alan Rugman (ed), *The Oxford Handbook of International Business* (2nd edn, Oxford University Press 2009) 183–204.

134 Vanhonnaeker (n 60); Dani Rodrik, *Has Globalization Gone Too Far?* (Institute for International Economics 1997); Dani Rodrik, *Straight Talk on Trade: Ideas for a Sane World Economy* (Princeton University Press 2018) 13–14.

135 Frieden and Martin (n 108).

136 Leblond and Labrecque (n 111); Globerman, Hensyel, and Shapiro (n 49).

137 John Goodman, Debra Spar, and David Yoffie, 'Foreign Direct Investment and the Demand for Protection in the United States' (1996) 50 *International Organization* 565.

138 A notable exception is Nathan M Jensen, Glen Biglaiser, Quan Li, Edmund Malesky, Pablo M Pinto, Santiago M Pinto, and Joseph L Staats, *Politics and Foreign Direct Investment* (University of Michigan Press 2012), Chapter 5 ('Political Institutions and the Effectiveness of MNE Lobbying').

26 J Anthony VanDuzer et al.

5.4 Host-state characterization

Political science research looks at the state as a constellation of social interests. Policy is determined by the mediation of these interests through domestic institutions. Most political scientists assume that states want to maximize public welfare, though they acknowledge that the policies needed to do so depend on the state's circumstances, including its position in the international economy and its relative power. With few exceptions, political science research is not very developed in relation to how international investment policy is determined.[139] The chapter by Leblond and Labrecque in this volume makes a useful contribution in that regard.[140]

It is also the case that political scientists sometimes make what Frieden and Martin call 'heroic assumptions and simplifications' about the nature of the state in the interests of developing tractable analysis.[141] For example, analysts may 'reduce domestic institutions to an executive and a legislature or reduce domestic interests to a median voter'.[142] In looking at the interaction between states and the international system, most work takes the characteristics of states as given and not nationally specific.[143]

5.5 Impact in host state

As noted, investment is generally considered to be positive for economic growth and welfare in the political science literature. The political impact of investment, however, is examined in few studies. The current literature focuses almost exclusively on investors' entry. Few political scientists have explored the impact of IIAs (and indirectly of FDI) on policy change, including whether IIAs actually produce regulatory chill.[144]

6. Moving beyond disciplinary silos

The profiles sketched above reveal both commonalities and differences across disciplines. Undoubtedly, in some respects, the differences are overstated. While we have sought to avoid presenting a caricature of economics, international business, law, and political science, we could not do justice fully to each discipline's complexity and diversity. As well, the borders between disciplines are

---

139 Poulsen (n 64) concludes that 'scholarly attention to the politics of the investment treaty regime has just begun' (10).
140 Leblond and Labrecque (n 111).
141 Frieden and Martin (n 108) 125.
142 ibid 136.
143 ibid 137.
144 A notable exception is Christine Côté, 'A Chilling Effect: The Impact of International Investment Agreements on National Regulatory Autonomy in the Areas of Health, Safety and the Environment' (PhD Thesis, London School of Economics 2014).

increasingly blurred and porous as specialists in one discipline investigate questions and use methodological techniques from others. This is most evident, perhaps, in the attention recently paid by all four disciplines to the question of whether IIAs actually encourage inward investment into the countries that sign them. Many scholars in international business have enthusiastically embraced multi- and interdisciplinary study, though even here, the practice of interdisciplinarity lags the expressed enthusiasm. It is still the case that most research proceeds from a single disciplinary perspective. Indeed, within each discipline the approaches taken often focus only on a limited aspect of foreign investment activity. Investment lawyers' failure to consider the work of trade, tax, and development lawyers is an obvious example.

Looking at international investment through a policy lens, the comparison in this introductory chapter suggests a number of areas in which employing more than one discipline could be useful. International business scholarship has developed a deep contextual understanding of MNE behaviour. By contrast, law and political science largely treat firms as homogenous. Incorporating international business's firm-specific insights would improve our understanding of the effects of legal instruments like IIAs on firm behaviour, which would usefully inform policy choices about how to attract and manage international investment, including whether a country should sign IIAs and, if so, what their content should be. Political science analysis on investment policy has been largely limited to whether states are open to foreign investment but could be employed to understand the political economy of more finely-grained policy choices. Economics is informed by firm heterogeneity in only a limited way and could be made more policy relevant by importing a more heterodox conception of the firm based in international business research.

A related area for interdisciplinary enquiry is particular host-country characteristics and how they interact with investor location choice and post-investment behaviour. Some work on this has been done in political science, economics, and, especially, international business, though policy relevance has not been a goal of most international business research until recently. International investment lawyers' understanding of questions like whether a country needs to commit to ISDS could benefit greatly from a better understanding of particular host-state characteristics.

At the same time, lawyers' deep and rigorous understanding of legal instruments could be marshalled to assist economists and international business scholars. The latter have identified factors like good governance and the protection of property rights as host-state characteristics that are attractive to investors. But for this kind of evidence to be practically useful to policy-makers, these concepts first need to be unpacked and given specific content by lawyers. Then, their particular features can be analysed by international business scholars in terms of how they affect investors' decision-making. Political scientists, for their part, could focus their attention on the process to create these specific legal institutional characteristics and the determinants of various institutional outcomes.

28 J Anthony VanDuzer et al.

The discussion profiled above also reveals gaps in our understanding of international investment policy. A key issue for host-state policy-makers related to foreign investment activity is its social, environmental, and other non-economic effects. While economics research has addressed some of the economic effects of foreign investment and political scientists have engaged in a limited study of the implications of these effects for policy preferences, all disciplines need to do more to understand the non-economic effects of international investment on host states as well as their implications for the process and outcomes of host-state policy-making related to foreign investment.

In the book's final chapter, we expand on these and other areas in which interdisciplinary research can provide a richer understanding of foreign investment activity as it relates to policy-making by states.

Part I

International investment's changing context

2 Trade and foreign direct investment in the 21st century

Ari Van Assche

1. Introduction

The past 30 years have seen an information and communication technology (ICT) revolution that has transformed the way companies conduct international business. An exponential growth in computing power and telecommunications network capacity has dramatically reduced the cost of transmitting information over long distances. Companies have reacted to the drop in communication costs by redesigning their production processes, abandoning the practice of concentrating their value chain in a single location. Through outsourcing and offshoring, they have sliced up their production processes and dispersed their production activities across multiple countries, leading to global value chains (GVCs).

In the past, international trade primarily involved the exchange of final products, but now trade in intermediate inputs accounts for roughly two-thirds of all international trade.[1] Furthermore, countries increasingly rely on imported inputs to produce their exports. Johnson and Noguera estimate that the import content embedded in gross world exports rose significantly between 1970 and 2008.[2] This growth accelerated over time, with the import content of exports increasing roughly three times faster after 1990 than in the 1970s and 1980s. There is some evidence, however, that this trend has stagnated after the Great Recession of 2008–2009, owing to rising global uncertainties.[3]

Traditional models of trade and foreign direct investment (FDI) are poorly equipped to explain GVCs. Conventional theories treat the production technologies that allow firms to transform inputs of production into final goods as completely localized. That is, a US export is assumed to be entirely 'Made in the USA', while a Chinese export is considered 'Made in China'. In these traditional

---

1 Robert C Johnson and Guillermo Noguera, 'Accounting for Intermediates: Production Sharing and Trade in Value Added' (2012) 86 *Journal of International Economics* 224.
2 Robert C Johnson and Guillermo Noguera, 'A Portrait of Trade in Value Added over Four Decades' (2017) 99 *The Review of Economics and Statistics* 896.
3 Byron Gangnes, Alyson C Ma, and Ari Van Assche, 'Global Value Chains and the Trade-income Relationship: Implications for the Recent Trade Slowdown' in Bernard Hoekman (ed), *The Global Trade Slowdown: A New Normal?* (CEPR Press London 2015) 111–126.

32 *Ari Van Assche*

frameworks, the sole reason why companies conduct international business is to reach foreign consumers, or to tap into foreign-based resource pools.

Recently, economists have incorporated insights from the field of supply chain management into traditional theories, thereby shedding new light on GVCs. In these studies, production processes are modelled as a sequence of tasks that are combined to produce a final good. This new research stream enriches our understanding of trade and FDI in three ways. First, it helps explain which new motives firms have adopted to conduct international business. Second, it describes new patterns of trade and FDI that have emerged in recent decades. Third, it highlights how the rise of GVCs has shifted traditional preferences that firms and workers have towards trade and FDI liberalization.

What follows is a brief overview of these new trends in the literature, and how they improve our understanding of the multinational firm in the 21st century. In Section 2, we describe the traditional models of trade and FDI. In Section 3, we discuss new theoretical frameworks that allow for the emergence of GVCs. Section 4 provides concluding remarks.

2. National production paradigm

In a recent book, Baldwin built a useful framework to reflect on globalization. He divides history into three periods: the *pre-globalization period* (before 1820) when both transportation and communication costs were high, the *first unbundling period* (1820–1990), when transportation costs dropped but communication costs remained high, and the *second unbundling period* (1990-present), when both trade and communication costs became low.[4] He argues that each period has organized production and consumption in a different way, affecting trade and foreign investment flows.

Traditional trade and FDI theories were built to explain international business in the *first unbundling period* when transportation costs were low, but communication costs remained high. Indeed, much of trade and FDI theories have been characterized by what is called the 'national production paradigm', whereby final goods are considered tradable in world markets but production inputs are non-tradable.[5] In other words, a core assumption in most traditional trade and FDI theories is that value chains are local, but markets are global. That is, the entire production process of goods takes place within a single country (due to high communication costs), but companies can sell goods globally (due to low transportation costs).

While the 'national production paradigm' seems innocuous at first glance, it has conditioned scholars' thinking on trade in important ways. If firms need to source all production inputs from within a country's frontiers, then firms only have

---

4 Richard Baldwin, *The Great Convergence: Information Technology and the New Globalization* (Belknap Press 2016).
5 Ronald W Jones, *Globalization and the Theory of Input Trade* (MIT Press 2000).

a single motive to conduct international trade: reaching foreign consumers through exports. In such a setting, trade is all about expanding a firm's consumer base internationally. Domestic firms use exports to reach foreign clients. Imports are a reflection of foreign firms' actions to reach domestic customers.

The 'national production paradigm' has also shaped traditional thinking on FDI. If value chains are local, then there are two motives for firms to conduct outward FDI: to move the entire production process close to consumers (market-seeking FDI) or to locate production close to natural resources (resource-seeking FDI). In the remainder of this section, we discuss in greater detail how the 'national production paradigm' has conditioned our understanding of trade, trade politics, FDI, and FDI politics.

2.1 Traditional trade theory

The 'national production paradigm' plays a key role in the derivation of some of the most well-known predictions on trade. Take the traditional Heckscher–Ohlin model as an example. It supposes that countries have different factor endowments and investigates which countries should specialize in the production of which goods. Building on the explicit assumption that value chains are local, the model predicts that countries specialize in the export of goods that intensively use production factors that are relatively abundant in the country. Conversely, they import goods that require production factors that are relatively scarce.

The 'national production paradigm' is also a central principle in the so-called new trade theory models. To explain the large amount of intra-industry trade that occurs between countries with similar endowments (e.g. United States and Canada), economists have introduced scale economies and product differentiation into their theoretical frameworks.[6] This new trade theory proposes that, in differentiated goods industries such as automobiles, countries with similar endowments each specialize in the production and export of certain varieties of goods since it allows companies to increase the scale of their production. For example, Germany exports Volkswagen and Audi cars, while the United States exports Fords and Teslas. In these models, the entire production process of varieties is assumed to take place within a firm's home country. Here again, the sole reason why firms in this model conduct international trade is to reach foreign consumers through exports.

2.2 Traditional trade politics

The 'national production paradigm' has helped shape the main tenets of traditional trade politics, with firms, workers, and consumers each adopting different views on trade policy. To illustrate this, we focus on the trade politics

6 Paul Krugman, 'Increasing Returns, Monopolistic Competition and International Trade' (1979) 9 *Journal of International Economics* 469.

34 *Ari Van Assche*

that derive from the Heckscher–Ohlin model. Firms' trade preferences are shaped by the industry in which they operate. Companies in import-competing industries (i.e. comparative-disadvantaged sectors) benefit from import restrictions that protect them from foreign competition. In skill-abundant countries such as the United States, it is firms in labour-intensive sectors that prefer import restrictions. In labour-abundant countries such as Mexico, it is companies in skill-intensive industries that lobby for import tariffs.

Such firm-level trade preferences influence trade politics since governments not only care about national welfare, but also about industry support. Indeed, a government that cares about political contributions has the incentive to unilaterally impose import tariffs as long as the financial support that they obtain from companies in import-competing industries outweighs the welfare losses that consumers face due to higher prices.[7]

Firms in exporting industries (i.e. comparative-advantage sectors) have opposing trade preferences. They gain from heightened foreign market access since it increases their export opportunities and strengthens their competitiveness in foreign markets. As a result, they want foreign countries to reduce tariffs on their goods. In skill-abundant countries, for example, firms in skill-intensive industries benefit from a tariff reduction on foreign imports. In labour-abundant countries, it is the firms in labour-intensive industries that care about reductions in foreign countries' import tariffs.

Governments do not have the power to unilaterally reduce the import tariffs of foreign countries, but they can enter into trade agreements with foreign countries, which lead to reciprocal tariff reductions. In such a trade liberalization scenario, the government inevitably loses political support from its firms in import-competing industries, but it gains political support from its firms in exporting industries.[8] Government may thus decide to enter into trade agreements if the political support gained from exporting industries (as well as from consumers) exceeds the loss in political support of import-competing industries. We have summarized the trade preferences with regards to liberalization of different types of firms in Table 2.1.

Workers' trade policy preferences are aligned with those of the companies for which they predominantly work. In developed countries, skilled workers benefit from trade liberalization since it leads to an expansion of skill-intensive industries, which increases the real wages of skilled workers. Unskilled workers, on the other hand, favour trade protection since trade liberalization leads to a contraction of labour-intensive industries, reducing unskilled workers' real wages (see Table 2.1).

For their part, consumers benefit from trade liberalization in both types of country since lower tariffs lead to lower prices and thus increase overall

---

7 Gene M Grossman and Elhanan Helpman, 'Protection for Sale' (1994) 84 *The American Economic Review* 833.

8 Donald H Regan, 'Explaining Trade Agreements: The Practitioners' Story and the Standard Model' (2015) 14 *World Trade Review* 391.

Trade and foreign direct investment 35

Table 2.1 Stakeholders' trade and FDI preferences in traditional trade and FDI models

Stakeholder	Trade liberalization	FDI liberalization
SKILL-ABUNDANT COUNTRY		
Consumers	√	√
Firms		
Skill-intensive sectors	√	√
Labour-intensive sectors	X	X
Workers		
Skilled workers	√	X
Unskilled workers	X	√
LABOUR-ABUNDANT COUNTRY		
Consumers	√	√
Firms		
Skill-intensive sectors	X	X
Labour-intensive sectors	√	√
Workers		
Skilled workers	X	√
Unskilled workers	√	X

Note: √ indicates if a stakeholder is in favour of a type of liberalization, while X suggest it is unsupportive. The results are opposite if we consider stakeholders' preferences for trade and investment protection.

consumption opportunities. It is important to point out, however, that political economists generally discount the weight of consumers in trade politics since consumers face a collective action problem.[9] That is, while consumers as a group benefit from trade liberalization, individual consumers have little incentive to lobby for it because the benefits from free trade are small compared to the cost and time required to advocate free trade. This renders the political support that consumers provide for trade liberalization limited.

2.3 Traditional FDI theory

The 'national production paradigm' is also a central piece in traditional models of the multinational firm, which have mostly focused on market-seeking and resource-seeking motives for FDI.[10]

---

9 Mancur Olson, *The Logic of Collective Action* (Harvard University Press 1965).
10 John H Dunning, 'Location and the Multinational Enterprise: A Neglected Factor?' (1998) 29 *Journal of International Business Studies* 45.

36   *Ari Van Assche*

Traditional FDI studies, based on Dunning's eclectic Ownership, Location, and Internalization (OLI) framework,[11] have focused on two main motives for firms to conduct outward FDI. First, a company has a strong product technology that is desired by foreign consumers, but trade costs make it cheaper for the firm to produce its goods close to foreign consumers rather than exporting them from the home country. Finally, they are better off setting up their own plant rather than outsourcing production to an external firm. This type of FDI is called market-seeking FDI. Alternatively, a company may have a strong expertise in exploiting natural resources and be better off keeping their operations within company borders, but the natural resources it wants to exploit are located in a foreign county. This type of FDI is called resource-seeking FDI.

Markusen and Venables have derived additional results related to the OLI framework by introducing multinational firms in a Heckscher–Ohlin trade model.[12] Based on the assumption that firms need to pay an initial fixed cost to set up a company and an additional fixed cost for each production plant that it builds, they show that multinational firms (and the accompanying FDI flows) are particularly likely to arise if the initial 'set up' fixed costs are large relative to plant-level fixed costs, and when trade costs are high. This is because, on the one hand, high 'set up' fixed costs imply that there are significant firm-level economies of scale that favour concentrating production at home. On the other hand, the high trade costs favour the setup of multinational subsidiaries to avoid the high costs of shipping from the home country. Brainard has famously called this the proximity-concentration trade off in FDI decisions.[13] Firms are more likely to choose FDI over exports if trade barriers or transportation costs are high (e.g. automobiles), leading to *proximity* to consumers. In contrast, companies are more likely to *concentrate* production at home if economies of scale are high at the firm-level relative to the plant level, leading firms to choose exports over FDI.

More recent studies have included firm-level heterogeneity into traditional models to investigate which type of firms are more likely to become multinationals. Helpman, Melitz, and Yeaple show that it is easier for high-productivity firms to pay for the fixed cost of setting up a production plant than it is for low-productivity firms since they generate larger economies of scale.[14] As a consequence, only the 'better' high-productivity companies self-select into

---

11 For a discussion of Dunning's OLI framework, see J Anthony VanDuzer, Patrick Leblond, and Stephen Gelb, 'Introduction to international investment policy and rationale for an inter-disciplinary approach', Chapter 1 in this volume.

12 James R Markusen and Anthony J Venables, 'Multinational Firms and the New Trade Theory' (1998) 46 *Journal of International Economics* 183; James R Markusen and Anthony J Venables, 'The Theory of Endowment, Intra-industry and Multi-national Trade' (2000) 52 *Journal of International Economics* 209.

13 Lael S Brainard, 'An Empirical Assessment of the Proximity-concentration Trade-off between Multinational Sales and Trade' (1997) 87 *The American Economic Review* 520.

14 Elhanan Helpman, Marc J Melitz, and Stephen R Yeaple, 'Export Versus FDI with Heteroge-neous Firms' (2004) 94 *American Economic Review* 300.

becoming multinational firms, whereas less productive firms remain exporters. Yeaple provides empirical evidence that the most productive US firms indeed invest in a larger number of foreign countries and sell more in each country in which they operate.[15]

Markusen finally illustrates that comparative-advantage forces affect the type of country and industry in which multinational firms are most likely to emerge.[16] Since the fixed cost of setting up a firm is generally skill-intensive, multinational firms tend to concentrate in skill-abundant countries. Furthermore, investment liberalization induces firms in the skill-abundant country to conduct horizontal FDI to labour-abundant countries, effectively crowding out local firms even more.

2.4 Traditional FDI politics

Traditional FDI models predict that firms' preferences related to FDI liberalization are similar to their trade preferences (see Table 2.1). Firms in industries with the comparative-advantage will lobby for FDI liberalization since it increases their opportunities to reach foreign consumers through outward FDI, particularly if trade costs are high and firm-level economies of scale are significant. Conversely, firms in comparative-disadvantaged sectors oppose FDI liberalization since inward FDI restrictions protect them from competition from local subsidiaries of foreign firms.[17]

The FDI policy preferences of workers, however, are now opposite from those of firms (see Table 2.1). In skill-abundant countries, skilled workers support trade liberalization, but do not support FDI liberalization because the ability of domestic firms to substitute exports with market-seeking FDI would displace home-country production plants, hurting skilled workers. Unskilled workers in skill-abundant countries, then again, support FDI liberalization since the ability of foreign firms to conduct inward FDI in the domestic economy can lead to employment gains despite the potential crowding out of local firms.[18]

Reich illustrated this divergence in FDI policy preferences between firms and workers by asking readers to consider two types of firms:[19]

- Corporation A is headquartered in the United States, its top managers are US citizens, and American investors hold a majority of its shares. But Corporation A primarily sells to its foreign consumers through its foreign production plants.

---

15 Stephen Yeaple, 'Firm Heterogeneity and the Structure of US Multinational Activity' (2009) 78 *Journal of International Economics* 206.

16 James Markusen, 'Trade versus Investment Liberalization' (2017) National Bureau of Economic Research Working Paper No 6231 <www.nber.org/papers/w6231.pdf> accessed 18 June 2019.

17 ibid.

18 ibid.

19 Robert B Reich, 'Who is Us?' (1990) 68 *Harvard Business Review* 53.

38 *Ari Van Assche*

- Corporation B is headquartered abroad, its top managers and directors are foreign citizens, and foreigners hold a majority of its shares. But Corporation B conducts inward FDI to produce in the United States.

He points out that Corporation A's managers will not necessarily make decisions that are better for American workers than those of Corporation B. According to Reich, it is the foreign firm that hires most American manufacturing workers. In line with Table 2.1, he therefore argues that a country should open its borders to investors from around the world to encourage the entrance of foreign multinationals rather than favouring companies that simply fly the US flag.

2.5 Summary

Taken together, it becomes clear that the 'national production paradigm' has helped feed two commonly heard views about trade and FDI policy. First, it points to a mercantilist view of trade policy among firms and workers: exports are good and should be promoted since they strengthen a country's production and employment in comparative-advantage sectors; imports are bad and should be constrained since they weaken production and employment in sectors that have a comparative disadvantage. According to this view, governments in skill-abundant countries should only accept trade liberalization if the foreign country's tariff reductions garner sufficient political support among skilled workers and skill-intensive firms (as well as consumers) to overcome the loss in political support from unskilled workers and labour-intensive firms.

The 'national production paradigm' also means that firms and workers have diametrically opposing views about FDI policy. Workers favour inward FDI since it can increase a country's production and employment while they oppose outward FDI because it allows companies to substitute local employment with foreign jobs. In contrast, firms consider outward FDI positively because it provides them with more options to reach foreign markets while they see inward FDI negatively because it reduces their competitiveness in their home country. These opposing preferences towards FDI liberalization may explain why countries generally do not have well-established FDI policy agendas compared to trade policy programmes.

3. Globalization of production

Advances in communication technology have made the national production paradigm outdated, because they make it easier for firms to coordinate geographically separated tasks that are part of the same value chain.[20] These technological changes have made it easier for firms to transform production designs and processes into an electronic format. As a result, many companies

---

20 Ari Van Assche, 'Modularity and the Organization of International Production' (2008) 20 *Japan and the World Economy* 353.

now rely on sophisticated computer-aided design (CAD) technologies and business-to-business systems to share codified information between tasks. In other words, we have entered Baldwin's second unbundling period where both transport and communication costs are low.[21]

3.1 Implications for trade

To explain the rise of GVCs, economists have begun opening up the black box of production in a literature referred to as the 'task approach to trade'.[22] Instead of modelling production as a singular activity, they have started to exhibit the production process as a sequence of stages, or tasks, that need to be combined to produce a final good. These tasks can be performed at a distance from other tasks, albeit at a communication cost that needs to be paid to coordinate different production activities. A company's core challenge is thus to decide how to allocate tasks to firms and subsidiaries that now potentially can be located in different countries.

It is instructive to start with Porter's concept of 'value chain' to understand the economic logic of slicing up production and dispersing activities to different locations around the globe (see Figure 2.1).[23] A value chain is a sequence of activities or tasks that a company performs to design, produce, sell, deliver, and support its products. It not only consists of the physical transformation processes (so-called primary activities) that go into producing a good, but also includes support activities such as research and development, procurement, and human-resource management.

A quick glance at the various activities of a value chain suggests they are heterogeneous in two dimensions: input requirements and communication linkages. The first determines the benefit of dispersing value-chain tasks across countries; the latter identifies the cost of coordinating value-chain tasks at a distance.

3.1.1 Input requirements

One characteristic of a task that affects where to locate the task is its input requirements. The production of a task requires a mix of labour inputs, technology, fixed assets, working capital, and various types of information, and this mix can differ greatly for tasks along the value chain. R&D and marketing, for example, are skill-intensive tasks that require lots of specialized knowledge. In contrast,

---

21 Baldwin (n 4).

22 Gene M Grossman and Esteban Rossi-Hansberg, 'Trading Tasks: A Simple Theory of Offshoring' (2008) 98 *The American Economic Review* 1978; Ari Van Assche, 'Global Value Chains and the Rise of a Global Supply Chain Mindset' in Stephen Tapp, Ari Van Assche, and Robert Wolfe (eds), *Redesigning Canadian Trade Policies for New Global Realities* (McGill-Queen's University Press 2017) 183–208.

23 Michael E Porter, *Competitive Advantage: Creating and Sustaining Superior Performance* (Simon and Schuster 1985).

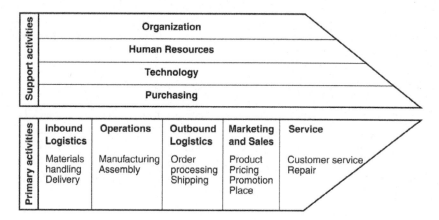

Figure 2.1 Porter's Value Chain

manufacturing assembly is generally a standardized, repetitive, and labour-intensive task. In line with the traditional theory of comparative advantage, firms have an incentive to move tasks that use certain inputs intensively to countries that are abundant in these inputs.

Jones and Kierzkowski were among the first to formally illustrate the logic of task-level comparative advantage.[24] Suppose that production consists of two tasks that are geographically separable: a skill-intensive headquarter service and a labour-intensive manufacturing activity. For simplicity, assume that only the skill-abundant country consumes the final products. If communication costs are high (first unbundling period), companies locate both its headquarter services and manufacturing in the skill-abundant country. In this case, value chains are local and there is no trade. If communication costs are low (second unbundling period), however, companies have an incentive to offshore manufacturing to the labour-abundant country, while keeping headquarter services in the skill-abundant country. In that case, comparative-advantage forces lead to trade in tasks, where the skill-abundant country exports headquarter services while the labour-abundant country exports manufactured final goods. Note that none of this trade is motivated by firms' desire to reach foreign consumers; rather, it is driven by firms' decisions to reduce production costs.

More recent studies have made predictions about the type of firms that develop GVCs. Antràs and Helpman show that if companies located in skill-abundant countries differ in their productivity and face a fixed cost of offshoring

---

24 Ronald Jones and Henryk Kierzkowski, 'The Role of Services in Production and International Trade: A Theoretical Framework' in Ronald Winthrop Jones and Anne O Krueger (eds), *The Political Economy of International Trade: Essays in Honor of Robert E. Baldwin* (Blackwell 1990) 31–48.

manufacturing, only high- productivity firms can profitably jump over the fixed-cost hurdle of offshoring, whereas low-productivity firms remain better off manufacturing at home.[25] In other words, firms with local value chains and global value chains can coexist in an industry, with the latter being more productive than the former. This prediction has been supported by empirical evidence that Japanese firms that offshore production activities tend to be more productive than those that source locally.[26]

Described in this way, the task trade approach does not sound particularly new, but rather simply a rehash of the standard theory of comparative advantage – although at the task level instead of the goods level.[27] Indeed, international production fragmentation allows countries to specialize in finer-grained value-chain slivers instead of entire industries, thus improving the fit between firms and locations as resources are assigned more efficiently towards those activities in which the countries have a comparative advantage.

There are important differences, however, from traditional models. In a GVC world, it is no longer the case that trade and FDI are solely driven by market-seeking or resource-seeking reasons. In other words, firms not only conduct international business to locate their entire production process in the vicinity of foreign consumers or natural resources but they also do so to fragment their production process and make their supply chain more efficient.[28] Here are three new motives that companies adopt for conducting international business that were not present in traditional models:

Efficiency-seeking: By conducting tasks in other countries, firms can reduce input costs and increase their overall productivity.[29] There is ample supporting evidence to back this up: Amiti and Konings, for example, show that a 10 percentage point drop in input tariffs leads to a 12 per cent productivity gain for Indonesian firms that import their inputs.[30] Of course foreign firms can also increase their productivity by locating activities in low cost jurisdictions, endangering the competitiveness of domestic firms.

Flexibility-seeking: Conducting tasks in other countries allows firms to reduce supply chain risks. There are many events that can negatively affect a local value chain. For example, a sudden exchange-rate appreciation might significantly

---

25 Pol Antras and Elhanan Helpman, 'Global Sourcing' (2004) 112 *Journal of Political Economy* 552.

26 Eiichi Tomiura, 'Foreign Outsourcing, Exporting, and FDI: A Productivity Comparison at the Firm Level' (2007) 72 *Journal of International Economics* 113.

27 Ari Van Assche, 'Global Value Chains and Canada's Trade Policy: Business as Usual or Paradigm Shift?' (2012) Institute for Research on Public Policy Study No 32 <https://irpp.org/wp-content/uploads/assets/research/competitiveness/global-value-chains-and-canadas-trade-policy/IRPP-Study-no32.pdf> accessed 18 June 2019.

28 Van Assche (n 22).

29 Grossman and Rossi-Hansberg (n 22).

30 Mary Amiti and Jozef Konings, 'Trade Liberalization, Intermediate Inputs, and Productivity: Evidence from Indonesia' (2007) 97 *American Economic Review* 1611.

42   *Ari Van Assche*

increase the relative cost of performing a task in a particular location. A natural disaster such as an earthquake or tsunami might make it prohibitively expensive to carry out production locally for a certain period of time. In that case, a firm's ability to circumvent the shock depends on its ability to obtain the task rapidly elsewhere. As Kogut and Kulatilaka illustrate, companies can build resilience and operating flexibility into their value chain by carrying out similar tasks in different foreign locations.[31] If a shock hits one supplier, the firm can then import the task from another supplier.

Knowledge-seeking. Conducting tasks in other countries allows firms to tap into knowledge that is not available locally.[32] Once the external knowledge is obtained, the company can then use it to enhance the parent firm's innovation and productivity in its headquarter location.[33] For instance, Keller shows that international trade and FDI are major channels for international technology diffusion.[34]

The emergence of these new motives for trade and FDI suggests that companies in GVCs increasingly adopt a 'supply chain mindset' when conducting international business.[35] For firms, global business is no longer about the destination (selling to foreign markets), it is also about the journey (production process). Companies view international business as a way to reduce production costs, connect to stronger partners, access foreign technology, and diversify their exposure to supply chain shocks. As a result, GVC firms tend to favour trade and investment policies that facilitate the development of their production networks, such as import tariff reductions that facilitate their ability to collaborate with foreign value-chain partners.

3.1.2 Communication linkages

The location decision of a task depends not only on the cost of production in a country but also on the inherent communication links that exist between the task and other value-chain nodes. To execute a task, a firm generally requires information that has been generated and transferred from other value-chain activities. A US subsidiary in Canada, for example, might rely on financing from its headquarters in the United States, inputs made in Mexico and information from its R&D centre in, say, Ireland. The cost of obtaining these goods, capital, people, and know-how tends to increase with distance, which acts as a countervailing force against the geographic dispersion of GVC tasks.

---

31 Bruce Kogut and Nalin Kulatilaka, 'Operating Flexibility, Global Manufacturing, and the Option Value of a Multinational Network' (1994) 40 *Management Science* 123.
32 Heather Berry, 'Global Integration and Innovation: Multicountry Knowledge Generation within MNCs' (2014) 35 *Strategic Management Journal* 869.
33 ibid; Wilber Chung and Stephen Ross Yeaple, 'International Knowledge Sourcing: Evidence from US Firms Expanding Abroad' (2008) 29 *Strategic Management Journal* 1207.
34 Wolfgang Keller, 'International Technology Diffusion' (2001) National Bureau of Economic Research Working Paper No 8573 <www.nber.org/papers/w8573.pdf> accessed 18 June 2019.
35 Van Assche (n 22).

A growing body of literature has investigated the type of information that is most easily transferred from a distance with little loss of productivity. Routine tasks, such as performing simple calculations, are more easily sent offshore since they can be specified in simple instructions and taught to foreign workers with little misunderstanding.[36] Non-routine tasks, such as customer care, require complex thinking, judgement, human interaction, and language skills, and are more difficult to transfer.

Blinder counters, however, that it is not that the task needs to be routinizable, but that the communication linkage between tasks needs to be codifiable – that is, expressed digitally – and thus easily transferred over the internet.[37] Tasks such as computer programming that rely intensively on codifiable information from other value-chain activities can therefore be performed more easily at a distance. In contrast, tasks such as hairdressing and legal advice, which rely intensively on tacit information and cannot be conveyed in symbols, require frequent face-to-face contact, making them difficult to offshore.

The existence of these communication costs highlights the growing focus of firms on the complexities of moving goods, people, and information across international borders. Communication linkages remain far from being free and safe. International transportation costs, border-related trade costs, and behind-the-border trade costs continue to create headaches for firms that are integrated in GVCs.

3.1.3 Empirical evidence

The second unbundling process has now been widely documented empirically. There is vast evidence that production chains for goods and services are not concentrated within single countries but are now increasingly fragmented, with corporations dispersing activities across multiple countries and companies.[38] Countries increasingly specialize in the production and exports of slivers of the value chain, not of entire goods.[39] Furthermore, firms increasingly connect with foreign value-chain partners to produce final goods and services.

Companies can connect with foreign value-chain partners in two directions. Upstream, they can import intermediate goods and services from their foreign partners, which they then use in their own production (backward participation). Downstream, firms can export intermediate goods and services to their foreign

---

36 David H Autor, Frank Levy, and Richard J Murnane, 'The Skill Content of Recent Techno-logical Change: An Empirical Exploration' (2003) 118 *Quarterly Journal of Economics* 1279; Runjuan Liu, Dorothee J Feils, and Barry Scholnick, 'Why Are Different Services Outsourced to Different Countries?' (2011) 42 *Journal of International Business Studies* 558.

37 Alan S Blinder, 'Offshoring: The Next Industrial Revolution?' (2006) 85 *Foreign Affairs* 113.

38 Robert C Feenstra, 'Integration of Trade and Disintegration of Production in the Global Economy' (1998) 12 *The Journal of Economic Perspectives* 31; Johnson and Noguera (n 1).

39 Grossman and Rossi-Hansberg (n 22).

44 *Ari Van Assche*

value-chain partners, which in turn use them to make their own exports (forward participation).

The Trade in Value Added (TiVA) dataset compiled by the OECD and the WTO allows us to gain insights into the extent of a country's backward and forward participation in GVCs.[40] By combining input–output data for multiple countries with trade statistics, the dataset allows a country's gross exports to be decomposed into two parts: (1) domestic value added, which is generated in the exporting country; and (2) foreign value added, which comes from outside the exporting country. Foreign value added depicts a country's backward participation in GVCs. Domestic value added can be further decomposed into two subparts: domestic value added consumed in the destination country and domestic value added embodied in a foreign country's exports. The latter term captures a country's forward participation in GVCs.

The foreign value-added share embodied in gross exports is an indicator of a country's backward participation in GVCs, since it indicates how heavily a country relies on imported inputs to produce its exports. In Table 2.2, we focus on the importance of GVCs in the trade of NAFTA countries. In 2015, GVCs accounted for 10 per cent of US exports, 21 per cent of Canadian exports and 36 per cent of Mexican exports.[41] In other words, for the three NAFTA countries, foreign inputs account for one-tenth to more than a third of their gross export value.

Table 2.2 Integration in global value chains, NAFTA countries, 2005 and 2015

	Share of foreign value added in gross exports		Domestic value added embodied in foreign exports as share of gross exports		GVC trade as share of gross exports	
	2005	*2015*	*2005*	*2015*	*2005*	*2015*
United States	10.8	9.5	22.5	22.2	33.3	31.7
Canada	19.6	21.2	12.6	15.3	32.2	36.5
Mexico	34.0	36.1	8.3	8.8	42.3	44.9

Source: author's calculations using the OECD-WTO TiVA database

40 Koen De Backer and Sébastien Miroudot, 'Mapping Global Value Chains' (2014) European Central Bank Working Paper No 1677 <www.ecb.europa.eu/pub/pdf/scpwps/ecbwp1677.pdf> accessed 16 October 2019.

41 The significantly smaller foreign value-added share for the United States should not come as a surprise. The large size of the US economy implies that firms have a substantially bigger pool of local intermediate input providers in their proximity to draw on than smaller countries such as Mexico and Canada. Consequently, there is less need to partner with foreign suppliers to produce goods or services.

Trade and foreign direct investment 45

Firms also export intermediate goods to foreign value-chain partners, which use them to produce their own exports. For example, a Canadian aerospace company may export an intermediate good to Seattle, which Boeing then uses to produce and sell planes around the world. Table 2.2 shows that a significant portion of NAFTA countries' exports are in the form of intermediate goods that are used in the exports of other countries. In 2015, forward participation accounted for 9 percent of Mexico's gross exports, 15 percent of Canada's gross exports, and 22 percent of US gross exports.

3.2 Implications for trade politics

The fact that firms no longer concentrate their entire production process in a single country changes trade politics. To demonstrate this, consider once again two countries: a skill-abundant and a labour-abundant country. Assume also that the production of a good requires the combination of two tasks: skill-intensive headquarter services that are always produced in a firm's home country and manufacturing that can be produced in either of the two countries.

Consider first the trade preferences of firms in the skill-abundant country. If manufacturing is skill-intensive, there is no incentive for firms to move their manufacturing plant overseas since the skill-abundant country has a comparative advantage in manufacturing. In that case, all firms in the industry adopt local value chains and the trade preferences end up being the same as in the traditional model: skill-intensive firms support trade liberalization since it improves their ability to reach foreign consumers (see Table 2.3).

In labour-intensive industries, in contrast, firms' trade policy preferences shift due to the fact that they now have the ability to offshore their manufacturing plant to the labour-abundant country. Instead of opposing trade liberalization, their position on trade policy is now mixed. On the one hand, they continue to oppose tariff reductions on imports from their foreign competitors since these import tariffs sustain their competitiveness. On the other hand, they favour a reduction on trade barriers to and from their own production plants and value-chain partners since such tariff cuts reduce production costs, thereby increasing their competitiveness. Taken together, these opposing preferences on trade liberalization imply that the political support of labour-intensive firms for import protection is, if anything, lower than in traditional models.

Firm preferences are opposite in labour-abundant countries. In labour-intensive industries, firms have no incentive to offshore manufacturing and so their trade preferences are similar to traditional models; they support trade liberalization. In skill-intensive industries, they support protection against imports from their competitors, but not from their subsidiaries or value-chain partners.

The trade preferences of workers are largely similar to those in the traditional model. In skill-abundant countries, skilled workers favour trade liberalization, while unskilled workers oppose it. Conversely, in labour-abundant countries, unskilled workers prefer trade liberalization, while skilled workers oppose it.

46 *Ari Van Assche*

Table 2.3 Stakeholders' trade and FDI preferences under global value chains

Stakeholder	Trade liberalization	FDI liberalization
SKILL-ABUNDANT COUNTRY		
Consumers	√	√
Firms		
Skill-intensive sectors	√	√
Labour-intensive sectors	?	?
Workers		
Skilled workers	√	?
Unskilled workers	X	X
LABOUR-ABUNDANT COUNTRY		
Consumers	√	√
Firms		
Skill-intensive sectors	?	?
Labour-intensive sectors	√	√
Workers		
Skilled workers	X	X
Unskilled workers	√	?

Note: √ indicates if a stakeholder is in favour of a type of liberalization, while X suggests it is unsupportive. Stakeholders' preferences for trade and investment protection are opposite.? indicates that preferences are mixed or indeterminate.

Finally, consumers prefer trade liberalization since it reduces prices and thus increases consumer welfare.

Taken together, these results suggest one big change in trade politics: the trade policy coalition between firms and workers that originally supported the mercantilist view of trade has now broken down.[42] Workers who are relatively scarce in an economy have lost an important ally in their quest for trade protectionism: the companies they work for in comparative-disadvantaged industries. For these firms, import tariffs are no longer a boon that acts as a protective buffer against foreign competitors, but rather a hindrance that negatively affects their own competitiveness. To meet corporate objectives, they thus have an incentive to lobby for import liberalization, even if this disproportionately helps foreign workers to the detriment of domestic blue-collar workers.

3.3 *Implications for FDI*

FDI theories have also changed in light of GVCs' emergence. Studies of the multinational firm now recognize that firms have multiple motives for

---

42 Ari Van Assche and Byron Gangnes, 'Global Value Chains and the Fragmentation of Traditional Trade Policy Coalitions' (2019) 26 *Transnational Corporations* 31.

conducting FDI. Dunning pointed out early on that, besides market-seeking and resource-seeking purposes, companies also have efficiency-seeking motives for conducting FDI.[43] In this case, they move a part of the value chain to a foreign country in order to take advantage of differences in production costs. Markusen studied the drivers of market-seeking (horizontal) FDI versus efficiency-seeking (vertical) FDI by introducing both forms of multinational activity into a model with both labour- and skill-abundant countries.[44] He showed that market-seeking FDI primarily occurs between similar countries since this supports production of the multinational firm's good in both countries. Efficiency-seeking FDI, however, is greatest when countries have very different factor endowments, since it creates large differences in factor prices. Finally, Yeaple argued that FDI may emerge for a combination of both market-seeking and efficiency-seeking reasons,[45] leading to export-platform FDI.[46] In this case, a company may set up a labour-intensive manufacturing plant in a labour-abundant country that is located in the vicinity of a large third-country market.

Early empirical studies found little evidence of efficiency-seeking FDI. Brainard as well as Carr, Markusen, and Maskus suggested that most FDI originating from developed countries was market-seeking FDI.[47] More recent studies, however, point out that the share of efficiency-seeking FDI is much higher than previously thought, even within developed countries. Alfaro and Charlton, for example, found that a significant amount of efficiency-seeking FDI has been misclassified as market-seeking in previous studies.[48]

Other studies have suggested that FDI between developed countries may also be misclassified as market-seeking. Some developed-country companies conduct foreign investment in other developed countries to gain access to foreign knowledge, not markets. The starting point in these studies is that countries differ markedly in their knowledge profiles[49] and that firms can benefit from tapping into different knowledge hotspots since knowledge diversity catalyzes

---

43 Dunning (n 10).

44 James Markusen, *Multinational Firms and the Theory of International Trade* (MIT Press 2002).

45 Stephen Yeaple, 'The Complex Integration Strategies of Multinationals and Cross Country Dependencies in the Structure of Foreign Direct Investment' (2003) 60 *Journal of International Economics* 293.

46 Karolina Ekholm, Rikard Forslid, and James Markusen 'Export-Platform Foreign Direct Investment' (2007) 5 *Journal of the European Economic Association* 776.

47 Brainard (n 13); David L Carr, James Markusen, and Keith Maskus, 'Estimating the Knowledge-Capital Model of the Multinational Enterprise' (2001) 91 *American Economic Review* 693.

48 Laura Alfaro and Andrew Charlton, 'Intra-Industry Foreign Direct Investment' (2009) 99 *American Economic Review* 2096.

49 John Cantwell and Simona Iammarino, 'MNCs, Technological Innovation and Regional Systems in the EU: Some Evidence in the Italian Case' (1998) 5 *International Journal of the Economics of Business* 383; Chung and Yeaple (n 33).

48   *Ari Van Assche*

innovation.[50] Therefore, many firms deliberately conduct FDI to similar countries to gain access to complementary knowledge pockets that are not available locally.[51] Once new knowledge is tapped into, the company can use reverse knowledge transfers to enhance the parent firm's innovation in its home country.[52] Taken together, these new, second unbundling theories suggest that firms also increasingly adopt a global supply chain mindset towards FDI. Besides market-seeking, they conduct FDI to reduce costs and access foreign knowledge pockets, which help strengthen their competitive advantage. Firms, therefore, favour FDI policies that facilitate their ability to move value-chain stages to different countries.

3.4 Implications for FDI politics

Firms' changing mindset towards international investment influences FDI politics. Consider again the scenario where firms need to produce their skill-intensive headquarter services in their home country but can locate manufacturing at home or abroad. Firms' preferences towards FDI liberalization continue to be broadly similar to their preferences towards trade liberalization, even though they have changed compared to traditional models (see Table 2.3). In skill-abundant countries, firms in skill-intensive industries continue to produce their entire value chain in their home country, and so they support FDI liberalization, since outward FDI increases their options to reach foreign consumers. Firms in labour-intensive industries, then again, have mixed feelings about FDI liberalization. On the one hand, they support lowering restrictions on outward FDI since it allows them to offshore labour-intensive manufacturing to the labour-abundant country. On the other hand, they oppose lowering restrictions on inward FDI since it increases competition from foreign firms. These mixed preferences suggest that labour-intensive firms' opposition to investment liberalization is more ambiguous than in traditional models. Note that, once again, the results are opposite in labour-abundant countries.

Workers' FDI policy preferences now also become ambiguous (see Table 2.3). In skill-abundant countries, skilled workers do not like that FDI liberalization makes it easier for skill-intensive companies to conduct market-seeking FDI, since it allows firms to substitute exports with foreign production, but they like that FDI liberalization promotes efficiency-seeking FDI, since the productivity rise that goes hand-in-hand with this type of FDI increases the demand for skilled workers.[53] Unskilled workers like that FDI liberalization

---

50 John Cantwell, *Technological Innovation and Multinational Corporations* (Basil Blackwell 1989).

51 John Cantwell and Grazia D Santangelo, 'The Frontier of International Technology Networks: Sourcing Abroad the Most Highly Tacit Capabilities' (1999) 11 *Information Economics and Policy* 101.

52 Berry (n 36); Chung and Yeaple (n 33).

53 Ann Harrison and Margaret McMillan, 'Offshoring Jobs? Multinationals and US Manufacturing Employment' (2011) 93 *Review of Economics and Statistics* 857.

increases foreign firms' ability to conduct employment-generating inward FDI. However, they dislike that FDI liberalization increases home-country firms' ability to offshore labour-intensive activities. This latter effect has been a major concern for unskilled workers, who are largely opposed to FDI liberalization.

Consumers are the only stakeholder for which preferences remain the same: they continue to benefit from investment liberalization (see Table 2.3).

3.5 Summary

A comparison of the results in Tables 2.1 and 2.3 suggests that trade and FDI politics have changed in significant ways in the second unbundling period. First, the rise of global value chains has, to an extent, undermined the traditional mercantilist view of trade and trade policy. Second, the FDI policy preferences of firms and skilled workers are more aligned towards FDI liberalization than in traditional models. Taken together, these two trends suggest that unskilled workers in skill-abundant countries are increasingly isolated in their quest for both trade and investment protection. The accompanied feeling of disenfranchisement may help explain the rise in populism that several countries have experienced in recent years.[54]

4. Concluding remarks

In this paper, we have evaluated how economists' thinking of trade and FDI has evolved as they have started abandoning the assumption that production processes are localized (the national production paradigm). We have argued that scholars increasingly view trade as an exchange in tasks, not goods. That is, they recognize that firms not only conduct trade to reach foreign consumers but also to build efficient value chains. They also recognize that FDI is not only a tool to locate production in the proximity of consumers or natural resources, but also to build efficient global value chains.

We have discussed how these changes have allowed scholars to recognize that firms have developed new views of trade and investment policy. It is no longer the case that firms merely ask governments for help in accessing foreign natural resources and foreign markets. Firms now also lobby policymakers to help facilitate connections with their foreign value-chain partners or set up foreign production plants. Furthermore, firms no longer want governments to primarily focus on building trade and investment relations with other developed countries. Instead, firms now also want governments to build trade and investment agreements with developing countries. On the trade side, these new demands for connectivity include requests for tariff elimination on intermediate imports, as well as measures for trade facilitation. On the investment side, these

---

54 Dani Rodrik, 'Populism and the Economics of Globalization' (2018) 1 *Journal of International Business Policy* 12.

requests include demands for investor–state dispute settlement systems, particularly with developing countries.

We have also analyzed the implications of GVCs' emergence for trade and FDI politics. We have demonstrated that the ability to fragment production processes internationally has made firms more favourable towards trade and investment liberalization. Blue-collar workers in developed countries and skilled workers in developing countries, however, are hurt by reductions in trade and investment barriers, which to an extent may explain the recent rise in populism.

3 Actors, institutions, and policy in host countries

Krista Nadakavukaren Schefer

1. Introduction

Scholars typically approach the law of international investment protection as a subject that pertains distinctly to international law – an area of law that centres around the rules written by states and binding to states. The international law-centric position is understandable, because international investment law *is* a part of general international law. As in all areas of international law, state actions are central to investment law's overall existence; states negotiate, draft, and ratify the treaties containing most of the promised protections for investors; states are the actors that can be held to account on the international level for any violations of the promises made in these treaties. While some of international investment law's features make it clearly different from other areas of international law, these features make it a specialized area of general international law rather than taking it out of the international law system entirely.[1]

Yet, solely examining investment law as international law ignores a great deal of the legal context facing both foreign investors and the government agents responsible for working with foreign investors. The law of foreign investment is inextricably tied to domestic laws and institutional structures. Investors have long recognized this, of course, but it is easy for people working mainly with the public international law aspects of investment to forget this. This chapter highlights the more general legal context of foreign investment by pointing out the domestic contributors to the development and implementation of the rules protecting foreign investors. This is important because the investor and the host agencies responsible for regulating any particular investment relationship are

---

1 For example, the protection obligations contained in international investment law instruments provide direct rights of access to dispute settlement mechanisms to non-state actors. Private parties do not usually have the right to sue a state for violations of international law. See Lukas Vanhonnaecker, 'International investment agreements', Chapter 10 in this volume; J Anthony VanDuzer and Patrick Dumberry, 'Investor–state dispute settlement', Chapter 11 in this volume.

52 *Krista Nadakavukaren Schefer*

primarily bound to work within the host's domestic legal framework for the life of the investment.

Legal systems, however, are not hermeneutically separated from one another. Even if a particular set of rules is not invoked in a given legal dispute, it may well lend substantial influence over those rules that are being interpreted and applied. The influence can be direct; domestic court judges, for example, may refer to standards set forth in international treaties when evaluating domestic law arguments brought before them. Judges may also, however, simply adopt such standards indirectly and without saying so, either by applying the factors set forth in international law to a case decided in another area of law as a matter of legal reasoning or by adapting analytical frameworks from one legal context into another distinct legal context. Thus, the general norms or values of one legal regime may cross-fertilize a separate regime: international law may fertilize domestic law, and domestic law concepts may enter international law.

These types of legal interactions occur where domestic investment rules and the international protections afforded foreign investors are concerned. National criminal laws prohibiting bribery, for example, may be a source of domestic law that international investment tribunals rely upon when determining whether they have jurisdiction over a claimant. Whether an investor has made an 'investment' for the purposes of an investment treaty and is eligible for protection may rest on whether the investor concluded a legal contract upon entering the market.

The influence of international law on domestic law decision-making exists as well, but garners less attention in the academic literature on international investment policy-making. Yet, the means by which international law instruments of investment protection impact the actors, institutions, and policies of host countries is arguably as important for the system of international law as it is for the individual domestic system considered.

It is intuitive to think that the continual flow of influence between the material laws of the international and domestic investment regimes is significant for the systems. There is a larger issue, however, that may get overlooked if one is looking at the rules only as instruments of practical usage: how do the forms of interaction of investment rules affect the legitimacy of the investment law system? A complete answer to this question would require a thorough analysis of the specifics of investment and host-country legal frameworks, which is beyond this chapter's scope. Instead, I point out a number of issues that determine the answer's contours. I begin with a short introduction to the international legal system. Next, I explain the idea of 'sources' of international investment law. This is relevant because, in international law, process is an aspect of the definition of 'sources' of law, but it is often neglected in the practice of identifying sources. In the third part I say a few words about which sources of domestic law are most likely to be relevant to foreign investment activities. Finally, I discuss the relationship between international and domestic law and, by doing so, bring up a theoretical inquiry into the nature of the 'sources' of law to which we should attend in investor–state disputes and other investment contexts.

2. International law: the basics

Defining international law is a growing challenge. While once it would have been more or less accurate to call it the rules governing a state's behaviour toward other states, today international law includes interstate rules plus a variety of rules that govern states' relationships with non-states – formal international organizations (e.g. the United Nations or World Trade Organization), informal organizations (e.g. terrorist networks), groups (e.g. indigenous tribes), and legal persons (corporations and similar legal entities), and individuals (the law of human rights).[2] What's more, international lawyers are also increasingly looking at whether and how non-states' self-generated rules bind those (or other) non-state actors in their international activities.[3] Thus, topics such as 'soft law'[4] and corporate social responsibility[5] are of great interest to the international legal world as well as to those focusing on national law systems.

2.1 Basic tenets of international law

2.1.1 Sovereignty

The basic tenets of international law remain firmly entrenched in the notion of state sovereignty. Sovereignty is one of the most fundamental – but also most disputed – concepts of international law.[6] 'Internal sovereignty' means the government's power in relation to other entities within a state (and often to the residual power of the citizens); 'external sovereignty' designates the power of the government in relation to other entities outside the state.[7] In international law, state sovereignty refers to the power of the state vis-à-vis other states (and other international actors) to determine everything about itself – from how it is governed to what rules it is governed by. Thus, a state must consent to any restriction on its actions.

---

2 Malcolm N Shaw, *International Law* (8th edition Cambridge University Press 2017) 32–36.

3 The literature on the governance of non-state actors is large and growing, e.g. Anne Peters, Lucy Koechlin, Till Förster, and Gretta Fenner (eds), *Non-State Actors as Standard Setters* (Cambridge University Press 2009).

4 Soft law is the term given to instruments that are non-binding but influential. See Shaw (n 2) 87–88.

5 The term 'corporate social responsibility' (CSR) refers to the duties of corporations to serve needs of the public – by protecting social, environmental, and labour rights – as well as the needs of their shareholders. For an introduction to how CSR relates to international law, see Jennifer A Zerk, *Multinationals and Corporate Social Responsibility: Limitations and Opportunities in International Law* (Cambridge University Press 2006).

6 Stephen D Krasner, *Sovereignty: Organized Hypocrisy* (Princeton University Press 1999).

7 Christina Eckes, 'The Reflexive Relationship between Internal and External Sovereignty', *UCD Working Papers in Law, Criminology & Socio-Legal Studies, Research Paper No 0506121314* (6 December 2013) available at <http://ssrn.com/abstract=2439186> accessed 16 June 2019.

54 *Krista Nadakavukaren Schefer*

Because states are sovereign, the first rule of international law is that states are equal. The Charter of the United Nations clearly sets forth 'the principle of the sovereign equality of all [states]' as the first principle listed as a means of achieving its purposes of maintaining peace and fostering cooperation and the promotion of human rights.[8] No state is legally 'superior' to another. This, in turn, leads to the second rule of international law: the principle of non-interference in domestic affairs of a state.[9] Because states are equal and sovereign, no state can make a rule limiting another state's choice of how to govern itself or behave. Finally, the prohibition on the use of force, a third pillar of international law, is in fact an extension of the principle of non-interference.[10]

2.1.2 Rules of behaviour

The result of these tenets is that the international legal system consists of a network of voluntarily-accepted rules channelling state behaviour. The rules may be consciously created – such as in treaties – or they may arise over time through the consistent practice of states, which leads to a belief in their obligatory nature. The latter is called 'customary law'.[11] Unless a rule of customary law is protested during its emergence,[12] even a state that does not accept the rule will be considered bound by it.

Finally, general principles can be rules by virtue of their existence in numerous national legal systems or rules that can be gleaned from the existence of the international legal system itself.[13] Courts often announce the first type in the absence of other rules to guide their decision-making. Thus, the International Court of Justice (ICJ) held that indirect evidence to prove a case is admissible even if there is no body of international evidence rules.[14] It based this finding on the fact that domestic legal systems throughout the world all accept indirect evidence in legal proceedings. The second type of general principle is qualitatively different from the first type. The principles stemming from the nature of international law as a legal system are those that are essential

---

8 UN Charter, art 2.1, available at <www.un.org/en/sections/un-charter/un-charter-full-text/> accessed 10 December 2018. See also UN Charter art 1 (listing the purposes of the United Nations).

9 UN Charter, ibid, arts 2.4 and 2.7 contain the provisions ensuring each state the right to be free of interference in its physical integrity and in its authority to determine its domestic affairs.

10 UN Charter, ibid, art 2.4.

11 Customary international law rules are generally considered rules that attain their legal characteristic through long-term, consistent, and widespread state practice combined with *opinio juris* indicating that states adhere to them out of a sense of obligation. See Section 3.1 ('Sources of international law') below.

12 *Asylum Case* (Colom. v Peru), 1950 ICJ Reports 266, 277–278 (Judgment of 13 June 1950); *Fisheries Case* (U.K. v. Nor.), 1951 ICJ Reports 116, 131 (Judgment of 18 December 1951).

13 Shaw (n 2) 73–74.

14 *Corfu Channel case* (merits), ICJ Reports 1949 (Judgment of 9 April 1949) 4, 18.

Actors, institutions, and policy 55

to its functioning. Good faith adherence to treaty obligations is perhaps the most widely-recognized general principle of international law – for without a belief in each state's promises to abide by the law, no legal system could exist.[15]

2.1.3 Hierarchy of international laws

International law's rules in treaties, customs, or general principles as well as the way the rules emerge, or come to exist, are called the 'sources' of international law. Significantly, with the exception of a set of peremptory, or non-derogable, norms (called *'jus cogens'* norms, such as the prohibitions on slavery, genocide, piracy, and torture[16]), all sources of international law are, at least theoretically, hierarchically equal. That is, treaties, customary law, and general principles are equally 'binding' on states, even though the state's explicit consent is only given to treaty-based rules.

2.1.4 State responsibility

While a state cannot be forced to accept a treaty that limits its freedom to act (or to refrain from acting), it must adhere to those limitations that it does accept. The principle of *pacta sunt servanda* (that is, that agreements are to be upheld) demands that states are internationally 'responsible' for doing (or not doing) that which they agreed to do (or not do). The 59 Articles on the Responsibility of States for Internationally Wrongful Acts[17] can be crystallized for our purposes into two principles:

1. States are responsible for their own wrongful acts;[18]
2. States are responsible for the wrongful acts of their agents.

The principle that a state is liable for breaching any of its international obligations holds even when a state has contradictory obligations stemming from two treaties.[19] If an obligation of free trade in Treaty A would prevent the state from stopping imports of any goods from another territory but the obligations of Treaty B prohibit the importation of endangered species, the state's decision to act in adherence with Treaty B by imposing a bar to the importation of tiger pelts could leave it responsible for its violation of Treaty A. Significantly, the same is true if the

---

15 See Robert Kolb, *Good Faith in International Law* (Hart Publishing 2017).
16 See M Cherif Bassiouni, 'International Crimes: "*Jus Cogens*" and "*Obligatio Erga Omnes*"' (1996) 59 *Law & Contemporary Problems* 63–68.
17 Articles on the Responsibility of States for Internationally Wrongful Acts (United Nations 2005) (text as adopted by General Assembly Resolution 56/83 of 12 December 2001, and corrected by document A/56/49(Vol. I)/Corr.4) [ASR].
18 ASR ibid, art 1.
19 ASR ibid, Chapter V (Circumstances Precluding Wrongfulness).

56 Krista Nadakavukaren Schefer

state acted in accordance with its national constitutional obligations but in doing so violated one of its international law duties.[20]

A second important aspect of state responsibility is that the rules on responsibility apply to all agents of state authority.[21] That is, anything that any branch of government or any level of government does is considered a 'state action'.[22] This principle is enormously significant for investment law. The passage by a national legislature of a law subjecting investors to new public health regulations,[23] an unjustified refusal to issue a permit to a foreign investor by a municipal administrative agency,[24] or even a refusal by a state-run company to pay a supplier for work performed[25] could cause the 'state' as a whole to be found internationally responsible for having acted wrongfully. Potential liability can also arise from an action taken by a private entity under the authority of the state.[26] Thus, a private security company's misdeeds when administering a military prison would be considered the actions of the state and implicate the state's responsibility, because the running of a prison is an act of governmental authority.[27]

With this background to international law, we turn now to our main focus: the sources of international investment law.

3. Sources of international investment law

3.1 Sources of international law

A source of law is an instrument (a document, finding, or other legal act of the state) or process from which legal rights and obligations can be determined. Most of the

---

20 ASR ibid, art 3 ('The characterization of an act of a State as internationally wrongful is governed by international law. Such characterization is not affected by the characterization of the same act as lawful by internal law'.).

21 ASR ibid, Chapter II (Attribution of Conduct to a State).

22 ASR ibid, art 4.1.

23 The cases brought by the cigarette maker Philip Morris against governments that implemented regulations intended to reduce smoking offer the clearest example of how legislative attempts to protect health may generate investor backlash; e.g. *Philip Morris Brands Sàrl, Philip Morris Products SA and Abal Hermanos SA v Oriental Republic of Uruguay*, ICSID Case No ARB/10/7, Award (8 July 2016); *Philip Morris Asia Limited v The Commonwealth of Australia*, UNCITRAL, PCA Case No 2012–2012, Award on Jurisdiction and Admissibility (17 December 2015).

24 *Metalclad Corporation v The United Mexican States*, ICSID Case No ARB(AF)/97/1, Award (30 August 2000) paras 99–100, 104.

25 The famous case of *Salini v Morocco* involved a complaint by an Italian construction company for non-payment of its contracted price by a company established as a separate entity from the Moroccan state. *Salini Costruttori SpA and Italstrade SpA v Kingdom of Morocco*, ICSID Case No ARB/00/4, Decision on Jurisdiction (31 July 2001). The tribunal found, however, that the Moroccan company was functionally and structurally part of the state, and thus attributed its actions to Morocco (ibid para 35).

26 See particularly ASR (n 17), arts 5, 8, 9 (attributing responsibility to private persons acting in the exercise of governmental authority, at the direction of a state, or in the absence of state authority if the act is one that would have been in the exercise of authority but for the default).

27 ASR ibid, art 5.

Actors, institutions, and policy 57

attention in modern international law examines the definition, characteristics, and role of the three sources named by the Statute of the International Court of Justice.[28]

3.1.1 The legal instruments

The ICJ Statute's Article 38 lists treaties (also called 'conventions'), customary international law, and general principles of law as the primary sources of law available to the judges to assess international legal questions before them. Article 38(d) sets forth additional (so-called secondary) sources that can be consulted should the primary sources not provide the necessary clarity. Decisions of other tribunals (whether arbitral tribunals or tribunals from other fields of international law) and the writings of eminent scholars are also of relevance in determining the content of the law.[29] Though Article 38 is binding only on the ICJ itself, its contents have been much more widely applied. International trade, human rights, and investment tribunals consistently look to treaties, custom, and general principles for rules upon which to base their decisions.

These three sources of 'hard' law, however, are no longer the only instruments to which the international lawyers and judges look for rules. The international community of states has turned to drafting documents that are explicitly quasi-legal and the international activities of non-state actors, which have been producing international guidelines, codes, principles of action, and other law-like documents.

The term 'soft law' is often used to describe instruments that propose rules of behaviour or rights and which often actually influence behaviour, but which have not been accepted by states as international law. Soft law can come into existence in various ways. Like treaties, some soft law rules can be the result of a conscious effort by different actors to agree on them in a written – but non-'treaty' – instrument. The standards promulgated by international financial regulatory institutions, such as the Basel Committee on Banking Supervision[30] and the Financial Stability Board,[31] are examples of negotiated instruments specifically designed to be influential on rule-makers rather than being the rules

---

28 The International Court of Justice is the judicial authority created by the Charter of the United Nations to hear disputes between states and issue advisory opinions to five United Nations (UN) organs (including the Security Council and General Assembly) and certain UN specialized agencies.

29 Alain Pellet, 'Art 38' in Andreas Zimmermann, Christian Tomuschat, and Karin Oellers-Frahm (eds), *The Statute of the International Court of Justice: A Commentary* (2nd edition Oxford University Press 2012) 731–870, 734–748.

30 See Pierre Panchaud, 'Bank for International Settlements' in Thomas Cottier and Krista Nadakavukaren Schefer (eds), *Encyclopedia of International Economic Law* (Edward Elgar 2017) 90–93, 92.

31 See Eva Hüpkes, 'Financial Stability Board (FSB)' in Cottier and Nadakavukaren Schefer ibid 100–103.

themselves.[32] Other soft law rules are more comparable to custom in that they are simply considered the 'right' thing to do, but not because of a legal obligation to adhere to them. Most international codes of behaviour, such as the International Bar Association's 2014 Guidelines on Conflicts of Interest in International Arbitration,[33] and corporate codes of conduct are all 'soft' instruments – acting as persuasive tools rather than binding ones.

The strict legal view of soft law rules and instruments varies. Some courts treat such documents as interpretive aids rather than as 'law', given their ambiguous nature, while other decision-makers deny their relevance to the judicial process.[34] In either case, the soft law instruments provide evidence of the existence of emerging global norms and can contribute to shifts in attitude among decision-makers as to the international community's goals.

Significantly, the difference between hard and soft law is not a question of bindingness. While hard law is often binding and soft law is not binding, hard law instruments can be non-binding as well. Beyond the preambular language of treaties, which is agreed to be non-binding but is nevertheless a part of an acknowledged 'hard law' instrument, and reservations exempting a party from a particular obligation that binds other parties, the use of the term 'should' in treaty texts is interpreted as permitting a state party to ignore the related obligations without incurring international responsibility. The difference between the two, instead, rests largely on the (in)existence of state consent to the particular rule or instrument.

Hard law is based on the consent of states – explicit in the case of treaties, implied in the case of customary law, and inferred in the case of general principles. Soft law is not. Even where soft law rules are actually applied, they are applied because they are normatively persuasive, efficient or logical, or strategically important. They are not applied by virtue of the fact that governments have agreed that they have a legal quality. In fact, many soft law instruments become instruments only because they have no legal quality. Many are composed by non-state actors: e.g. organizations, committees of experts, think tanks, civil society, and business firms. A states' role, therefore, in the creation of such rules, is not determinative.

---

32 Chris Brummer, *Soft Law and the Global Financial System: Rule Making in the 21st Century* (2nd edition Cambridge University Press 2015).

33 IBA, *Guidelines on Conflicts of Interest in International Arbitration* 12 (23 October 2014) (setting forth in the 6th introductory provision that 'These Guidelines are not legal provisions and do not override any applicable national law or arbitral rules chosen by the parties. However, it is hoped that, [...] the revised Guidelines will find broad acceptance within the international arbitration community, and that they will assist parties, practitioners, arbitrators, institutions and courts in dealing with these important questions of impartiality and independence').

34 Elina Mereminskaya, Bofill Mir, and Alvarez Jana Abogados, *Results of the Survey on Use of Soft Law Instruments in International Arbitration* (6 June 2014) available as http://arbitra tionblog.kluwerarbitration.com/2014/06/06/results-of-the-survey-on-the-use-of-soft-law-instruments-in-international-arbitration/?_ga=2.165223673.733400174.1516796515-1962678513.1516796515 accessed 24 January 2018.

3.1.2 The process of rule creation

Before we turn to international investment law, it is worth noting that the discussion of international law sources generally revolves solely around the instruments of law. That is no doubt because the provisions of Article 38 of the ICJ Statute are focused on the *instruments as vessels* that contain binding legal obligations of states. However, a number of scholars of international law include a second aspect of sources in their discussion: the *process* of producing these rule-containing instruments.[35] The emergence of rules through interpretation, for example, makes the interpretive act also a source of law.[36] Equating Article 38 with the sources of international law, therefore, can be faulted for omitting half of the sources of law doctrine: the rule-making process. I come back to this in my discussion of the legitimacy of sources, as legitimacy rests on the entirety of sources. Thus, legitimate processes of rule-making are as important as (and in fact cannot be separated from) the legitimacy of the instruments.

3.2 Sources of investment law

Today's law of investment protection, as a part of international law generally, also relies on Article 38 of the ICJ Statute's doctrine of international legal sources. Currently, international investment agreements (IIAs) form the main source of investment law, with around 2,400 bilateral investment treaties (BITs) and a growing number of free trade agreements (FTAs) containing investment protection chapters in force. Yet, the other sources of international law play an as-yet under-researched role in shaping the system.

3.2.1 Treaties

As treaties, IIAs are instruments from which international tribunals glean rights and obligations of the parties to the agreements. These treaties' content, including the relationship among the rights and obligations contained within them, has been the focus of most of the scholarship of international investment law.[37]

Other treaties can also be a source of international investment law. Although not an investment protection agreement, the General Agreement on Trade in Services (GATS) can be important for investors and potential investors.[38] A state's GATS obligation to provide market access to foreign service suppliers in sectors listed in their national schedule of commitments in the form of 'mode

---

35 Hugh Thirlway, *The Sources of International Law* (Oxford University Press 2014) 3.
36 Ingo Venzke, *How Interpretation Makes International Law* (Oxford University Press 2012).
37 See Vanhonnaecker (n 1).
38 General Agreement on Trade in Services, in force 15 April 1994, Marrakesh Agreement Establishing the World Trade Organization, Annex 1B, (1994) 1869 UNTS 183, 33 ILM 1167 [GATS].

60 Krista Nadakavukaren Schefer

3' commitments (i.e. to allow foreign service suppliers to establish a presence in the territory of that member) may be considered an investment provision.[39] Offering investors the right to operate on host territory is a significant concession of the traditional right of states to deny the entry of investments and, as such, complements the traditional post-establishment investor protections found in BITs.[40]

The non-discrimination principles in GATS include national treatment[41] and most-favoured-nation treatment.[42] These principles require the host to treat foreign services investors no less favourably than investors from the host state or from other states once the investment is operational. Enforceable through the WTO's state-to-state dispute settlement mechanism, GATS rights can be particularly significant for new investors who may encounter difficulties in competing on the marketplace but do not have the resources to launch an investor–state claim themselves or who cannot access investor–state dispute settlement (ISDS).

The Agreement on Trade-Related Investment Measures (TRIMs) is another WTO agreement that is a source of investment obligations on host states.[43] TRIMs aims to prevent investment regulations from distorting trade flows. Thus, TRIMs requires members to ensure that any regulations applying to investment not discriminate against foreign investors' trade in goods and not restrict imports and exports of goods.[44] TRIMs lists a number of examples of measures that would violate its provisions, including the use of local content requirements, and export restrictions on goods produced by a foreign investor.[45] Even though a foreign investor cannot call on TRIMs obligations of a host state directly in ISDS, TRIMs provisions are subject to the state-to-state dispute settlement in the WTO.[46] However, some investment treaties incorporate TRIMs obligations or prohibit the kinds of performance requirements that would breach TRIMs. Investors benefiting from these treaties

---

39 GATS ibid, art XVI. Market access is defined as the absence of identified restrictions on foreign participation in the national market, like caps on foreign ownership levels.

40 Bart De Meester and Dominic Coppens, 'Mode 3 of the GATS: A Model for Disciplining Measures Affecting Investment Flows?' in Zdenek Drabek and Petros C Mavroidis (eds), *Regulations of Foreign Investment: Challenges to International Harmonization* (World Scientific Publishing 2013) 99–152.

41 GATS (n 38) art XVII. Like market access, national treatment applies only in relation to services sectors listed in a country's national schedule of commitments and subject to any limitations inscribed in the schedule.

42 GATS ibid, art II.

43 Agreement on Trade-Related Investment Measures, in force 15 April 1994, Marrakesh Agreement Establishing the World Trade Organization, Annex 1A, (1994) 1868 UNTS 186 [TRIMS].

44 TRIMs ibid, art 2.1.

45 TRIMs ibid, Annex.

46 TRIMs ibid, art 8.

Actors, institutions, and policy   61

can pursue claims in ISDS.[47] As well, TRIMs rules could be indirectly relevant to claims under an IIA by informing the interpretation of expected behaviour of a host state.

Treaties outside of the international economic law spheres play a lesser but growing role in investment law. Environmental law agreements (such as the Convention on Climate Change and its protocols[48]) have been a source of inspiration for disputants, as have agreements on human rights (e.g. the Convention against Racial Discrimination[49]) and public health (such as the Framework Convention on Tobacco Control[50]), each invoked as interpretive assistance when tribunals need to decide the scope of permitted governmental regulation of investors.

3.2.2 Customary law and general principles

Customary law and general principles of law, the other classic sources of international law, also play a role in investment. These two sources offer tribunals a way to justify their findings where treaty language is absent or ambiguous. We may forget, however, just how relevant custom and general principles are beyond the dispute settlement context. Existing often as gap-fillers, both custom and general principles should actually be more important in the creation of a treaty than in its future interpretation. This is because the state parties presumably know that non-treaty sources of international law form the context for discussion of treaty content.

The ability to presume custom and general principles as applicable to international relations is, in effect, a shortcut to concluding a consensual agreement. Treaty drafters may assume that each negotiating party is acting in good faith and will fulfil any obligation it accepts, because good faith and *pacta sunt servanda* (the obligation to adhere to an agreement) are both general principles of law, applicable to every state. Knowing that any international tribunal will apply the universally-recognized concept that a disputant will have to prove the affirmative assertions it makes – a customary rule of international law – drafters can skip writing specific rules into the treaty to cover that. This

---

47 e.g. Agreement between the Government of Canada and the Government of the Peoples' Republic of China for the Promotion and Protection of Investments, signed 9 September 2012, entered into force 1 October 2014, *Canada Treaty Series* 2014/26, art 9; North American Free Trade Agreement, signed 17 December 1992, in force 1 January 1994, reprinted in (1993) 32 ILM 670, art 1106.

48 Multiple investment treaty-based claims have been lodged against Spain for its revocation of a subsidy for renewable energy producers.

49 *Mike Campbell (Pvt) Ltd and Others v Republic of Zimbabwe* (2/2007) [2008] SADCT 2 (28 November 2008) (referring to the jurisprudence of the European Court of Human Rights, the Inter-American Court of Human Rights, the African Commission on Human and Peoples' Rights, and the Constitutional Court of South Africa on the question of access to justice and effective remedy and to the United Nations Human Rights Committee on racial discrimination).

50 *Philip Morris v Uruguay* (n 23).

62 Krista Nadakavukaren Schefer

leaves more time to focus on those aspects of international law that are clearly not custom, or that are norms whose characterization as custom or general principle is contested. For example, negotiators frequently include a provision in IIAs stating explicitly that a host state's expropriation of a foreign investor's property must be accompanied by 'full' compensation (a contested norm).

Where non-investment norms become relevant to an international investment dispute, customary rules and general principles may also be invoked to justify a tribunal's decision. One example would be the reference to transnational public policy by tribunals denying an investor's claim where the investment was secured by a bribe.[51] Another example would be references to 'sustainable development' as a limit on the state's obligations to the investor. While sustainable development is regarded by some as an emerging principle of international law, the lack of consensus on this characterization has led states to start including a reference to it in the preambles of IIAs, setting it out as a goal of the parties' investment relationship. This permits tribunals to interpret the firm treaty obligations in a way that fosters sustainable development.[52]

3.2.3 Other legal instruments

The characteristics of international investment law, however, allow for a much broader range of legal instruments to influence tribunals than generally-recognized hard and soft international legal sources. Perhaps the most obvious additional source of law that investment tribunals have are investor contracts with the host state. The precise status of these contracts is the subject of some disagreement, as they are often drafted with national law as the 'applicable law' for purposes of their legal effect. Nevertheless, an IIA may provide for the international protection of any contractual agreements between the host and investor (a so-called 'umbrella clause'). The contractually-agreed-upon standards, in turn, may implicate the domestic norms of the host state, as the arbitrators will look to host-state law to interpret such standards.

Domestic law itself is an additional source of international dispute resolution in the context of investments. Because the investment is, by definition, 'in' the host state, any specific national foreign direct investment legislation adopted by the host state will create rights or obligations on the investor. This obviously means that host-state legislation may become a source of law in an investment dispute brought on the international level. For example, domestic law may breach investor-protection provisions in a treaty.

The current evolution of legal rules in home states to hold corporations accountable for their actions abroad also promises to affect the sources available

---

51 *World Duty Free Company v Republic of Kenya*, ICSID Case No Arb/00/7, Award (4 October 2001) para 157.

52 For a discussion on the inclusion of sustainable development provisions in IIAs, see Vanhonnaecker (n 1).

Actors, institutions, and policy **63**

to investment tribunals by adding home-state laws to the body of international and host-state legal sources.[53] Investor claims of host-state violations of their rights may be adjudged more critically if the investor itself failed to fulfil its own obligations toward its home authorities.

So just what are these laws that apply? Who are the relevant actors? What are the relevant institutions? The next section surveys sources of domestic law applicable to foreign investment.

4. Domestic law of foreign direct investment

The protection enjoyed by foreign investors has expanded throughout history from a solely national law basis to an element of international contracts between the investor and host state and an element of state-to-state treaties. Where IIAs give investors the opportunity to bring complaints about treaty violations against the host in international arbitration, investors are given rights that extend beyond the rights of domestic investors, and are allowed to benefit directly from rules of a treaty between states without being bound to any particular obligations in the treaty. This inequality between investor rights and state obligations has become one focus of the current debates about the relative value of the ISDS mechanism more generally.[54] The following sections address the nature and sources of domestic law with a discussion of how domestic law is relevant to foreign investment.

4.1 Domestic legal systems in general

Domestic law is the law applying only within a single state. The state's authority to create a legal system of its own choosing is an aspect of its sovereignty. Many domestic systems provide for divided competences, giving certain powers to national law-makers and other competences to subnational and municipal legislators. Moreover, a domestic system may provide for administrative rule-making and enforcement as well as for passing laws by legislative bodies.

While national legal systems differ significantly among each other in how laws are made, the common difference between national law and international law among all jurisdictions is the existence in national systems of an ultimate authority (the state) with the power of law enforcement. International law has no multilateral 'police', so the legal responsibility of states to halt their wrongful behaviour and to compensate for damages caused is binding but ultimately unenforceable. Domestic laws, on the other hand, can be legitimately enforced by state authorities: the police can physically interfere with an individual's

---

53 e.g. the French 'Duty of Vigilance' law for corporations was passed in February 2017, placing companies incorporated in France under an obligation to manage and report on the impacts of their supply chains on human rights, the environment, and health and safety.

54 See Vanhonnaecker (n 1) and VanDuzer and Dumberry (n 1).

64   Krista Nadakavukaren Schefer

movements; regulators can issue fines or revoke licences of businesses; and courts have compulsory jurisdiction and can order the attachment of the assets of a natural or legal person who violates domestic law.

In considering the sources of investment law, one must not forget that states have domestic sources of obligation that must be upheld at the same time as their international investment-related obligations. National legislation protecting basic rights, disadvantaged groups, labourers, the environment, cultural or educational programmes, or the integrity of the government may all exist in parallel to international investment protection obligations. The state's actions to uphold these obligations may conflict with obligations to protect foreign investors, yet both sets of obligations must be upheld. In this regard, it is important to recall that while the relationship between international and domestic laws may differ among national jurisdictions, from the perspective of international law, international law is superior. The key point is that the whole spectrum of a state's domestic law responsibilities needs to be kept in mind when thinking about the state's investment law framework.

4.2 Domestic investment law

Domestic sources of foreign investment law include the entire set of laws and regulations that affect what sectors of the economy permit foreign participation (and to what extent), any incentive programmes offered foreign investors, the rules on administrative procedures required for investors to gain permission to engage in an economic activity, and any rule particularly affecting investors activities (which may include generally-applicable regulations or individual contracts between the investor and the state). Domestic rules include both national and local laws.

The relevant domestic actors and institutions in investment law are those that make, apply, and enforce these laws. This includes legislative bodies (parliaments or other bodies representing the population), which pass general legislation binding within their territory; administrative agencies that issue permits, licences, rules, and regulations and may have their own enforcement powers; and possibly policing authorities. Courts and administrative tribunals are also very significant institutions for domestic investment law. Finally, offices and agencies responsible for state procurements as well as state-owned enterprises might be sources of state investment obligations due to their potential role as a contractual partner with the investor.

4.2.1 Legislatures

Law-making is a core governmental function. The legitimacy of laws depends to a large degree on law-making occurring in accordance with established procedural rules. Legislative structures will determine the exact procedures by which laws can be enacted – whether by majority-voting by representatives of the population (such as in a congressional system), by a consensus of the

Actors, institutions, and policy 65

majority party (such as in a parliamentary system), by a popular citizen vote (such as an initiative or referendum), or by some other method.

Within the legislative process, an institution of tremendous importance for the development of a law is the legislative committee. Given the number of bills proposed to legislatures, most state legislatures have a number of subgroups to address bills prior to their consideration by the full legislature. Varied in number, composition, and practices across systems, legislative committees are procedural sources of the rules affecting investment, as it is within committees that decisions regarding a proposed law's (sometimes called a 'bill') general characterization, basic content, and, indeed, ultimate viability are made.[55]

Another legislative source of investment law may be political parties. Again, practices vary from state to state, but where political parties strongly influence the voting of legislators, the internal decision-making processes of the parties can be regarded as an important procedural source of investment law as it is nearly equivalent to the general legislative process itself. As well, the significance of the parties' general ideologies will often help determine the legislative history of a law, itself a source of inspiration for courts and – directly or indirectly – tribunal interpretations of it.

Finally, bills, like laws, evolve from some pre-legislative process – but this process is generally much more amorphous than the bill-to-law process. Stemming from the ideas of an interest group, an individual, or even an indefinable public feeling, a proposal for a law may arrive on the official governmental agenda in any number of ways that often lack in transparency in the reasons for and means of sponsorship.

4.2.2 Executive offices

4.2.2.1 THE EXECUTIVE

The executive branch of government enforces laws that are promulgated by the legislature. As the enforcer of laws, the executive of a state therefore plays a crucial role for the investor. For example, the activities of the police – as enforcer of general legislation – may be the target of investigations regarding the host state's obligations of 'full protection and security' to protect the investor from third-party actions that harm the investment.

The executive itself, however, can also be an important source of law. Executive decrees and executive orders may bind a host-state internationally as well as domestically. While the contours of the domestic legality of executive statements that purport to bind the state internationally may be unclear, there is

---

55 For an overview of the structure and practices of legislative committees in a number of jurisdictions, see Meg Russel, Bob Morris, and Phil Larkin, *Fitting the Bill: Bringing Commons Legislation Committees into Line with Best Practice 30–41* (UCL Constitution Unit 2013).

66   Krista Nadakavukaren Schefer

little controversy that international law may hold such statements as binding.[56] The International Law Commission's work on unilateral acts of states sets forth draft principles that confirm, first, that '[e]very State possesses capacity to formulate unilateral acts in accordance with international law' (Principle 2) and that '[b]y virtue of their office, Heads of State, Heads of Government and ministers for foreign affairs are considered to represent their State and to have the capacity to formulate unilateral acts on its behalf' (Principle 3.1).[57] Unsurprisingly, then, statements by heads of state are fully attributable to the state under the rules of state responsibility and have been found relevant in determining the characterization of whether host-state actions breach IIA obligations.[58] As a result, the influence of a strong executive opinion on the development of host-state law is clearly an element that should be considered when examining a procedural source of law.

4.2.2.1 ADMINISTRATIVE AGENCIES

Most modern states permit the legislature to delegate regulatory powers to administrative agents. Given the technical nature of many of the rules applying to investors and investments, administrative agencies and ministries are therefore also important sources of domestic investment law. While administrative agencies are technically within the executive branch of government, they typically have law-making powers as well as enforcement competences. Besides generating rules and regulations regarding investors' operations and activities, agencies may issue initial approvals for the investor to enter the state as well as licences and permits that may be necessary to continue operating.

Agency decision-making may be granted an elevated level of deference by the domestic court system. The practice of affording deference to agency decisions is followed in international investment law as well, with ISDS tribunals regularly pointing out (most often, but not only, in an analysis of allegations of 'unreasonable' host-state conduct) that their opinions as to the legal 'correctness' of a domestic decision are not relevant, but rather that the extent of their review rests with their view of the reasonability of the decision.[59]

---

56 *Case concerning Armed Activities on the Territory of the Congo* (New Application: 2002), Judgment of 3 February 2006, Jurisdiction of the Court and Admissibility of the Application, para 46. See also ILC, 'Guiding Principles applicable to unilateral declarations of States capable of creating legal obligations, with commentaries thereto', art 4 and Commentary (in (2006) II *Yearbook of the International Law Commission 2006*, part 2).

57 See ILC, Unilateral Acts of States, Ninth report on unilateral acts of States, A/CN.4/569 and Add.1 (6 April 2006) (report by Special Rapporteur Víctor Rodríguez Cedeño).

58 Vengeful comments of an executive, for example, have been held to violate the public purpose element of an expropriation in several cases; e.g. *British Caribbean Bank England v The Government of Belize*, PCA Case No 2010-2018, Award (19 December 2014) para 240.

59 The tribunal *in Paushok v Mongolia* was explicit about its standard of review: '[the allegedly discriminatory measure] may have been a poor instrument to achieve the objectives of the Great Khural and the Tribunal has no evidence to the effect that they were in fact achieved. It

Actors, institutions, and policy 67

4.2.2 *The judiciary*

Finally, domestic judges and courts can be relevant actors for foreign investment activities. Domestic court is the investor's most available forum for claims of mistreatment by the host-state government because the jurisdictional authority to hear complaints is clear. Interpretations by judges are a formal source of law,[60] by declaring a meaning to legal terms as applied to specific facts.

Domestic judges' level of competence can vary, as can the court system's efficiency and effectiveness. Still, some national court systems (or particular courts within a national system) may have a high level of experience with investment issues, and so should not be ignored when the investor is investigating its protection options.

In common law jurisdictions, the judiciary is also a source of law, owing to the institutions of precedent and *stare decisis*. In such a system, the decisions of previous courts are explicitly taken into account, and the opinions of higher courts are binding on lower courts. Investment laws must therefore be applied in such a way as to be compatible with the interpretations given to them by precedent and any higher judicial authority.

4.3 *Non-governmental sources*

A wide range of non-governmental actors and institutions will also influence domestic investment law. In the same way that soft law and non-state actors help shape international law, interest groups (for-profit or not-for-profit) and individuals can have a decisive effect on the domestic legal environment facing investors.

The methods through which these actors and institutions make themselves heard and become involved in the legal process differ from jurisdiction to jurisdiction. In systems providing for citizen initiatives and referenda (such as Switzerland and the State of California[61]), individuals and non-governmental organizations may directly influence the creation or modification of legislation.

Most often, however, actors unrecognized on the international legal plane become 'sources' of investment law considered by international tribunals because they influence the domestic political process so as to shape their state's obligations and actions toward foreign investors. Public movements in democracies can sway legislatures through elections, which in turn may

---

is not the role of the Tribunal to weigh the wisdom of legislation, but merely to assess whether such legislation breaches the Treaty' (*Sergei Paushok et al v Mongolia*, UNCITRAL, Award on Jurisdiction and Liability (28 April 2011) para 316).

60 See Venzke (n 36).

61 The Venice Commission reported on European countries' popular vote mechanisms. See European Commission for Democracy Through Law (Venice Commission), Referendums in Europe – An Analysis of the Legal Rules in European States, Study No 287/2004, CDL-AD (2005)034 (2 November 2005).

68 Krista Nadakavukaren Schefer

determine the direction of administrations and even courts. Such movements, however, can also have a significant – even if indirect – influence on international law. Treaty law, clearly, is strongly shaped by national public movements.[62]

Less visibly, some non-state actors can influence the application of treaty law by influencing the organizations responsible for overseeing the treaties' applied. Because the secretariats of international organizations such as the International Centre for the Settlement of Investment Disputes (ICSID), the Permanent Court of Arbitration (PCA), and the Energy Charter Treaty can shape the law as applied, (at least certain) member states' preferences in funding and staffing decisions can result in shifts in the international investment protection environment.

The current discussions taking place on topics such as enhancing the transparency of ISDS, broadening the scope of participation in such proceedings, and heightening the accountability of investors for their actions in host countries make it clear that the wider international investment community – one composed of non-governmental organizations, representatives of indigenous peoples, academics, and activists connected through social media networks – must be regarded as sources of investment law as significant as states and international organizations. This is doubly important because, while the norms of transparency, participation, and accountability all contribute to the substantive legitimacy of investment law, the openness to impulses from those affected by and concerned with such norms contributes to the procedural legitimacy of the system – and thus to the overall legitimacy of investment law (international or domestic).[63]

5. The relationship between international law and domestic law

As noted, domestic rules cannot justify violations of international law. Thus, from the point of view of international law, the domestic laws and institutional structures governing international investment law should be subordinate to the international law demands of investor protection in IIAs.[64] This supremacy would hold true for protections found in any type of international law – general principles, customary international law, or treaties. The reasoning for such a position is clear: if domestic obligations could override contrary international law, then there would be a very limited scope for international rules to be considered 'binding'. In fact, the promises hosts made to investors in a bilateral

---

62 The anti-ISDS demonstrations across Europe and Canada, which led to the ISDS mechanism in the Comprehensive Economic and Trade Agreement (CETA) being replaced with a different dispute resolution mechanism are a prominent example of how displeased citizens can lead to fundamental structural changes in the norms governing state obligations toward investors and the mechanisms in place for settling investor–state disputes.

63 These discussions are addressed in Vanhonnaeker (n 1) and VanDuzer and Dumberry (n 1).

64 ASR (n 21) art 3.

Actors, institutions, and policy 69

treaty, for example, would be ineffective if domestic rules could declare the international rules unenforceable.

5.1 *The theory*

While the hierarchy of international law versus domestic law is clear enough, the relationship between international and domestic law is not so simple to diagram. On the level of international law theory, this relationship is traditionally understood as defined by two archetypal forms of domestic constitutional orders: monism and dualism.[65] A purely monist system assumes a single system of law governs the relevant jurisdiction.[66] Both international law and domestic law will be valid within the jurisdiction, but, typically, monist jurisdictions will hold that international law will prevail over any inconsistent domestic law. A dualist system, on the other hand, assumes that international law must be integrated into the domestic system before it can be applied as law within the territory of the state.[67] Thus, international law is 'transformed' into domestic law by an act of the legislature and only then is it domestically binding. There can be no internal conflict between international and domestic law in such a system.

The monists prefer international law on one of two theoretical grounds. It may be seen that international law is the only way to ensure the superiority of the individual over the government, because it requires the law to provide for protections against the state.[68] Others consider monism a logical consequence of having international rules govern interstate relations.[69] Dualism prefers to regard the state as the ultimate author of consensual rules in the international community.[70] This view places more weight on the sovereignty of the state by seeing international law and national law as two separate, but equal, systems of law.

In practice, not only are the labels monist and dualist inadequate to describe the legal realities of most nations' positive rules on how international laws are to be applied by their courts but they also do not reflect states' practice in a straightforward way.[71] Monist countries, such as the United States, may require legislative action to make an investment treaty effective – certainly if it is

---

65 See Madelaine Chiam, 'Monism and Dualism in International Law', Oxford Bibliographies (last modified 27 June 2018) available at <www.oxfordbibliographies.com/view/document/obo-9780199796953/obo-9780199796953-0168.xml> accessed 4 November 2018.

66 ibid.

67 ibid. Chiam notes that some scholars use the term 'pluralism' rather than 'dualism'.

68 See AFM Maniruzzaman, 'State Contracts in Contemporary International Law: Monist versus Dualist Controversies', (2001) 12 *European Journal of International Law* 309, 312–313.

69 Shaw (n 2) 98.

70 ibid 97–98.

71 For a good introduction to the theory and practice of states regarding domestic application of international law, see David Sloss, 'Applying Treaties in Domestic Law' in Duncan Hollis (ed), *The Oxford Guide to Treaties* (Oxford University Press 2012) 367 available at <http://digitalcommons.law.scu.edu/facpubs/635> accessed 8 January 2018.

70   Krista Nadakavukaren Schefer

a chapter of a free trade agreement, often if it is a bilateral investment treaty. At the same time, in dualist countries, such as Canada, an international investment agreement can be declared effective without any legislation if parliament sees no need for implementing acts, but an individual may only rely on the treaty provisions in a Canadian court to the extent that the protections are implemented in domestic law.[72]

Moreover, even where a treaty is accepted as effective, national courts in dualist states will often approach international law as a source of law rather than as law. That is, the national judge may read international law as a place from which she can look for rights and obligations rather than as statements of rights and obligations that are in fact immediately binding as such. Judges can, for example, interpret national texts in light of international obligations in order to find a way of ensuring that domestic law does not conflict with international law or they can support their findings with references to international court decisions without accepting that the international norm is itself binding within that jurisdiction.

At the same time, the processes by which an international treaty was made are rarely investigated by the courts or tribunals that consult them. This is not different from how international decision-makers usually proceed in applying a clear text setting forth a treaty obligation; nevertheless, it can be important to take such processes into account because the legitimacy of the instrument depends in part on the legitimacy of the process from which it emerged.

6. The legitimacy of the sources of investment law

This brings me to a final set of considerations surrounding the actors, institutions, and processes of domestic investment law: the legitimacy of the 'sources' of investment law on the domestic and international levels and what it may say about their relationship. Recall that according to conventional understandings, a 'source of law' is either an instrument containing law or a process through which rules are made law. If processes are also sources, they need to be identified and evaluated as well.

6.1 Politics as process

Relying on Philip Allott, I suggest that whereas international treaties are perhaps a 'source' of domestic law they (and customary international law) are 'not the sources of International Law. They *are* International Law'.[73] The true source of treaties (and customary international law), Allott convincingly argues, is politics.

---

72 *Attorney-General for Canada v Attorney-General for Ontario* [1937] AC 326 (PC).
73 Philip Allott, 'Interpretation – an Exact Art' in Andrea Bianchi, Daniel Peat, and Matthew Windsor (eds) *Interpretation in International Law* (Oxford University Press 2015) 373–392, 385.

Actors, institutions, and policy 71

In other words, a treaty is a statement of international law while also being a contributor to what is domestic law. The origin – the source – of international law, however, is the politics leading to the creation of the rule. Politics, in turn, is the dialogue among participants that leads to the writing down of the law. Again, process is key. As a result, the legitimacy of a norm must rest on the legitimacy of its process to becoming a rule as much as on the legitimacy of the rule itself.

6.2 Legitimacy of process

The question of whether international treaty law is a source of law or law itself is just as relevant on the domestic level as it is on the international level because the legitimacy of a legal norm (a substantive 'source') depends to a large degree on the legitimacy of its procedural origins (a procedural 'source') – that is, for domestic courts to apply an international investment rule, that rule's substantive fairness is a necessary but not sufficient factor for the legitimacy of the domestic legal rule emerging from it.[74]

On the question of what makes a law legitimate, there seems to be general agreement that both transparency and the participation of all affected stakeholders in the law-making process are prerequisites.[75] Transparency means that the law-making is done in a way that the public knows the content of the matters discussed and of the rules promulgated and the method by which the decisions are made. Participation means that all of those affected by the decision regarding what the rule will be are able to express their views and have those views considered. While not all views can always be integrated into the final rule, participatory mechanisms ensure that all aspects of the rule's consequences have been considered appropriately.

Even more intriguing than the insights into the importance of procedural norms to the legitimacy of a rule are the psychological studies that demonstrate that the participation-representational aspects of procedural fairness may contribute more to public acceptance of a legal ruling than the functional role of procedure in ensuring 'correct' results.[76]

Although considered aspects of good governance, transparent and legitimate rule-making procedures are often burdensome on state resources. Promulgating legitimate rules often takes longer, costs more, and requires more active effort of state officials than ones that are agreed upon in secret or within a closed

---

74 Thomas Franck, *Fairness in International Institutions* (Clarendon Press 1995).

75 e.g. Ian Clark, *Legitimacy in International Society* (Oxford University Press 2005); Rüdiger Wolfrum and Volker Röben (eds) *Legitimacy in International Law* (Springer 2008); David D Caron, 'Investor State Arbitration: Strategic and Tactical Perspectives on Legitimacy' (2009) 32 *Suffolk Transnational Law Review* 513, fn 1 and accompanying text.

76 Tom R Tyler and Justin Sevier, 'How Do the Courts Create Popular Legitimacy? The Role of Establishing the Truth, Punishing Justly, and/or Acting Through Just Procedures' (2013/2014) 77 *Albany Law Review* 1095.

72   *Krista Nadakavukaren Schefer*

group. Nevertheless, beyond any ethical commitment to an ideal of legitimacy, rules that are perceived as legitimate are more likely to be well accepted even by those who disagree with the specific content and adherence to them is more likely.[77] If the source of the treaty was not legitimate, then the domestic legal ruling based on the treaty (using the treaty as its source) cannot be legitimate. Looking at investment law from the 'sources' perspective is interesting because it indicates not only that the relationship between rights and obligations of each level must be determined, but that the variety of methods that can lead to rights and obligations must also be regarded comprehensively.

6.3 *Legitimizing the procedural aspects of investment law sources*

Clearly, negotiations among states that lead to treaties can be a source of international law. The consistent, widespread, and repeated actions of states over time (combined with a belief that the legal bindingness of these actions leads to customary rules) can also be a source, just as domestic legal principles applied separately in all of the world's legal jurisdictions can be found to be a source of international law (as a general principle).

Thus, the actors and institutions relevant to forming international law are more numerous than simply the delegates at international treaty negotiations, international tribunals, and a handful of particularly eminent scholars. They include the entire administrative staff of all of the states' relevant agencies, all of the parliaments that must ratify treaty texts, all of the diplomats who may respond to actions or inactions of other states (whether they respond or not can also be significant), all of the planners of state-owned enterprises signing contracts with foreign suppliers, and all of the domestic courts that develop legal principles in their national systems that might be generalizable on the global scale. This opens the study of sources to a large number of individuals and groups, each of which is relevant to shaping what rules should influence what is considered applicable law.

But the process-based sources of law may be even broader: what about the one-time actions of particular significance? And what about international commissions' work to inform policy-makers about the extent of a particular problem or the potential consequences of taking certain actions and not others? What about the non-state actors' consistent, widespread, and repeated calls for change? Or the individual's complaint to her national courts about actions taken by a company that harms her interests? Are these also 'sources'? I cannot claim to answer these questions, but I bring them out to demonstrate the complexity of the issues we need to struggle with.

---

77 See Tom R Tyler, *Why People Obey the Law* (Princeton University Press 2006).

7. Final thoughts

As a prospective investor, the sources of investment law are vast, extending much beyond only the regulations determining whether and which investments can be made. The numerous branches of government and the interaction of the multiple domestic non-state actors, institutions, and processes are all relevant. So, too, however, is the international investment law framework.

So far, international investment law has not delved deeply into the issue of international–domestic law interaction. While some disputes before arbitral tribunals have clarified certain individual items within this relationship (e.g. that domestic investment protection legislation must be interpreted according to the interpretive standards applied in international law,[78] but that determining whether a contractual obligation can be enforced by international investment law depends on whether there was a contract affording a right as per the host's domestic law[79]), the deeper connection between the systems has only begun to be addressed.[80] We need to grapple with it, however, because the answers – whatever they are – must then be taken into account when the domestic sources of investment law look at IIA provisions. The parliaments, agencies, and courts, the business associations, the civil society groups, and the individual activists that refer to or rely on international rules must also consider that the source of the international rule they are applying is the international political process, and that the rule is therefore only as legitimate as the process itself was. Perhaps, simply by bringing this analysis into discussion, investment law will become more legitimate.

Many of us who are mainly interested in international law may not sufficiently scrutinize the procedural legitimacy of both the national and international legal rule-making systems when we analyse and comment upon the investment regime as a whole. Yet, with a broad range of domestic actors and institutions affecting the development of national legal practices, the legitimacy of the system as a whole is clearly affected by these actors'/institutions' legitimacy as well.

---

78 e.g. *OPIC Karimun Corporation v Bolivarian Republic of Venezuela*, ICSID Case No ARB/10/14, Award (28 May 2013), paras 70–76 (setting out a chain of tribunal decisions in which international rules determined the interpretation of a domestic foreign investment law).

79 e.g. *Rusoro Mining Limited v Bolivarian Republic of Venezuela*, ICSID Case No ARB(AF)/12/5, Award (22 August 2016), paras 289–344 (analysing whether the claimant's investment was legal according to Venezuela's legislation, court decisions, and policy practice).

80 Jarrod Hepburn, *Domestic Law in International Investment Arbitration* (Oxford University Press 2017).

4 State-owned enterprises and sovereign wealth funds

An economic assessment

Steven Globerman, Phillip Hensyel, and Daniel Shapiro

1. Introduction

A prominent phenomenon that has been the source of increasing attention and concern on the part of many politicians and business leaders, especially in the United States and other developed countries, is the role of state-owned enterprises (SOEs) and sovereign wealth funds (SWFs) in the international economy. The direct and indirect linkages between SOEs and SWFs and their national governments raise important public policy issues, especially in the context of international trade and investment flows. Governments in developed Western countries have become increasingly sceptical of the net benefits of allowing government-owned (or influenced) companies to invest in their economies. The broad concern is that government ownership results in organizations pursuing 'non-commercial' objectives, which may not only undermine their efficiency but may also do economic harm to the host economy. Non-commercial objectives might even include carrying out espionage or sabotage in host countries that are potentially or actually engaged in conflict with the SOEs' home states.[1] A related concern has been raised about unfair trade practices linked to financial or other subsidies received by SOEs.

Government ownership of businesses has also raised concerns surrounding their indirect impacts on international trade and investment. Specifically, government-owned enterprises, especially in strategic sectors, are seen as being shielded by home governments against takeovers by foreign multinationals, as well as enjoying tariff and non-tariff protections against competitive imports.[2] These concerns are leading to growing calls for reciprocity in the form of restrictions on state-owned enterprises from buying domestically-owned companies or otherwise being allowed to invest in host countries.

---

1 For a discussion of national security and international investment policy, see Patrick Leblond and Sébastien Labrecque, 'National security and the political economy of international investment policy', Chapter 9 in this volume.

2 PWC, 'State-Owned Enterprises: Catalysts for Public Value Creation?' (PWC 2015) <www.pwc.com/gx/en/psrc/publications/assets/pwc-state-owned-enterprise-psrc.pdf> accessed 16 June 2019.

The concerns identified above rest upon two related presumptions. One is that state ownership, per se, results in organizations behaving and performing differently than they would if they were privately owned. A second is that the relevant differences in behaviour and performance are not mediated by market competition because state-owned organizations have access to direct and indirect government subsidies that are not reliably available to privately-owned companies. State-owned organizations might be expected to behave and perform differently than privately-owned firms because the former have different organizational goals than the latter and/or because the two types of organizations differ in terms of how efficiently they pursue their objectives.

The bulk of the literature focusing on state ownership, and particularly on the activities of SOEs, discusses why one would expect state ownership to change the behaviour and performance of organizations, primarily by making the state, rather than private investors, the principal or residual claimant of those organizations. We shall briefly review this literature; however, since others have extensively articulated the key arguments, our primary focus will be on two related issues of which theory and what evidence has been less well integrated into the literature. The first issue is whether and how the nature and extent of government ownership affect the behaviour and performance of organizations. In particular, is the performance of organizations systematically linked to the share of government ownership and, if so, how? The second issue is whether and how the relationship between government ownership and organizational performance is mediated by other characteristics of government-owned organizations, such as whether the latter are participating in foreign markets or in specific industries, or the countries in which they are headquartered.

SWFs and especially SOEs constitute a heterogeneous group of organizations with respect to characteristics such as their share of government ownership, their participation in international markets and the location of their corporate headquarters, among other things.[3] This heterogeneity suggests that the relationship between government ownership and economic performance is likely to be complex and, perhaps, relatively specific to individual groups of organizations. In the next section of this chapter, we identify the scope of government ownership of SWFs and SOEs.

The third section briefly outlines the main conceptual arguments that link government ownership to an organization's behaviour and performance while the fourth section reviews empirical studies primarily focusing on how organizational performance is related to the extent of government ownership. In doing so, we pay particular attention to whether the relationship is mediated or moderated by factors such as the location of the organization's headquarters,

---

3 Garry D Bruton, Mike W Peng, David Ahlstrom, Ciprian Stan, and Kehan Xu, 'State-owned Enterprises Around the World as Hybrid Organizations' (2015) 29 *Academy of Management Perspectives* 92.

76 Steven Globerman et al.

where else the organization does business and what type of business it does. The fifth and final section provides a summary and policy conclusions.

2. Overview of SWFs and SOEs

Before presenting data on SWFs and SOEs, it is useful to define what they mean. According to the Sovereign Wealth Fund Institute, a SWF is a state-owned investment fund or entity that is commonly established from balance of payments surpluses, official currency operations, the proceeds of privatizations, government transfer payments, and/or fiscal surpluses and/or receipts from resource exports. This definition excludes, among other things, foreign currency reserves held by monetary authorities for traditional balance of payments or monetary policy purposes, state-owned enterprises in the traditional sense (see below), government-employee pension funds (funded by employee/employer contributions), or assets managed for the benefit of individuals.[4] The Organisation for Economic Cooperation and Development (OECD) defines an SOE as an enterprise where the state has significant control through full, majority, or significant minority ownership. This encompasses SOEs that are owned by the central or federal government, as well as those owned by regional and local governments.[5]

2.1 SWFs

Table 4.1 lists the ten largest SWFs as of September 2017. The Sovereign Wealth Fund Institute, which is the source of the data reported in the table, estimates that the total assets held by 79 SWFs as of September 2017 were approximately US$7.42 trillion. The assets of the ten largest SWFs listed account for almost three-quarters of all SWF assets. Hence, SWF asset holdings are concentrated in a small number of funds.

Several other observations might be made about the SWFs listed in Table 4.1. Five of the funds have their origins in oil and gas revenues.[6] The assets held by these five funds accounted for around 57 percent of all SWF assets as of September 2017. The four largest non-commodity-based funds are headquartered in China and account for around 27 per cent of all SWF assets. Hence, one can conclude that significant changes in the price of oil or in China's overall trade balance could substantially alter the overall importance of SWFs as a source of global financial capital.[7]

---

4 This definition is provided by the Sovereign Wealth Fund Institute, 'Sovereign Wealth Fund Rankings' <www.swfinstitute.org/sovereign-wealth-fund/> accessed 16 June 2019.

5 PWC (n 2).

6 The five are: 1) Norway's Government Pension Fund; 2) Abu Dhabi's Investment Authority; 3) Kuwait's Investment Authority; 4) Saudi Arabia's SAMA; 5) Qatar's Investment Authority.

7 Further to this point, the Sovereign Wealth Fund Institute identifies 44 SWFs of the 79 listed as having their origins in oil and gas.

State-owned enterprises and wealth funds 77

Table 4.1 Ten largest SWFs as of September 2017

Fund name	*Home country*	*Assets (US$ billion)*
Government Pension Fund-Global	Norway	954
Abu Dhabi Investment Corporation	UAE – Abu Dhabi	828
China Investment Corporation	China	814
Kuwait Investment Authority	Kuwait	524
SAMA Foreign Holdings	Saudi Arabia	514
Hong Kong Monetary Authority Investment	China – Hong Kong	457
SAFE Investment Corporation	China	441
Government of Singapore Investment Corporation	Singapore	359
Qatar Investment Authority	Qatar	320
National Social Security Fund	China	295

Source: Sovereign Wealth Fund Institute, Sovereign Wealth Fund Rankings

Another observation worth making about SWFs is that they are a relatively recent phenomenon. Specifically, the Sovereign Wealth Fund Institute estimates that around two-thirds of all SWFs were created in the post-2000 period and almost 22 percent were created post-2010.

Perhaps the most important point to make about the empirical data surrounding SWFs is that they are still relatively minor participants in the global asset allocation process. This point is underscored by the fact that US investment companies alone at the end of 2016 managed around US$19.2 trillion.[8] This is almost three times the value of total assets managed by all SWFs. Table 4.2, which lists the ten largest asset managers worldwide, further illustrates SWFs' relatively modest size. In this case, private-sector asset management companies had over four times the value of assets under management than the ten leading SWFs.

While other data can certainly be presented regarding the activities of SWFs, they would not alter the main point that SWFs play a relatively modest overall role in allocating financial capital on a global basis. Furthermore, given their origins in the energy sector and China's trade surplus, a case can be made that their relative importance will diminish in the future. Hence, any concerns about the activities of SWFs should be tempered by this observation.

8 See Figure 1.1 of Investment Company Institute, *2017 Investment Company Fact Book: A Review of Trends and Activities in the Investment Company Industry* (57th edn, Investment Company Institute 2017).

78   *Steven Globerman et al.*

Table 4.2 Largest asset managers worldwide as of 31 December 2016 versus largest SWFs as of September 2017

Largest asset managers	Assets under management (US$ billion)	Largest SWFs	Assets under management (US$ billion)
Blackrock (US/UK)	5,138	Government Pension Fund	954
Vanguard (US/UK)	3,920	Abu Dhabi Investment Corporation	828
State Street (US/UK)	2,460	China Investment Corporation	814
Fidelity (US)	2,240	Kuwait Investment Authority	524
BNY Mellon (US/UK)	1,596	SAMA Foreign Holdings	514
JP Morgan (US/UK)	1,555	Hong Kong Monetary Authority	457
Pimco (US/ Germany/UK)	1,479	SAFE Investment Company	441
Capital Group (US)	1,474	Singapore Investment Corporation	359
Prudential (US)	1,263	Qatar Investment Authority	320
Goldman Sachs (US/UK)	1,175	National Social Security Fund	295
Total	**22,300**		**5,506**

Source: Statista, The Statistics Portal (www.statista.com/statistics/322452/largest-asset-man agers-worldwide-by-value-of-assets/)

2.2 SOEs

There are two main sources of data identifying the largest SOEs. One standard data source is UNCTAD's World Investment Report.[9] This source focuses on SOEs that have foreign affiliates, i.e. that qualify as multinational enterprises (MNEs). For 2016, UNCTAD identified close to 1,500 state-owned MNEs with more than 86,000 foreign affiliates operating around the globe. As a share of all MNE activity, SOEs account for a relatively small share. Specifically, they accounted for around 1.5 percent of the universe of MNEs and about 10 percent of all foreign affiliates. However, SOEs tend to be relatively large MNEs with 15 of the top 100 non-financial MNEs being SOEs. They also tend to be headquartered predominantly in emerging economies. In this regard, 41 of the top 100 MNEs from developing and transition economies are state-owned.

9 See UNCTAD, *World Investment Report 2017: Investment and the Digital Economy* (United Nations 2017).

State-owned enterprises and wealth funds 79

Table 4.3 Fifteen largest non-financial state-owned MNES (2016)[10]

Company	Home country	Industry	State-ownership percentage	Total sales (US$ million)
Volkswagen	Germany	Motor Vehicles	20	240,366
China State Construction Engineering	China	Construction	100	140,099
Nippon Telephone and telegraph	Japan	Telecom	32.4	92,218
Deutsche Telecom	Germany	Telecom	17.4	80,866
EDF	France	Utilities	84.6	78,773
Enel	Italy	Utilities	23.6	75,898
Engie	France	Utilities	32.0	73,724
Airbus Group	France	Aircraft	11.1	73,660
China Minmetals	China	Metal Products	100	68,913
China National Offshore Oil	China	Petroleum	100	67,789
Deutsche Post	Germany	Transportation	24.9	63,430
Petronas	Malaysia	Petroleum	60.6	63,322
Eni	Italy	Petroleum	25.8	61,690
Peugeot	France	Motor Vehicles	13.7	59,774
Renault	France	Motor Vehicles	15.0	56,691

Table 4.3 lists the 15 largest state-owned MNEs in 2016. It can be seen that the majority of these largest state-owned MNEs have minority state ownership, except for the China-headquartered ones, which are entirely state-owned. The majority of the companies listed in Table 4.3 are headquartered in Europe, and they are predominantly in telecom, utilities, and motor vehicles. These industrial sectors have historically been seen as 'strategic' by national governments. The fact that Asian state-owned MNEs, particularly those headquartered in China, are majority or wholly government owned, while those headquartered in Europe tend to be minority owned, suggests that it might be difficult to identify the separate influence of government ownership from the influence of headquarters' location on SOE performance. We shall return to this point later in the chapter.

The data reported by UNCTAD suggest that governments tend to hold majority ownership shares in home-country MNEs. In fact, it reports that for

10 ibid Annex Table 24.

80 *Steven Globerman et al.*

all state-owned MNEs for which data are available over one third were fully owned by their home governments, while another 29 percent were controlled through majority ownership. In 21 percent of cases, the home government owned between 25 and 50 per cent of the MNEs' equity; however, even when it is a minority shareholder, the government is typically the largest single shareholder. The government also has significant influence over the board of directors and corporate strategy. Indeed, it might be argued that, at least in the case of China, the government can and does influence corporate strategy even without owning equity in the relevant companies. An example is the Chinese Communist Party's directive to the giant entertainment company, Wanda, to invest domestically and reduce its investment abroad. However, some amount of equity ownership is, apparently, useful. China again provides an example. Notwithstanding the control that the Chinese government exerts over content distributed by privately-owned Internet companies, the Chinese government has been pushing China's privately-owned technology companies to offer the state an ownership stake and a direct role in corporate decisions.[11]

2.3 Summary

SWFs and SOEs play a potentially significant role in the global economy, although they still account for a modest share of financial and real international economic activity.[12] Any analysis of SWFs and SOEs necessarily includes a substantial amount of activity carried out by Chinese companies. Hence, it is important to try to assess whether the behaviour and performance of Chinese SWFs and SOEs differ from that of their non-Chinese counterparts and, if so, whether the differences are due to government ownership patterns or to other factors that may be unique to China.

3. The influence of government ownership: theory

As Dewenter and Malatesta assert, for many policy analysts it is an article of faith that government-owned firms must be less efficient or, at least, less

---

11 Li Yuan, 'China Seeks Stakes in Tech Titans' *The Wall Street Journal* (11 October 2017) <www.wsj.com/articles/beijing-pushes-for-a-direct-hand-in-chinas-big-tech-firms-1507758314?mod=searchresults&page=174&pos=7> accessed 17 June 2019; Richard McGregor, 'China Takes on the Tycoons' *The Wall Street Journal* (13 October 2017) <www.wsj.com/articles/china-takes-on-its-new-tycoons-1507916358> accessed 17 June 2019.

12 Grzegorz Kwiatkowski and Pawel Augustnowicz, 'State-Owned Enterprises in the Global Economy- Analysis Based on Fortune Global 500 List' (2015) *Managing Knowledge and Learning Conference* 1739 <https://www.researchgate.net/publication/323733942_State-Owned_Enterprises_In_The_Global_Economy_-_Analysis_Based_On_Fortune_ Global_500_List> accessed 20 January 2020.

profitable than privately-owned ones.[13] The fundamental justification for this assertion is the principal-agent problem arising from the fact that the principal is a government (or set of governments) department(s) or agency(ies). The main problem in this case is that the residual cash flows of firms are not readily transferable to individual owners as they would be in the case of private companies. The government principals who head the departments and agencies that own the state-owned enterprises are themselves managers and not owners.[14] Hence, unless the managers can somehow extract (directly or indirectly) most or all of the profits earned by state-owned companies, their incentive to monitor the managers of those companies is impaired, which, ultimately, should degrade the performance of those companies.

This relatively narrow view of government officials' impaired incentive to act as effective residual claimants in state-owned companies suggests that measures of profitability and efficiency will be lower in government-owned organizations than in privately-owned ones. However, not all researchers agree with this argument. In particular, the OECD points out that there is both an income and a substitution effect at work in government-owned enterprises.[15] The substitution effect references the attenuation of government officials' incentives to monitor managers. That is, it supports the view that government officials have impaired incentives to monitor managers effectively. The income effect refers to the possibility that the managers of state-owned companies substitute pecuniary for non-pecuniary managerial pursuits, which arises if managers can increase their personal wealth by increasing the wealth of the organizations that they manage.

The failure of shareholders to act as effective monitors of managers in privately-owned companies has also been extensively discussed in the literature.[16] The basic argument here is that ownership of private companies is often so dispersed among large numbers of shareholders that individual shareholders have weak incentives to play a monitoring role, since the costs of monitoring outweigh their expected individual financial benefits. The growth of passive investing through index funds has strengthened concerns that principal-agent problems lead to reduced profitability and efficiency even in privately-owned firms. As a result, Dewenter and Malatesta argue that whether government-owned firms are more or less efficient than private firms is primarily an empirical issue.[17]

---

13 Kathryn Dewenter and Paul Malatesta, 'State-Owned and Privately-Owned Firms: An Empirical Analysis of Profitability, Leverage and Labor Intensity' (2001) 9 *American Economic Review* 320.

14 Cuervo-Cazurra, Inkpen, Musacchio and Ramaswamy identify this as the 'double management' problem (Alvaro Cuervo-Cazurra, Andrew Inkpen, Aldo Musacchio, and Kannan Ramaswamy, 'Government as Owners: State-Owned Multinational Companies' (2014) 45 *Journal of International Business Studies* 919).

15 OECD, *State-Owned Enterprises in the Development Process* (OECD 2015).

16 The relevant arguments are extensively discussed in Andrei Shleifer, 'State versus Private Ownership' (1998) 12 *Journal of Economic Perspectives* 133.

17 Dewenter and Malatesta (n 13).

82 Steven Globerman et al.

We shall review some evidence on whether government ownership is associated with reduced efficiency in the next section of this chapter, as well as whether the linkage between government ownership depends on the extent of ownership or on other factors. At this point, we note that state-owned companies are likely to be less profitable than privately-owned companies because the former are more likely than the latter to forego maximum profits in the pursuit of social and political objectives. They are also more likely to have lowered measured efficiency than privately-owned firms given specific social objectives. For example, if an important objective of government is to maintain employment, measures of labour productivity in government-owned enterprises are likely to be lower than in privately-owned ones. Indeed, conventional measures of productivity might be impaired by the pursuit of a number of other social objectives, such as reducing pollution or developing rural areas.

Privately-owned companies are also typically constrained to promote the interests of other stakeholders besides their owners. For example, growing pressure by NGOs and social action groups on private businesses to act in a socially-responsible manner might effectively constrain the maximization of profits in private companies, as well as creating private-sector inefficiencies as the quid pro quo for public benefits and a social licence to operate. Moreover, direct regulation by governments can and does constrain profit maximization on the part of privately-owned companies and may often oblige those companies to operate in ways that are less privately efficient than would be the case if they were free to maximize profits.

In short, both government-owned and privately-owned companies are unlikely to operate as unconstrained profit maximizers and will be directly or indirectly obliged to pursue additional social goals.[18] The pursuit of those social goals is likely to result in reduced profitability and efficiency. Hence, as in the case of the traditional principal-agent problem discussed above, the extent to which non-profit-related obligations affect the profitability and efficiency of government-owned enterprises relative to privately-owned enterprises might be a matter of degree. Again, the relationship between profitability and government ownership, on the one hand, and efficiency and government ownership, on the other hand, is an empirical issue.

Several other conceptual arguments have been raised in support of the notion that government ownership will affect the performance of organizations. One such additional argument is that the quality of managers will be systematically lower in government-owned businesses because such firms will be pressured by government to hire 'politically-connected' people, rather than those best

---

18 By definition, if profit maximization were the only goal of society, government-imposed con-straints on profit maximization would make no sense. In an economy free of market failures, profit maximization would contribute to higher standards of living, which is certainly one major social objective.

qualified to perform the desired tasks.[19] Certainly, in the case of China, membership in the Communist Party is an important criterion for senior managerial posts. This does not mean, however, that government-owned businesses will ordinarily be less profitable than privately-owned ones, other things being constant. Indeed, political connections may be an important determinant of profitability in many countries, and not just in the case of government-owned businesses.

Another argument is that government ownership provides for 'soft-budget' constraints, which effectively allows managers in government-owned enterprises to operate less efficiently and profitably than their counterparts in privately-owned companies for long periods of time, if not indefinitely. This assertion is equivalent to an argument that government-owned enterprises enjoy access to financial capital subsidies, since competitive capital markets provide hard budget constraints in the form of inter-firm competition for financial capital. A related concern about SWFs is that they are a source of subsidized capital, particularly for home-country SOEs. Again, we are talking about differences in degree, since many privately-owned firms directly or indirectly enjoy government-financed subsidies.

3.1 Extent of ownership

PWC argues that one should not expect to find a consistent relationship between the extent of government ownership and the behaviour and performance of government-owned organizations.[20] It is possible that the government can exercise significant operating control over an organization, even though it owns a relatively small share of the company, as in cases when governments own 'golden shares'. The government can also exert influence over organizations in its role as regulator or allocator of capital. An example in this regard is the Chinese government effectively forcing privately-owned steel mills to reduce capacity in order to generate higher prices for steel produced in SOEs. The key point made by PWC is that government influence is not necessarily equivalent to the state's ownership share.[21] Nevertheless, PWC proposes the general hypothesis that as the state dilutes its effective ownership and influence over firms, one would expect to find those firms following strategies and actions that are more likely to focus on financial performance over social and political objectives.

This viewpoint effectively argues that mixed-ownership enterprises should perform better than enterprises that are wholly owned by government. Vining

---

19 Anne Krueger, 'Government Failures in Development' (1990) 4 *The Journal of Economic Perspectives* 9.

20 PWC (n 2).

21 ibid.

84 *Steven Globerman et al.*

and Weimer among others, reject this argument.[22] Specifically, they argue that public-private hybrids exhibit tension among owners over both goals and strategy. As a result, it creates managerial dissonance that contributes to organizational failure. Inoue, Lazzarini, and Musacchio take a position in between these two, albeit in the specific context of developing countries.[23] They argue that minority state-owned investment can have a positive effect on firms' returns on assets by helping to boost entrepreneurial activity through investments in projects that would otherwise remain unfunded. Given the minority nature of the government stakes, majority control will be in the hands of profit-oriented shareholders, which, as PWC argues, should mitigate the agency distortions associated with fully state-owned enterprises. However, the authors put forward the caveat that the positive effects of minority stakes will be attenuated when the minority state-owned firms are part of privately-owned business groups, because minority state-owned capital might be used to support other companies in the business group. In addition, institutional improvements that reduce market failures will also attenuate the benefits offered by minority state ownership.

In short, the PWC perspective leads to the prediction that the performance of government-owned organizations improves monotonically as private ownership increases relative to government ownership. On the other hand, Vining and Weimer's position leads to a prediction that the performance of SOEs deteriorates as private ownership replaces public ownership, at least up until the point where private owners are the sole, or dominant, principals of the organization. Inoue, Lazzarini, and Musacchio caution that the positive impact of minority state ownership on firm performance is mediated by the quality of governance institutions and the identities of the majority private owners.

3.2 Ownership forms

Shapiro and Globerman discuss different government ownership models. Specifically, they mention three models of the state's ownership function: the centralized model, the decentralized model, and the dual model.[24] In the centralized model, there is one government body, a ministry or a holding company, responsible for the government's stake in all SOEs. In the decentralized model, SOEs are the responsibility of different ministries. In the dual form, responsibility is shared between a sector ministry and one

---

22 Aidan Vining and David Weimer, 'The Challenge of Fractionalized Property Rights in Public-Private Hybrid Organizations: The Good, the Bad and the Ugly' (2016) 10 *Regulation and Governance* 161.

23 Carlos Inoue, Sergio Lazzarini, and Aldo Musacchio, 'Leviathan as a Minority Shareholder: Firm-Level Implications of Equity Purchases by the State' (2013) 56 *Academy of Management Journal* 1775.

24 Daniel Shapiro and Steven Globerman, 'The International Activities and Impacts of State-Owned Enterprises' in Karl Sauvant, Lisa Sachs, and Wouter Schmitt Jongbloed (eds), *Sovereign Investment: Concerns and Policy Reactions* (Oxford University Press 2012).

single central ministry, such as the ministry of finance. They suggest that centralization permits greater consistency and transparency in SOE governance, which should produce better performance, other things constant.

Alternatively, Huang, Guangrong, and Xu, in the specific context of China, distinguish decentralization based on what level of government has the oversight function for state-owned businesses (e.g. higher or lower levels of government).[25] They note that decentralization was one of the methods for SOE reforms beginning in the second half of the 1990s. Decentralization, in general, did not change the objectives and responsibilities of the oversight government. Delivering growth and/or tax revenues have been the key priority of different levels of government, including local government; however, because the cash flow rights were transferred to the local government after decentralization, the local government would internalize more of the costs and benefits of governing the decentralized SOEs. The authors argue that this internalization should result in an improvement in SOE performance. They also posit that decentralization is likely to have a stronger impact on governance for SOEs that are partially owned (30 to 49 per cent) than for those that are fully owned (100 per cent). This is because, in partially-owned SOEs, there are other governance mechanisms to obtain information about SOE behaviour and performance so that direct information available to government, which is presumably more accessible to local governments than to governments physically further away from the SOEs they own, is of less importance to the management of those SOEs.

PWC argues that the linkage between centralization of ownership and SOE performance is not clear-cut.[26] On the one hand, creating a single body responsible for the state's commercial assets allows for the development of specialized capabilities to monitor and evaluate SOE performance. It also promotes clearer accountability for the performance of SOEs. However, centralization might also lead to inefficiencies, owing to a weaker link between performance and control rights, and it might act as a magnet for corruption. They also assert that organizations that are indirectly owned by the government via SWFs, state pension funds, or state banks are more likely to follow similar behaviours to privately-owned firms because the government has a limited ability to direct their behaviour, as it is not a direct owner. Moreover, such organizations are likely to be more focused on achieving high levels of financial performance than other state-owned organizations because the SWFs have the mandate to achieve a certain return on their investments.[27]

---

25 Zhangkai Huang, Luxing Guangrong, and Lixin Xu, 'Hayek, Local Information and Commanding Heights: Decentralizing State-Owned Enterprises in China' (2017) 107 *American Economic Review* 2455.

26 PWC (n 2).

27 A very similar set of claims is found in Cuervo-Cazurra, Inkpen, Mussachio and Ramaswamy (n 14).

86 *Steven Globerman et al.*

3.3 Geographic distribution of activities

In some discussions of state ownership and organizational performance, the geographical distribution of the organization's activities is seen as conditioning the relationship between the two. In particular, whether or not the government-owned enterprise is a multinational company or not has been suggested to influence the linkage between state ownership and performance. In one version of the argument, state-owned multinational enterprises (SOMNEs) are likely to perform better (by commercial standards) than domestic state-owned organizations because the host government can impose laws and regulations on the former that oblige them to behave in ways similar to other host-country firms, including increased transparency, which might assist any private shareholder, particularly in the host country, to monitor SOMNE managers. This might be particularly true for SOMNEs that are listed on host-country stock exchanges.[28]

On the other hand, even if some SOMNE investments are made with profitability in mind, home governments may oblige SOMNEs to make investments abroad to achieve political or other non-commercial objectives. Obviously, in the latter cases, home governments will likely need to subsidize the SOMNEs, since the latter are likely to suffer from firm-specific disadvantages in the host country. Alternatively, SOE internationalization may be pushed by managers, seeking to enhance their prestige; therefore, they may overpay for foreign assets or buy unprofitable target companies.[29] Again, this should worsen the relationship between government ownership and organizational performance.[30]

3.4 Summary

While the preponderance of opinions on the issue would maintain that government ownership leads to poorer performance in terms of the standard commercial objectives such as profitability and efficiency, the opinions are not uniform. That is, some authors have put forward arguments that the principal-agent problems that influence the behaviour and performance of government-owned enterprises also affect the performance of privately-owned enterprises. Hence, even if government-owned organizations pursue non-economic objectives (more so than privately-owned organizations), it is not theoretically clear that the former will be less profitable or less efficient than the latter. In short, much, if not most, of the

---

28 Megginson and Fotak argue specifically in the case of SWFs that performance is closely related to whether a fund operates in a transparent or non-transparent manner. Also relevant is whether a fund is sponsored by a democratic or non-democratic nation (William Megginson and Vijko Fotak, 'Rise of the Fiduciary State: A Survey of Sovereign Wealth Fund Research' (2015) 29 *Journal of Economic Surveys* 773).

29 Cuervo-Cazurra, Inkpen, Musacchio and Ramaswamy (n 14)

30 While this risk might also apply to privately-owned companies, competition for financing in private capital markets makes this behaviour on the part of private-sector managers less likely.

conceptual arguments surrounding SWFs and SOEs do not lead to reliable determinative conclusions and, ultimately, are empirical issues.

4. The influence of government ownership evidence

In this section, we summarize evidence on the profitability and efficiency of SWFs and SOEs compared to their privately-owned counterparts, as well as factors that condition the comparison. We look first at SWFs and then at SOEs.

4.1 The performance of SWFs

Since SWFs are fiduciary agents investing financial capital for the government, it is sensible to assess their performance by the value they create for the government shareholders. To be sure, the value might encompass a broad range of social and economic outcomes, including economic development and greater financial market stability. Of course, similar benefits might be created by the activities of privately-owned asset managers, albeit less directly. As a practical matter, if one is going to compare the performance of SWFs to that of privately-owned asset managers, one needs to focus on relatively narrow and measurable criteria. In evaluating asset management, the standard measures of performance is risk-adjusted returns created for shareholders. Asset managers create higher risk-adjusted returns in several ways: 1) by identifying and investing in assets that are 'undervalued'; 2) by improving the performance of the underlying companies in which they invest through active and effective monitoring of management; 3) by reducing the covariance of asset returns[31] through efficient asset diversification.

To the extent that one believes in efficient markets, identifying and investing in undervalued assets is unlikely to be a major differentiator of performance when comparing SWFs to privately-owned asset managers. Furthermore, since SWFs are supposedly investing for all citizens, their portfolio diversification decisions are unlikely to be segmented from other sources of income earned by citizens. For example, SWFs created primarily through oil and gas revenues should arguably be 'underweighted' in terms of investing in energy assets compared to investment benchmarks, since their ultimate shareholders (citizens) derive a disproportionate share of their incomes by working directly or indirectly in the oil and gas sector. On the other hand, privately-owned asset managers may or may not invest according to industry investment benchmarks (i.e. they may or may not be passive investors). Any active investor will be motivated by its clients' investment objectives rather than the relative importance of different industries in the nation's gross domestic product.

In light of these issues, it can be argued that the most meaningful comparison of SWFs to privately-owned asset managers should focus on the impact that investments made by the two types of organizations have on the financial and

---

31 A positive covariance means that asset returns move in the same direction at the same time while a negative covariance means that they move in opposite directions.

operating performances of target companies. Specifically, do investments by SWFs result in improved financial performances by the firms in which they invest compared to investments by private asset managers? If so, one can argue that SWFs should do a better job than private asset managers in acting as fiduciary agents for their shareholders. As a result, host governments should welcome the investment activities of SWFs in their domestic companies.

A possible caveat is that any actual or anticipated improvement in the financial performance of SWFs' target investments might reflect actual or anticipated advantages bestowed on those target investments by the SWF's home governments. Thus, investors might interpret an investment by an SWF in a specific company as a signal that the home government wants that company to expand and prosper financially and, further, that the company will be the recipient of direct or indirect home-government financial assistance. In this case, an above-average stock price appreciation for that company should not be interpreted as investors' assessment that the SWF will improve the efficiency of the company through active and effective agency.

The practical relevance of this caveat cannot be dismissed, but it is considerably mitigated by the fact that SWFs make large investments outside their home countries. Such investments are unlikely to receive home-country support. For example, Megginson and Fotak report that foreign investments represent 82 per cent of all SWF investments by number and around 69 per cent by value over the period 1989–2012.[32] They also report that most SWF equity investments in publicly-traded companies involve purchases of sizeable minority stakes in target companies. These observations suggest that if companies in which SWFs invest financially outperform similar investments made by private investors, the superior performance reflects superior agency on SWFs' part.

One way in which the impacts of SWF investments have been identified is by looking at how the stock market reacts to announcements by SWFs of prominent investments (or divestments) in companies. Above-average price appreciation of stocks after announcements of their purchase by SWFs suggests that other investors believe that SWF ownership will improve the performances of the companies in which the investments are made. Conversely, announcements of divestments that are followed by an above-average appreciation of the stock prices of the divested companies indicate that eliminating SWF ownership is expected to result in improved financial performances of the relevant companies.

Hesse and Sun assess whether and how stock markets react to the announcements of investments and divestments by SWFs.[33] They evaluate the short-term financial impact of SWFs' activities on selected public equity markets by calculating the

---

32 Megginson and Fotak (n 28).

33 Heiko Hesse and Tao Sun, 'Sovereign Wealth Funds and Financial Stability – An Event Study Analysis' (2009) International Monetary Fund Working Paper No 09/239 <www.imf.org/en/Publications/WP/Issues/2016/12/31/Sovereign-Wealth-Funds-and-Financial-Stability-An-Event-Study-Analysis-23370v> accessed 16 June 2019.

State-owned enterprises and wealth funds 89

abnormal return associated with SWF investment. The latter is calculated as the difference between the actual returns due to the SWF action and the estimated normal returns in the absence of SWF action. Results suggest that average abnormal returns are positively associated with SWFs' share purchases but not significantly negatively associated with their divestments. Moreover, significant share price responses to SWF investments are confined to developed economies.

Kotter and Lei show that the cumulative abnormal return of SWF investments has an announcement effect similar to the effect of investments by hedge funds and institutional investors on stock returns.[34] In addition, investments by more transparent SWFs have about a 3.5 per cent larger cumulative abnormal return, suggesting that voluntary disclosure might serve as a signalling device to investors. The authors also identify a significant negative, albeit small, announcement effect from SWFs' divestitures. Conversely, Beck and Fidora find no significant negative impact of divestiture announcements by Norway's SWF on the stock prices of divested companies.[35]

Finally, Megginson and Fotak find universal support for a post-announcement stock price increase of 1 per cent to 3 per cent; however, this is significantly less than the 5 per cent abnormal return documented for stock purchases by comparable privately-owned financial investors, suggesting a SWF stock price discount.[36]

Several studies examine the actual performance of assets acquired by SWFs. For example, Knill, Lee, and Mauck find that target firms' returns decline following SWF investment.[37] This suggests that SWFs may not provide some of the benefits that are offered by other institutional investors. Similarly, Bortolloti, Fotak, and Megginson show that SWFs' investment targets suffer from declining return on assets and sales growth over a three-year period following the SWF investment. Larger declines are associated with SWFs taking seats on boards of directors and with SWFs under strict government control acquiring greater shares.[38]

In short, while there is mixed empirical evidence regarding the expected performance of SWFs relative to privately-owned asset managers, the balance of evidence tends to show an inferior performance for SWFs. Nevertheless, the evidence is sufficiently mixed such that it does not support a high level of concern about the non-commercial performance of SWFs.

34 Jason Kotter and Ugur Lei, 'Friends or Foes? The Stock Price Impact of Sovereign Wealth Fund Investments and the Price of Keeping Secrets' (2008) Board of Governors of the Federal Reserve System International Finance Discussion Papers No 940 <www.federalreserve.gov/pubs/ifdp/2008/940/ifdp940.pdf> accessed 16 June 2019.

35 Roland Beck and Michael Fidora, 'The Impact of Sovereign Wealth Funds on Global Financial Markets' (2008) European Central Bank Occasional Paper Series No 91 <www.ecb.europa.eu/pub/pdf/scpops/ecbocp91.pdf> accessed 16 June 2019.

36 Megginson and Fotak (n 28).

37 April M Knill, Bong Soo Lee, and Nathan Mauck, 'Sovereign Wealth Fund Investment and the Return-to-Risk Relationship of Their Target Firms' (2012) 21 *Journal of Financial Intermediation* 315.

38 Bernardo Bortolloti, Veljko Fotok, and William L Megginson, 'The Sovereign Wealth Fund Discount: Evidence from Public Equity Investments' (2015) 28 *Review of Financial Studies* 2993.

90 *Steven Globerman et al.*

4.2 The performance of SOEs

Several studies comparing the performance of SOEs to privately-owned companies use data from the Fortune Global 500 list. As noted earlier, this list includes large SOEs that are not necessarily publicly traded but that provide financial statements. In this regard, Kwiatkowski and Augustnowicz compare the financial performances of SOEs and privately-owned entities drawn from the Fortune list over the period 2005–2014.[39] They use several accounting measures of profitability, including return-on-assets (ROA), return-on-sales (ROS), and return-on-equity (ROE). They find that the mean ROA is roughly the same for SOEs and private entities over the full period. The same finding applies for the ROS measure; however, the mean ROE for SOEs remains below the mean ROE for private companies throughout the period.

Boardman and Vining use the same data but distinguish SOEs by whether or not the state is a majority equity owner of the enterprise (minority ownership is identified as a mixed enterprise).[40] They find that SOEs and mixed enterprises are significantly less profitable and less efficient than privately-owned companies after controlling for other factors such as size, main industry, and age of the organization. Profitability measures include ROA, ROS, and ROE. Efficiency measures include sales per dollar of assets and sales per employee. Specifically, with respect to profitability mixed enterprises perform about the same or worse than SOEs, while in terms of efficiency mixed enterprises perform about the same or slightly better than SOEs. Dewenter and Malatesta also use data from the Fortune Global 500 list and find, using profitability measures, that government-owned firms are less profitable than privately-owned ones. They also conclude that government-owned firms use relatively more labour than do privately-owned ones (i.e. they are less efficient).[41]

Several studies use other financial data sets to compare the performances of government-versus privately-owned firms. For example, Florio uses data from the Forbes Global 2000 list of the world's largest 2,000 companies covering the business year 2010–2011 augmented with information from the Orbis database.[42] He concludes that the average SOE (where the government or a public authority holds more than 50.1 percent of the firm's shares) performs better than the average Forbes-list company: SOE's ROS is 8.8 percent while the average ROS is 7.2 percent.

---

39 Kwiatkowski and Augustnowicz (n 12).

40 Anthony Boardman and Aidan Vining, 'Ownership and Performance in Competitive Environments: A Comparison of the Performances of Private, Mixed and State-Owned Enterprises' (1989) 12 *The Journal of Law and Economics* 1.

41 Dewenter and Malatesta (n 13).

42 Massimo Florio (2014), 'The Return of Public Enterprise' (2014) SSRN <https://ssrn.com/abstract=2563560> accessed 19 October 2019. These data are more comprehensively discussed in Przemyslaw Kowalski, Max Buge, Monika Sztajerowska, and Matias Egeland, 'State-Owned Enterprises: Trade Effects and Policy Implications' (2013) OECD Trade Policy Papers No 147, 4.

State-owned enterprises and wealth funds 91

Inoue, Lazzarini, and Masacchio use financial data reported by publicly-traded firms in Brazil to compare the financial performance of firms in which government holds minority equity stakes to those of privately-owned firms.[43] They find a positive relationship between minority government ownership and a firm's return on assets. However, the difference is substantially reduced when equity stakes are allocated to business group affiliates and as local public institutions develop. Funkhouser and McAvoy employ data from a sample of Indonesian SOEs and private enterprises and show that SOEs have lower profit margins than private enterprises.[44] They also find that the former have higher costs, which suggests that SOEs are less efficient than private enterprises; however, when output levels in state-owned and private enterprises are similar, cost differences disappeared. Hence, one cannot infer that SOEs are necessarily less efficient than private enterprises, although one can infer that the former do not set profit-maximizing prices. Estrin, Hanousek, and Svejnar report mixed evidence regarding the performance of SOEs in China, where performance is focused on productivity. Perhaps their most important conclusion is that mixed enterprises in China seem to do better than private firms or wholly state-owned firms.[45] Chen, Firth, and Xu find that SOEs affiliated with the central government outperform other firms in China, including private firms and SOEs affiliated with other levels of government.[46]

There are also numerous studies of individual industries that contrast the performance of government- and privately-owned firms. The studies are too numerous to review here in any comprehensive way. Suffice to say that the findings are mixed.[47]

In summary, there are hundreds of studies that compare the performances of state-owned and privately-owned enterprises operating in a variety of industries. While it seems fair to conclude that the balance of evidence shows that privately-owned firms are more efficient and profitable than government-owned ones, a substantial number of studies draw the opposite conclusion or fail to find evidence of any difference in performance. There is only limited systematic evidence bearing upon the factors that

---

43 Inoue, Lazzarini, and Musacchio (n 23).
44 Richard Funkhouser and Paul McAvoy, 'A Sample of Observations on Comparative Prices in Public and Private Enterprises' (1979) 16 *Journal of Public Economics* 353.
45 Saul Estrin, Evzen Kocenda, and Jan Svejnar, 'Effects of Privatization and Ownership in Transition Economies' (2009) 47 *Journal of Economic Literature* 1.
46 Gongmeng Chen, Michael Firth, and Liping Xu, 'Does the Type of Ownership Control Matter? Evidence from China's Listed Companies' (2009) 33 *Journal of Banking and Finance* 171.
47 Anthony Boardman and Aidan Vining, 'Ownership and Performance in Competitive Environments: A Comparison of the Performance of Private, Mixed, and State-Owned Enterprises' (1989) 32 *Journal of Law and Economics* 1; Aidan Vining and Anthony Boardman, 'Ownership versus Competition: Efficiency in Public Enterprise' (1992) 73 *Public Choice* 205; Holger Muhlenkamp, 'From State to Market Revisited: A Reassessment of the Empirical Evidence Efficiency of Public (and privately-owned) Enterprises' (2015) 86 *Annals of Public and Cooperative Economics* 535.

92   Steven Globerman et al.

might condition the ownership-performance linkages observed. Even here, the evidence is inconclusive. Perhaps the most widely reported finding is that the competitive conditions surrounding an industry matter. However, there are differences in the findings. Specifically, some studies report that the efficiency performance of state-owned firms improves relative to privately-owned firms when an industry is relatively competitive; others report that privately-owned firms outperform government-owned ones under competitive conditions.

We conclude that the available evidence is limited and inconsistent with regard to how government ownership conditions the relative performance of SOEs. Specifically, some studies find that mixed public–private ownership harms the performance of organizations compared to full-government ownership, while other studies find the opposite. Finally, there is some (limited) evidence that the performance of SOEs relative to privately-owned companies is worse in developed countries than in developing countries.[48] Recent evidence from China suggests that this may occur because in institutionally weak environments governments provide access to critical resources that promote the SOEs' success.[49]

4.3 Evidence from privatization

Another broad approach to identifying differences in the performances of government- versus privately-owned firms focuses on how newly-privatized companies performed after privatization as compared to before privatization. Again, this encompasses a large literature, which precludes us from providing a comprehensive review. Hence, we focus on several studies that provide reviews of the relevant literature.

Megginson and Netter provide perhaps the most frequently cited review of privatization's outcome.[50] They conclude that the evidence supports the proposition that privatization is associated with improvements in the operating and financial performance of divested firms. This basic finding is repeated in Ginglinger and Megginson;[51] however, a more recent review by Arcas and Bachiller of some 28 studies published from 1992–2007 provides a more equivocal conclusion.[52] Although the majority of these studies conclude that

---

48 Shapiro and Globerman (n 24); Johan Wilner, 'Ownership, Efficiency, and Political Interference' (2001) 17 *European Journal of Political Economy* 723.

49 Kevin Zheng Zhou, Gerald Yong Gao, and Hongzin Zhao, 'State Ownership and Firm Innovation in China: An Integrated View of Institutional and Efficiency Logic' (2017) 62 *Administrative Science Quarterly* 1.

50 William Megginson and Jeffrey Netter, 'From State to Market: A Survey of Empirical Studies on Privatization' (2001) 39 *Journal of Economic Literature* 321.

51 Edith Ginglinger and William Megginson, 'The Evidence on Privatization Around the World' (2010) 108 *Bankers, Markets and Investors* 56.

52 Maria-Jose Arcas and Patricia Bachiller, 'Operating Performance of Privatized Firms in Europe: Organizational and Environmental Factors' (2010) *International Journal of Public Administration* 487.

SOEs significantly improve their efficiency after privatization, a significant minority provides conflicting evidence such that the authors conclude that the evidence concerning the effects of privatization on performance is inconclusive.

Both Megginson and Netter and Arcas and Bachiller review studies of privatizations in developed and developing countries. Other studies have focused on privatization in transition economies where a substantial amount of privatization took place in the 1980s and 1990s. Shapiro and Globerman characterize the outcome of these studies as ambiguous.[53] They state that this outcome is unsurprising given that privatization in transition economies was often accompanied by other major changes in the political and economic environment. Furthermore, transition privatization was accomplished in a variety of ways and was applied to a large number of firms, many of which report only limited data. They also conclude that privatization was more likely to improve firm performance in Central and Eastern Europe than in the former Soviet Union, where insider privatization, particularly in Russia, tended to result in concentrated managerial ownership, often to the detriment of firm performance.

Given the prominence of state ownership in China, as noted earlier, the outcome of privatization efforts in China is of particular interest. Much of that country's privatization has been relatively recent and is complicated by the complex ownership structure of Chinese companies. In particular, since the mid-1990s, many large SOEs in China have been commercialized (i.e. made to operate as independent commercial entities) while some shares in them have been sold, resulting in a large number of mixed enterprises. Li and Xu report that management buyouts accounted for nearly half of the total privatization programmes in China after its accession to the WTO, and that this privatization technique achieved the most prominent progress in terms of business performance.[54] However, the outcome of management buyouts varied from case to case. In cases of many small SOEs, attributes of a state enterprise were retained after privatization. As a result, privatization had only a modest influence on corporate governance with some mild improvement in productivity, as employment was generally reduced. More substantial improvements in efficiency and profitability were identified for larger SOEs after privatization. However, the authors caution that governments were more likely to privatize firms with greater profit-making potential.

Dewenter and Malatesta reinforce Li and Xu's caution that before-and-after privatization comparisons can be affected by actions taken prior to privatization.[55] Specifically, returns on sales and on assets increased for the sample of firms after privatization. However, differences in returns on equity before-and-after privatization were statistically insignificant. They conclude that there is not much evidence that

---

53 Shapiro and Globerman (n 24).
54 Shansan Li and Ningxiang Xu, 'The Influences of WTO Accession on China's State-Owned Enterprises' (2015) 3 *Open Journal of Business and Management* 192.
55 Dewenter and Malatesta (n 13).

94 Steven Globerman et al.

privatization itself increases firm profitability; however, there is evidence suggesting that governments efficiently restructure some firms before selling them.

The empirical evidence from privatization experiences does not much change our earlier assessment of studies comparing the performances of privately- and state-owned companies. Namely, the balance of evidence supports a conclusion that private ownership leads to better financial and operating performance, but the conclusion is a weak one given a significant amount of evidence to the contrary. The variety of experiences limit our ability to generalize the results of privatization. In addition, governments may strategically improve the performance of firms prior to privatization, which implies that the governance of SOEs can be improved, but that improvements may not require private ownership.

5. Summary and conclusions

The economics literature surrounding SWFs and SOEs is truly voluminous. Hence, in a relatively short essay, it is necessary to focus on a narrow set of issues. In this chapter, we essentially focus on the issue of whether, and to what extent, government-owned businesses are less commercially successful than privately-owned ones. This issue goes to the heart of the concerns that many Western governments have raised about state enterprises, especially SOEs from other countries. Namely, the concern is that such enterprises receive direct and indirect subsidies from home-country governments in order to enable them to compete against privately-owned companies. This, in turn, is seen as contributing to trade abuses such as dumping, as well as takeovers of privately-owned domestic companies by foreign-based SOEs, while SOEs in foreign countries are able to survive without foreign capital investment.

While there are theoretical reasons to expect state-owned enterprises to be less efficient and profitable than their privately-owned counterparts, whether they are in fact less efficient and profitable is ultimately an empirical question. While there are a robust number of empirical studies that address this issue, the conclusions one can draw are both tentative and limited. Specifically, while the balance of evidence points to state-owned enterprises being less profitable and efficient than privately-owned ones, there is a substantial amount of empirical evidence that contradicts this conclusion. The empirical evidence bearing upon the efficiency of SWFs relative to private-sector asset managers is similarly ambivalent: while the balance of evidence points to private companies being more efficient, results vary across studies.

In addition, there is no basis in the empirical literature for drawing firm and generalizable conclusions about factors that might mediate or moderate the linkages between state ownership and organizational performance. In particular, there is no consistent relationship between the share of government ownership and the performance of SOEs. There is also no clear-cut evidence that a more competitive industrial environment reduces the performance gap between state- and privately-owned firms. Finally, studies that focus on SOEs' home countries offer some support for the conclusion that any performance advantage of privately-owned firms is greater in developed economies, although there is again contrary evidence.[56]

In sum, while state ownership is becoming increasingly controversial in international economic relations, the evidence supporting the notion that SOE operates on non-economic terms is weak. Moreover, it can be argued that most of the costs of any non-commercial behaviour by SOEs are borne by their owners, which should further reduce the degree of controversy among government administrations about the issue. In our view, the implication of these results is that governments should focus more on trade and investment rules, and less on the ownership structure of foreign investors and trade partners in negotiating trade agreements.

---

56 Shapiro and Globerman (n 24).

Part II

Promoting international investment

5 The economics of foreign direct investment and international investment agreements

Eugene Beaulieu and Kelly O'Neill

1. Introduction

> Economists pronounce on legal matters at their peril: law, even international law, is a discipline all its own, with a jargon just as impenetrable as ours is to them.[1]

The magnitude and the nature of foreign direct investment have gone through momentous changes over the past two decades. The tremendous growth in FDI has changed the landscape of the global economy. The patterns of FDI have changed in terms of the sources of FDI and the location of FDI. The nature of FDI has been transformed as globalized production has intrinsically linked trade and investment through global value chains (GVCs).[2] There has been a commensurate transformation in the field of international economics over the past two decades in both the theoretical and empirical analysis of FDI. The theory has evolved from an approach that focuses on country-level analysis to one that focuses on firm-level analysis. Rather than focusing on why and how *countries* trade and invest, the focus has shifted to why, where, and how some firms engage in international trade and investment while others do not. This focus on the firm has changed how economists think about and understand FDI and international trade. Empirical analysis has also evolved to exploit firm-level data, and the gravity model of international trade and investment has emerged as the workhorse model for empirical analysis in international economics. At the same time, international policy governing trade and investment has evolved. International investment agreements have expanded dramatically as countries have looked to these agreements as a tool to attract foreign investment and/or to protect firms' investments in foreign locations.[3]

The above quote from Nobel Laureate Paul Krugman reflects economists' view of international trade policy prior to these momentous changes in the economics and policy of international investment. This chapter examines the

---

1 Paul Krugman, 'What Should Trade Negotiators Negotiate About?' (1997) 35 *Journal of Economic Literature* 113.
2 See Ari Van Assche, 'Trade and foreign direct investment in the 21st Century', Chapter 2 in this volume.
3 See Lukas Vanhonnaeker, 'International investment agreements', Chapter 10 in this volume.

100 *Eugene Beaulieu and Kelly O'Neill*

economics of IIAs in the context of a rapidly transforming landscape of international trade and investment and major developments in the theory and empirics of international economics.

The chapter is organized as follows. Section 2 presents an overview of the new economics of multinational firms: global value chains, trade, and investment. Section 3 reviews the economic rationale for adopting policies that promote international investment with a particular focus on international investment agreements. Section 4 examines the empirical evidence on whether IIAs promote FDI. The last section draws some conclusions.

2. The new economics of multinational firms: global value chains, trade, and investment

In order to understand the economics of international investment, it must be put in the context of globalization in general and GVCs in particular. The OECD defines the phenomenon of GVCs as a situation 'where the different stages of the production process are located across different countries (whereby) companies (are motivated) to restructure their operations internationally through outsourcing and offshoring of activities'.[4] Although multinational enterprises (MNEs) have been organizing their activities in the form of GVCs for many years, the phenomenon has largely been absent from economic analysis and policy discussions until very recently.[5] In fact, surprisingly, although the 'GVC' acronym is prevalent in the business-economics discourse, academic economists and the economics literature still do not widely use the term 'global value chains'. In the most recent *Handbook of International Economics*, the phrase 'global value chains' does not appear in the index.[6] This is not uncommon in the field of economics as academic economists prefer to refer to GVCs as vertical FDI, outsourcing, or as fragmented production. Although economists seem loath to use the GVC moniker, they have made considerable advances in understanding GVCs' key features.[7] An important

---

4 OECD, 'Global Value Chains (GVCs)' (OECD 2016) <www.oecd.org/sti/ind/global-value-chains.htm> accessed 9 May 2019.

5 For a detailed discussion of GVCs and their evolution, see Ari Van Assche (n 2).

6 Gita Gopinath, Elhanan Helpman, and Kenneth Rogoff, *Handbook of International Economics* (vol 4 Elsevier 2014).

7 The best work on this topic is summarized by Pol Antràs and Stephen Yeaple, 'Multinational Firms and the Structure of International Trade' in ibid Gopinath, Helpman, and Rogoff. These are some of the key academic references in this field: Gene Grossman and Elhanan Helpman, 'Integration versus Outsourcing in Industry Equilibrium' (2002) 117 *Quarterly Journal of Economics* 85; Pol Antràs, 'Firms, Contracts, and Trade Structure' (2003) 118 *Quarterly Journal of Economics* 1375; Elhanan Helpman, Marc J Melitz, and Stephen Yeaple, 'Export Versus FDI with Heterogenous Firms' (2004) 94 *American Economic Review* 300; Pol Antràs and Elhanan Helpman, 'Global Sourcing' (2004) 112 *Journal of Political Economy* 552; Elhanan Helpman, 'Trade, FDI, and the Organization of Firms' (2006) 44 *Journal of Economic Literature* 589; Pol Antràs, Luis Garicano, and Esteban Rossi-Hansberg, 'Offshoring in a Knowledge Economy' (2006) 121 *Quarterly Journal of Economics* 31; Gene Grossman and

The economics of FDI and IIAs 101

exception to economists' refusal to embrace the term 'global value chains' are economists working at international institutions such as the OECD, UNCTAD, and the WTO, where the terminology is much more widely used and accepted.[8] However, regardless of what you call them, economists have emphasized that international trade and investment are increasingly organized within GVCs and different stages of the production process are located across different countries. In particular, economists stress the interconnection of international trade, GVCs, and FDI. This is a fairly recent development in the literature and a deeper analysis of FDI requires improved efforts to measure the phenomenon. The OECD has undertaken extensive efforts to measure GVCs and estimates that MNE-coordinated GVCs account for an astounding 80 per cent of global trade.[9] This dispersion of the production process has spread internationally, and components of the value chain include such activities as design, production, marketing, distribution, and others.

Since FDI is closely tied to global value chains, it is important to understand this connection. Beaulieu and Dahlby provide a schema for how economists think about the connection between GVCs and FDI.[10] This matrix of global production is presented in Figure 5.1. The total value of inputs used in producing a given level of output can be represented by the large outside box. Production is organized and structured using intermediate inputs that can be produced by the firm (insourced) or by another firm (outsourced) and the input can be produced within the domestic economy (onshore) or produced in a foreign country (offshore). The box labelled 'Parent' represents the inputs or tasks that are performed by the firm that controls the production of the final product. Some inputs or tasks can be purchased at arm's length from other firms operating in the domestic economy (represented by the box labelled 'Domestic Suppliers'). Alternatively, a firm can obtain some of its intermediate inputs offshore; inputs supplied by a foreign subsidiary are represented by the box labelled 'Foreign Affiliate'. This source of inputs gives rise to foreign direct investment. Alternatively, the firm could obtain inputs from an outside firm operating in another country, which is represented by the box labelled 'Foreign

---

Esteban Rossi-Hansberg, 'Trading Tasks: A Simple Theory of Offshoring' (2008) 98 *American Economic Review* 1978.

8 OECD, WTO, UNCTAD, 'Implications of Global Value Chains for Trade, Investment, Development and Jobs' (2013) OECD, WTO, UNCTAD Joint Report Prepared for the G-20 Leaders' Summit Saint Petersburg (Russian Federation) 2 <https://unctad.org/en/PublicationsLibrary/unctad_oecd_wto_2013d1_en.pdf> accessed 17 June 2019; UNCTAD, *World Investment Report 2013: Global Value Chains: Investment and Trade for Development* (United Nations 2013).

9 ibid OECD, WTO, UNCTAD 23.

10 Bev Dahlby, 'Global Value Chains, Foreign Direct Investment, and Taxation' in Aaron Sydor (ed), *Global Value Chain Impacts and Implications: Trade Policy Research* (Foreign Affairs and International Trade Canada 2011); Eugene Beaulieu and Bev Dahlby, *Foreign Direct Investment and Taxation* (unpublished manuscript 2016).

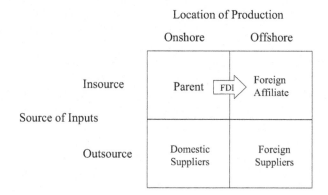

Figure 5.1 Location and sources of inputs in the global value chain

Suppliers'. FDI's role in the GVC is determined by the boundaries defining the production by the 'Parent', 'Domestic Suppliers', and 'Foreign Suppliers'.

Arguably, given the growth in FDI and MNE activity, there is a greater need to coordinate trade and investment policies and to pay greater attention in both contexts to trade in services, as well as to re-examine the existing forms of investment and trade treaty commitments. This analysis needs to include the definitions of both foreign investment and investor in IIAs[11] and to ensure that investors are responsive to states' interests in promoting investment in businesses within GVCs. Additional legal analysis is required to identify the role of law and the need for reform of domestic and international rules to take account of GVCs. Although the legal aspects of MNEs and GVCs are beyond the scope of this chapter, it is noteworthy that the legal literature has not progressed very far in this regard but is evolving rapidly.[12] Here, we focus instead on some key trends and developments in FDI and MNE activity.

There are some key trends in FDI/GVCs that are important to highlight. Antràs and Yeaple highlight six key features of multinational firms operating in the global economy.[13]

---

11 See Vanhonnaeker (n 3).
12 For an overview of the research agenda on legal aspects of GVCs, see The IGLP Law and Global Production Working Group, 'The role of law in global value chains: a research manifesto' (2016) 4 London Review of International Law 57. For a summary of the economics of GVCs, see David Dollar and Matthew Kidder, 'Institutional Quality and Participation in Global Value Chains' in World Bank (ed), *Measuring and Analyzing the Impact of GVCs on Economic Development* (International Bank for Reconstruction and Development & The World Bank 2017) 161; Sherry Stephenson, 'Global Value Chains: The New Reality of International Trade' (2013) E15 Expert Group on Global Value Chains: Development Challenges and Policy Options Compilation Report 1 <http://e15initiative.org/wp-content/uploads/2015/09/E15-GVCs-Stephenson-Final.pdf> accessed 17 June 2019.
13 Antràs and Yeaple (n 7).

1. Although there has been tremendous growth of FDI into and out of emerging and lower-income countries, multinational activity is still primarily concentrated in developed countries and most of it is two-way in nature. Developing countries are beginning to become larger players in this activity but are still generally more likely to be a destination of FDI than a source of FDI (at least on a net basis).
2. Activity by multinational firms is more concentrated in capital-intensive and R&D intensive goods and services and also tends to be intra-industry in nature.
3. Distance matters for foreign investment and for international trade in goods and services.
4. Firms engaged in international trade and investment tend to be larger, more productive, and more R&D intensive than other firms. Also, firms that engage in foreign investment are also more likely to engage in international trade.
5. Within multinational firms, the parent firms are relatively more engaged in R&D and affiliates are more engaged in selling goods in foreign markets.
6. Most FDI is made up of cross-border mergers and acquisitions (M&As) rather than new (greenfield) investment, and this is particularly true for FDI in developed economies.

As discussed above, economists have been reluctant to adopt the GVC terminology, but the economics literature has evolved with 'new, new trade theory' and theories and analyses of 'fragmented production'. The phrase 'fragmented production' reflects that production may take place within or outside firms as well as onshore or offshore. The key feature is that, increasingly, international trade is made up of firms exchanging intermediate inputs rather than simply sending final goods across international borders.

Economists often refer to fragmented production as vertical FDI. There is a well-developed literature in economics that identifies two main types of FDI: horizontal and vertical FDI. In horizontal FDI, the affiliate replicates the production process (that the parent firm undertakes in its domestic facilities) elsewhere in the world. In vertical FDI, the production chain is broken up and parts of the production processes are transferred to affiliate locations. Vertical FDI is mainly driven by production cost differences between countries (for the parts of the production process that can be performed in another location). Vertical FDI is growing rapidly and is an important factor behind the large increase in FDI inflows to developing countries. The vertical FDI decision also involves a trade-off between cost savings and the fixed cost of setting up an additional production facility. Cost savings related to local comparative advantage make some stages of production cheaper in other countries. One way to measure GVCs is by measuring the trade in value-added exports. Figure 5.2 shows how the share

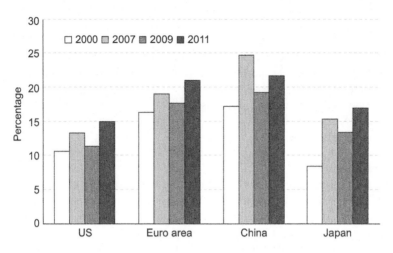

Figure 5.2 The share of foreign value-added in the exports of major economies (percent of total exports, 2000–2011)[14]

of international trade in value-added exports has increased in the United States, the euro area, China, and Japan between 2000 and 2011.

This section examined the economics of international investment and put it in the context of globalization in general and GVCs in particular. It discussed the evolution of the way economists think about foreign investment and how FDI investment has become inextricably linked to GVCs. It highlighted the conceptual advances in economics with respect to GVCs and foreign investment and discussed the research that needs to be done to understand the rapidly changing world of foreign investment. Organizations such as the OECD, UNCTAD, and the WTO have been developing tools to measure and understand globalized trade and investment with GVCs and the research agenda continues to evolve. The next section looks at IIAs and examines their impact on the pattern of investment.

3. Location promotion: the economics of FDI and international investment agreements

Reduced obstacles to trade and FDI and the possibilities that they open up for MNEs to disperse production activities within integrated international production systems create new opportunities for countries. The challenge is

---

14 Filippo di Mauro 'How are Global Value Chains Shaping the World's Economy?' (World Economic Forum, 10 September 2015) <www.weforum.org/agenda/2015/09/how-are-global-value-chains-shaping-the-worlds-economy/> accessed 9 May 2019.

The economics of FDI and IIAs 105

to attract FDI and then to maximize the benefits associated with it in order to realize the opportunities arising from the new environment.[15]

As the above quote illustrates, FDI is considered a positive element of economic growth and development and countries are encouraged to reduce obstacles to FDI and find ways to harness its positive impact. One of the approaches countries have used to reduce obstacles, or at least signal they are open for FDI, is to sign bilateral investment treaties (BITs) and free trade agreements (FTAs) with investment chapters (referred to here as international investment agreements or IIAs).[16] For instance, there was a dramatic increase in IIAs beginning in the 1990s.[17]

Before discussing the increase in IIAs and their impact on attracting international investment, however, it is important to consider the impact of FDI on economic growth and development. Attracting FDI has become a key policy objective of many governments. This trend is, at least in part, related to the positive impact that FDI can have on economic development. Given the six stylized facts on multinational firms outlined above, there is good theoretical and empirical evidence that FDI can contribute to economic growth and development. However, the evidence suggests that FDI is necessary but not sufficient for economic growth and development. That is, although FDI and international trade may be necessary conditions for growth and development, other factors (e.g. good institutions) are necessary for trade and investment to contribute significantly to economic growth and development.[18] Economists point out that FDI contributes to economic growth through technology spillovers, export spillovers, and productivity spillovers. That is, MNEs bring technology and a propensity to import and export (see key feature #4 above) as well as higher levels of productivity. For developing countries, the potential economic benefits associated with higher levels of FDI have been widely researched and the evidence is well understood. Capital investment is required to sustain development in these countries where local capital markets are often weak or very thin.[19] In theory, foreign investment can promote technology

---

15 UNCTAD, *World Investment Report 1996: Investment, Trade and International Policy Arrangements* (United Nations 1996).

16 Note that the economics literature sometimes refers to IIAs as BITs even if the former also refers to investment chapters found in FTAs. We will use IIAs throughout this chapter.

17 UNCTAD, *World Investment Report 2015: Reforming International Investment Governance* (United Nations 2015) 106.

18 e.g. Robert J Barro, *Determinants of Economic Growth: A Cross-Country Empirical Study* (MIT Press 1998); Daron Acemoglu and James Robinson, 'The Role of Institutions in Growth and Development' (2008) Commission on Growth and Development Working Paper No 10, 1 <http://documents.worldbank.org/curated/en/232971468326415075/pdf/577100NWP0Box31UBLIC10gclwp10101web.pdf> accessed 17 June 2019.

19 Gordon H Hanson, 'Should Countries Promote Foreign Direct Investment?' (2001) United Nations Conference on Trade and Development G-24 Discussion Paper Series No 1 <https://core.ac.uk/download/pdf/7043195.pdf> accessed 17 June 2019.

106 *Eugene Beaulieu and Kelly O'Neill*

transfers, productivity advancements, higher wages, and indirect positive externalities.[20] For instance, the host economy may experience a decline in market prices within a sector as a result of increased competition, which would benefit consumers. The price drop is an externality not appropriated by the foreign investor, but occurs as a result of FDI.[21] There is also some theoretical and empirical evidence that these firms not only bring technology and productivity to their foreign affiliates but that there is also a spillover of these benefits to domestic firms operating in host countries. The issue of FDI spillovers has not yet been resolved. Some, such as Lipsey,[22] report a positive impact of FDI on wages, productivity, exports, and the introduction of new industries compared with domestic firms. However, the evidence on FDI's spillover effect is mixed – partly because spillovers are difficult to measure.[23] This is still a very active area of research and a careful review of this literature is beyond the scope of this chapter.

Given that FDI is generally considered good for the economy, governments put in place policies to attract such investments.[24] One such policy is the signing of IIAs. The key question, then, is whether or not these agreements are effective in attracting FDI. A fundamental challenge of attracting international investment is the promotion of the location. Economists have identified a range of location-specific factors relevant to firm decision-making such as good governance and the protection of property rights.[25] Management scholars stress the importance of location branding strategies that they claim are crucial for attracting foreign investment.[26] Finally, in many locations, reinforcing location-specific advantages requires domestic policy reform. For example, there is a rich literature on the impact of institutions such as the rule of law on FDI.[27] This is particularly important in the context of GVCs because they typically require extensive contracts, which in turn depend on strong legal institutions for their enforcement. For our purpose, we will focus our attention on the evidence with respect to the role played by IIAs in attracting international investment.

IIAs are generally designed to address the risk of undertaking foreign investment in countries where there may be uncertainty in treatment by host-country

---

20 Brian Aitken, Gordon H Hanson, and Ann Harrison, 'Spillovers, Foreign Investment, and Export Behavior' (1997) 43 *Journal of International Economics* 103.

21 Theodore H Moran, Edward Graham, and Magnus Blomstrom, *Does Foreign Direct Investment Promote Development?* (Peterson Institute for International Economics 2005).

22 Robert E Lipsey, 'The Role of Foreign Direct Investment in International Capital Flows' (2000) National Bureau of Economic Research Working Paper No 7094 <www.nber.org/papers/w7094.pdf> accessed 17 June 2019.

23 Hanson (n 19) 23.

24 See J Anthony VanDuzer, Patrick Leblond, and Stephen Gelb, 'Introduction to international investment policy and rationale for an interdisciplinary approach', Chapter 1 in this volume.

25 For a summary, see Dollar and Kidder (n 12).

26 See Leila Hamzaoui-Essoussi, Nicolas Papadopoulos, and Alia El Banna, 'Attracting foreign direct investment: Location branding and marketing', Chapter 6 in this volume.

27 Dollar and Kidder (n 12).

governments.[28] Theory and empirical evidence highlight that an important prerequisite for a high level of FDI is that investors view the political risk of the host country as manageable. Political risk may, for example, comprise the danger of expropriation of the investment without adequate compensation. IIAs are considered important legal instruments in international investment law to mitigate this kind of risk. The enormous variation in regulatory regimes between states as well as weak institutions threaten the ability of internationally-oriented firms to safely invest abroad. Governments tout IIAs as effective frameworks for host economies to attract needed capital, and for MNEs to better integrate globally through FDI. But, as IIAs become the preferred method for bilateral investment cooperation, an understanding of their influence on FDI remains unclear.

In general, developed-country governments have signed IIAs with developing countries to protect the investments in the developing country by firms from the developed country. For their part, developing countries have generally signed IIAs in order to attract FDI from developed countries. The first IIA was signed by Germany with Pakistan in 1959. Since then, IIAs have grown dramatically, especially in Europe and East Asia.[29]

The Canadian example is worth looking at because it demonstrates a recent and concerted effort by its federal government to expand its investment treaty programme. Canada was a relative latecomer in contrast to some European jurisdictions, negotiating the majority of its early IIAs throughout the 1990s. In the following decade, Canada focused less attention on investment agreements. But, since 2009, a renewed effort has resulted in Canada ratifying eight IIAs.[30] In 2016, 57.1 per cent of Canadian direct investment abroad was protected under 33 IIAs and Canada was negotiating IIAs with 12 other countries.[31] Consequently, the value of Canadian country-pair foreign investment that is governed by IIAs is set to increase dramatically as current investment and trade agreements conclude and come on stream. This concentrated uptick in Canadian IIA activity comes at a time when global IIA ratification has stalled or levelled off.[32] Canada's foreign trade and investment strategy, in contrast to other jurisdictions like Australia, appears to include IIAs as an essential

---

28 For a discussion of IIAs from a legal perspective, see Lukas Vanhonnaeker (n 3).

29 UNCTAD (n 17).

30 UNCTAD, 'The Role of International Investment Agreements in Attracting Foreign Direct Investment to Developing Countries' (2014) UNCTAD Series on International Investment Policies for Development 1 <https://unctad.org/en/Docs/diaeia20095_en.pdf> accessed 17 June 2019; UNCTAD, 'Investment Policy Hub' (2019) UNCTAD Division on Investment and Enterprise <https://investmentpolicyhubold.unctad.org/IIA/CountryBits/35#iiaInnerMenu> accessed 9 May 2019.

31 Note that IIAs in Canada are known as Foreign Investment Protection Agreements (FIPAs). See Katie Meredith and Alexandre Gauthier, 'Canada's International Trade and Investment Agreements: A Variety of Options' (2012) 32 Canadian Library of Parliament Publication No 2012-32-E <https://lop.parl.ca/sites/PublicWebsite/default/en_CA/ResearchPublications/201232E> accessed 21 June 2019.

32 UNCTAD (n 17).

component for promoting reciprocal FDI flows.[33] For instance, Canada has predominantly been using IIAs to target emerging economies on a case-by-case basis, where local conditions are attractive to Canadian MNEs.[34]

The Canadian case is also instructive for understanding the motivation for signing IIAs and assessing the impact of IIAs on foreign investment. The Canadian IIA programme is motivated by reducing investment market risk for its MNEs and increasing outward foreign investment to specific localities.[35] The Canadian government's policy is driven by the understanding that outward foreign investment produces net economic benefits for Canada.[36] The reasoning is that by facilitating the integration of Canadian MNEs globally, it creates opportunities to diversify asset holdings, access human capital, enter markets, strengthen supply channels, and reduce operating risks. Research indicates that firms with an outward focus are more productive than their domestically-focused counterparts, and the economies in which they are headquartered receive potential spillover benefits.[37]

In practice, developed countries like Canada establish IIAs with developing/ emerging economies based on specific commercial and economic factors such as: existing investor protections, likelihood of country engagement, quality of rule of law and institutions, and the probability of ratifying a treaty. Canada's preference for establishing IIAs with developing nations is to ensure that Canadian MNEs receive 'fair and equitable treatment' within host countries that lack institutional quality or political stability when investing. Specific provisions of importance include preserving the ability of governments to enact legitimate public policy programmes, creating a clear set of investment standards and protections (such as protection against expropriation), and the inclusion of a dispute-settlement process (also called investor–state dispute settlement process).[38] In effect, a clear set of rules and due process are meant to promote bilateral investment flows by reducing the risk associated with international investment. Dolzer and Schreuer support the sentiment that IIAs add clarity to international investment regimes, stating that the

> purpose of investment treaties is closely tied … to the removal of obstacles (the 'obstacles' being market uncertainties and institutional weakness found in developing countries) that may stand in the way of allowing and channelling more foreign investment into the host states.[39]

---

33 Meredith and Gauthier (n 31).
34 ibid.
35 ibid.
36 ibid.
37 Someshwar Rao, Marc Legault, and Ashfaq Ahmad, 'Canadian-Based Multinationals: An Analysis of Activities and Performance' (1994) Industry Canada Working Paper No 2 <www.ic.gc.ca/eic/site/eas-aes.nsf/vwapj/wp02e.pdf/$file/wp02e.pdf> accessed 16 June 2019.
38 ibid.
39 Rudolf Dolzer and Christoph Schreuer, *Principles of International Investment Law* (2nd edn, Oxford University Press 2012) 22.

The economics of FDI and IIAs 109

This rationale for IIAs harkens back to the aforementioned 1996 quote from UNCTAD on obstacles impacting FDI.

IIAs may also attract FDI by signalling other pro-investment changes in domestic regimes. Investors generally believe that investment agreements are closely tied to liberalizing market reforms in developing economies and strengthen perceived, or actual, weakness in domestic institutions.[40] IIAs can influence the content of domestic investment law where that is consistent with host government policy.[41] Host governments typically consider increases in FDI a benefit to their economy and may react by reforming domestic laws to replicate IIAs. Further, MNEs may lobby for domestic reforms once political channels become established in the host country, which in turn may attract further investment.[42] Moreover, developing countries, in the process of investment reforms, may complement their domestic policies by seeking to encourage foreign investment. Foreign investors can stabilize economies since they are less likely than lenders to divest during periods of economic hardship.[43]

IIAs also improve investment markets in developing countries by stabilizing cross-border investment environments with international law. With an IIA present, even if domestic reforms remain poor or never occur, MNEs can assume a level of protection by host governments guaranteed by IIAs regardless of dynamic shifts in policy and have access to coercive recourse if treaty provisions are broken.[44] Developing country governments benefit from accommodating MNEs in this way by signalling to international markets their willingness to mitigate foreign investor risk as a policy priority. This willingness to reduce risk for MNEs can potentially reverberate through global markets and attract FDI from other nations as well, since it can be assumed that the host government's intention is to treat all foreign investors with similar protections.[45] Apart from attracting more FDI, entering into an IIA can also be symbolic of a government's openness to negotiating other international treaties.[46]

---

40 Jeswald W Salacuse and Nicholas P Sullivan, 'Do BITs Really Work? An Evaluation of Bilateral Investment Treaties and Their Grand Bargain' (2005) 4 *Harvard International Law Journal* 76.

41 Beth A Simmons and Lisa L Martin, 'International Organizations and Institutions,' in Walter Carlsnaes, Tomas Risse-Kappen, and Beth A Simmons (eds), *Handbook of International Relations* (Sage Publication 2002) 202. Also, see Vanhonnaeker (n 3).

42 Nathan M Jensen, Glen Biglaiser, Quan Li, Edmund Malesky, Pablo M Pinto, Santiago M Pinto, Joseph L Staats, *Politics and Foreign Direct Investment* (University of Michigan Press 2012) 115.

43 Lipsey (n 22).

44 Eric Neumayer and Laura Spess, 'Do Bilateral Investment Treaties Increase Foreign Direct Investment to Developing Countries?' (2005) 33 *World Development* 1567.

45 Jennifer Tobin and Susan Rose-Ackerman, 'Foreign Direct Investment and the Business Environment in Developing Countries: The Impact of Bilateral Investment Treaties' (2005) Yale Centre for Law, Economics and Public Policy Research Paper No 293, 8.

46 Neumayer and Spess (n 44) 1571; ibid Tobin and Rose-Ackerman 14.

4. Do international investment agreements promote FDI in practice?

Although IIAs may have broader objectives than simply attracting FDI, the latter is seen as the key motivating factor driving such agreements, and the primary question is whether IIAs actually affect the flows of FDI. Perhaps a better way to phrase this question is: what role do IIAs play in determining the pattern and magnitude of FDI? A number of research papers quantifying the relationship between FDI flows and IIAs have been produced over the last 15 years. In many cases, subsequent papers improved on earlier work by conducting more in-depth analyses. As a result, the literature provides some mixed evidence of IIAs' impact on FDI. An overview of the literature finds differing methodologies, sample sizes, time series, variables, and data sources. Further, earlier studies had significant shortcomings, including limited sample sizes and the unaddressed issue of endogeneity or reverse causation. This is explained in more detail below.

There are a number of other important questions about IIAs that we will also address in this section:

- Are IIAs more effective in some contexts than in others? For example, do IIAs affect FDI from developed to developing differently than from developing to developing?
- Do IIAs tend to act as a complement to domestic rules and regulations or as a substitute for them?
- Has the proliferation of IIAs affected their impact?

The first research on the impact of IIAs that we are aware of is from UNCTAD and Hallward-Driemeier.[47] These studies did not find a strong, statistically significant effect of IIAs on FDI.[48] UNCTAD initiated the empirical conversation on IIAs by analyzing FDI data from countries where IIAs had been ratified, conducting a cross-sectional analysis of 133 countries in the year 1995.[49] It

---

47 UNCTAD, *World Investment Report 1998: Trends and Determinants* (United Nations 1998); Mary Hallward-Driemeier, 'Do Bilateral Investment Treaties Attract Foreign Direct Investment? Only a bit … and they could bite' (2003) World Bank Development Research Group Investment Climate Research Working Paper No 3121 <http://documents.worldbank.org/curated/en/113541468761706209/pdf/multi0page.pdf> accessed 17 June 2019.

48 There is also a nice overview of these by Jan Peter Sasse, *An Economic Analysis of Bilateral Investment Treaties* (Gabler Verlag 2011) 69.

49 A cross-section analysis in this case refers to having FDI and IIA data for each country. That is, countries are the unit of analysis and there is one observation for each country – it is a cross-section of countries. This type of data allows the researcher to observe correlations between, say in this case, signing IIAs and flows of FDI across countries, but it is not possible to identify a causal relationship. To establish causation, it is important to observe data over time and across countries this is referred to as panel data – a panel of data across countries and over time.

The economics of FDI and IIAs 111

concluded that there was a weak relationship between FDI flows and ratifying an IIA. It is crucial to understand that there are some important conceptual and statistical/data problems with identifying a causal relationship between signing an IIA and attracting FDI. These problems highlight the difference between a correlation and a causal relationship. Almost all of the studies find a correlation between FDI and IIAs, but this does not always imply that a new IIA between two countries will cause or generate new FDI. The key empirical challenge is known as endogeneity, which can result from either 'reverse causality' (i.e. FDI causes IIAs) or from 'omitted variables' (i.e. factors not controlled [or accounted] for that are responsible for causing both IIAs and FDI). A good way to think about reverse causality is to suppose that a firm from a developed country is investing in a developing country and, to help protect its investment, it gets its home government to negotiate an IIA with the host government.[50] In the data, this would be observationally equivalent to a new IIA leading to new FDI. However, the IIA could have resulted from the proposed FDI in the first place. Moreover, it is also possible that there is an omitted variable that is correlated with FDI and the signing of an IIA. For example, suppose a host country adopted a new rule or regulation that was attractive to foreign investors and also increased the likelihood that the country would sign an IIA. This situation would create what is called a 'spurious' correlation between FDI and IIAs. Again, this is an example of endogeneity bias where empirically it looks like an IIA is driving FDI, but this may not be the case.

Another important challenge with attempting to quantify the impact of IIAs on FDI is with data and measurement. It is extremely difficult to measure FDI consistently across countries and over time. The statistics on the value of FDI, establishing ownership and location of ownership, measuring stock of FDI versus flow of FDI, and how to define and measure FDI continues to be a challenge for researchers and policymakers. These data limitations have meant that some studies focus on specific countries or specific types of country. If the sample of countries that are included in the study systematically excludes countries with certain attributes, then there could be sample-selection bias in the analysis.[51]

It is important to keep these data and empirical challenges in mind while considering the evidence. In general, some of the earlier studies were affected by the aforementioned data and empirical limitations more than the recent studies. For example, cross-country studies are not able to deal with the endogeneity problem discussed above. That is, countries may sign IIAs with

---

50 If the investment is conditional on the negotiated IIA, however, then there is no reverse causality since the IIA remains the 'cause' of the investment.

51 Sample selection bias means that rather than a random sample the data represents countries with particular observable characteristics. That is certain countries are 'selected' in the data gathering process and basing statistical analysis on this type of data will bias the results of the analysis. This means that a researcher may find a correlation in data with sample selection bias does not exist in the general case.

112   *Eugene Beaulieu and Kelly O'Neill*

other countries where their firms are already planning on investing. The cross-section analysis does not allow the researcher to control for this endogeneity, whereas a panel data approach – where the researcher observes data across countries and over time – does allow the researcher to statistically address the endogeneity problem.

There are statistical techniques to manage the challenges with sample-selection bias and endogeneity. Hallward-Driemeier employs these techniques and statistically tests whether IIAs increase FDI from developed economies to developing economies when an IIA was ratified.[52] Her analysis used panel data from 20 OECD countries and 31 developing countries between 1980 and 2000. She found that IIAs improve the likelihood of attracting FDI in countries where institutional quality was high, suggesting that IIAs were complementary to effective government institutions and not a good substitute (no statistically significant relationship was found between IIAs and FDI to developing countries where institutional quality was low).

Tobin and Rose-Ackerman conducted a similar study.[53] Their analysis addresses whether the number of IIAs signed by low- or middle-income countries attract larger shares of FDI from all countries by acting as a signal to foreign investors. The panel data, broken down into developed and developing economies, comprised up to 176 countries between the time periods of 1984 and 2000. In addition to testing the signalling effect, they tested whether IIAs acted as a substitute for institutional quality. Controlling for endogeneity, the results indicate, as with Hallward-Driemeier, that IIAs are not good substitutes for jurisdictions with high political risk (i.e. low institutional quality) and, by themselves, impact FDI very little.

In contrast to the aforementioned research, even though they followed similar statistical modelling approaches, Salacuse and Sullivan, as well as Neumayer and Spess, found strong evidence that IIAs significantly increase FDI flows to developing countries.[54] Salacuse and Sullivan found a strong relationship between IIAs and developing countries that ratify agreements with the United States; however, IIAs with all other OECD countries had a weak relationship. They attribute this finding to stronger protections in the US agreements. The results obtained by Neumayer and Spess differ in that they find evidence of a positive relationship between the number of IIAs a developing nation has with OECD countries and increased FDI. However, their study fails to address reverse causality in their assessment, which may lead to overstated effects on FDI. Gallagher and Birch test subregion relationships between the United States and Latin America.[55] Contrary to Salacuse and Sullivan, they find that

---

52 Hallward-Driemeier (n 47).
53 Tobin and Rose-Ackerman (n 45).
54 Salacuse and Sullivan (n 40); Neumayer and Spess (n 44).
55 Kevin Gallagher and Melissa Birch, 'Do Investment Agreements Attract Investment? Evidence from Latin America' (2006) 7 *The Journal of World Investment and Trade* 961.

IIAs in general do increase FDI, but they do not find that this effect is stronger for IIAs between the United States and subregions in Latin America.

So, the empirical evidence is somewhat mixed. It does show a strong correlation between IIAs and FDI, but different samples of countries, different years of analysis, and different statistical approaches do present a more nuanced perspective. More recent research, however, begins to form a consensus that IIAs are significant determinants of FDI in developing countries.[56] Tobin and Rose-Ackerman's study is of particular interest, since the authors revisited the IIA topic to find contrasting results to those of their original study, mentioned above. Two hypotheses were tested: developing country IIAs with developed countries increase FDI; and the marginal impact of IIAs decreases as more treaties are ratified. When the authors tested the effect of IIAs this time, they found support for both hypotheses. That is, they found that IIAs with developed countries attract FDI to the developing countries; however, the impact of IIAs on FDI is weaker as more treaties have been ratified.

Lejour and Salfi conduct a large and more recent analysis of IIAs' effect on FDI.[57] Their sample size contains data from 217 countries, including data measuring FDI flows between OECD country pairs as well as between OECD countries and non-OECD countries. The time series for the analysis is from 1985 to 2011. The authors found an average increase in bilateral FDI stocks of 35 per cent for country pairs where IIAs existed. Further, their analysis found that lower-middle- and low-income countries, specifically in East Asia and Middle and Eastern Europe, realize larger FDI stock gains from establishing an IIA.

To date, it appears that the earlier studies found mixed evidence on the impact of IIAs on investment, but more recent studies have found that IIAs increase investment. Bellak takes a more systematic approach to the analysis of the evidence to date, by conducting a comprehensive review of current IIA literature in a meta-analysis of 33 (out of 37) studies published between 1998 and 2012.[58] The meta-

---

56 Tobin and Rose-Ackerman (n 45); Christian Bellak, 'How Bilateral Investment Treaties Impact on Foreign Direct Investment: A Meta-analysis of Public Policy' (2013) MAER Network Colloquium University of Greenwich <https://how-bilateral-investment-treaties-impact-on-foreign-direct-investment-a-meta-analysis-of-public-policy-by-christian-bellak-vienna%20(1).pdf> accessed 17 June 2019; Axel Berger, Matthias Busse, Peter Nunnenkamp, and Martin Roy, 'Do Trade and Investment Agreements Lead to more FDI? Accounting for Key Provisions Inside the Black Box' (2013) 10 *International Economics and Economic Policy* 247; Arjan Lejour and Maria Salfi, 'The Regional Impact of Bilateral Investment Treaties on Foreign Direct Investment' (2015) CPB Netherlands Bureau for Economic Policy Analysis Working Paper No 298, 2 <www.cpb.nl/sites/default/files/publicaties/download/cpb-discussion-paper-298-regional-impact-bilateral-investment-treaties-foreign-direct-investment.pdf> accessed 17 June 2019; Rod Falvey and Neil Foster-McGregor, 'North-South FDI and Bilateral Investment Treaties' (2015) Maastricht Economic and Social Research Institute on Innovation and Technology Working Paper No 2015–010 <https://pdfs.semanticscholar.org/9405/a282f454b729d30f9d1c79ab42ec15a3628f.pdf> accessed 17 June 2019.
57 ibid Lejour and Salfi.
58 Bellak (n 56).

114   *Eugene Beaulieu and Kelly O'Neill*

analysis is a statistical analysis of results from empirical studies measuring the impact of IIAs on FDI. Bellak finds that over three-quarters of the papers (76 per cent of them) find a positive and statistically significant impact of IIAs on FDI. To summarize, Bellak's meta-analysis finds that the literature examining the impact of IIAs on FDI reveals a positive relationship between IIAs and FDI overall.

It is also important to put the evidence on the impact of IIAs on FDI in the context of a broader literature on the determinants of FDI. There is a substantial body of empirical research examining the determinants of FDI. One problem with this literature is that the studies tend to focus on one particular FDI determinant. In this chapter, for instance, we have been focusing on how IIAs affect FDI. For their part, other studies have examined the effects of taxation and other host-country characteristics on FDI.[59] It is, therefore, crucial to bring these different literatures together and put them within the broader context of the determinants of FDI.

Two recent studies by Blonigen and Piger and Eicher, Helfman, and Lenkoski systematically examine the body of evidence on the determinants of FDI.[60] They carefully examine what factors are most likely required to explain the pattern of FDI. They confirm that the results do depend on the type of FDI and the set of countries examined and that, in general, the factors that are most likely to drive FDI are traditional gravity variables such as distance and economic size as well as cultural distance factors (whether countries share language and culture histories), relative labour endowments, and trade agreements. They find evidence that host- and source-country characteristics such as lower tax regimes and high levels of productivity generate more FDI and that there are differences in the determinants of FDI between developing and developed countries. Their results are consistent with the results from the

---

59 James R Hines, 'Lessons from Behavioural Responses to International Taxation' (1999) 52 *National Tax Journal* 305; Thomas Gresik, 'The Taxing Task of Taxing Transnationals' (2001) 39 *Journal of Economic Literature* 800; Roger Gordon and James Hines, 'International Taxation' in Alan Auerbach and Martin Feldstein (eds), *Handbook of Public Economics* (vol 4 Elsevier 2002) 1935; OECD, 'Tax Effects on Foreign Direct Investment' (2007) Organization for Economic Cooperation and Development Policy Studies No 17 <www.oecd.org/ctp/tax-policy/39866155.pdf> accessed 17 June 2019; Ruud De Mooji and Sjef Ederveen, 'What a Difference Does It Make? Understanding the Empirical Literature on Taxation and International Capital Flows' (2006) European Commission Economic Papers 2 <http://ec.europa.eu/economy_fi nance/publications/pages/publication578_en.pdf> accessed 17 June 2019; Michael Devereux, 'The Impact of Taxation on the Location of Capital, Firms and Profit: A Survey of Empirical Evidence' (2007) Oxford University Centre for Business Taxation 1 <www.sbs.ox.ac.uk/sites/default/files/Business_Taxation/Docs/Publications/Working_Papers/Series_07/WP0702.pdf> accessed 17 June 2019. For a legal discussion of taxation policy and international investment, see Allison Christians and Marco Garofalo, 'Tax competition as an investment promotion tool', Chapter 8 in this volume.

60 Bruce A Blonigen and Jeremy Piger, 'Determinants of Foreign Direct Investment' (2014) 47 *Canadian Journal of Economics* 775; Theo Eicher, Lindy Helfman, and Alex Lenkoski, 'Robust FDI Determinants: Bayesian Model Averaging in the Presence of Selection Bias' (2012) 34 *Journal of Macroeconomics* 637.

literature that shows that IIAs are correlated with FDI, and that IIAs are complementary to other key host-country characteristics and not substitutes for other factors attracting FDI. That is, signing an IIA can attract FDI when the host country has characteristics that are attractive to foreign investors. Countries will not attract FDI by signing an IIA if they have low productivity, weak institutions and rule of law, high political risk, and are small economies far away from and lacking good connections with the source country.

5. Conclusions

The IIA regime is experiencing a legitimacy crisis and many governments and other stakeholders are calling for reform of the system, including ISDS procedures and investor protection standards (like fair and equitable treatment [FET] and most-favoured nation [MFN] treatment).[61] Some critics have argued that the system of international investment agreements should be scrapped because such agreements may adversely affect state sovereignty, and may not be very useful in attracting FDI. This chapter examines the economics of FDI and IIAs and summarizes the evidence on the impact of IIAs on FDI.

The chapter begins by examining the economics of IIAs and provides an overview of their evolution. There are strong claims that IIAs are not effective at attracting FDI; however, the theory and evidence suggests that IIAs have an important role to play in international economics. We point out that economic principles underpin international trade and investment law rules and document that trade and investment has undergone dramatic changes over the past number of decades. Moreover, the field of international economics has also undergone fundamental changes; the way we model and think about trade and investment has changed dramatically. The changing nature of trade and investment and the transformation of thinking in international economics has led to important changes in the architecture of investment treaties and the investment components of trade agreements. More research is being done in this regard and recent efforts are confronting the challenges of the emergence of SOEs and their impact on FDI.

The chapter then examines the empirical evidence on the effectiveness of IIAs in attracting FDI. The evidence makes it very clear that signing IIAs is positively correlated with FDI, but that a causal relationship is difficult to determine. The evidence suggests that countries with ambitions to expand bilateral FDI tend to sign IIAs and this may play a hand in increasing FDI. However, host and source-country characteristics are key drivers of FDI and IIAs are complementary to these factors. Perhaps ironically given the original motivation of IIAs to drive FDI by protecting investment, the evidence is clear that IIAs are not substitutes for weak laws and institutions that facilitate FDI. Countries

---

61 See Vanhonnaeker (n 3); J Anthony VanDuzer and Patrick Dumberry, 'Investor–state dispute settlement', Chapter 11 in this volume.

with ambitions to attract FDI have to work hard to improve the economic climate, reduce political risk, and build strong ties with source countries; an IIA can only complement these actions to attract FDI. The determinants of FDI depend on the type of FDI and the set of countries examined. However, in general, the factors that are most likely to drive FDI are traditional gravity variables such as distance and economic size as well as cultural distance factors, relative labour endowments, and trade agreements. Host- and source-country characteristics such as lower tax regimes and high levels of productivity generate more FDI. IIAs are complementary to other key host-country characteristics and not substitutes for other factors attracting FDI. That is, signing an IIA can help attract FDI when the host country has characteristics that are attractive to foreign investors.

6 Attracting foreign direct investment

Location branding and marketing

Leila Hamzaoui-Essoussi, Nicolas Papadopoulos, and Alia El Banna

1. Introduction

Globalization and other contemporary forces have brought about major economic, social, and political transformations around the world. One of the most noteworthy recent developments has been the unprecedented growth, in both volume and importance, of foreign direct investment worldwide as its benefits to both developed and developing host countries are being widely recognized.[1] As a result, a growing number of potential investment locations are actively seeking to attract it and the roster of places competing for investment has grown significantly.

Competition for FDI is now more intense than ever before and involves various different jurisdictional levels, from countries to provinces or states, regions, and individual cities.[2] In light of the goal of not only working actively to *make* a place attractive for investors but also to *present* it as such, governments have been focusing on improving the actual business environment as well as, of specific interest in this chapter, on improving the *investment image* of the places they represent more systematically than before through promotional efforts.

Research shows that the reputation of potential investment locations and investors' image of them has a direct impact on their perceived attractiveness.[3] The location images investors have may not necessarily match (and need not match) some 'objective reality', howsoever this may be defined. What matters is that, to a great extent, these images influence their location decisions. While

---

1 For details on FDI growth, see Ari Van Assche 'Trade and foreign direct investment in the 21st century', Chapter 2 in this volume and Eugene Beaulieu and Kelly O'Neill, 'The economics of foreign direct investment and international investment agreements', Chapter 5 in this volume.

2 For simplicity, in this chapter we use 'place' and 'nation' or 'country' as interchangeable generic terms, letting the context define the meaning and using other specific terms only when they are expressly relevant.

3 Ying Fan, 'Branding the Nation: Towards a Better Understanding' (2010) 6 *Place Branding and Public Diplomacy* 97.

118 Leila Hamzaoui-Essoussi et al.

developed countries typically have an established positive image, developing economies[4] generally tend to suffer from a poorer or poorly defined image notwithstanding any FDI-specific strengths they may have.

The importance of place image, and the growth of inter-country competition for FDI, have made *nation branding*, defined as the strategic representation of a country based on its economic, political, social, and/or cultural capital,[5] an important practice internationally in efforts to attract foreign investment. For instance, annual spending on FDI promotion activities has been growing significantly[6] and establishing a centralized investment promotion agency (IPA) has become a popular institutional approach in FDI attraction.[7]

Research on the FDI decision making process and location choice is voluminous, as is research on the importance of place image in such contexts as tourism attraction and export promotion. However, studies on the two strands together are virtually nonexistent and so our understanding of the point at which they intersect, 'nation branding for FDI', is poor. This chapter's overall aim is to examine the nature and role of investment promotion, nation branding, and image management for FDI attraction, and to do so in the context of FDI decision making and the factors that influence investors in choosing investment locations.

Following this introduction, the next section summarizes key concepts on FDI and related location decisions; the next two sections examine the place image and branding concepts in relation to FDI and review promotional efforts to attract foreign capital; and the last two sections synthesize existing knowledge on nation branding challenges and opportunities for FDI attraction and provide concluding comments.

2. Foreign direct investment: background and location choice decision process

Places feel the need to market themselves as 'investment products' that investors can 'buy' by electing to locate there. This means attempting to tilt the balance of both the actual and perceived environment so as to highlight location-specific advantages and de-emphasize disadvantages. Considering the ongoing search for 'best FDI locations' by investors, places try to market themselves using a variety of means that until recently were virtually unknown to them. Over time, such efforts have become more sophisticated and

---

4 For simplicity, emerging, less developed, transitional, and emerging economies will be referred to collectively in this chapter as 'developing' unless otherwise specified.

5 Gyorgy Szondi, 'The Role and Challenges of Country Branding in Transition Countries: The Central and Eastern European experience' (2007) 3 *Place Branding and Public Diplomacy* 8.

6 Bjorn P Jacobsen, 'Investor-based Place Brand Equity: A Theoretical Framework' (2009) 2(1) *Journal of Place Management and Development* 70.

7 For a detailed discussion of how IPAs work, see Matthew Durban, 'FDI policy advocacy and investor targeting', Chapter 7 in this volume.

systematic, moving from primitive conceptions of marketing, which considered it synonymous with selling or advertising, toward contemporary views that differentiate between tactical subparts, such as selling and promotion, and strategic marketing and branding.

Since promotional approaches used to attract foreign investment are, by definition, aimed at the mind of the investor, it logically follows that to make the former effective presupposes a good understanding of the latter. Systematic investment promotion calls for a better and deeper understanding of the complexity and challenges associated with investors' location choices. This section reviews findings on FDI decision making, the role of incentives, the elements that cause variations in investor behaviour, and emotional versus rational factors in FDI location choices.

2.1 Decision making in FDI

A common misconception is that FDI decisions are a matter of choosing among alternative locations, rather than also, and in many cases *primarily*, being a matter of *choosing among alternative modes of operation*. This is because location choice normally *follows* a firm's decision to invest abroad. The process involves three distinct steps, of which location choice is usually the last: Deciding *whether or not* to expand internationally; if yes, deciding *how* to go abroad (the 'mode of entry' (MOE) decision), which may take one of four main forms, namely exporting, contractual arrangements, international alliances, or investment; and if FDI is chosen over some other MOE, then the *where* question comes up and presents a number of alternative possibilities. These include investing in the target market itself, expanding existing or establishing new facilities at home or at other locations where the firm already has production plants, or, conversely, considering whether investment in the selected target location may in fact be expanded so that it can serve as a hub for servicing other nearby markets.

The *reason* for a firm's decision to go abroad in the first place is probably the most important consideration in this discussion. Possibilities include gaining access to foreign markets, new technology, skilled labour, and capital or natural resources, as well as enabling the firm to take advantage of the political, taxation, operational flexibility, and other benefits from operating in various different jurisdictions. It logically follows, therefore, that a company may or may not consider FDI as a MOE option. For instance, resource-seeking mining firms must by necessity invest wherever these resources are available, whereas market-seekers have many more MOE options including direct or indirect exports and licensing.

The relevance of this line of thought is that working to attract FDI typically must, but rarely does, target two different types of investors, each with very distinct needs and decision making processes: Firms that *must* invest, and whose only question therefore is '*where* to go'; versus firms that can *choose* the MOE they prefer, whose question is not just where to go but also '*how* to get there'.

120   *Leila Hamzaoui-Essoussi et al.*

For the first type of investor, much of the attractiveness of a country depends on such factors as its natural resource advantages, which are 'givens' (a company that needs bauxite will go to where bauxite is available). For the second type, which comprises the majority of potential investors, most firms adopt sequential MOEs, beginning with exports and gradually moving to investment if they can and if the target market warrants it. Since these firms tend to expand internationally in incremental steps, investment attraction efforts may be directed fruitfully toward *companies that already have some involvement* in the target country. This may include the population of firms that already export to the country, or have contractual arrangements there, or have production facilities that have worked well to date and may be candidates for expansion.

Large numbers of researchers have tried to understand the base factors that lead firms to undertake FDI in particular countries and how the location choice process works, and interest in this area has grown in line with the growth of FDI worldwide.

2.2 *Determinants of FDI*

Dunning's[8] well-known framework comprising Ownership (O), Locational (L), and Internalization (I) advantages (OLI) examines both macro (country-specific) and micro (firm-specific) variables. Ownership and Internalization advantages are firm-specific, while Locational factors reflect the 'where' of FDI, are country-specific, and, according to Dunning,[9] depend on whether the firm is a resource-, market-, efficiency-, or strategic asset-seeker.

International business research on the determinants of FDI has focused mainly on location-specific advantages and such factors as labour costs and production efficiencies, political stability, proximity, and market size and growth rate.[10] A distinction has also been made in regard to the factors that drive FDI toward developing versus developed countries. For instance, a study of 71 developing countries found that those in Sub-Saharan Africa received a lower FDI share compared to other regions because of an 'adverse regional effect' attributed mainly to the continent's overall poor image.[11] Another study concluded that some factors that affect FDI patterns in developed countries, such as exchange rate variations and source country size, do not apply in the

---

8 John H Dunning, 'Exploring Changing Patterns of International Production: In Defense of the Eclectic Theory' (1979) 41 *Oxford Bulletin of Economics and Statistics* 31.

9 John H Dunning, 'Location and the Multinational Enterprise: A Neglected Factor?' (1998) 29 *Journal of International Business Studies* 45.

10 Yigang Pan, 'The Inflow of Foreign Direct Investment to China: The Impact of Country-specific Factors' (2003) 56 *Journal of Business Research* 82; Nuno Carlos Leitao and Horacio Faustino, 'Determinants of Foreign Direct Investment in Portugal' (2010) 11 *Journal of Applied Business and Economics* 2007.

11 Elizabeth Asiedu, 'On the Determinants of Foreign Direct Investment to Developing Countries: Is Africa Different?' (2002) 30 *World Development* 107.

Attracting foreign direct investment 121

developing world; moreover, geographic distance seems to be more important for firms engaging in resource-seeking instead of market-seeking activities.[12]

To summarize, many different factors affect investors' decisions: Specific factors are relevant only in certain ways and for certain types of businesses or investment settings, only to a limited and variable extent, and mostly for investors at specific steps of their decision-making process.

2.3 The role of policy measures in location choice

Investors usually have much more leverage than governments in FDI transactions, since the location of the latter is a given whereas in many cases the former can choose which of the 'givens' suits them best. This leads governments to establish specific advantages aimed at enhancing their location's competitiveness, including tax holidays, grants, and other incentives, and to promote, as applicable, the availability of skilled labour, low business operating costs, and other production factors. The effectiveness of such policies and characteristics depends largely on how they compare against similar ones at competing jurisdictions, and some studies (e.g. PricewaterhouseCooper)[13] provide comparative information on government incentives, worker compensation and fringe benefits, office space, ISDN connections, business and income taxes, accounting, consulting, IT and legal services, transportation, and other investment-related attributes.

Despite the potential attractiveness of technical characteristics, previous research suggests that they are not among the most effective,[14] that the influence of incentives depends on the type of investment (e.g. companies looking to decrease costs will be more sensitive to financial incentives than market-seekers),[15] and that tax credits and incentives do better at *retaining* present investors than in *attracting* new ones.[16] Importantly, incentives and business costs are more likely to be considered by investors only after a shortlist of otherwise-desirable destinations has been selected.[17]

It is also necessary to know the decision process at the investor's organization in order to identify the *stage* where it will be most receptive to various different

---

12 Pan (n 10).
13 PricewaterhouseCoopers, 'Comparison of High-Tech Industries in Major North American Metropolitan Areas' (2000).
14 Barry M Rubin and C Kurt Zorn, 'Sensible State and Local Economic Development' (1985) 45 *Public Management Forum* 333.
15 Michael Overesch and Georg Wamser, 'Who Cares About Corporate Taxation? Asymmetric Tax Effects on Outbound FDI' (2009) *World Economy* 1657.
16 Louis T Wells and Alvin G Wint, 'Marketing a Country: Promotion as a Tool for Attracting Foreign Investment' (2000) The International Finance Corporation Revised Edition FIAS Occasional Paper No 13
17 Rubin and Zorn (n 14).

122 *Leila Hamzaoui-Essoussi et al.*

marketing efforts. These stages include[18] identifying the project's location determinants and the country factors that influence them; creating a list of eight to 20 locations that fit the key determinants well; assessing each location in detail to shorten the list to no more than five candidates, at which point the incentives offered by countries may be considered;[19] further reducing the list to perhaps three locations based on information from site visits and more detailed financial and other considerations; and selecting the location for entry. Considering these steps in location choice, place marketers are called to develop FDI promotion strategies in light of sufficient background knowledge on the factors that affect their potential investors' behaviour, not only in general but also depending on the stage of the location choice process.

2.4 Variations in FDI behaviour by investor, investment and location characteristics

From a marketing perspective it is also important to distinguish the following factors that affect investment decisions.

2.4.1 Type of business and type of FDI

While most of the determinants discussed above are applicable to practically any firm, Tiits[20] and others stress that additional or different factors are at play when examining FDI decisions by technology-intensive firms. Such firms value supportive knowledge-intensive environments (e.g. higher education, science parks) and focus on modes of operation centred around business networks that emphasize innovation and include producers, their suppliers and contractors, R&D institutions, skilled labour, and distributors. The successful evolution of California's Silicon Valley, for example, has been attributed to such factors as the availability of business support services, skilled labour, and venture capital, together with defence spending, access to knowledge organizations, and the presence of a leading entrepreneur or firm.[21]

The services sector is another type of investor with unique characteristics and needs. For example, Raff and Von der Ruhr[22] investigated outward FDI by US service producers and found that factors related to market structure (often

---

18 Jacobsen (n 6).
19 Nicolas Papadopoulos and Louise A Heslop, 'Country Equity and Country Branding: Problems and Prospects' (2002) 9 *Journal of Brand Management* 294.
20 Marek Tiits, 'Technology-intensive FDI and Economic Development in a Small Country – The Case of Estonia' (2007) 11 *Trames Journal of the Humanities and Social Sciences* 324.
21 Paul A Herbig and James E Golden, 'The Rise of Innovative Hot Spots: Silicon Valley and Route 128' (1993) 10 *International Marketing Review* 35.
22 Horst Raff and Marc von der Ruhr, 'Foreign Direct Investment in Producer Services: Theory and Empirical Evidence' (2001) CESifo Working Paper No 598.

Attracting foreign direct investment 123

monopolistically competitive), level of cultural (dis)similarity, and the paucity of needed information (e.g. service quality assessment) act as potential barriers to foreign market entry by service firms.

Another key difference in investor behaviour arises from the choice between greenfield investment, international joint venture (IJV), or merger and acquisition (M&A) as the FDI mode, which is linked to the international expansion objectives discussed earlier. Investors choosing M&As tend to focus more on the *company* they want to engage with than on the *country/location* of that company.[23] This unique characteristic of M&A (and sometimes IJV) related behaviour means that investment promotion is likely to be less effective (if at all) if it emphasizes the country's investment climate than if it focuses on the quality of existing firms that might partner with a foreign firm.

2.4.2 *Investor nationality and cultural distance*

A 23-country study[24] found that a country's stock of FDI in a target market is positively related to the existing level of exports from the former to the latter, but negatively related to the cultural and geographic distance between the two countries. This highlights a 'visibility' and critical mass advantage from pre-existing close involvement of foreign firms in a given market, and buttresses a point made earlier: Since expansion is a sequential process, exporters and other firms with local involvement may constitute prime targets for future investment attraction.

As well, the mode of investment has been found to be significantly related to the investor's culture of origin,[25] as cross-cultural differences influence managers' perceptions about the costs and risks of alternative modes as well as organizational practices and expectations, thereby increasing the likelihood of a firm to favour one expansion mode over another. Similarly, a study of FDI determinants in China[26] examined the role of market size, labour cost, labour quality, and technological capability, and its findings contrasted markedly by investor origin: Western investors were sensitive to attractive 'pull' factors of the *foreign environment*, while Asian-origin FDI showed

---

23 Nicolas Papadopoulos, Vijay Jog, Louise Heslop and Ritoo D'Souza, 'The Investment Climate in Canada: Foreign Investor Experiences and Perceptions' in Stephen Preece and P Woodcock (eds), *International Business* (Administrative Sciences Association of Canada International Business Division 1997) 37.

24 Robert Grosse and Len J Trevino, 'Foreign Direct Investment in the United States: An Analysis by Country of Origin' (1996) 27 *Journal of International Business Studies* 139.

25 Bruce Kogut and Harbir Singh, 'The Effect of National Culture on the Choice of Entry Mode' (1988) 19 *Journal of International Business Studies* 411.

26 Chengqi Wang, Jeremy Clegg and Mario Kafouros, 'Country-of-origin Effects of Foreign Direct Investment: An Industry Level Analysis' (2009) 49 *Management International Review* 179.

124   Leila Hamzaoui-Essoussi et al.

a greater influence of 'push' factors that reflected the *investors' needs* and perhaps their cultural proximity to China.

2.4.3 Additional key location characteristics

An important component that affects FDI decisions is the evolution of most emerging countries as they move from underdeveloped or command-based structures to market economies that can make them *bona fide* competitors on a global scale. FDI in emerging markets is responding to new strategic opportunities arising from their growing investment in human capital, technological infrastructure, and R&D capabilities. At the same time, the nature of these opportunities and the level and type of response of foreign companies to them is influenced by, as well as influences, the evolution of FDI-related policies. Indeed, distinct episodes in the evolution of policy can be identified in which sectoral FDI restrictions (e.g. foreign ownership) are either tightened or loosened over time.[27] Therefore, factors affecting FDI decisions can be industry- as well as country- and time-specific.

Another important characteristic is the location level that tries to attract foreign investment. One thinks of investing in 'America' differently from 'New York' versus 'Oklahoma', and in 'Britain' differently from 'London' versus 'Aberdeen'. Different location levels approach the investment promotion task differently, which serves to further accentuate the differences between them as viewed from by investors.

2.5 Emotional versus rational factors in FDI location choice

The research reviewed so far addresses the 'rational' part of FDI decision making. Except for occasional minor or passim references, the extant literature does not deal with soft factors that may also influence FDI and reflects the long-standing and ongoing debate over the distinction between rational, emotional, or hybrid decision making.[28]

Cechella[29] examined commonly cited rational factors but also whether cultural affinity – including a shared language, culture, and/or history – is considered in location choices found and that it is an important determinant in the early stages of internationalization. Still, the notion of culture can be considered a rational 'hard' factor which is *external* to the firm and can be measured and observed. For instance, a population's level of fluency in foreign languages is statistically measurable, and so language variables are often included

---

27 ibid.

28 Jorge E Araña and Carmelo J León, 'Do Emotions Matter? Coherent Preferences Under Anchoring and Emotional Effects' (2008) 66 *Ecological Economics* 700.

29 Cristiano Cechella, 'The Influence of Cultural Affinity for the Boost of Brazilian Investment in Portugal' (2010) 3 *Regional Science Inquiry Journal* 59.

Attracting foreign direct investment 125

in FDI location choice decisions. On the other hand, 'soft' factors, namely, emotions and affect, are *internal* to the individuals making the decision and may influence them to a similar, lesser, or greater degree than rational, cognitive considerations. An Argentine firm may decide to invest in Spain, for example, because of cultural similarities between the two countries that can be measured relatively easily – but this does not mean that all Argentine investors *like* Spain and its people, and so in cases of negative affect a different decision may be made.

The five-stage FDI decision process described earlier[30] calls for extensive information gathering and processing, which is rather unrealistic if 'all' potential opportunities and locations in the world (countries, cities, regions ...) were to be included. The costs associated with such a task are prohibitively high, which makes an 'all-points search' in the initial stage of the process factually impossible. This means that rational analysis is influenced by emotional factors, or the reverse: That the latter may in fact determine how the former will proceed. Emotional factors influence *which locations* and *what types of information* will be entered into the initial choice set, *how* the information will be *interpreted*, and *how* will location candidates be *analysed* throughout the process.[31]

Emotions can be seen as complements to rational choice processes in FDI decisions, since, in a situation of cognitive limitation, investors need a device to contain their range of options.[32] Emotions can be that device, whether the manager is or is not consciously aware that they do. More specifically, network theory and learning theory are providing tools to help investors make investment decisions. The former[33] relates to the economic value attached to one's social network, which includes personal and business relationships both at home and in FDI target locations as well as other countries. This network may be important and germane to an investment decision by providing information, local connections, and other inputs. As well, learning theories[34] relate to the decision maker's direct or indirect experience with and learning about the host country, with investing internationally, and with international business in general, which may be drawn upon to help make better investment decisions.

Van de Laar and De Neubourg[35] illustrated the role of emotional factors in FDI decisions based on their study of 219 Dutch firms (79 investors and 140 non-investors) in relation to countries in Central and Eastern Europe. Their

---

30 Rubin and Zorn (n 14).
31 Papadopoulos and Heslop (n 19).
32 Mindel van de Laar and Chris de Neubourg, 'Emotions and Foreign Direct Investment: A Theoretical and Empirical Exploration' (2006) 46 *Management International Review* 207.
33 Ronald S Burt, 'The Network Structure of Social Capital' in RI Sutton and BM Staw (eds) *Research in Organizational Behaviour* (vol 22 JAI Press 2000).
34 John Martin, *Organizational Behaviour* (Thomas Learning 2001); Van de Laar and De Neubourg (n 32).
35 Van de Laar and De Neubourg ibid.

126 *Leila Hamzaoui-Essoussi et al.*

model includes personal relations with relatives, friends, or businesses in the host country; personal involvement or interest arising from an employee's nationality of, or willingness to work in, the target country; language knowledge; and positive personal experience with the country. These variables were present in FDI-related decisions, with 12.5 per cent of the investor sample stating that at least one important factor in their decision making was of a personal nature and 28 per cent of the investors had not made any fact-based investment analysis. This is in line with Loewenstein,[36] who showed that investors' cognitive evaluation of risks may often diverge from their emotional reaction *to those same risks*, and that emotions will largely influence their decision (e.g. economic analysis may favour investment in a country notwithstanding political instability and a high-risk rating, but a manager's affective assessment of having to live there to implement and manage the investment may counter this and lead to a no-go decision).

To summarize, the both the 'how' (MOE) and the 'where' (location) factors that influence FDI decisions are greater in number and considerably more varied than is typically taken into account in place marketing for investment attraction. Importantly, by focusing on 'rational' factors, traditional explanations of FDI behaviour do not account for the impact of soft factors that influence the perceived images of places by investors. Since an investor cannot possibly consider all the available FDI possibilities, decision-makers limit the range of alternatives to a set of options that can be reasonably investigated. From the outset, and in subsequent stages of the decision process, the alternative locations for which information is collected are triaged to arrive at ever-shorter shortlists and so places and their images become an important variable to consider. The affective part of the investment process has to deal with place images and the emotions they engender, and since leveraging people's emotions is one of the core functions of branding, the role of place branding in FDI promotion has to be considered more extensively.

3. Investment promotion, place marketing, nation branding

Contemporary research in psychology has confirmed the primacy of emotion over cognition, and FDI 'where' decisions, i.e. which location to 'buy', are influenced by emotional factors similarly to consumers' decisions on 'which brand to buy', from within the choice sets of, respectively, investment locations and commercial brands. Therefore, FDI decisions can be influenced, at least partly, by the creation of 'location brands'. Recent policy shifts in many countries aimed at enhancing their attractiveness for FDI have brought about a rise in competition and, inevitably, a greater degree of homogeneity across

---

36 George Loewenstein, 'Emotions in Economic Theory and Economic Behavior' (2000) 90 *American Economic Review: Papers and Proceedings* 426.

investment environments – which makes branding even more relevant than before both cross-nationally and also among places within the same country.

3.1 Investment promotion and the role of investment promotion agencies

Investment promotion has been defined[37] as a portfolio of activities with several subparts including advertising, investment seminars and missions, participation in trade shows and exhibitions, distribution of literature, one-to-one direct marketing efforts, facilitating visits of prospective investors, matching prospective investors with local partners, help with obtaining permits and approvals, and services for investments that are already operational. These activities are most commonly conducted by IPAs, which have become a popular institutional approach in the strategic promotion of FDI.

As of 2001, there were more than 160 national and over 250 subnational IPAs,[38] of which 85 per cent were located in developing countries and were established in 1980 or later.[39] These agencies were initially seen primarily as 'information providers',[40] but over time their activities have expanded and now include (a) image building, aimed at improving investors' views of a country; (b) investment generation, aimed directly at enlarging the inward flow of capital; and (c) investment servicing activities, concerned with facilitating investors after an investment is made.[41]

3.2 From promotion to place branding and marketing

Traditional promotion campaigns and marketing efforts used by IPAs, such as brochures, investment guides, or advertisements aimed at raising investor awareness of a region, have become less effective over time.[42] A growing number of cities, provinces, states, nations, and subnational or supra-national regions have in the past few decades adopted marketing and branding concepts and tools to attract tourists, workers, investors, sports, or other mega-events, and so on. A prolific body of literature dedicated to country image, place marketing and place branding, and more recently nation branding, underscores the growing importance of the area for scholars and practitioners.

---

37 Wells and Wint (n 16).
38 UNCTAD, *World Investment Report: The World of Investment Promotion at a Glance* (UNCTAD 2001).
39 World Bank, *Census of Investment Promotion Agencies* (World Bank 2005).
40 Joel I Deichmann, 'Foreign Direct Investment in the Czech Republic: The Role of Origin Effects and Government Promotion Abroad' (2010) 52 *Comparative Economic Studies* 249.
41 Wells and Wint (n 16); Deichmann ibid.
42 Craig Young, 'Meeting the New Foreign Direct Investment Challenge in East and Central Europe: Place-Marketing Strategies in Hungary' (2005) 23 *Environment and Planning Government and Policy* 733.

128 *Leila Hamzaoui-Essoussi et al.*

Following the initial notion of 'country-of-origin' and a product's broader 'place of association',[43] place branding emerged when intense global competition helped to convince place authorities that marketing has a critical role to play in helping to improve overall place welfare.[44] In tourism, governments, sector associations, and individual operators have long been involved in systematic place marketing.[45] This could also be the case for investment since, similarly to tourism, in deciding where to invest the investor is the buyer and the location is the product. Investment attraction can thus benefit from systematic marketing, which has led to image-based place brand marketing by several countries to attract FDI. However, research in this area is in its infancy and there is a dearth of studies on the role of nation branding in attracting FDI.

Drawing from various definitions that evolved over time, a 'brand' can be thought of as some combination of verbal and design elements which identify an item and differentiate it from its competitors, 'brand image' refers to the mental schema that represents the item in a person's mind, and 'place branding' is used when, simply, the 'item' in question is a place.[46]

The notion of a brand encapsulates the totality of the well known and most central paradigm in marketing, the 'marketing mix' or '4Ps' construct, which comprises four elements: The *Product* or service itself, including its design and packaging; its *Price*, whether expressed in monetary, time, psychic, or other terms; the *Place* to which it is distributed and the channels used to get it there; and *Promotion*, which may include advertising, personal selling, incentives, word of mouth, and other means of communication. Taken together, these four elements are used to create the attributes of a brand and, since they all are subject to interpretation by the buyer, they underscore and highlight the importance of brand image in the buyer's mind.

Branding places is usually more complex than branding most commercial products, because of the great diversity of attributes and variety of stakeholders involved in the place context. The image of a brand rarely matches what its marketers had in mind, since people interpret inputs in whichever way they choose, and this is especially so in the case of place brands, for which the targeted publics receive many more inputs than those emitted as part of place strategy. For instance, we learn about places in school, through travel, from the media, and so on. As places began realizing that 'perception is everything' not only to consumers but also to business buyers, they became increasingly sensitized to their image. A strong positive brand image can help places to

---

43 Nicolas Papadopoulos, 'Of Places and Brands' in Andy Pike (ed), *Brands and Branding Geographies* (Edward Elgar Publishing 2011).

44 Simon Anholt, *Brand New Justice: The Upside of Global Branding* (Butterworth-Heinemann 2003).

45 Nicolas Papadopoulos, 'Place Branding: Evolution, Meaning, and Implications' (2004) 1 *Place Branding* 36.

46 David A Aaker, *Managing Brand Equity* (The Free Press 1991).

Attracting foreign direct investment 129

differentiate themselves from others or, stated differently, a place's prosperity and progress can only be ensured through creating and maintaining positive brand images.

3.3 Place image and place branding

Given the complexity of 'place', creating place brands should typically involve a more sophisticated process than is the case with most commercial products. In fact, since place names are omnipresent, their representations in mental schemata are strengthened over time and become ever more complex. People accumulate inputs in memory through experiences in education, the media, travel, or exposure to product category labels (e.g. Scotch whisky, Berber rugs). Such inputs *identify* objects in relation to a place and *distinguish* them from others, and may reflect comparative advantages ('Swiss Timing' in sports) or disadvantages ('Balkanization' in politics). While in earlier times branding most often resulted from habit or inertia (e.g. 'Cathay Pacific', 'Norway Sardines', 'Joe's Garage'), in the contemporary era it has become a key strategic issue.

In practice, place images have been considered important traditionally in areas ranging from tourism to international relations, exports, and the protection of local industries from imports through 'buy domestic' campaigns. In research, the literature on the effects of place images on buyers – which is referred to as the 'made-in', 'country-of-origin', or 'Product-Country Image' (PCI) effect[47] – has been voluminous. Specific findings of interest here pertain to: (1) The influence of place images on investors and industrial buyers; (2) a focus by most PCI studies on developed market economies; and (3) a preference by consumers in developing countries for brands from industrialized ones, on the assumption that they are of higher quality and/or carry more prestige compared to domestic products and those from other nations in the developing world.[48]

A positive and powerful reputation acquired by a product or a place can be an asset of high value – even more valuable than tangible assets. That is why the concept of *place brand equity*, drawing on the equivalent definition for commercial products by Aaker,[49] is conceptualized as 'the real and/or perceived assets and liabilities that are associated with a place (country) and distinguish it from others'.[50] For example, systematic efforts by African countries to brand themselves for tourism must contend with prevailing images of the so-called

---

47 Nicolas Papadopoulos, 'What Product and Country Images Are and Are Not' in Nicolas Papadopoulos and Louise A Heslop (eds), *Product-Country Images: Role and Implications for International Marketing* (The Haworth Press 1993).
48 Leila Hamzaoui-Essoussi and Dwight Merunka, 'Consumers' Product Evaluation in Emerging Markets: Does Country of Design, Country of Manufacture or Brand Image Matter?' (2007) 24 *International Marketing Review* 409.
49 Aaker (n 46) 43.
50 Papadopoulos (n 45).

130   *Leila Hamzaoui-Essoussi et al.*

'continent effect' that paints the entire region as one characterized by strife, poverty, and disease.[51]

In relation to FDI, place branding has to link these place assets and values with the intention of the potential investor to invest. Governments have begun to realize that each place has an image, and that marketing it systematically as a brand can help to achieve their objectives. A key feature of the place branding process is that a brand strategy can help to fuse public and private sector interests and change how a place is perceived, and so an important issue for strategists is the need to understand the nature of branding and adapt it for their use.

3.4 Nation branding

Nation branding has been of interest to many researchers and practitioners, owing to the potential benefits of establishing a positive country image. Its objective is to create 'reputational capital'[52] through marketing activities addressed to both international as well as domestic audiences, and therefore to enhance a country's export, investment, and tourism attraction positions.

In the face of significantly intensifying global competition, the importance of how countries are perceived by their target markets led to the growing interest in *systematic* nation branding over the past quarter-century. People's views about a country may be favourable or unfavourable, and may be grounded in strong or weak beliefs and reflect various levels of precision or be very diffuse. Importantly, a nation brand exists with or without any conscious branding efforts on the part of the brand owner, since brand images exist in people's minds and can be constructed with information from many sources. People often create stereotypes of places, reflecting interlinked mental networks of associations, which lead to inferences when considering buying products from, travelling to, or investing in a specific country.

Nations may manage their images for specific purposes, such as attracting tourists, investors, or skilled workers, but nation branding would be guided by, and expressed in, an overall brand strategy that incorporates all characteristics of a place regardless of the specific task at hand in one campaign or another. That is, a nation branding strategy should not be seen as an array of separate strategies developed for various different purposes, but as a nation's strategic orientation based on a competitive identity that encompasses the nation's various facets. Then, depending on the context, the nation brand may evoke a specific combination of these

---

51 Nicolas Papadopoulos and Leila Hamzaoui-Essoussi, 'Place Images and Nation Branding in the African Context: Challenges, Opportunities, and Questions for Policy and Research' (2015) 1 *Africa Journal of Management* 54.

52 Szondi (n 5).

facets, or be considered as a corporate brand that endorses many sector brands, such as tourism, exports, or FDI.

Certain characteristics of place marketing present unique difficulties, including the need to reconcile the often-competing interests of different stakeholders (e.g. 'untouched wilderness' for tourists versus 'advanced manufacturing' for investors). Their socio-political objectives typically are broad and diffuse, and therefore harder to operationalize and measure than 'sales and profit'. Their governments lack full authority and control over inputs and outputs (a tourism board may promote 'friendly people' but cannot command the people to be friendly). Finally, places (especially in developing countries) face severe constraints in both resources and marketing know-how.

The national image of many countries is linked to their past: They are viewed through the prism of their specific history and are identified with a stereotype. This is also the case for most developing economies, whose image is often assessed in a more negative light than their actual conditions might suggest. For example, perceptions of countries not only in Africa but also in Latin America contain negative elements from a history of political instability both on a country-by-country basis as well as because of an overall 'continent effect'. Such markets lack the critical mass benefits enjoyed by their major global competitors (e.g. strengths in everything from fashion to finance interact in the case of New York, thus providing synergistic benefits for all its sectors). Many developing countries also lack a well-established professional public service, which are musts for systematic decision making and success in place branding that is typically led by government.

When properly developed, a country's brand relies on its core competencies, its competitive position, and relevant macro trends that might affect it.[53] There are several elements of the nation branding concept that reflect its two-fold nature, within the context of the marketing mix that was highlighted above – the promotional aspects, from simple advertising to strategic nation branding, and the elements of the product itself, which call for government policies on product design (e.g. institutional infrastructure), price (e.g. investment incentives), and distribution (e.g. efficient supply chains). Interestingly, the recent growth in FDI flows to emerging economies might reflect image shifts in the eyes of potential investors resulting from improvements in both promotion (nation branding) and the product itself (government initiatives). Furthermore, companies with existing investments in a country may serve as 'goodwill ambassadors' and contribute to promoting positive changes in its perceived attractiveness, thus helping it to become part of investors' location choice set.

---

53 F Gilmore, 'A Country – Can it be Repositioned? Spain – the Success Story of Country Branding' (2002) 9 *Brand Management* 281.

4. Implications and discussion: location branding for foreign investment attraction

While many different factors affect investors' decisions, none alone is enough to achieve a country's desired goals. In addition, research has found that many such factors are less important than commonly thought or more appropriate in certain cases than in others. For instance, much of the information from consulting organizations which compare the operating cost base across various cities is useful but only in certain ways and for certain types of businesses, and often mostly for investors who have already shortlisted cities for possible investment. Likewise, research has shown that the relative effectiveness of government incentives tends to wane as more and more jurisdictions begin offering them in order to compete.

Successful branding is more the result of true marketing know-how, hard work, sufficient funding, and careful positioning, than of developing 'slogans' or 'advertising campaigns'. Many of the strategy recommendations made to countries for branding purposes tend to be based on incomplete understandings of the meaning and functions of various marketing tools, ranging from branding itself to the usefulness of advertising or personal selling. For instance, some studies include recommendations for 'avoiding advertising' for investment, apparently pursuant to the belief that foreign investors are too 'rational' to be influenced by it. However, as shown by the studies reviewed here, this view more often than not reflects a misunderstanding of the functions of advertising. While neither business executives nor end-consumers might readily admit to being influenced by it, the evidence is that it has a significant influence providing that it is properly executed (which in itself is a tall order) and is used with clear objectives as to its intended results.

An overview of national promotional campaigns today (e.g. *Crafted With Pride in America, CzechInvest*) shows that (a) advertising and other forms of promotion are widely used and (b) any country is facing a steep uphill battle to differentiate itself because of the billions spent on PCI-based campaigns by jurisdictions around the world. This, of course, does not mean that campaigns should not be undertaken. Failing to develop a desired brand image leaves the target market free to create whatever stereotype it wishes. An image will emerge one way or another, but, without attention by the place itself, it will often be based on misconceptions that are likely to have negative short- and long-term consequences.

4.1 Opportunities in location branding: leveraging soft power

Opportunities for attracting FDI based on nation branding are directly linked to evaluating the existing qualities the country possesses, deciding whom to target, and then using the most efficient tools for implementation. This does not apply to developing and developed countries in the same manner, and if a nation has some advantages because of its favourable country image, this is very often

Attracting foreign direct investment 133

confined to one specific sector(s) rather than covering the entire country. For developed countries, this is often extended to many sectors that in turn affect the overall country image. For developing countries; however, the number of sectors with competitive advantages is usually small, and their nation brand identity has not yet been actively defined or communicated. Anholt[54] proposes that these countries could establish their identity by promoting their strong export brands and other nation-specific advantages (e.g. coffee exports and/or wildlife tourism in the case of African countries).

Whereas there is a belief, especially in developing countries, that nation branding is the sole responsibility of the government, the private sector can also engage in public-private sector partnerships that can contribute to the country's perceived competitiveness and thus trigger the process of image building. This in turn enhances the chances of success in placing export products in international markets, which will help to enhance the country's overall image among consumers and tourists as well as investors.

These considerations directly link to an important aspect of FDI attraction strategies: Sector targeting and higher FDI inflows have been shown to be statistically correlated.[55] Countries must define the industries they want to attract to build clusters, as companies, depending on their objectives, tend to look for business networks and interconnected organizational environments when choosing where to invest.

As a country's 'window to the world', IPAs can help to 'put it on the map' of potential investors. To succeed, IPAs should, at the least, move from just 'promotion' to a fuller *marketing*-oriented and services-driven consultancy organization focusing on investor needs, develop links with the private sector, cooperate with regional partners to strengthen local networks, and keep pace with how new media have changed communications with investors.[56] In general, IPAs' commitment to attracting investors can translate into a proactive approach, as illustrated by Nicaragua's agency, PRONicaragua, which invited potential investors to visit the country at its expense. Among other results, a German systems manufacturer chose to invest in the country even though it was not in the firm's initial list of favourite countries in the region.

An examination of sector-specific investment promotion efforts in 124 countries, note that investment promotion decreases information asymmetries, lessens the bureaucratic/procedural burden, and leads to higher FDI flows to developing countries.[57] For developed countries, however, investment promotion has less impact because they are likely to experience such problems

---

54 Anholt (n 44).

55 ECORYS, *Exchange of Good Practice in Foreign Direct Investment Promotion Final Report* (ECORYS Netherlands BV 2013) 156.

56 World Bank, *Global Investment Promotion Best Practices* (World Bank Investment Climate Department 2012).

57 Torfinn Harding and Beata S Javorcik, 'Roll out the Red Carpet and they will Come: Investment Promotion and FDI Inflows' (2011) 121 *The Economic Journal* 1445.

134　*Leila Hamzaoui-Essoussi et al.*

to a lesser degree. Furthermore, the size and maturity of a country's own market will influence its effectiveness at nation branding. For instance, small and newly-emerging European countries tend to spend a good portion of their budget on image-building activities, whereas bigger and more mature economies focus more on inter-regional networking and furthering the implementation of their nation branding strategy.

Countries may use a combination of image-building techniques for enhancing their perceived attractiveness for FDI. The most common techniques are advertising in general or in sector-specific media, investment exhibitions, conducting general information missions to potential investment source countries, and general information sessions on investment opportunities.[58] Taking advantage of a country's online presence, which requires resources and know-how, can make a strong positive impression and help to establish a level playing field against competitors. As noted by El Banna et al.,[59] some countries have been showcasing their location advantages online to promote FDI to investors and have some of the best websites in terms of their overall design and content (e.g. South Africa).

4.2 Branding places: local and global difficulties and complications

Place marketing has been practised in various different contexts, such as export promotion and tourism, and by various different players such as companies, trade associations, and local and national governments, independently and with little or no coordination among them, often resulting in fragmented and conflicting image marketing.[60] Perhaps the biggest challenge of nation branding is to create a harmonious and coherent value chain throughout a nation – that is to say, how to consistently aggregate the separate purchasing decisions of a variety of 'customers' across a vast spectrum of unrelated needs and intentions. For example, a potential investor may learn about a country while visiting it as a tourist, or vice-versa, resulting in a holistic perspective even though tourists and investors do not share the same interests.

Another common difficulty is that even if there is synergy and collaboration among the dimensions of nation branding, a country can be more successful in one dimension than in others. Whereas destination branding for tourism has been conducted mainly by tourism organizations, the situation is more complex in the case of FDI. Attracting investment covers many economic sectors and calls for greater coordination by multiple bodies. The large number of organizations engaged in nation branding can hinder the process, which makes

---

58　Wells and Wint (n 16).

59　Alia El Banna, Leila Hamzaoui-Essoussi and Nicolas Papadopoulos, 'A Comparative Cross-National Examination of Online Investment Promotion' (2017) 25 *Journal of Euromarketing* 131.

60　Fan (n 3).

Attracting foreign direct investment 135

strategic coordination highly important. Nevertheless, some IPAs have become a flagship for country brands – as in the case of *CzechInvest*, which managed to move from simple promotional campaigns to a more complex strategy addressing investors' specific needs.[61]

The complexity of defining a nation branding strategy is also linked to the growing competition not only between nations but also at the intra-national level, with cities and subnational regions competing against each other. Places at any level have the potential to be successful at attracting FDI commensurate with their characteristics, but this depends on a good understanding of where they fit within the location categories from the investors' perspectives. Although they compete against each other, subnational locations can also capitalize on one another's and their country's branding strategy to enhance their international visibility. Hampering such efforts, however, is the lack of coordination across jurisdictional levels, which often results in conflicting messages across regions in the same country.

As seen previously, different promotional tools have different effects depending on when, where, and how they are used, as well as for which specific target. Government agencies must always be aware of the basic information foreign companies are looking for when searching for a location, which might concern the local labour market, supplier networks, infrastructure, quality of life, or taxes and regulations. This means that making relevant, accurate and timely information easily available to investors requires agencies that have both the needed financial resources as well as the necessary know-how. Another important challenge to developing an effective FDI branding strategy is uncontrollable political and economic factors that can put all other efforts on hold, such as continuing or increasing socio-political instability in a country (e.g. Tunisia and other countries after the Arab Spring across North Africa).

Overall, alongside efforts on the promotional side of nation branding, a country needs to provide the right micro and macro economic climate required to nurture a successful business environment. Since the investor is the 'buyer' and the place is the 'product', in marketing terms this type of activity is part of the 'product design' element of the marketing mix. For example, FDI inflows in African countries have been on the rise as a result of changes in their infrastructures accompanied by targeted investment promotion. Once improvements to the business environment are in place they need to be communicated to target audiences, making both product and promotion an integral part of nation marketing.

Finally, it is important to stress that successful country branding does not stop with the launching of a successful campaign and involves much more than just 'a campaign'. It is vital for places to *measure their existing image* in advance, to be able to *measure the achieved outcome* of efforts to enhance it.

---

61 Young (n 42).

136 *Leila Hamzaoui-Essoussi et al.*

Those that develop image tracking systems are better able to monitor investors' perceptions and act upon them. It is also important for a place to know who its competitors are and what image investors hold of the complete competitive pool of alternative locations, in order to develop appropriate marketing strategies for success. This obviously refers to *systematic, long-term* tracking systems rather than one-shot, *ad hoc* studies, which is what most countries that undertake this type of research tend to do.

5. Conclusion

Taken together, all the points made so far about the nature of the FDI decision-making process lead readily to the conclusion that there is much more to that process than meets the eye. The current state of affairs in advertising, promotion, branding, or marketing for FDI leads to the conclusion that government organizations working on investment attraction have not even begun to scratch the surface of what 'nation branding' means and how its various facets can be capitalized upon. Most current efforts for attracting FDI betray a lack of understanding of the factors that influence investor decisions and fail to grasp the importance of strategic marketing considerations that are key behind any successful branding effort.

Developments over the last few decades have led to a growing integration of the global economy, leading many places to realize that they need to compete aggressively and systematically for the limited pool of available FDI capital. Traditional major recipients of foreign investment, such as the US and EU, have reacted with efforts to maintain their relative competitive positions, while such key developing countries as China and India took significant steps to be part of the emerging global economy. The rise of the developing world has brought more opportunities to pursue but also more countries pursuing these opportunities. This has changed the conceptualization of what is needed to attract FDI, from 'promotion' (or, worse, 'advertising') to one of 'marketing' (or at least 'branding').

In this context, many economies are increasingly interested in improving their standing on a large variety of factors that influence FDI location choices, including transaction costs, infrastructure, financial incentives, and supply chains. Previous research has shown that such factors are not all considered at the same stages of the investors' selection process. They vary by the position of FDI in the broader set of MOE alternatives, the stage in the decision process *if* FDI is decided upon, the type of business, investment, and investor, cultural distance, and characteristics of the investment location. Moreover, places have to deal with international and subnational competition, which significantly expands the range of options for investors and highlights the importance of the effect that a place's image can have on FDI attraction.

Nation branding is a relatively new field that has become a 'must' in enabling countries and their firms to effectively promote exports, attract tourism and investment, and, more generally, manage their images. This is turning

Attracting foreign direct investment 137

governments into active participants in business decision-making processes, and thus presents significant and major opportunities and challenges. The role of agencies tasked with investment attraction is certainly set to increase and to enhance the importance of branding, but the lack of strategic marketing know-how and the often-conflicting objectives of the diverse organizations and institutions that are engaged in nation branding can hinder the process.

More research is clearly needed to examine the prerequisites for successfully establishing or enhancing country equity in FDI, particularly from two main perspectives. First, developing a better understanding of the influence of nation branding on investment location choice and of the soft factors that can significantly affect that choice, namely, investors' perceptions and considerations of the images of countries and other places. Second, identifying the determinants of strategic nation branding activities undertaken by various stakeholders, in order to capitalize on the interaction and needed consistency between FDI-oriented and other nation branding efforts such that each leverages and reinforces the others. In turn, this will help determine the factors that influence investors' decisions of where to locate, focusing on the extent to which they consider, or take advantage of, nation branding programmes for attracting FDI.

7 FDI policy advocacy and investor targeting

Matthew Durban

1. Introduction

The increased importance of foreign direct investment (FDI) for economic development, coupled with greater competition between locations, has made investment promotion a growing activity of governments, not only in developed countries, but also in developing countries and economies in transition. Today, there are very few governments that do not have an institution that deals directly with the promotion of inward investment from overseas.[1]

Arguably, these institutions can only do an effective job if their efforts are combined or preceded by an opening up of the economy and liberalization of the investment regime. Foreign investors will quickly dismiss the opportunity if the reality demonstrates a record of arbitrary regulation, untenable sovereign risk, and unstable economic fundamentals.

This chapter seeks to explain the role and purpose of FDI policy and advocacy from the perspective of a national investment promotion agency and the outworking of such policy into sector and investor targeting. IPA examples are used from secondary literature but also the author's direct experience of investment promotion and attraction over some 20 years, more recently with the Australian Trade and Investment Commission (Austrade) and Indonesia's Badan Koordinasi Peranaman Modal or Investment Coordination Board (BKPM).[2] There are four sections plus conclusion in which the content of investment policy, policy advocacy (including integration with trade), investor targeting, and future directions are considered.

---

1 The World Association of Investment Promotion Agencies (WAIPA) was established in 1995 and is registered as a non-governmental organization (NGO) in Geneva. In 2014, the Association had 249 member agencies from 157 countries reflecting not only the growth in IPAs: World Association of Investment Promotion Agencies: The Global Reference Point for FDI 'WAIPA Menu' <http://waipa.org/> accessed 6 September 2015.

2 The views expressed in this paper are the author's own and not the institutions with which he was affiliated.

2. The content of investment policy: context and benchmark strategies

2.1 Context

In conditions of perfect competition, where exchange and coordination costs are zero and there are no externalities, transactions tend to be determined by market forces. In practice, such perfect competition has rarely existed and to some degree all markets contain failures or imperfections. In general, these fall into two types: structural and transactional.[3] Structural imperfections refer to the structure of the market and industry in which a firm operates and thus involve issues of market shares and market power that each firm commands. Market concentration can impair market efficiency and create barriers to entry. Transactional imperfections refer to imperfections in knowledge and, in particular, to the asymmetry of information between buyer and seller, which lead to business transaction costs. There are also other types of costs incurred in carrying out transactions, such as legal costs for the stipulation of contracts.[4]

IPAs seek to address such market imperfections and, by various gradations of activity and behaviour, signal to foreign investors that they have been addressed and/or seek to help foreign investors overcome such failures and realize their investment projects. Successfully overcoming market imperfections, especially transactions costs, however, requires much more than the simple opening up a country to foreign investors and general promotion of a country's advantages. Increasing competition for both location and market share, together with rapid technological advances and difficult budgetary circumstances, have resulted in a plethora of policy responses and often increased the sophistication of service offerings. IPAs are adopting more targeted approaches by focusing on selected industries, countries, and companies. Investment promotion covers a wealth of services, ranging from the provision of market information to the undertaking of feasibility studies and environmental impact assessments. The level of ambition partly reflects the resources available to the various IPAs and the presence of other complementary bodies that can provide services to foreign investors but also the degree of market failure that is perceived to hinder inward FDI.

According to the United Nations Conference on Trade and Development (UNCTAD), IPAs in OECD countries have applied a focused approach to investment promotion with investor targeting and 'aftercare' as prime functions.[5]

---

3 John H Dunning and Alan M Rugman, 'The Influence of Hymer's Dissertation on the Theory of Foreign Direct Investment' (1985) 75 *American Economic Review* 228; Frederick T Knickerbocker, *Oligopolistic Reaction and Multinational Enterprise* (Harvard Press University1973).

4 Grazia Ietto-Gillies, *Transnational Corporations and International Production* (2nd edn, Edward Elgar 2012).

5 UNCTAD, 'The World of Investment Promotion At A Glance: A Survey of Investment Promotion Practices' (2002) United Nations Conference on Trade and Development ASIT Advisory Studies No 17 <https://unctad.org/en/Docs/poiteipcd3.en.pdf> accessed 18 June 2019. Aftercare means helping the investor establish their business after the decision to invest has been made and potentially helping them to expand their operations.

140   *Matthew Durban*

IPAs in the category 'other developing countries' followed this pattern while IPAs in 'economies in transition' tended to take up more tasks. IPAs in 'developing countries' had by far the largest portfolio of services, reflecting their relatively larger challenges in attracting investment. Across the board, investor targeting and investment policy advice were the first and second most-frequently mentioned core functions. There was little evidence, however, that the IPAs in question proactively identified domestic market gaps on their own; instead, they responded to government priorities.

In many countries, FDI policy priorities have moved from the liberalization of FDI regimes towards an open market with a focus on investment promotion and industry targeting; however, many countries are now calling for more 'sustainable' FDI in the future.[6] The national government's view of economic development and the part or otherwise that foreign capital or expertise can play in the process are the overriding considerations driving state policy on foreign investment. Most governments have to balance concerns of national security and (often) ambivalent community feeling towards foreign investment with national economic priorities.[7]

Another key consideration regarding investment policy is the linkage between investment and trade.[8] For policymakers, the rise of intra-firm trade in global value chains underscores the benefits of trade liberalization for domestically-owned affiliates located abroad and foreign-owned companies in the domestic economy. It also leads to investment liberalization being not only a substitute for trade liberalization but also encouraging further trade openness.[9]

Policy may also be determined by the extent to which businesses are entering, integrating with, and moving up global value chains; the formulation of policy must also consider the extent of market failure as well as the desire of state actors to shift the relative importance of particular industries in their economies.

---

6 Columbia Center for Sustainable Investment, 'Five-Pillar Framework for Sustainable International Investment' <http://ccsi.columbia.edu/about-us/five-pillar-framework-for-sustainable-international-investment-2/> accessed 20 June 2019; UNCTAD, 'Investment Policy Hub' (United Nations 2015) <http://investmentpolicyhub.unctad.org/ipfsd>) accessed 18 June 2019.

7 See Patrick Leblond and Sébastien Labrecque, 'National security and the political economy of international investment policy', Chapter 9 in this volume.

8 See Ari Van Assche, 'Trade and foreign direct investment in the 21st century', Chapter 2 in this volume; Eugene Beaulieu and Kelly O'Neill, 'The economics of foreign direct investment and international investment agreements', Chapter 5 in this volume.

9 Mark Casson, David Barry, James Foreman-Peck, Jean-Francois Hennart, Dennis Horner, Robert A Read, and Bernard M Wolf, *Multinationals and World Trade: Vertical Integration and the Division of Labour in World Industries* (Routledge 1986); John Dunning (ed), *From the Common Market to EC 92: Regional Economic Integration in the European Community and Transnational Corporations* (UN Transnational Corporations and Management Division 1993); John Cantwell, 'The Relationship Between International Trade and International Production' in David Greenaway and L Alan Winters (eds), *Surveys in International Trade* (Wiley-Blackwell 1994); UNCTAD, *World Investment Report: 2013: Global Value Chains: Investment and Trade for Development* (United Nations 2013).

FDI policy advocacy and investor targeting 141

The latter is a particular challenge in resource-dominated economies: how to develop or generate ever more sophisticated services industries, research, education spillovers, and skill upgrades.

The policies that are most likely to be effective are those that encourage positive interaction between the locational strategies of multinationals and national economic development, such as modern infrastructure or the up-skilling of labour.[10] None of this can be 'fixed' in the short term. Policies are generally costly with benefits not realized until well-beyond average government terms of office. Balancing host-country demands with investor needs is often a trade-off:

> Multinational enterprises tend to respond to the comparative advantage of country and its locational assets. Governments, on the other hand, seek not only to exploit their countries' current comparative advantage but also seek to build new, dynamic comparative advantages and to strengthen the competitiveness of their firms, encouraging firms on their territories to engage in a consistent upgrading of their activities.[11]

2.2 Benchmark strategies

Moran has described a four-part strategy for investment promotion or attraction: the first step is to create a 'good' investment climate.[12] The list of 'ingredients' – low inflation, stable exchange rates, steady economic growth, reliable infrastructure, high literacy rates, liberalized trade, minimal corruption, stable and transparent political institutions, etc. – are well documented. These are perhaps necessary conditions for investment but they are not sufficient. The second component is to overcome information asymmetries around host-economy opportunities. International investors in emerging markets rarely have access to reliable or accurate information or analysis. Small markets or small populations also compete with larger markets for share of voice. It is instructive that even in a developed country such as Australia, the services of the national trade and investment promotion agency (Austrade) are focused on addressing information provision and market intelligence. A third category of strategies includes directed public expenditure on infrastructure and training designed to

---

10 UNCTAD (n 5).

11 Santi Chaisrisawatsuk and Wisit Chaisrisawatsuk, 'Imports, Exports and Foreign Direct Investment Interactions and Their Effects' in Economic and Social Commission for Asia and the Pacific, *Towards Coherent Policy Frameworks: Understanding Trade and Investment Linkage* (2007) United Nations Studies in Trade & Investment No 62 <www.unescap.org/sites/default/files/tipub2469.pdf> accessed 16 June 2019.

12 Theodore H Moran, *Harnessing Foreign Direct Investment for Development: Policies for Developed and Developing Countries* (Center for Global Development 2006) <www.cgdev.org/sites/default/files/9781933286099-Moran-harnessing-fdi.pdf> accessed 18 June 2019.

142 *Matthew Durban*

attract specific FDI. The fourth and final strategy is the provision of financial or fiscal incentives for relocation.

Integrating these components into a single coherent strategy presents a significant challenge, particularly with overlapping ministerial responsibilities and competition for government resources. A coordinating body to either make the case for or see through the implementation of such projects can therefore be advantageous. For instance, Indonesia's investment promotion agency, BKPM, has that expressed function. It reports on a day-to-day basis to the vice-president and is charged with economic coordination of the ministries of finance, industry, trade, agriculture, environment and forestry, labour, state-owned enterprises, public works and public housing, agricultural and spatial, cooperatives and SMEs. Austrade, in contrast, operates as a junior agency within the portfolio of the Department of Foreign Affairs and Trade with limited policy influence.

2.3 Indonesian investment promotion

To attract inward FDI and administer foreign investment legislation, the Indonesian government established BKPM in 1973 as a central body to screen investment applications, grant licences and permits, and offer investment incentives. However, a Regional Autonomy Law, introduced soon after the 1997–1998 Asian financial crisis, also empowered the regencies and municipalities, amongst other bodies, to order and spend their own budgets, including administer and allocate investment by subnational investment bodies known as *Badan Koordinasi Penanaman Modal Daerah* or BKPMD. During this period, the Indonesian government was forced to take many measures to promote economic recovery in line with IMF emergency-funding loan conditions. It also reoriented FDI policies and initiated reforms in areas related to private investment, including the legal system.

The Indonesian government promulgates a detailed negative investment list that states the degree to which foreign investment is permitted in specific sectors of the economy.[13] For example, sectors in which investment is prohibited include goods and services prohibited by Indonesian law, those considered dangerous or polluting, and those considered 'strategic for national security or heritage' (this covers variously defence and alcohol production). In other areas, such as higher education, 100 per cent investment is possible but subject to special permits and licences. Foreign training companies, for example, can only hold 49 per cent of local operations.

BKPM maintains a matrix of investor projects in progress and the deputy chair is responsible for a review of regulations and making recommendations to improve

---

13 Badan Koordinasi Penanaman Modal, Investment Opportunities, Priority Sectors <https:// twbusiness.nat.gov.tw/files/201707/%E5%8D%B0%E5%B0%BC1-Draft%20Paparan%20Dir %20KDUI_.pdf> accessed 21 June 2019.

FDI policy advocacy and investor targeting 143

the investment climate. There is no formal structure, mechanism or standing committee for this, however.[14] It has the authority to issue investment licences and advise on the best investment climate, as measured by the World Bank's Doing Business Index. Indonesia has coordinating ministries that supposedly test BKPM recommendations and proposed regulations for the impact on tax, labour, domestic trade, industry, and agricultural interests. In practice, whole-of-government support for investment is required while regulations and policies can be contradictory, especially in an environment where the bureaucracy and general public may be sceptical of the benefits of FDI.

A key problem in Indonesia is that inter-island transport costs are very high. This pushes up the general cost structure, particularly for remote areas, leading to large inter-regional price differences. On logistics performance, Indonesia lags all ASEAN neighbours bar the Philippines.[15] Underinvestment has contributed to the low quality and quantity of infrastructure. Regulatory constraints on competition and inefficient service provision compound these problems, as does a strong post-financial crisis aversion to foreign borrowing, which means successive governments have not availed themselves of much of the long-term concessionary finance on offer.[16]

The Indonesian government, through BKPM, is keen to attract investment that drives economic growth, brings capital, and transfers both technology and skills. There is a preference for investment in advanced manufacturing rather than production focused on consumer goods, such as luxury goods and processed foods. One solution, favoured by BKPM, is to encourage the development of trading houses with a view to capitalizing on the growth in intra-firm trade and value chains.[17]

2.4 Australian investment promotion

In Australia, foreign investment is screened by the Foreign Investment Review Board (FIRB). Australia's foreign investment policy provides guidance to foreign investors in understanding the government's approach to administering the Foreign Acquisitions and Takeovers Act 1975. The policy also identifies investment categories that need to be notified to the government for prior approval, even if the Act does not appear to apply. The Australian Treasurer can block proposals that are

---

14 Information cited outside BKPM's website is derived from the author's meetings with various BKPM executives in December 2014. The author is particularly indebted to Vice Chairman Pak Himawan and Deputy Director Pak Nurul Ichwan.
15 World Bank, 'Logistics Performance Index' (2014) <https://lpi.worldbank.org/international/global/2014> accessed 18 June 2019.
16 Haryo Aswicahyono and Hal Hill, 'Is Indonesia Trapped in the Middle?' (2015) University of Freidburg Department of International Economic Policy Discussion Paper Series No 31 <www.vwl-iwipol.uni-freiburg.de/iwipol/REPEC/fre/wpaper/DP31_Aswicahyono_Hill_Is_Indonesia_Trapped_in_the_Middle.pdf> accessed 18 June 2019.
17 That is, businesses that import, export, and finance. On closer scrutiny, BKPM's definitions are akin more to the conglomerate model endemic in Korean or Japanese business, where a single conglomerate controls multiple and related businesses.

144 *Matthew Durban*

contrary to the national interest or apply conditions to the way proposals are implemented to ensure they are not contrary to the national interest.

All foreign government investors must notify the government and get prior approval before making certain direct investments in Australia, regardless of the value of the investment. This requirement extends to starting a new business or acquiring an interest in land (including an interest in rural land), as well as any interest in a prospecting, exploration, production, or mining tenement. As well, foreign persons need to notify and get prior approval before acquiring a substantial interest in, or control of, an Australian business that is valued above A\$252 million (a threshold that is indexed annually on 1 January). Consistent with Australia's treaty commitments, higher thresholds apply to country-specific investors commensurate with free trade agreements (e.g. Chile, Japan, Korea, New Zealand, and the United States).

Austrade is separate from the FIRB. It is responsible for attraction (proactive targeting of investment and outreach to investors), promotion, and facilitation. Nevertheless, both Austrade and FIRB can advise investors *before* a final application is made to reduce the likelihood of disappointment. Austrade has an important education outreach function in this regard.

Austrade reincorporated an investment promotion function in 2007–2008, following an almost ten-year exclusive focus on trade promotion. Prior to this, a separate agency, Invest Australia, funded investment promotion positions in selected countries (focused on the US and Europe) and was supported by an office in Sydney. Aside from the appeal of cost reductions, the integration with trade was seen as generating significant synergies, particularly since one of the performance indicators by which Austrade measured its success was the estimated export sales value of any foreign investment. Austrade is charged with:

> identifying potential foreign investors and presenting the business case for investing in Australia; introducing leads to states and territories and 'Commonwealth partners' with a view to 'attracting productive foreign direct investment to Australia'.[18]

This involves daily cooperation with federal, state, and territory government departments, both onshore and offshore. The investment cycle starts with strategies developed with partner agencies at a federal and state level, before Austrade undertakes promotion offshore. A National Investment Advisory Board, chaired by Austrade, is the key planning and reporting mechanism by which Austrade works with state and territory investment promotion agencies on strategy implementation, investment promotion and facilitation, and staff training and development. Under the auspices of the Board, Austrade delivers the 'Winning Investment for Australia' training programme, which aims to build

---

18 Australian Trade Commission, *Annual Report 2013–2014* (Australian Trade Commission 2014) 15 <www.austrade.gov.au/AR-201314/about-austrade.html> accessed 18 June 2019.

a professional and global team approach to investment promotion, attraction and facilitation across government.[19]

Austrade seeks to attract investment in five areas jointly agreed by Australian and state and territory governments: agribusiness and food, major infrastructure, tourism infrastructure, resources and energy, and advanced manufacturing, services, and technology. Within the last area, Austrade focuses on 'growth opportunities' for investment in medical and materials sciences and technologies, and digital technologies.[20]

Investment resources at Austrade are predominantly focused on North America, Europe, India, Singapore, and China. Within those regions, Austrade investment teams assess foreign capability and prioritize outreach (e.g. ICT from West Coast USA and India, financial services from the United Kingdom).

3. Policy advocacy: mechanisms, screening, and facilitation, integration with trade

One function of IPAs is policy advocacy, though the form that it takes may vary. The most basic meaning of advocacy is to represent, promote, or defend some person(s), interest, or opinion. According to UNCTAD, policy advocacy by IPAs

> serves three major functions for overall national development: (a) it helps shape the investment climate to attract greater inflows of foreign direct investment (FDI); (b) it promotes policies that allow greater benefits to be extracted from that FDI; and (c) it builds national competitiveness in a global economy ... done well, policy advocacy also has the effect of enhancing dialogue and policy review with stakeholders, including the investor community, thereby contributing to good governance in investment promotion.[21]

Advocacy regarding FDI is designed to:

> effect changes in regulations, laws, government policies and their administration, pertaining to fields such as investment, trade, labour, immigration, real estate, taxes, infrastructure, technology and education. The immediate goal is to shape a climate conducive to attracting and benefiting from FDI.[22]

IPA legislation in general gives little autonomy to set policy and develop goals, if it says anything at all about them. National legislation and policies in

19 ibid 60.
20 Australian Trade and Investment Commission, 'Opportunities' (Australian Government) <www.austrade.gov.au/International/Invest/Opportunities> accessed 20 October 2019.
21 United Nations Conference on Trade and Development (UNCTAD), 'Investment Promotion Agencies as Policy Advocates' (2008) UNCTAD Investment Advisory Series A, No 2, 5, 11 <https://unctad.org/en/Docs/iteipc20076_en.pdf> accessed 18 June 2019.
22 ibid 7, 15.

146   *Matthew Durban*

Australia, the United Kingdom, and Canada follow this approach. In Indonesia, however, the BKPM chairman recommends sectoral priorities to cabinet ministers, the uptake of which is a reflection of the chairman's own persuasive powers at the discretion of other ministries, rather than through a prescribed consultative process with clear criteria, debate, and issue of discussion papers. Austrade, as with other Australian government agencies, responds to a 'letter of expectation' from the responsible portfolio minister with a 'letter of intent'. The agency sets out at a high level how it will respond to the priorities of the government of the day.

The World Bank IPA benchmark survey suggests that the principal role of IPAs in policy advocacy is to improve the investment climate through representation of the views of investors commensurate with consistent treatment of all companies ('the level playing field') as well as national interest or security concerns, which will reflect variously the country's security architecture and community reaction to perceived or real market domination by particularly countries or companies.[23] In other words, IPAs should canvass and feed back to governments the experience of actual and potential investors in the country: the barriers and obstacles to be overcome, a comparison with competing locations within or outside the country, and the regulatory experience – often with overlapping jurisdictions.[24] Governments must weigh and balance such feedback with their economic development policy objectives and national sentiment/public opinion. Multinational companies are more likely to seek assistance from government/the IPA if there is a policy impediment or tax issue rather than a capital or information deficit, whereas smaller firms without such networks or in-house capability often need help in both areas.

The World Bank's IPA benchmark survey, the secondary literature, and the author's experience suggest that IPA leadership in improving the overall investment climate over other ministries and line departments is a combination of advice, coordination and influence. The best performing IPA will not only be able to attract and facilitate FDI, but also directly advise on improvements to the legal and policy environment for both local and foreign investment. The veracity and credibility of this advice is based on feedback from the IPA's investor clients. This can be obtained using a variety of methods: individually, as each contact is made or each project developed, but also via public sector forums, advisory councils, aftercare services including site visits, investor surveys, and via foreign investor association relationships in source countries.[25] For

---

23 World Bank, *Global Investment Promotion Best Practices 2012* (World Bank 2012) <http://docu ments.worldbank.org/curated/en/532231468343733823/pdf/907580WP0v20Bo0n0Best0 Practices0web.pdf> accessed 18 June 2019.

24 ibid 19.

25 UNCTAD (n 21) 46.

example, most European Union IPAs have a board of directors or advisory council with private sector representatives.[26]

The use of benchmarking (e.g. the World Bank's 'Doing Business' index and UNCTAD's investment policy reviews) and of consultants (e.g. GDP Global's mystery shopping exercises in various countries) can be invaluable. Feedback can be collected during and at the end of the process but the most valuable information is perhaps at intervals along the investment continuum. This can take years as the business develops and milestones are reached but it is arguably the most valuable as serious reflection and comparison can be made with other locations. Structured interviews with or surveys of investors from their initial expression of interest through to business registration, after the first few months of operations and on significant anniversaries, can be built into service-level agreements between the IPA and company. Austrade and its predecessor body Invest Australia incorporated such data collection into aftercare programmes. Regard must be given to competitive integrity, however. Investors will be loath to divulge strategic information in a public forum or accept attribution in the public domain. Nevertheless, the better the IPA understands the industries to which it attaches priority, the more nuanced and accurate will be its advocacy.

It is hard to find detailed examples of direct foreign investor advocacy directly resulting in policy changes outside government reaction to screening. In Australia, foreign investors such as IBM and the global accounting firms successfully advocated for the retention of a modified R&D tax deduction available to both domestic and foreign companies. Such examples are rare. Indonesian–Singaporean sugar refiner Wilmar has been less successful in trying to break into Australia's pool sugar export marketing arrangements.[27]

Streamlining approvals and fast-tracking projects do not amount to policy change, but nevertheless can save the foreign investor time and money. Indonesia's BKPM has responded to investors 'doing business' issues primarily by attempting to streamline business registration procedures through a 'single window' style arrangement, reducing the number of permits through negotiation with each line ministry, and providing a single point of contact in the agency to handhold large investors through the process. This has been in response to investor concerns expressed directly to BKPM, to government, and via prolific business organizations (e.g. the peak indigenous business chamber *Kamar Dagang dan Industri Indonesia* (KADIN); foreign business associations, such as the American and European Chambers and the Indonesia–Australia Business Council).

---

26 ECORYS, 'Exchange of Good Practices in FDI Promotion: A Study Carried out Under the Framework Contract ENTR/2009/033' (2013) *ECORYS* 37 <http://ECORYS-exchange-of-good-practice-in-Foreign-Direct-Investment-promotion_en.pdf> accessed 18 June 2019.

27 Financial Review, 'Sugar Industry politics threaten $3b in foreign investment' (*Financial Review*, 10 June 2015) <www.afr.com/brand/chanticleer/sugar-industry-politics-threaten-3b-in-foreign-investment-20150609-ghk4bt> accessed 22 September 2015.

148　*Matthew Durban*

IPAs can seek to improve a country's international competitiveness but few are policy originators or makers, an aspiration for which they are typically not resourced. The author is hesitant to recommend an increased 'policy-making' capability role for IPAs, based on experience and the specific IPA examples cited in this chapter. After all, FDI is but one element of economic policy.

3.1 Combining investment and trade promotion?

While there are clear linkages between investment and trade, this should not be seen as a prima facie case for integrating international promotion efforts. Import restrictions and foreign business establishment restrictions can both hinder access for foreign investors. Local content or employment requirements may protect nascent domestic companies but can have a negative impact on production costs and thereby reduce export competitiveness.

In practice, however, there are differences in mandate and operational functions between investment and export promotion, which can translate into institutional friction and conflict within agencies. Trade or export promotion is more often transactional in nature, typically dominated by large commodity deals. The investment process is more often based on relationships of trust, lengthy due diligence, and project timelines. Export promotion has its own special needs. For example, agencies must often work closely with local firms to find out what they can deliver, and to assist them in attaining 'export readiness' in terms of skills, capacity, and finance. As a result, officials involved must have a thorough understanding of the local business community's capabilities. In contrast, and somewhat surprisingly, understanding the capabilities of local businesses and training local managers play a relatively minor role in the job of investment promotion.[28] This difference in mandate could be mitigated with strong interagency and ministry liaison.

4. Investor targeting: staged approaches, priority sectors, and incentives

The World Bank's Global Investment Promotion Best Practices project surveys the world's investment promotion agencies triennially to collect examples of best practices and provide an objective measure of agency competitiveness.[29] According to such information, investment promotion is increasingly seen to be client-oriented. A commonly-held view amongst IPAs is that personal contacts with investors are preferable to non-personal methods of promotion.[30] Hence,

---

28　Frank Sader, 'Promoting Investment and Trade: How Different are these Functions?' (2002) *Foreign Investment Advisory Service* 2.

29　World Bank (n 23).

30　This reflects the author's experience of and conversations with investment practitioners in government organisations in Australia, Canada, and the UK.

FDI policy advocacy and investor targeting   149

a considerable share of promotional budgets are devoted to arranging meetings with foreign companies and third parties as well as networking to generate leads and insights, attending conferences and trade fairs, and undertaking missions abroad. This may appear to be common sense for any organization involved in client or customer service but it is by no means common for government departments to be involved in outreach particularly to foreign nationals. Similarly, studies have shown that IPAs that target sectors attract more FDI than those that do not. One study found that sector targeting increased the growth rate of FDI inflows into that sector by 41 per cent. Another study found that, in developing countries, targeted sectors received 155 per cent more FDI than non-targeted sectors.[31]

In practice, IPAs need sector expertise to remain credible and generate information of high value to investors, although this can be supplemented by secondments from other agencies or departments or private consultants. It is difficult for any IPA to be an expert in all sectors. It is, therefore, necessary to identify a few sectors of priority to national development and focus on those.[32] IPAs must also understand investor determinants and motivation to be effective and provide a targeted service. This is particularly important when large firms have decentralized decision-making, a consequence of tax-effective structuring, multi-country operations, procurement, stock market access, or all of the above. The result is that FDI can be a serendipitous mix of the deliberate, sequential, and opportunistic.[33]

Investor targeting combines supply and demand factors but is led by the former. In general, the host government, in consultation with a range of public and private sector interests, both domestic and foreign, determines industry priorities. Business associations can lead the way, but government can also call for submissions or policy papers. Not all recommendations will necessarily be in favour of FDI.

Ideally, the IPA or equivalent commercial service will be able to advise on the efficacy or wisdom of promoting and attracting investment into the industry priorities determined by the government of the day. This will depend on enabling legislation and the IPA's influence on government policy-making.

Harding and Javorcik have suggested that firms confront four stages throughout the process of deciding where to invest abroad.[34] First, a long list of 8 to 20 potential host countries (encompassing popular FDI destinations,

---

31 World Bank (n 23) 20.

32 ibid.

33 Aihie Osarenkhoe, 'A Study of the Enablers of Non-Sequential Internationalization Process among Small and Medium-Sized Firms' (2008) 3 *International Journal of Business Science and Applied Management* 2; Paola Conconi, Andre Sapir, and Maurizio Zanardi, 'The Internationalisation Process of Firms: From Exports to FDI' (2016) 99 *Journal of International Economics* 16.

34 Torfinn Harding and Beata S Javorcik, 'Foreign Direct Investment and Export Upgrading' (2012) 94 *The Review of Economics and Statistics* 964.

150 *Matthew Durban*

countries close to existing operations, and emerging FDI destinations) is created.[35] In reality, the initial corporate selection process is a mix of responses to opportunistic inquiries and existing relationships, management intuition, cold-call-style pitches from third parties, and analytical assessment. In the second stage, about five sites are selected from the long list, based on the trade-off between costs and the quality of the business environment. The accessibility of the information about potential host countries plays a crucial role, as sites under consideration are rarely visited during this stage. IPAs that have up-to-date, detailed, and accurate data on their websites and are willing to prepare detailed answers to investors' enquiries can increase the chances of their countries being included in the shortlist. In the third step, the investor typically visits the host country, giving the IPA an opportunity to emphasize the advantages of locating there, present potential investment sites, and facilitate contacts with the local business community. The provision of information by local experts (tax, accountancy, law) can help with community buy-in but is also designed to transfer project due diligence from the host government to the private sector. Austrade, for example, has a referral registration process in each market upon which investors (and exporters) can draw for advice. IPAs can also play a role in the fourth and final stage by providing information on investment incentives and offering help with project registration.

IPAs stimulate FDI inflows by facilitating access to information and reducing the burden of red tape. More specifically, investment promotion is more effective in countries where English is not an official language and in countries that are more culturally distant from the United States.[36] Also, investment promotion works better in countries with less effective governments, higher corruption, and a longer time period required to start a business or obtain a construction permit, which is consistent with investment promotion alleviating problems of red tape.[37]

IPAs need to target investors by industry and by country, taking into account multinational decision-making that is often dispersed. In practical terms, this involves the identification of countries in which target industries of interest are located and assignment of business development resources to research, introduce, and market the opportunity – the focus being on those countries/industries that have a clear competitive advantage and a strong value proposition.[38]

The following examples from Australia and Indonesia illustrate how sectoral policies and priorities were translated into investor promotion, targeting, and

---

35 See Leila Hamzaoui-Essoussi, Nicolas Papadopoulos, and Alia El Banna, 'Attracting foreign direct investment: Location branding and marketing', Chapter 6 in this volume.

36 Harding and Javorcik (n 34).

37 Torfinn Harding and Beata S Javorcik, 'Roll Out the Red Carpet and They Will Come: Investment Promotion and FDI Inflows' in Karl P Sauvant and Jennifer Reimer (eds), *FDI Perspectives: Issues in International Investment* (2nd edn, Vale Columbia Center on Sustainable International Investment, 2012) 34–35.

38 World Bank (n 23).

facilitation. In Australia, from 2008, the government implemented a series of policies to promote the development of renewable energy culminating in an emissions trading scheme in 2012–2013. An emissions reduction target was set and the country's IPA was charged with securing FDI in the country's nascent industry. Invest Australia, Austrade's predecessor body for investment promotion, targeted Spanish company Acciona to invest in wind farms. The financial crisis of 2007 had left many European companies with sound balance sheets operating in moribund domestic markets whereas Australia was attractive with a 20-year record of constant economic growth and supportive government policies. Acciona has since expanded into infrastructure, becoming a lead partner in the Transcity consortium building the A\$1.5 billion Legacy Way tunnel in Brisbane.[39] As of mid-2017, the company employed more than 1,000 people directly and was participating in more than 20 infrastructure projects in Australia.[40] Similar economic climate drivers proved attractive to Spanish company Ferrovial's subsidiary, Cintra, which joined forces with Australian superannuation fund REST in 2012 to invest and operate selected toll-road projects in Australia.[41]

IBM considered a range of locations for a new research and development laboratory in late 2009. With Austrade and Department of Industry facilitation, IBM decided to co-locate a lab within the University of Melbourne. The lab focuses on computational life sciences, notably natural resource assistance, natural disaster management, healthcare, and life science analytics. According to IBM, the decision was based on the university's research reputation and the government's policy decision to invest in high-speed broadband.[42]

Indonesia, for its part, had until late 2014 a more comprehensive list with few sectors untouched: infrastructure (some 27 public–private partnership projects were listed), food and agriculture (palm oil, rubber, and cacao), energy (gas, coal, and oil with a focus on in-country beneficiation), and industry (petrochemicals). Following the change of government in October 2014, BKPM's new chairman promulgated a revised list of investment priorities: electricity generation, labour-intensive industries (food and beverage, textiles, footwear, toys, and furniture), agriculture (palm oil, rubber, and cocoa), maritime (integrated fish processing, auction houses, and cold storage), import substitution (generic medicine production in particular with demand driven by the new healthcare scheme), and downstream mineral processing (oil refining and smelters).[43] BKPM is also keen to attract investment that improves Indonesia's regional supply chain access such as in the growing automotive

---

39 Australian Trade and Investment Commission, 'Austrade Investor Case Studies', <https://austrade.gov.au/AR-201314/program-1-1.html> accessed 18 June 2019.
40 Acciona Australia, 'Projects' <www.acciona.com.au/projects/> accessed 30 October 2017.
41 Austrade Investor Update <http://m.austrade.gov.au/International/Invest/Investor-Updates/2012/1108-Super-fund-REST-invests-in-transport-infrastructure≥ accessed 23 August 2015.
42 Australia Trade and Investment Commission (n 39).
43 BKPM (n 13).

152 *Matthew Durban*

manufacturing and assembly business. To that end, BKPM executives consider outward investment in areas of competitive advantage such as cement, plantations (rubber and palm oil), and food and beverage processing as an important part of this strategy.

The Indonesian government has sought to attract foreign investors to deliver turnkey projects in energy and transport, areas in which Indonesia is seriously deficient. French company GDF Suez, in partnership with PT Supreme Energy and Sumitomo Corporation, completed successful drilling for geothermal energy in Sumatra in 2013 and sold an offtake to state-owned electricity distributor Perusahaan Listrik Negara (PLN). The project benefited from a power purchasing agreement guaranteeing a 50 per cent offtake purchase by PLN, a risk exploration fund, and various tax holidays. More recently, the Central Kalimantan governor and president director of PT Perkeretaapian Tambun Bungai signed a joint agreement in Palangkaraya for the construction of a 425-kilometre railway track from Pucuk Cahu to Batanjung. PT Bungai represented the China Railway Consortium Group, which won the US$5.5 billion project tender. According to the joint agreement, the consortium has been given four years to construct the railway and 50 years to operate it, before it is handed over to the provincial administration.[44]

Although BKPM uses a 'FDI Markets' (produced by the *Financial Times*) subscription service to track and identify target investors by country, there is no proactive outreach beyond ad hoc events. Anecdotal evidence suggests that foreign investors are aware of the infrastructure and energy deficits and use their financial clout (and sometimes their diaspora links, as with the Chinese) to pitch turnkey solutions to government. Tenders, if there are any, often reflect the specification of the preferred supplier.

While, domestically, BKPM works closely with Indonesian business and employer groups to identify potential partners for foreign investors, particularly in the small and medium-sized enterprise sector, regulatory barriers are however significant. BKPM provides, therefore, an important interlocutory role as the first point of contact for investors, providing advice as to process, procedure, and available support and incentives. Depending on the type of FDI activity, line ministries need to be consulted and permits or licences obtained. This can take many months with the investor required to undertake liaison between ministries.

Developed country IPAs such as Invest Canada, UK International Trade, and Austrade, in partnership with Australian states and territories, also include aftercare in recognition of the importance of reinvestment, expansion and, of course, the widely-held belief that it is better to keep and grow an existing customer than to find a new one.

---

44 Both project references courtesy of BKPM, 'BKPM Badan Koordinasi Penanaman Modal', <www2.bkpm.go.id/> accessed 18 June 2019.

4.1 Challenges remain

While there is a considerable body of literature asserting the growth benefits of FDI, the literature around the most attractive policy settings is more equivocal. Research by Blonigen and Piber suggests there is little robust evidence to support government policies to encourage FDI, such as reducing multilateral trade costs, business costs, or improving infrastructure; the exceptions include policies that result in negotiated bilateral trade and investment agreements.[45] Similarly, there is scant evidence to suggest a statistical correlation between the measures that a developed country adopts to attract FDI and the actual value of FDI recorded.[46] Yet, countries continue to offer fiscal or financial incentives – including tax holidays, accelerated depreciation schemes, duty exemptions, and grants. Again, there is little evidence to suggest these have anything but a deleterious effect on host-country budgets.[47] So the reason countries, particularly developing ones, continue to offer such measures may be a signalling effect. Nevertheless, no amount of cash incentive is going to support a multinational million-dollar investment if the opportunity is unclear and profit repatriation uncertain.[48]

Bellak and Leibrecht have suggested that countries seeking to attract FDI generally focus on two policies: improving infrastructure or lowering taxes.[49] Of course, such actions also help domestic firms and must be considered within constrained budgets. Their findings suggest taxes are somewhat less important as an allocation factor. In fact, information and communication infrastructure was rated as more important than transport infrastructure or electricity-generation capacity.[50] National or local tax regimes have a negative impact when the infrastructure endowment is considered inadequate. In other words,

---

45 Bruce A Blonigen and Jeremy Piber, 'Determinants of Foreign Direct Investment' (2011) National Bureau of Economic Research Working Paper No 16704 <www.nber.org/papers/w16704.pdf> accessed 18 June 2019.

46 Harding and Javorcik (n 34).

47 Jacques Morisset, 'Does a Country Need a Promotion Agency to Attract Foreign Direct Investment: A Small Analytical Model Applied to 58 Countries' (2003) World Bank Foreign Investment Advisory Service Working Paper No 3028, 3 <http://documents.worldbank.org/curated/en/977191468739488998/pdf/multi0page.pdf> accessed 18 June 2019.

48 Hans Christiansen, Charles Oman, and Andrew Charlton, 'Incentives-Based Competition for Foreign Direct Investment: The Case of Brazil', (2003) Organisation for Economic Cooperation and Development Working Paper No 2003/1 <www.oecd-ilibrary.org/docserver/631632456403.pdf?expires=1560882822&id=id&accname=guest&checksum=5DF63F1AE392AEEAEF2BFD5EB7C91F4A> accessed 18 June 2019; Fergus Cass, 'Attracting FDI to Transition Countries: The Use of Incentives and Promotion Agencies' (2007) 16 *Transnational Corporations Journal* 77.

49 Christian Bellak and Markus Leibrecht, 'Improving Infrastructure or Lowering Taxes to Attract Foreign Direct Investment' in Karl P Sauvaunt, and Jennifer Reimer (eds), *FDI Perspectives: Issues in International Investment* (2nd edn, Vale Columbia Center on Sustainable International Investment 2012).

50 ibid.

154   *Matthew Durban*

infrastructure has specific locational advantages that allow for higher taxes on profits without discouraging investment.[51]

5. Future directions for investment promotion

Based on the author's experience and the IPA literature, there are a number of areas where investment promotion could be used more effectively and applied more strategically.

5.1 *Value-chain integration*

Many agencies, including Austrade and BKPM, have now adopted value-chain terminology in IPA charters. This is both a recognition that value chains drive globalization but also an attempt to educate SMEs as to the benefits of participating in such chains, especially given domestic protectionist tendencies, and, thereby, win international business contracts and upskill local businesses. Depending on the extent of market failure, the government via the IPA can provide an end-to-end service: attracting the investor and ensuring supply inputs integrate the investor's operations into the local business environment or supply chain.

In practice, this has been harder to facilitate with few sustained success stories outside aircraft, automobile, and electronics fabrication. Moreover, implementation of an IPA approach based on value chains requires detailed mapping on where priority industries are currently integrated, where they could do more, and how success might be measured (e.g. statistics recording exports, imports, outward investment, inward investment, and other variables).

There are, nonetheless, examples where governments have set up vendor development or supply capability programmes. This is where foreign investors are effectively used as 'talent scouts' to invite and leverage local firms into the supply chain, contributing management, quality control, and production planning. The foreign investors advise the local participants in terms of what equipment, machinery, and training are needed to lift local performance and increase local content.[52] Both Malaysia and Singapore owe much of their industrial development to SME development boards, which helped coordinate the provision of infrastructure facilities, financial assistance, advisory services, market access, and other support programmes.[53] Moran describes how Singapore's Economic Development Board subsidized the salary of an engineer

---

51 See Allison Christians and Marco Garofalo, 'Tax competition as an investment promotion tool', Chapter 8 in this volume.

52 Moran (n 12) 22, 23.

53 United Nations Conference on Trade and Development (UNCTAD), 'Best Practices in Investment for Development' (2011) Investment Advisory Series <https://unctad.org/en/pages/publications/Investment-Advisory-Series-B-(FDI-Case-Studies).aspx> accessed 18 June 2019.

or a manager within foreign affiliates for two to three years to select and assist local firms to become suppliers.[54] The objective was for the host country to appeal to foreign investors' own self-interest in finding low cost, reliable local suppliers. In the first decade of this century, the Australian Departments of Industry and Defence similarly worked with Australian industry to pursue work opportunities identified in the US Joint Strike Fighter Industry Participation Plan with Lockheed Martin, Pratt & Whitney, General Electric, and Rolls-Royce.

5.2 Promoting overseas FDI through national or multilateral political risk insurance

Often official political risk insurance from a national or multilateral provider can help provide credibility to host-country commitments around the treatment of foreign investment projects, especially politically-sensitive ones.[55] Such insurance overcomes the market failure associated with imperfect contracts by limiting the exposure to opportunistic behaviour by governments (e.g. retrospective legislation, sudden import bans on essential raw materials or equipment). Institutions that offer such insurance include the Multilateral Investment Guarantee Agency (MIGA), the Asian Development Bank and, at a national level, Australia's Export Finance and Insurance Corporation (EFIC).

This kind of financial support does not extend to a discounted policy premium rate, however. According to Moran, political risk insurance policies offered by public institutions have higher premiums than those on offer private ones.[56] EFIC, for instance, seeks to recover its cost on commercial terms, and generates a sizeable surplus each year.

A new role for EFIC has been in outward investment where, in a departure from underwriting export transactions, the agency can provide finance to help SMEs establish overseas subsidiaries as long as net benefit criteria are met (e.g. demonstrated return to Australia). This is especially useful for SMEs that lack collateral, particularly those that are service-based and do not have physical collateral to provide surety. The benefits are not just risk mitigation but also signalling to investors that the host country is serious about economic development and is seeking investment partners of calibre. Insurance can and is provided by source or home country organizations such as Australia's EFIC, but the net domestic benefit of this kind of public service has yet to be established. Some governments may be unwilling to subsidize what can be egregiously seen as offshoring.

54 Moran (n 12).
55 ibid 117.
56 ibid.

156   *Matthew Durban*

5.3 Mechanisms to avoid the double taxation of profits earned abroad

Equitable tax treatment is influential in multinational relocation or expansion.[57] IPAs can play an important part in determining the efficacy of such arrangements in a competitive bidding for investment. While noting that in recent years the proclivity of multinational companies to move earnings and revenue through multiple jurisdictions to avoid tax has generated little public sympathy for such mechanisms, international corporations frequently cite double taxation as a barrier to FDI.[58] There is a positive correlation between double taxation treaties and FDI stocks.[59] Reduced tax is more likely to attract investors into less developed countries than developed ones.[60] The message for an IPA is perhaps that national treatment of investors is attractive so long as greater transparency is reciprocated at a country-to-corporation level.

5.4 Using regulation to combat bribery and corruption to enhance national reputations

Increasingly, barriers to entry are rarely about tax alone. Setting up a business can vary enormously in complexity and efficiency.[61] In Singapore and Australia, a business can be registered within days. In Indonesia, the official lead-time is just over 50 days. Overlapping regulation and jurisdiction, and multiple permits from different ministries are a recipe for *Bleak House*-style[62] inefficiency but also corruption. 'Facilitation for a fee' is increasingly a broader issue in investment matters. Corruption was listed by 30 per cent of SMEs in Southeast Asian economies as a significant barrier to doing business. Theft and disorder were mentioned by 24.5 per cent of respondents.[63] Other identified obstacles for SMEs operating in Southeast Asia relate to a variety of anti-competitive activities, including smuggling, price-fixing, and poaching of skilled workers.

---

57 Christians and Garofalo (n 51).
58 ibid.
59 Fabian Barthel, Matthias Busse, and Eric Neumayer, 'The Impact of Double Taxation Treaties on Foreign Direct Investment: Evidence from Large Dyadic Panel Data' (2010) 28 *Contemporary Economic Policy* 1; Arjan Lejour, 'The Foreign Investment Effects of Tax Treaties' (2014) Oxford University Centre for Business Taxation Working Paper No 1403 <www.cpb.nl/sites/default/files/publicaties/download/dp265-foreign-investment-effects-tax-treaties.pdf> accessed 18 June 2019.
60 Paul L Baker, 'An Analysis of Double Taxation Treaties and their Effect on Foreign Direct Investment' (2014) 21 *International Journal of the Economics of Business* 341.
61 Doing Business, *Doing Business 2019* (World Bank Group Flagship Report Index Series 2019) <www.doingbusiness.org/reports> accessed 18 June 2019.
62 I am referring to the legal machinations described in Charles Dickens's *Bleak House*.
63 Ganeshan Wignaraja, 'Factors affecting entry into Supply Chain Trade: An Analysis of Firms in Southeast Asia' (2015) 2 *Asia and the Pacific Policy Studies* 636.

The OECD's Anti-Bribery Convention (officially, the Convention on Combating Bribery of Foreign Public Officials in International Business Transactions) is aimed at reducing corruption primarily in developing countries by encouraging sanctions against bribery in international business transactions carried out by companies based in the Convention-member countries.[64] Many governments have also introduced anti-bribery legislation. In Australia, the *Australian Criminal Code* is in place, the US has the *Foreign Corrupt Practices Act*, and the United Kingdom has a Bribery Act.[65] All have implications as to the way organizations operate sustainably and legally across international borders. The national IPA, along with country diplomatic and commercial services, is in pole position to observe and advise on compliance with such legislation. Poor behaviour by a government department, investor or investee, particularly during a transaction facilitated by an IPA, can incur significant reputational risk for a country. All parties need to be aware of the implementing legislation. They must also establish and provide training in effective compliance mechanisms as well as independently monitor performance..[66] IPAs could take a leadership role in providing training to the private sector in such governance. Austrade, for example, visits offshore and onshore Australian businesses to update them on anti-bribery legislation.

5.5 Using the banking network

Finally, a more effective promotional service can be provided if international banks and other financial institutions are involved in the investment process as early as possible, since they can provide high-quality business information and market intelligence. Involving such organizations in both investment and trade promotion can help reduce the fixed costs of government-deployed resources.[67] A majority of companies cite insufficient quality information as a significant barrier to doing business in overseas markets.[68] For most SMEs, however,

---

64 OECD, 'Convention on Combating Bribery of Foreign Public Officials in International Business Transactions' (1999) Organization for Economic Co-Operation and Development (OECD) <www.oecd.org/daf/anti-bribery/ConvCombatBribery_ENG.pdf> accessed 18 June 2019.

65 Foreign Corrupt Practices Act 1977 (US); Bribery Act 2010 (UK).

66 The OECD has a suite of publications that cover all aspects of responsible multinational business practice: OECD, 'OECD Guidelines for Multinational Enterprises-Responsible Business Conduct Matters: Annual Reports' (OECD 2018) <https://mneguidelines.oecd.org/responsible-business-conduct-matters.htm> accessed 18 June 2019.

67 Sebastian Krautheim, 'Heterogeneous firms, exporter networks and the effect of distance on international trade' (2012) 87 *Journal of International Economics* 27; Tomohiko Inui, Keiko Ito, and Daisuke Miyakawa, 'With a little help from my bank: Japanese SMEs' export decision' (*VoxEU*, 6 January 2016) <https://voxeu.org/article/little-help-my-bank-japanese-smes-export-decision> accessed 18 June 2019.

68 Australia's International Business Survey 2014 noted that 59 percent of businesses cited 'lack of information about local culture, business practices and language' as a barrier to doing business overseas: <www.export.org.au/pdf/research/aibs-2014/AIBS-2014-FULL-Report-FINAL-20140730-web.pdf> accessed 21 Jun 2019.

158 Matthew Durban

involvement of an international bank is not an option, since they have limited access to finance due to the high cost of borrowing and limited availability of financing from commercial banks.[69]

6. Conclusion

On the whole, FDI does not lead but is rather led by host-country policies and strategies. Policy advocacy by IPAs would appear to have an important but not defining influence. Influential and effective FDI policy advocacy needs to take into account both host-country advantages and corporate-targeting strategies. A developed market with best-practice business registration and a strong, stable macroeconomic climate rarely needs to sell location. Investment-ready projects become the *casus belli* for investors. Developing countries, however, have to tackle both economic climate and define projects. The IPA's ability to handhold investors through the latter, particularly when English is not the preferred language and the cultural context is complex, can add significant value.

Both Austrade and BKPM have an outward investment focus, albeit with indeterminate measures of success. Their activities should be more complementary than it is in practice. One country's outward investment is another country's inward investment but sector priorities are different and resources are often poorly matched. Nevertheless, it is encouraging to note that both institutions host delegations from the other and share advice on the optimum economic climate. This kind of cooperation could be extended within sectors across countries to ensure a similar optimum application of resources and increase the likelihood of success. A more formal cooperative framework would be advisable, however, either as part of economic partnership agreements or investment treaties.

Increasingly, online transactions are reducing trade costs. However, service-based businesses, which so often characterize developed-economy exports, cannot avoid face-to-face interactions, and this can be challenging in high-context cultures where relationships, network-based trust, and personal introductions matter. This is where on-the-ground IPA support, using the badge of government to gain access and enhance credibility, can add the most value in investor targeting.

Closer alignment with the trade function could perhaps go further in policy and operational coordination, such as by ensuring that foreign businesses that invest and then export from that investment receive appropriate recognition and input into economic climate improvements. This would help capture more of the benefits associated with FDI and contribute to communicating more easily an investment project's merits to sceptical electorates.

Similarly, and largely absent from the FDI examples cited here, is any alignment with industry policy aside from high-level sector consultation. FDI

---

69 Wignaraja (n 63) 636.

can provide significant benefits in particular to SMEs, struggling with such constraints as a limited domestic market, inability to access offshore supply chains and finance, and inadequate skilled labour. An industry policy and subsequent IPA operational plan that recognize these constraints and seek to identify investment opportunities that can build capability to address such limitations will create a virtuous loop.

Finally, coordinated outreach by countries to companies for which global value chains are increasingly the norm requires an understanding of complementary economies and competitive advantage, coordination of facilitation with networks and partners nationally and overseas, and substantive access to useful information.

8 Tax competition as an investment promotion tool

Allison Christians and Marco Garofalo

1. Introduction

Perhaps the most popular mantra of international tax policy is that states that seek foreign investment cannot tax the returns to such investment because investors will either fight, by adopting increasingly aggressive tax avoidance practices, or flee, by moving their operations to some other, more favourable, location. The availability of favourable locations depends on lawmakers' will and ability to use their domestic tax regimes to lure and promote investment from elsewhere – that is, to engage in 'tax competition'.

Tax competition might be healthy – some argue it is an appropriate way to check the state's otherwise unrestrained tendency to expand itself. But the policies of some states can also undermine those of others, and even ultimately themselves. This results in less than optimal tax systems, but it also redirects investment through subsidy and preference. It is clear that states have adopted multiple kinds of tax measures expressly designed to gain investment advantages at the expense of other states. When this happens, the states that stand to lose investment and tax revenues to such measures may look for solutions by negotiating multilateral constraints. Often, there is no mutually advantageous equilibrium to be found.

Failing cooperation, might states seek recourse in other regimes? Over the years, some have explored how regional and international regimes might be used to draw a boundary around what constitutes acceptable use of the tax system as a tool for investment promotion. To understand the nature and significance of these efforts requires some foundational understanding of the design of the international tax system, and why it creates conflicts that states sometimes seek to solve by looking to other regimes. The goal of this chapter is to examine these foundations and locations for conflict resolution.

The second part presents a simple fact pattern that helps illustrate the competing pressures posed by the need for revenues and the desire for foreign investment. The third part considers how states have turned to European Union (EU) competition law as one response to these phenomena, while the final part considers how they have turned to the World Trade Organization (WTO) as another. Since taxation surely has some capacity to impact international trade

Tax competition as an investment promotion tool 161

and investment, it is expected that states will continue to seek ways to gain an advantage while also preventing others from doing the same. Whether the EU or WTO can ultimately serve as effective regulators of a workable consensus remains to be seen.

2. Using tax to lure capital in a global economy

Two key features drive every tax strategy designed to promote investment by luring foreign capital into a state. These are (1) relieving tax on the targeted investment and (2) ensuring that no other country imposes tax in the void. Both must be present in order for a tax-luring strategy to 'work'. As in any market, intermediaries find opportunities to intervene. Sometimes intermediaries facilitate transactions that would otherwise not occur, while other times they act as pure rent-seekers. Whether they are mainly capital-exporting, capital-importing, or acting as intermediaries or conduits, states tend toward policies that increase, rather than decrease, tax competition.[1] To understand why this is so, we first work through the basic components of income taxation and how they function in the global economy. Thereafter, we examine a simplified illustration of the causes of tax competition.

2.1 Taxing income: the fundamentals

No matter what kind of tax system a given state decides to use, it must determine who and what to tax, how to enforce its will, and how to deal with the impact of its tax policy choices on economic outcomes. In an economically integrated world, states do not legislate in a vacuum; instead, one state's answer to these questions may easily overlap or otherwise conflict with that of another.[2]

For example, when a person from State A invests in State B and the investment earns a return, State A may wish to tax the return because it claims the right to tax the person on income from any source, while State B may seek to do the same because the item of income arises within its territory. Both jurisdictional claims are generally accepted as legitimate. Accordingly, in the context of economic globalization, states must ask themselves whether and how they ought to act cooperatively to resolve conflicts when they occur.

The most obvious conflict is 'double taxation' – a term that is typically used to describe a situation in which a taxpayer is taxed by more than one state on the same income. In other areas of tax regulation, especially involving trade in goods (i.e. tariffs), states forged multilateral agreements to agree to specified

---

1 States do not fit neatly or exclusively into these categories but often have dual roles vis-à-vis other states, hence national interests are only rarely singular.
2 For an exploration into why these are the core principles and why they are difficult to achieve in practice, see Allison Christians, 'Sovereignty, Taxation, and Social Contract' (2009) 18 *Minnesota Journal of International Law* 99.

reductions and used institutions, especially the World Trade Organization, to police violations of agreed principles. But states did not create a multilateral regime to coordinate income tax conflicts in the same way.

Instead, states first devised unilateral strategies to relieve double taxation for their own taxpayers under certain conditions, and then developed bilateral (and on occasion multilateral) tax treaties to allocate tax revenues among themselves.[3] Unilaterally, states use either a credit or exemption method to prevent double taxation. The credit method provides domestic tax credit for foreign tax paid while the exemption method exempts all foreign income from tax regardless of whether it is taxed elsewhere.

To illustrate these unilateral and bilateral methods to relieve double taxation: suppose Company A from State A invests in State B, where it earns a profit of $100 (see Figure 8.1).

State B, as the host or 'source' state, may impose a tax on that $100, let us say at a flat rate of 30 percent, or $30. State A, seeking to tax income earned from any source by its residents, imposes its own rate of tax, say 35 percent. If the State A tax falls on top of that already imposed by State B, Company A would face a double tax (65 percent) of income derived from its activities in State B, but only 35 percent if it stays home. State A might decide that capital *should* stay home, and therefore do nothing. This is not likely because there are national gains to be achieved if capital expands overseas, so long as it doesn't

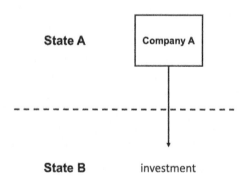

Figure 8.1 Basic cross-border direct investment

---

3 The OECD estimates that there are over 3,000 bilateral tax treaties currently in force; OECD, *Developing a Multilateral Instrument to Modify Bilateral Tax Treaties, Action 15–2015 Final Report* (OECD Publishing 2014). It recently developed a unique multilateral treaty to implement a set of agreed international tax standards under the auspices of the Base Erosion and Profit Shifting (BEPS) Initiative. OECD, 'Multilateral Convention to Implement Tax Treaty Related Measures to Prevent BEPS' (opened for signature 7 June 2017).

Tax competition as an investment promotion tool   163

flee all together. State A is therefore likely to seek some neutral tax policy to ensure its investors can invest internationally.

Neutrality comes in numerous and often mutually exclusive forms, however. For example, one option is for State A to exempt all foreign income earned by State A companies. In a two-state world, this would be considered neutral because State A investors would face the same tax rate as State B investors when investing in State B.[4] In choosing this kind of neutrality, however, State A makes domestic investment in State A more costly relative to investment in State B. That is, if Company A invests in State A, it will face a 35 per cent rate, while in State B, it faces only a 30 per cent rate. Assuming that Company A faces broadly similar risk and return expectations for investments made in State A and State B, tax exemption makes State A investors eager to export their capital to reduce their taxes.

State A might accept this outcome to help its large domestic companies expand into State B, but it will worry that State B's lower tax rate will induce capital flight. State A's second option is to seek neutrality between investors that invest domestically and those that invest abroad. The main mechanism for achieving this kind of neutrality is worldwide tax with a foreign tax credit: State A calculates its normal tax on Company A – here $35 – but deducts from this amount any income tax already paid to State B – here $30, so that Company A faces a total tax of 35 percent, as it would had it invested domestically. In a multi-state world, worldwide taxation with foreign tax creditability achieves this kind of neutrality so long as foreign tax rates do not exceed that of the home state.[5]

However, note State A's position vis-à-vis State B in this case: State B collected $30 in revenue and State A collected only $5. Company A is indifferent about this allocation assuming it faces a total rate of tax of $35 no matter what it does, but State A is not. State A may thus seek a tax treaty with State B to split the tax more evenly between them – for example, by State B reducing its rate to 20 percent so that State A's residual rate rises to 15 percent.

Tax treaties are accordingly a means for states to negotiate the reallocation of tax revenues between source and residence. The world's more than 3,000 existing bilateral tax treaties are based on a common model and related guidance primarily developed by the Organisation for Economic Cooperation and Development (OECD) for this purpose.[6]

---

4 See Richard Musgrave and Peggy Musgrave, *Public Finance in Theory and Practice* (5th edn, McGraw-Hill 1989) 15.

5 Capital import neutrality and capital export neutrality are mutually exclusive policies to the extent that the tax base and effective tax rate diverges among states, which is the current reality. As the policies cannot be reconciled, governments commonly revisit the balance they have struck and a reform in one country can have international impacts.

6 OECD, *Model Tax Convention on Income and on Capital* (OECD Publishing 2017). The UN model tax treaty discussed above is structurally parallel to the OECD model and serves as a second influence on many tax treaties in force. See Allison Christians, 'Tax Treaties for Investment and Aid to Sub-Saharan Africa: A Case Study' (2006) 71 *Brooklyn Law Review* 639.

164   *Allison Christians and Marco Garofalo*

Even as they negotiate the terms of revenue sharing among themselves, many states are in the business of adopting policies that intentionally allow taxpayers to reduce or eliminate taxation. This is, in effect, the strategy at work in all forms of tax competition. A state might, for example, seek novel ways to allow taxpayers to allocate income to its territory where it will be exempt from tax. When this happens, the state may be accused of using its taxing power not to raise revenue, but rather to siphon the tax base (i.e. capital) from other states.

2.2 Tax competition under different international approaches

States seeking foreign investment may reduce their source-based tax rates or narrow the tax base (or both), but in either case the strategy is ineffective if the taxpayer would face tax elsewhere on a residual basis. It will be futile for a host state to lower its tax if the taxpayer resides in a home state that taxes the income and provides a foreign tax credit. In that case, a host state that reduces its own tax would only cede the revenue to the residence state, not relieve it.

To illustrate with the example given above, in a world of only states A and B, if State A taxes its residents on income from any source, but gives credit for foreign taxes paid, then State B will not lower its tax on the income below State A's residual rate. To do so would merely allow State A to collect more revenue. Instead, State B would have an incentive to raise its rate to 35 percent, and deny State A its 5 percent residual as described above. It is for this reason that, in the early days of income taxation, critics called the unilateral foreign tax credit a 'present of revenue' to foreign states.[7]

If instead State A is an exemption state, State A investors would face no home country tax on their foreign investments while they would continue to face a 35 percent tax on their domestic investments. In a two-world state, State B would keep its rate just below that of State A's rate on domestic returns, but once there are more than two states, the competition to attract State A capital will intensify. Investors would evaluate State B's 30 percent tax rate against the tax that would apply if they invested in any state other than State A.

Accordingly, where there is no residual tax rate at residence, host countries compete for foreign investment with their source tax rates. Tax competition at source arises due to the collective decisions of capital-exporting residence states to either exempt or indefinitely defer the taxation of certain income earned in foreign states.

2.3 Tax competition at source: an illustration

The relationship that develops among States A, B, and others, depending on the exercise of taxation at residence and source, demonstrates why tax is a complex

---

7 Edwin R A Seligman, *Double Taxation and International Fiscal Cooperation* (MacMillan 1928) 132, 135.

tool when it comes to investment promotion. To understand tax competition requires an appreciation that between the supply of and demand for investment capital, a market of intermediaries naturally arises to take advantage of the relationship created by these forces. An example, while potentially cumbersome despite being grossly oversimplified, may help explain why this is so.

This example seeks to illustrate the challenges a resource-rich host country might face in taxing multinationals, even where the quality and scarcity of the targeted natural resources might suggest that taxation should not deter investment.

Imagine a resource-extracting company (REC) from State A, a high-tax jurisdiction, looking to extract a given natural resource that can be found only (or mostly) in States B, C, and D. Each of States B, C, and D seems poised to tax any investment in their natural resources sector because the resource is relatively scarce or hard to get to in other places. However, in the short term, each state faces the risk of losing investment to one of the other states and having to wait until some future date when its own stores become the best remaining option.

To avoid that possibility, each of States B, C, and D may wish to offer an attractive tax rate, or a specially-defined tax base, as an incentive to an initial investment by REC.[8] Imagine, therefore, that State B engages in investment promotion by offering an attractive package geared to attract foreign investment in its natural resource sector, including among its offerings a guaranteed tax rate of 6 percent on all profits derived from resource extraction in State B over a period of twenty years.[9]

If State A is a country that employs a worldwide tax with foreign tax credits and REC engages in the resource extraction business directly, REC would face the State A tax rate on its State B-sourced profits. As the country of source, State B would typically impose its 6 percent tax on the profits attributable to REC's operations in State B.[10] State A would then nominally impose its 35 percent tax on the same profits, and then give a tax credit for the 6 percent paid to State B. In this way, State A's residual tax would fully negate the effectiveness of State B's tax reduction; State B might as well have taxed at 35 percent, leaving nothing for State A.

---

8 See OECD, 'Action Plan on Base Erosion and Profit Shifting' (OECD Publishing 2013) 18 <www.oecd.org/ctp/bepsactionplan.pdf> accessed 18 June 2019. Lawmakers may narrow their source tax base using a variety of strategies, from straightforward business tax incentives (e.g. accelerated depreciation and generous research and development credits and subsidies) to duration-, geographic-, or sector-based tax 'holidays' and 'free zones'.

9 This is only one form of incentive. State B could equally offer: accelerated depreciation for capital expenditures, thus allowing companies to eliminate taxable income throughout the early years of their operations; 125 percent or 150 percent deductions for expenses; or 'refundable' tax credits (which are simply cash transfers delivered through the tax system).

10 This is generally referred to as profits attributable to a permanent establishment, following tax treaty principles; however, domestic law may impose different threshold rules for taxing business profits. See OECD (n 6) art 5 (defining a permanent establishment as the threshold for taxing business profits at source) and art 9 (explaining how to identify profits attributable to a permanent establishment).

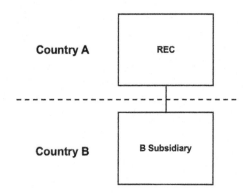

Figure 8.2 Basic Cross-Border Investment Via Subsidiary

The calculation changes if REC incorporates a subsidiary to run the operations in State B (see Figure 8.2).

Leaving aside anti-avoidance safeguards, REC gains an advantage by incorporating a State B subsidiary (BSub) because states do not generally tax the business income earned by foreign companies in foreign countries, even if they are owned and controlled by domestic shareholders. BSub is not a resident of State A for tax purposes, and so would not (generally) be taxed by State A in the same way as REC. Instead, State A would typically tax BSub in the same manner as it taxes other non-residents, namely only on their State A-source income (which is presumably zero in this type of scenario).[11]

In a two-state world, if the residence state fails to protect its base, such as by adopting deeming rules to tax the domestic shareholder of the foreign company, State B's policy choice to use the tax system to lure investment will be effective but the company will still pay tax: State B will attract investment from State A by maintaining a modestly lower rate. However, State B and State A are not alone in the world. Other countries, such as State C and State D in this example, also have reasons to enact policy choices to do the same thing that State B did, namely, offer generous tax incentives (each more generous than the next).

---

11 While in theory no legal regime prevents a country from claiming as its residents any corporation wherever incorporated or managed, the consensus under general principles is that the corporation must have some sort of recognizable tie to a state in order to be considered a resident and therefore a taxpayer. This is reflected in tax treaties, which assign residence according to a list of relevant nexus-producing factors (see OECD (n 6) art 4). In most states, the tie is legal incorporation or place of management and control (see Christians (n 2)). Where more than one state assumes that a corporate entity is resident, there is no international law to resolve the dispute unless a tax treaty applies (ibid). Where a treaty applies, it generally determines corporate residence by reference to its place of effective management (see OECD (ibid) art 4(3)).

Tax competition as an investment promotion tool 167

Resource states might reasonably form a cartel to stop their mutual destruction to the benefit of State A. Tax competition increases when the resources available investors include financial and legal services. Imagine a third country, State X, which has few or no relevant natural resources, but which does have a sophisticated legal and financial system that is well staffed with competent professionals and backed by savvy regulators and jurists. State X seeks to lure investment to its country in order to employ this local labour force. REC is a target if some of the profits from its global operations that would otherwise be taxed only by State B at source can instead be earned at a lower tax rate in State X before they return to State A in the form of repatriated profits. There are any number of ways State X can create the desired result for REC but any strategy it chooses will only work if it satisfies the same two rules that applied to successfully lure capital to State B in the first place: (1) relieve its own tax on the targeted investment and (2) ensure that no other country will impose tax in the void.

With a State X in the picture, one strategy for REC would be to create an intermediary in State X – let's call it XSub – to which income flows may be diverted from State B (see Figure 8.3).

XSub's role might be to purchase resources from State B at a low price and resell to final customers at a higher price, with the spread becoming XSub's profit belonging to XSub rather than BSub or REC. Alternatively, XSub might charge BSub various fees such as interest on loans, royalties for the use of

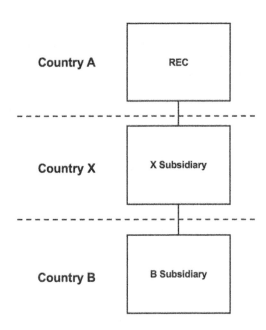

Figure 8.3 Cross-border investment via conduit and operating subsidiaries

168 *Allison Christians and Marco Garofalo*

trademarks, management and consulting fees, and the like. These fees would be deducted from BSub's income, which would reduce its State B tax, and be included in XSub's income, which State X may choose to tax more lightly than B or (more likely) not all. To the extent that State B did not entirely eliminate all tax on BSub's profits, State X's lure works: State X can (1) relieve tax of REC on the targeted investment in State B (profits from resource extraction) and (2) ensure that no other country imposes tax in the void.

Here, State A might intervene, for example, by deeming some of the profits earned by XSub to have been paid out to REC. It may do so on grounds that the underlying income earned in State X is not from the active operations involving natural resource extraction, but consists of highly mobile capital. However, it is very likely that State A will not intervene in practice, for various reasons. For example, domestic politicians might not wish to appear to be increasing the taxation of State A multinationals. Alternatively, State A may see the problem as one belonging to State B. Since State A had no intention of taxing BSub profits, it may see no reason to intervene when the income is earned by XSub instead. Finally, State A might be inclined to support the 'tax sovereignty' of States B and X to design their tax systems without interference, on the theory that State A itself wishes not to be disciplined by other countries for its own tax incentive structures.[12]

To the mixture of incentives and motivations already noted, there is added a massive and growing industry of tax professionals poised to assist multinationals with strategies that move income to favourable tax destinations. As a result, accommodating rules are likely to be continuously adopted and exploited as taxpayers seek to reduce their costs, including taxation, to the greatest possible extent. Thus, even if the State Bs of the world were to stop using their income tax systems to lure investment, taxpayers would continue their own efforts to divert profits to more favourable taxing states. The issue for investors is how much effort states are willing to expend to protect their tax bases. The more they are willing to do so, the higher tax costs investors ultimately face.

The ongoing struggle for coherence in international taxation signals that governments find it difficult to resist and to control tax competition. Lawmakers find themselves facing difficult policy choices with conflicting theoretical and empirical support: on the one hand they must work to protect the tax base from encroachment by other states while on the other, they reduce tax burdens specifically to lure inbound investment. Because this internal conflict plays out on an international stage, it raises the question of whether and when tax competition should actually be viewed as anti-competitive in the sense of being designed to gain unwarranted trade and investment advantages, and if so, what response, if any, arise in free trade or other international legal regimes. The next section explores the legal terrain.

---

12 There have been fluctuating periods of increased and decreased tolerance for tax sovereignty in the international community. See Sergio Rocha and Allison Christians (eds), *Tax Sovereignty in BEPS Era: Series on International Taxation* (Kluwer Law International 2018).

3. Declining to tax: a competitive or anti-competitive practice?

Since there is no singular supranational body tasked with policing how states use their tax systems to advantage themselves in investment, tax policymakers are constantly tempted to adopt ever more creative policies to gain advantage. It therefore should not be too surprising that some particularly visible tax practices eventually came to the attention of competition authorities, especially in the European Union where a pre-existing regime provides a mechanism to directly address such matters.

The EU's competition regime includes so-called 'fiscal state aid', a regime that prohibits member states from delivering tax subsidies in specified ways that distort competition within the EU's internal market.[13] The regime's existence, and the increasing willingness of the European Commission to test its boundaries, provide valuable insights into the kinds of tax strategies that states might use to lure foreign investment, as well as whether such strategies are, or should be, considered acceptable practices in a world in which free trade and investment are ostensibly broadly shared goals.

3.1 The state-aid framework

EU state-aid assessments involve six criteria, all of which must be satisfied in order for there to be a finding of prohibited state aid:[14]

(1) the existence of an *undertaking*,
(2) the existence of a *measure* attributable to the state,
(3) the grant of an *advantage* to the undertaking as a result of the measure,
(4) the financing of that measure through *state resources*,
(5) the *selectivity* of the measure, meaning that it is not a general grant of aid available to all, and
(6) its potential *effect on competition* and trade within the Union.

Fact patterns involving tax measures will usually satisfy all of the criteria, except for the 'selectivity' criterion. For example, providing a tax holiday to foreign investors in a particular industry or location would very likely be described under the first four and the sixth criteria. First, the criterion of 'undertaking' is broad, referring to any entity engaged in economic activity.[15] Second, a 'measure attributable to the state' includes situations in which the state provides a specific tax measure that advantages a specific company or

---

13 Consolidated Version of the Treaty on the Functioning of the European Union [2008] OJ C115/47, art 107(1).
14 See Commission Notice C/2016/2946 on the notion of State aid as referred to in Article 107(1) of the Treaty on the Functioning of the European Union [2016] OJ C 262.
15 ibid para 7; Joined Cases C–180/98 to C–184/98 *Pavlov and Others* [2000] ECR I–6451, para 74.

170 Allison Christians and Marco Garofalo

industry.[16] Third, reducing a specific company's tax burden may constitute an 'advantage' if it leads to almost any kind of tax reduction, whether by reducing the base or the applicable effective rate.[17] Fourth, the 'state resources' criterion includes most tax measures, regardless of which level of government enacted them and regardless of their administrative or legislative nature.[18] Finally, the official view of the 'effect on competition' criterion, also called 'distortion of competition', is affected whenever a state selectively grants an advantage to an undertaking.[19] Practically speaking, the criterion is assumed to exist once the other five elements are satisfied.

As a result, the analysis usually turns on whether or not the given tax measure is viewed as 'selective', which is defined to mean that the state grants an advantage to some economic actors and not others.

3.2 'Selectivity' as a fiscal issue

EU law distinguishes between two types of selectivity: regional (benefitting one region over another) and material (favouring certain sectors or firms).[20] Regional selectivity prohibits measures designed to lure investment to a specific geographic area.[21] States may, however, give local governments independence in implementing tax measures, which could have a similar effect.[22] Material selectivity is prohibited whether it is effected in law (*de jure*) or through its practical effects (*de facto*).[23] *De facto* selective measures are more difficult to detect.

Faced with a state-aid challenge, a member state may escape a finding of selectivity by showing that a measure is part of a general scheme. Thus, in a 1998 Notice, the Commission assured member states that 'purely technical tax

---

16 ibid Commission Notice para 51 ('A positive transfer of funds does not have to occur; foregoing State revenue is sufficient. Waiving revenue which would otherwise have been paid to the State constitutes a transfer of State resources'.).

17 European Commission, '1998 Notice on the application of State aid rules to measures relating to direct business taxation' COM (98) 384/03, para 9 (referring to base reductions such as special deductions, special or accelerated depreciation arrangements, or special reserves on the balance sheet, and rate reductions as either total or partial reduction, whether via exemption or credit, and including deferment, cancellation, or special rescheduling of tax debt).

18 ibid para 10; see also Case 248/84 *Germany v Commission* [1987] ECR 4013. The Commission thus implicitly recognizes that tax expenditures are equivalent, in budgetary terms, to government spending.

19 See Commission Notice (n 14) para 187 ('For all practical purposes, a distortion of competition … is thus assumed as soon as the State grants a financial advantage to an undertaking in a liberalised sector where there is, or could be, competition'.).

20 Commission Notice (n 14) para 119; see also Andreas Bartosch, 'The concept of selectivity?' In Erika Szyszczak (ed), *Research Handbook on European State Aid Law* (Edward Elgar 2011) 189.

21 Jakub Kociubiński, 'Selectivity Criterion in State Aid Control' (2012) 1 *Wroclaw Review of Law, Administration & Economics* 6.

22 Bartsoch (n 20) 176, 177.

23 Commission Notice (n 14) para 120.

measures' and certain measures pursuing general economic policy would be excluded from Commission investigations.[24] However, it can be quite difficult to demonstrate whether a tax measure forms part of a general scheme. The Court of Justice of the EU has stated that a measure that relieves a tax that would 'normally' have to be paid under the general scheme does not form part of the general scheme.[25] The analysis requires the court to determine a tax reference system – a base case – and identify whether a given measure deviates from it.[26] This is very much like the 'tax expenditure analysis' that many governments undertake to demonstrate how much revenue is foregone in enacting a given tax measure.

Like tax expenditure analysis, the entire state-aid analysis depends on the breadth of the base case. For instance, a country may seek to attract foreign investment by relieving the tax on interest paid to or by companies located abroad compared to that paid to or by domestic companies. Whether this constitutes selectivity will differ depending on whether the system of reference is the general corporate tax system or the taxation of income according to source.[27] For example, if the general corporate tax system features a tax rate of 15 percent but a particular taxpayer receives an administrative letter guaranteeing a maximum rate of 2 percent, this would clearly constitute selectivity. When different tax rates, inclusions, or exemptions apply to different types of income, the analysis is broader and more uncertain, creating risk for taxpayers that even if they merely avail themselves of the rules as written, their tax outcomes will not survive EU scrutiny.

Some commentators have found the Commission and the Court of Justice's approach to be overly broad, pointing to the landmark decision in *Adria-Wien Pipeline* as a prime example.[28] The Court of Justice of the EU found that an Austrian law granting an energy tax rebate for companies manufacturing goods, but not for companies providing services, was selective. The Court of Justice found the measure selective because both manufacturers and service providers might be 'major consumers of energy' and it was therefore inappropriate to

---

24 European Commission (n 17) para 13 ('tax measures of a purely technical nature (for example, setting the rate of taxation, depreciation rules, and rules on loss carry-overs; provisions to prevent double-taxation or avoidance); and measures pursuing general economic policy objectives through a reduction of the tax burden related to certain production costs (research and development (R&D), the environment, training, employment)'.).

25 Case C–173/73, *Italian Republic v Commission of the European Communities* [1974] ECR 709, para 33.

26 Claire Micheau, *State Aid, Subsidy and Tax Incentives Under EU and WTO Law* (Kluwer Law International 2014) 203; See Cases T-211/04 and T-215/04, *Government of Gibraltar* [2008] ECR II–3745. With respect to tax matters, we can note that the Commission takes 'such elements as the tax base, the taxable persons, the taxable event and the tax rates' into consideration when deciding on a system of reference (Commission Notice (n 14) para 134).

27 ibid Micheau 204.

28 Case C–143/99, *Adria-Wien Pipeline* [2001] ECR I-8365; see Bartosch (n 20) 179.

172   *Allison Christians and Marco Garofalo*

grant the energy tax rebate to one and not the other.[29] Whether or not one agrees with the *Adria-Wien* decision, the worry remains that there is no principled basis upon which the Court of Justice may determine an appropriate system of reference.[30] Finally, a measure can be selective if administrative discretion interferes with a measure otherwise forming part of a general scheme of taxation. This rule catches tax administrators that make side deals with specific taxpayers.[31]

Once a measure is considered materially selective, a state may still argue that it is 'justified by the nature or general scheme of that system'.[32] The Commission's view is that states may only claim intrinsic features of a tax system or its basic guiding principles as a justificatory factor, and not what it calls 'external policy considerations'.[33] For example, the Commission considers that such objectives as addressing 'fraud or tax evasion ... specific accounting requirements, administrative manageability, the principle of tax neutrality, the progressive nature of income tax and its redistributive purpose ... double taxation, and the objective of optimizing the recovery of fiscal debts' are acceptable justifications.[34] These objectives are internal to the general scheme of taxation because they are directed at preserving the integrity of the tax system. The system would become unmanageable if fraud or evasion was pervasive or if it were administratively unmanageable.

With respect to which external policy considerations are acceptable and which are not, some argue for a differentiation between permissible ('good') and impermissible (or 'bad') objectives. For example, ecological objectives are among the good objectives, as are 'other political motives based on considerations of a social, cultural or educational kind'; among the bad are targeted economic objectives, such as addressing 'unemployment in a particular region or the enhancement of the latter's attractiveness' to foreign investors.[35]

These distinctions may be explained by reference to the general principles of state-aid law. State-aid rules seek to avoid the distortion of competition in the European Union due to member states trying to pick economic winners. Thus, even though addressing unemployment in a particular region may have a social policy motivation, the relevant EU member state would still be trying to pick a 'winner'. On the other hand, state-aid law can more coherently accept an

---

29 ibid *Adria-Wien* para 50.
30 Bartosch (n 20); Micheau (n 26); Claire Micheau, 'Tax Selectivity in European Law of State Aid: Legal Assessment and Alternative Approaches' (2014) University of Luxembourg Working Paper No 2014–06 <https://papers.ssrn.com/sol3/papers.cfm?abstract_id=2499514> accessed 6 August 2019; Ruth Mason, 'When Are Tax Subsidies Illegal?' (2019) 69 *American University Law Review* (forthcoming).
31 Commission Notice (n 14) para 123.
32 ibid para 138.
33 ibid.
34 ibid para 139.
35 Bartosch (n 20) 187.

Tax competition as an investment promotion tool 173

advantage conferred in order to protect non-economic interests. In particular, 'protection of the environment constitutes one of the essential objectives of the Community'.[36]

The cases to date demonstrate that tax benefits in the form of state aid are not always at risk of EU intervention. Where investors engage in industries with permissible objectives, tax benefits may still be respected. The ongoing interest of the EU in member state tax policies means that tax benefits are likely to face scrutiny, causing member states to defend their policy choices. This fact may make member states more cautious about providing tax incentives, which may lead either to fewer such regimes overall, as the EU intends, or instead attention to designing more complex regimes that are less susceptible to anti-competition laws.

4. Tax as subsidy in the WTO

As Europe continues to work out the parameters of acceptable tax competition among its member states, the WTO regime on subsidies has had a broader impact on state practices. While taxes form part of the WTO regime, they are typically articulated in import/export language, such as in the case of the General Agreement on Tariffs and Trade (GATT) Most-Favoured-Nation (MFN) and National Treatment (NT) principles.[37]

It is not clear whether, and to what extent, these principles might constrain policy-makers seeking to use tax competition to attract foreign investment. In the EU state-aid context, importation and exportation of products is not relevant; what is at stake is the allocation of profits among jurisdictions without reference to underlying goods. The EU state-aid cases are, in this regard, different from the cases brought before WTO panels. Fundamentally, tax competition generally seeks to reduce the tax burden on capital, not raise it. Consequently, the MFN or NT principles in the GATT, along with the Agreement on Trade-Related Investment Measures (TRIMS), or the General Agreement on Trade in Services (GATS) appear inapposite to the task of curbing tax competition.[38]

Yet WTO instruments prevent states from imposing burdens on or discriminating between the goods or services of foreign nationals. In this respect, the Subsidies

---

36 Case C-487/06P *British Aggregates v Commission* [2008] ECR I-10,515 para 91.

37 General Agreement on Tariffs and Trade 1994 (in force 15 April 1994), Marrakesh Agreement Establishing the World Trade Organization, Annex 1A, 1867 UNTS 187, 33 ILM 1153 (1994) [GATT], arts I and III. For a discussion, see Michael Daly, 'WTO Rules on Direct Taxation' (2005) 9 WTO Discussion Paper No 9, 4 ('imported goods must be treated the same as or no less favourably than domestically produced-goods so as to ensure that discriminatory internal taxes are not used as a substitute for tariffs').

38 See Daly ibid 4–8; GATT ibid; General Agreement on Trade in Services (in force 15 April 1994), Marrakesh Agreement Establishing the World Trade Organization, Annex 1B, 1869 UNTS 183, 33 ILM 1167 [GATS]; Agreement: Agreement on Trade-Related Investment Measures (in force 15 April 1994), Marrakesh Agreement Establishing the World Trade Organization, Annex 1A, 1868 UNTS 186 [TRIMs].

174　*Allison Christians and Marco Garofalo*

and Countervailing Measures Agreement (SCM), though it applies to goods and not services, might most closely track the EU state-aid regime in terms of its potential to curb anti-competitive tax practices.[39]

4.1 WTO prohibition on subsidies

Although many of the concepts are similar, the WTO regime appears to grant states much more latitude to use the tax system strategically than appears to be allowed under the EU state-aid rules. The SCM prohibition on subsidies contains two components: the definition of a subsidy and the consequences that attach to different forms of subsidy. The three elements of a subsidy are:

(1) A financial *contribution*[40] that
(2) confers a *benefit*[41] with
(3) *specificity.*[42]

A financial contribution is similar to the EU state-aid concept of the 'existence of a measure attributable to the state'. A measure may constitute a 'financial contribution' under the SCM in multiple ways.[43] The criterion that 'government revenue that is otherwise due is foregone or not collected (e.g. fiscal incentives such as tax credits)' brings tax incentives into the scope of 'financial contribution' and therefore also subsidy scrutiny under WTO law.[44] A claimant alleging an infringement of the SCM must prove that the financial contribution provides a benefit, which is similar to the EU state-aid concept of 'an advantage'.[45]

Subsidies are only subject to WTO sanction if they satisfy the definition of 'specificity'.[46] The notion of 'specificity' in WTO law is similar to the notion of 'selectivity' in EU state-aid law in that they both prevent the state from

---

39　Agreement on Subsidies and Countervailing Measures (in force 15 April 1994), Marrakesh Agreement Establishing the World Trade Organization, Annex 1A, 1869 UNTS 14 [SCM]. This distinction means that only subsidies that affect the trade of goods are prohibited, whereas state aids that distort the market for anything are prohibited (see Micheau (n 26) 105, 106).

40　SCM ibid, art 1.1(a)(1).

41　SCM ibid, art 1.1(b).

42　SCM ibid, art 2.

43　SCM ibid, art 1.1(a)(1)(i) – (iv).

44　SCM ibid, art 1.1(a)(1)(ii).

45　SCM ibid, art 1.1(b). A benefit arises when a legal person or group of persons has received something beneficial. Appellate Body Report, *Canada – Measures affecting the export of civilian aircraft* (WT/DS70/AB/R,1999) 154; Micheau (n 26) 205. Similarly, an advantage may be any advantageous reduction in terms of tax base, liability, or enforcement. 1998 Notice (n 17) para 9; see also Micheau (n 26) 205.

46　SCM ibid, art 2. See also Micheau ibid 255.

Tax competition as an investment promotion tool 175

granting 'advantages' (in the case of the EU) or 'benefits' (in the case of the WTO) to individual enterprises or groups of enterprises.[47]

A subsidy can be specific in one of three ways. First, if access to the subsidy is explicitly limited by the state to certain enterprises, the subsidy is likely specific.[48] This is also known as *de jure* specificity, or specific as a matter of law.[49] Second, if the state provides objective criteria which are to be used in deciding whether to grant the benefit, this will decrease the likelihood of the subsidy being considered specific.[50] Objective criteria must be neutral, not favouring certain enterprises over others, economic in nature, and horizontal in application 'in relation to criteria like number of employees or size of the enterprises'.[51]

Third, the WTO regime prohibits *de facto* specific subsidies, or subsidies that are specific as a matter of fact.[52] This is necessary because lawmakers may use apparently objective or generalized criteria to mask what amounts to a specific subsidy. The criteria for determining a *de facto* subsidy include whether it is 'predominantly used' by certain enterprises and whether a 'disproportionately large' amount of the subsidy was used by certain enterprises.[53]

Predominant use must, of course, be assessed on a case-by-case basis. For example, an industry that is a main beneficiary of a subsidy in an economy in which there are few industries is less indicative of a subsidy than an industry that is the main beneficiary in a highly diversified economy.[54] The same principle applies to the length of the time that a subsidy programme has been in operation: conclusions cannot necessarily be drawn regarding the impact of a relatively new subsidy programme.[55] The disproportionately large criterion means that the subsidy may not be bigger than necessary in comparison to a given benchmark.[56] The appropriate benchmark will usually be relative to other subsidies given under the subsidy programme.[57]

---

47 ibid SCM, art 2.
48 ibid SCM, art 2.1(a).
49 Micheau (n 26) 256.
50 SCM (n 39), art 2.1(b).
51 Micheau (n 26) 256.
52 SCM (n 39), art 2.1(c).
53 ibid.
54 WTO Panel Report, *European Communities and Certain Member States – Measures Affecting Trade in Large Civil Aircraft*, WTO Doc WT/DS316/RW (22 September 2016) para 7.975.
55 ibid para 7.976.
56 ibid para 7.961.
57 ibid para 7.964. For example, the *EC – Countervailing Measures on DRAM Chips* case decided that a Korean subsidy programme was *de facto* specific when in practice, a disproportionately large amount of the subsidy was granted to a certain number of enterprises – namely, just 6 of 200 eligible companies used 41 percent of the available subsidy. WTO Panel Report, *European Communities – Countervailing Measures on Dynamic Random-Access Memory Chips from Korea*, WTO Doc WT/DS299/R (17 June 2005), para 7.223.

4.2 Implications for tax competition

Despite some similarity of terms, the EU rules seem overall more likely than the WTO rules to restrain the strategic use of tax measures to lure investment. In particular, the notion of specificity under WTO law appears weaker than the notion of selectivity under EU state-aid law.[58] In the EU, selectivity is a threshold to finding state aid regardless of any harm shown, but WTO rules only punish subsidies if the incentive affects international trade.[59] The EU approach presents a more comprehensive discipline on transfers to private organizations that can harm the market.

The WTO attaches legal consequences to 'prohibited' and 'actionable' subsidies, but these rules seem peripherally relevant to an inquiry about tax competition. For WTO purposes, prohibited subsidies are generally defined by reference to whether they burden or restrict the import (or encourage the export) of goods.[60] Tax competition, however, need not result in either: states may use tax competition to 'excessively' lower their domestic tax burden primarily to facilitate and increase the import of capital.[61] The measures described above as tax competition do not appear to be prohibited subsidies within the meaning of Article 3 of the SCM, even if the tax treatment of capital effectively impacts trade outcomes by advantaging some companies in some states over others.

Actionable subsidies appear similarly inapposite. These are defined as specific subsidies, and they are subject to WTO discipline only if they cause 'adverse effects' to other WTO members.[62] The three main types of adverse effects are (1) causing injury to another's domestic industry, (2) nullifying or impairing GATT 1994 benefits, and (3) causing serious prejudice to another's interests.[63] In terms of injury, the difficulty seems to be in tracing the effect of a tax subsidy in one state to the detriment of a company in another; indirect effects of this kind might plausibly occur but are difficult to square with the relevant language (besides likely being difficult to isolate in terms of the number of possible economic variables at play).[64] With tax competition, states often impose adverse effects on their own domestic industry (or, more likely, on their own tax revenues) in order to attract certain

---

58 The notion of selectivity is part of the definition of aid under EU state aid law, but specificity is not part of the definition of a subsidy.

59 Micheau (n 26) 262.

60 SCM (n 39), art 3 ('Except as provided in the Agreement on Agriculture, the following subsidies, within the meaning of Article 1, shall be prohibited: ... (b) subsidies contingent, whether solely or as one of several other conditions, upon the use of domestic over imported goods'.).

61 Micheau (n 26).

62 SCM (n 39), art 5.

63 ibid.

64 Injury is defined as 'any material injury to a domestic industry, threat of material injury to a domestic industry or material retardation of the establishment of such an industry'. It is determined by analyzing two impacts: (1) the volume of subsidized imported products and its effect on the price of like products in the domestic country, and (2) the 'consequent impact' on domestic producers of like products. Micheau (n 26) 114; SCM ibid notes 11 and 45.

economic activity. The harm occurs in the wrong place. Similarly, even if they might produce a similar economic effect as tariffs, income tax subsidies seem not to relate to GATT 1994 benefits.

'Serious prejudice', the third adverse effects category, occurs when states prop up certain industries through, among other means, *ad valorem* subsidies of products or forgiveness of government-held debt (which may include a tax).[65] However, the prejudice must bear on trade in a particular good.[66] As such, the 'serious prejudice' category may not be very helpful in addressing tax competition that targets the flow of capital. Even if a measure that allows multinationals to shift income to achieve tax benefits might be considered a subsidy, no WTO consequences would result unless trade in goods can be shown to have been impacted.

This point is illustrated by the application of WTO subsidy disciplines to tax measures in the context of the SCM case involving the US Foreign Sales Company (FSC) regime. Under this regime, the United States granted tax exemptions for certain 'foreign trade income' earned by US-headquartered foreign corporations.[67] The purpose of the FSC regime was to compensate US exporters for perceived tax disadvantages in the European market.[68] The United States claimed that it had created the FSC regime to correct a structural disadvantage, a permissible action under WTO rules. The WTO Panel did not agree. They held that the FSC exemptions constituted a subsidy contingent upon export performance, and therefore represented a prohibited subsidy.[69] The panel held that while WTO rules do not dictate the type of tax system a state may use, a member state cannot adopt a specific rule that violates WTO commitments simply because its system is disadvantageous to some constituents.[70]

The FSC case revealed the limitations of the SCM in responding to harmful tax competition. The United States lost this case because, having in place a tax system for worldwide income, it could not offer exceptions expressly designed to privilege exported products. Yet the decision makes clear that the United States may choose to exempt foreign income all together. If it did so (as it

---

65 SCM ibid, art 6.
66 WTO Panel Report, *United States – Subsidies on Upland Cotton*, WTO Doc WT/DS267/R (8 September 2004), para 7.1392.
67 WTO Panel Report, *United States – Tax Treatment for Foreign Sales Corporations*, WTO Doc DS108/R (8 October 1999) [*FSC*] para 2.1.
68 The first disadvantage was that the US nominally taxes the worldwide income of its tax residents, whereas some European countries only tax domestic source income (as discussed above, the reality of deferral for foreign subsidiaries means that worldwide taxation is easily avoided by US-based multinationals). The second disadvantage was that the EU had a value-added tax (VAT) whereas the US did not, leading some to argue that European exporters had a distinct advantage in selling goods in the US compared to US exporters selling goods in the EU. Daly (n 37) 9, 23.
69 *FSC* (n 67) para 7.130.
70 ibid para 7.122.

178   Allison Christians and Marco Garofalo

partially did with its 2017 tax reform), the WTO would be indifferent even though such a territorial system drives capital offshore and fosters tax competition among source states.

In particular, WTO Members may explicitly set their tax rates and their system of internal taxation as they wish, provided they do not distort the trade of goods by offering export subsidies. It seems that even very low or nil tax rates are likely acceptable under this standard. Companies can incorporate subsidiaries, lend money to each other, enter into agreements with each other, transfer property to each other, and shift profits among the group with great flexibility. Although distortion in the flow of capital results, the impact on trade is debatable and therefore apparently beyond the sanction of the WTO.

In contrast, the EU competition rules provide states with greater scope to tackle tax measures directly. The EU approach is to ask whether competition and trade effects are 'not inconceivable'[71] whereas the WTO approach requires proof of a quantifiable ascertained effect.[72] These are all part of the story of why and how states can use tax incentives to lure investment despite a broad notional international consensus that trade and investment flows ought to occur according to free-market principles.[73]

5 Conclusion

It is not always clear whether a state's use of its tax system to lure and promote investment should be seen as engaging in healthy or harmful tax competition. A state that reduces its overall tax base might be exercising appropriate fiscal restraint and setting an example for others. That kind of tax competition has mostly been viewed as appropriate by bodies such as the OECD, whose mantra was perhaps best summed up by former tax policy chief Jeffrey Owen's call for 'fair but fierce' tax competition among free-market economies.[74] On the other hand, governments might use their tax systems to capture global market share in ways that undermine, rather than foster, free-market competition. This kind of tax competition is sometimes referred to as harmful tax competition by OECD countries, but it has also become a battleground within other international regimes.

---

71 Case C–172/03, *Wolfgang Heiser v Finanzamt Innsbruck* [2005] ECR I–01627, para 35.
72 Micheau (n 26) 213.
73 This is evidenced by the core goals articulated in the OECD's constituting document signed in 1960, and reiterated since then across OECD tax reports, guidance, and other statements. These are, first, to promote growth, employment, and economic expansion of OECD member countries; second, to promote economic expansion of non-member developing countries, and third, to contribute to the expansion of world trade. Convention on the Organisation for Economic Co-operation and Development (adopted 14 December 1960), art 1.
74 Jeffrey Owens, *Fair Tax Competition: A Pillar of Positive Economic Reform* (INEKO International Conference on Economic Reforms for Europe, 2004).

Tax competition as an investment promotion tool 179

What might it mean to draw a line between acceptable tax competition and harmful or even anti-competitive practices in the context of other regimes? Within the EU, member states have seen their investment-luring tax incentives challenged by the European Commission as a form of state aid, expressly incompatible with internal competition law. Some of these cases involving large, highly visible US multinationals – Apple, Amazon, and Starbucks among them – have demonstrated the willingness of the European Commission to use state-aid rules to limit the ways in which European countries lure investment from outside the EU.

The story of state aid does not end with the EU, however. Instead, it raises the spectre of other bilateral and multilateral agreements meant to foster free trade having an impact on tax policies. If the process of luring with tax could be characterized as violating EU competition principles, it is not obvious why those same measures should pass muster under other regimes. The WTO agreements would seem to be a primary target for inquiry. The EU state-aid cases may have rekindled interest in the interplay between free trade and tax, but it is still difficult to explain with precision why one form of tax policy should be considered competitive while another should be considered anti-competitive.

With the terrain unsettled, it seems likely that some states will continue to seek recourse against specific tax measures within whatever international, regional, and even bilateral agreements or institutions provide viable processes to lodge complaints. Whether these complaints ultimately produce a coherent framework upon which national investment promotion policies can depend on remains to be seen.

Part III

Managing international investment

9 National security and the political economy of international investment policy

Patrick Leblond and Sébastien Labrecque

1. Introduction

Since the early 2000s, governments throughout the world, especially in Western countries, have become increasingly preoccupied with the impact that international investment may have on their country's national security and public safety. Such concerns are not new but governments have been invoking them more often to screen (and block) acquisitions of domestic firms by foreign investors. They have adopted policies to give national security a more prominent role when it comes to evaluating, approving, and managing foreign investment.[1] In 2018, according to an OECD report, more than 70 per cent of FDI around the world was destined to countries that apply cross-sectoral review processes for international investment, compared to half that percentage in the 1990s. Among 62 jurisdictions analysed by the same report, 87 per cent had some policy in place to manage national security interests related to acquisitions or ownership by foreign investors at the beginning of 2019.[2] As Wherlé and Pohl point out, 'investment policies motivated by national security considerations have stepped out of their niche and leapt onto newspapers' front pages'.[3] There appears to be an emerging polarization between countries when it comes to adopting specific policies to address national security with respect to international investment: some countries do not think that they are 'warranted at all' while others 'pay great attention to this policy area'.[4]

---

1 Joachim Pohl, 'Acquisition- and ownership-related policies to safeguard essential security interests: New policies to manage new threats: Research note on current and emerging trends' (2019) OECD Freedom of Investment Roundtable <www.oecd.org/investment/current-and-emerging-trends-2019.pdf> accessed 6 June 2019; Frédéric Wherlé and Joachim Pohl, 'Current trends in investment policies related to national security and public order'; (November 2018) Organisation for Economic Cooperation and Development <www.oecd.org/daf/inv/investment-policy/current-trends-in-oecd-natsec-policies.pdf> accessed 6 June 2019; Mark A Clodfelter and Francesca M S Guerrero, 'National Security and Foreign Government Ownership Restrictions on Foreign Investment' in Karl P Sauvant, Lisa E Sachs, and Wouter P F Schmit Jongbloed (eds), *Sovereign Investment: Concerns and Policy Reactions Sovereign Investment: Concerns and Policy Reactions* (Oxford University Press 2012).
2 ibid Pohl 12.
3 Wherlé and Pohl (n 1).
4 ibid.

184 *Patrick Leblond and Sébastien Labrecque*

How do we explain these two trends? More specifically, what are the factors driving the rise in national security concerns when it comes to international investment policy? Moreover, why is it not all states that worry a great deal about national security in relation to international investment? Finally, how should governments best address national security risks in their international investment policies? These are the questions that this chapter addresses. To do so, it adopts a political economy perspective, trying to identify the domestic and international economic and political factors that determine international investment policies when it comes to national security concerns.

Surprisingly, perhaps, political economy scholars have devoted very little attention to the issue of national security and international investment. More broadly, national security has not been much of a concern for political economy scholars while economic policy has not been the focus of security studies, although economics as a discipline has made significant methodological contributions to the latter.[5] As Alexandra Homolar points out:

> Scholars tend to remain separated by an ontological divide between different theoretical traditions as well as different units of analysis, including an artificial division between foreign policy and security issues on the one hand, and domestic and economic issues on the other.[6]

According to her, international security scholars continue to ignore the general policy-making process by assuming that 'national security is insulated from societal pressures and parochial interests'.[7] As such, national security is 'high politics' and the state is treated as a unitary actor acting on the international level; there is little or no role for domestic politics.

This means that we do not have a ready-made analytical framework to answer the aforementioned questions. Hence, we need to begin by reviewing how international investment policies are made in general and what factors have traditionally influenced them. We can then examine the political economy dynamics of rising national security concerns with respect to international investment policy and see how they compare to policies focused on inward investment. However, a detailed and systematic analysis of the national security dynamics with respect to international investment policy is beyond this chapter's scope; we only offer herein a first attempt at understanding these dynamics.

---

5 Ethan B Kapstein, 'Two Dismal Sciences Are Better Than One – Economics and the Study of National Security' (2003) 27 *International Security* 158.
6 Alexandra Homolar, 'The political economy of national security' (2010) 17 *Review of International Political Economy* 411.
7 ibid.

2. The political economy of international investment policy

In this section, we briefly review the literature on the political economy of international investment policy in order to try to identify factors that might help us explain why we have observed an increase in international investment policies to address national security concerns in the last decade.[8] In their international investment policies, governments pursue a number of objectives. They may want to attract FDI in order to promote economic development and growth, because foreign firms bring capital, technology, and knowledge.[9] Instead, they may want to restrict inward FDI to protect domestic firms from foreign competition, which they fear could lead to less overall investment, innovation, and job creation. They may restrict only certain types of international investment that threaten their country's national security, political stability, environment, culture, or heritage. Societal interests such as business, labour, environmental, or human rights groups may similarly have divergent views on international investment policies, depending on the effects that international investments have on them or those they support. Ultimately, the outcome in terms of policy is a function of the interaction between government and society. As Walter and Sen point out: 'even if most FDI had net positive welfare benefits for recipient countries, governments might still restrict it if some powerful domestic groups oppose entry by [multinational corporations]'.[10]

How the interaction between government and society plays out in terms of international investment policy depends on a number of factors: how societal interests are organized (e.g. centralized or not, sector-based or cross-sectoral) and able to express their preferences; the country's economic structure and performance (e.g. developing or developed, positive or negative growth); the government's public finances (e.g. the level of indebtedness); the nature of political institutions (e.g. democratic or authoritarian, federal or centralized, presidential or parliamentary); the quality of governance institutions (e.g. the level of corruption, the strength of the rule of law, the public administration's effectiveness and capacity); pressure by foreign governments or international organizations (e.g. the International Monetary Fund). Discussing in detail how all these factors affect international investment policy-making is beyond this chapter's scope. In this section, we focus our discussion of the literature on the political economy of international investment on a government's general policy stance towards inward FDI (allow or restrict) and the influence that societal

---

8 For an excellent review of literature, see Sonal S Pandya, 'Political Economy of Foreign Direct Investment: Globalized Production in the 21st Century' (2016) 19 *Annual Review of Political Science* 455.

9 For a discussion of the benefits associated with FDI, see Eugene Beaulieu and Kelly O'Neill, 'The economics of foreign direct investment and international investment agreements', Chapter 5 in this volume.

10 Andrew Walter and Gautam Sen, *Analyzing the Global Political Economy* (Princeton University Press 2009) 190.

186   Patrick Leblond and Sébastien Labrecque

interests, especially business and labour, have on a given stance. It needs pointing out that this is also where the political science literature has focused most of its attention when it comes to studying the political economy of international investment policy-making.[11]

International investment has grown rapidly since the 1980s, owing to states adopting policies to attract FDI and removing barriers to such investments. According to Sonal Pandya, one important reason for the liberalization of FDI policies around the world is democratization in developing countries.[12] She shows that, on average, democracies have fewer ownership restrictions than non-democracies. She argues that policy-makers in democracies have to pay more attention to workers' preferences, which are generally favourable to investment by foreign multinational firms, because the latter increase the demand for labour and tend to pay higher wages than local firms. As such, FDI increases the returns to labour, which is a relatively abundant resource in developing countries (compared to capital). In line with Pandya's results, Pablo Pinto finds evidence that labour-based (i.e. left-wing) governments are generally open to international investment and, as a result, adopt policies that are friendly to foreign investors, which in turn means that they attract more foreign investment than countries where governments rely on the support of domestic business owners.[13] Like Pandya, he argues that this is because 'FDI inflows are likely to decrease the return to [local] capital and increase the return to labor'.[14] Similarly, Jensen, Biglaiser, Li, Malesky, Pinto, Pinto, and Staats find that left-wing governments encourage international investment in sectors where labour and capital complement each other because FDI leads to increased wages; however, they restrict inward FDI in sectors where labour and capital are substitutes for one another, because the entry of foreign capital ultimately leads to job losses (right-wing [pro-business] governments, for their part, support inward international investment in those particular sectors).[15] These findings generally support the expected preferences of workers in both traditional and new global-value-chain FDI models, as presented by Ari Van Assche in Chapter 2 in this volume.[16] Van Assche argues that in labour-abundant (i.e. developing)

---

11 For details on the political science approach to studying international investment policy-making, see J Anthony VanDuzer, Patrick Leblond, and Stephen Gelb, 'Introduction to international investment policy and rationale for an interdisciplinary approach', Chapter 1 in this volume.

12 Sonal S Pandya, *Trading Spaces: Foreign Direct Investment Regulation 1970–2000* (Cambridge University Press 2014).

13 Pablo Pinto, *Partisan Investment in the Global Economy: Why the Left Loves Foreign Direct Investment and FDI Loves the Left* (Cambridge University Press 2013).

14 ibid 249.

15 Nathan M Jensen, Glen Biglaiser, Quan Li, Edmund Malesky, Pablo M Pinto, Santiago M Pinto, and Joseph L Staats, *Politics and Foreign Direct Investment* (University of Michigan Press 2012) 92.

16 See Ari Van Assche, 'Trade and foreign direct investment in the 21st century', Chapter 2 in this volume.

countries unskilled workers should favour (or have no preference towards) FDI liberalization, because it leads to more jobs and higher wages as a result of increased demand for their labour, while skilled workers should oppose it, because FDI leads to more capital that substitutes for their labour.

The situation may be different in developed democracies, however. For instance, Erica Owen finds empirical evidence that greater union density and concentration in such countries is associated with restrictions on FDI inflows.[17] She argues that the more workers are unionized and the more concentrated unions are, then the more influential unions will be in influencing policies towards international investment. According to Owen, unions will generally oppose FDI in developed democracies because they see it as having a negative impact on labour, especially less skilled labour: 'As multinationals gain market share at the expense of less productive domestic firms, an increase in economic productivity can reduce the overall number of jobs in the economy'.[18] Her finding and argumentation are in accordance with Van Assche's argument that unskilled workers in skill-abundant countries in a global-value-chain context will oppose FDI liberalization.[19] On the other hand, Pinto finds that left-wing governments generally have a positive view of FDI in developing as well as developed countries; however, this support is conditional on the investment increasing jobs and wages in the aggregate.[20]

Like workers, domestic firms worry that inward FDI may lead to their displacement by more productive foreign firms through greater competition. In a world economy driven by global value chains, Van Assche argues that this should be the case for firms in labour-intensive sectors in skill-abundant countries as well as firms in skill-intensive sectors in labour-abundant countries. On the other hand, he argues that firms in both categories should support the liberalization of outward FDI so that they can offshore labour-intensive activities to labour-abundant countries or skill-intensive activities to skill-abundant countries. This is why he concludes that such firms have mixed views on FDI liberalization in their sectors: yes to outward FDI but no to inward FDI. As for firms in skill-intensive sectors located in skill-abundant countries as well as firms in labour-intensive sectors located in labour-abundant countries, Van Assche argues that they should be favourable to policies liberalizing foreign investment because it gives them the flexibility to reach new markets through investment rather than trade or to tap into foreign knowledge as well as it makes it easier for supply chain partners to invest close to them.[21]

---

17 Erica Owen, 'The Political Power of Organized Labor and the Politics of Foreign Direct Investment in Developed Democracies' (2015) 48 *Comparative Political Studies* 1746.
18 ibid 1747.
19 Van Assche (n 16).
20 Pinto (n 13).
21 Van Assche (n 16).

188   *Patrick Leblond and Sébastien Labrecque*

As with labour unions, size and ability to coordinate are important factors in determining domestic firms' influence on a country's international investment policies. For instance, using data from India's reforms in the 1990s, Anusha Chari and Nandini Gupta find that firms in concentrated industries, which tend to be state-owned, are more likely to succeed at preventing the entry of foreign firms than privately-owned firms in less concentrated sectors (i.e. where they are more firms of a smaller size).[22] However, domestic political institutions also play an important role in channelling domestic firms' interests vis-à-vis policies on incoming international investment. As Jonathan Crystal argues: 'to make sense of the demands firms will put forth, one must understand how economic preferences are translated into policy demands through the filter of domestic politics'.[23] Looking at the United States, he finds that oftentimes firms will only put forth international investment policy demands for which domestic political institutions exist to channel those demands, even if they have broader (and possibly conflicting) demands.[24] In other words, if there is no administrative, regulatory, or legislative support for a demand that a firm would like to make to protect or promote its interests, then it does not put the demand forward; it only makes the demands for which there is a good chance of success. And this success is based on some kind of institutional alignment with the firm's particular preferences. As such, domestic political institutions serve as a filtering mechanism for firms demands regarding international investment policy.

In some situations, state priorities, rather than societal pressures, play a more important role in determining international investment policies. For instance, after an economic crisis, a government may need to attract FDI in order to jumpstart the economy since there is little domestic capital available. This is what happened with Chinese investment in the EU in the aftermath of the 2007–2012 banking and debt crises.[25] Often, opening up to international investment is one of the conditions imposed by international financial institutions like the IMF for providing financial assistance to the government. When the government is highly indebted as a result of a crisis, FDI liberalization is also often accompanied by the privatization of state-owned enterprises in order to generate funds to pay back government debt.[26] Foreign

---

22 Anusha Chari and Nandini Gupta, 'Incumbents and protectionism: The political economy of foreign entry liberalization' (2008) 88 *Journal of Financial Economics* 633.

23 Jonathan Crystal, 'A New Kind of Competition: How American Producers Respond to Incoming Foreign Direct Investment' (1998) 42 *International Studies Quarterly* 513, 537.

24 Crystal says that domestic firms, most especially multinational ones, have three main (and conflicting) economic interests with respect to international investment policies: (1) they want policies that protect them against foreign competitors; (2) they want policies that limit possible restrictions on their own investment activity abroad; and (3) they want policies to address the perceived injuries they sustain from such restrictions on their own international investment abroad (ibid 536).

25 Sophie Meunier, '"Beggars can't be Choosers": The European Crisis and Chinese Direct Investment in the European Union' (2014) 36 *Journal of European Integration* 283.

26 Walter and Sen (n 10) 192–193.

firms are usually the ones that end up buying these SOEs, since they are the only ones with the means to do so.

If some state priorities favour FDI liberalization, others such as acquiring technology and know-how, protecting and promoting the national culture, monopolizing revenues, or ensuring national security can have the opposite effect, requiring limits or constraints on international investment. For example, governments may impose ownership restrictions in certain sectors that they deem strategic. What is considered strategic varies from country to country but typical reasons for determining that a sector is strategic are: national security, public order (or political control), food security, culture, history, and economic development. For these reasons, there are some sectors where governments have traditionally limited foreign investors' involvement: e.g. agriculture, aviation, banking, media, energy, telecommunications, and transportation.[27] One rationale put forward for restricting ownership in such sectors is that they are deemed crucial for a country's sovereignty and independence. A state does not want to depend on foreigners for the provision of basic food necessities or critical services such as air transport and telecommunications, which can be vital for a country's national security in times of conflict. The government wants to be able to feed its population, summon commercial aircraft for the war effort or be able to communicate with citizens across the country or with the rest of the world. Another rationale for restricting foreign ownership is to support a country's industrialization through technology and knowledge transfers. For example, China has required that foreign investors enter a particular sector only through a joint venture with a domestic partner, with the latter owning at least 50 per cent of the venture. The main purpose of such a requirement is technology and knowledge transfers to the local partner.[28]

In terms of international investment policy-making, the political economy literature has focused most of its attention on explaining why countries have become more open to inward FDI by looking at the preferences and organization capabilities of domestic firms and workers and their increasing ability to influence policy-makers as states democratized.[29] It has been much less concerned with explaining why policy restrictions remain or are put in place by governments. In fact, we know very little about the political economy factors that lead to such restrictions. The state remains a sort of black box where 'government' makes policy based on certain pre-determined national priorities.

---

27 David Conklin and Don Lecraw, *Foreign Ownership Restrictions and Liberalization Reforms* (Routledge 1997).

28 Steven X Si and Garry D Bruton, 'Knowledge transfer in international joint ventures in transitional economies: The China experience' (1999) 13 *Academy of Management Perspectives* 83; Kun Jiang, Wolfgang Keller, Larry D Qiu, and William Ridley, 'International Joint Ventures and Internal vs. External Technology Transfer: Evidence from China' (2018) National Bureau of Economic Research (NBER) Working Paper No 24,455 <www.nber.org/papers/w24455> accessed 18 June 2019.

29 Pandya (n 8).

190   Patrick Leblond and Sébastien Labrecque

Our analysis of international investment policies and national security concerns below confirms this state of affairs.

3. International investment policies and national security concerns

Before we address the reasons behind the rise in national security concerns for international investment policies and why there is some variation across countries, we must gain a better understanding of how international investment can threaten a state's national security and what policy measures governments can be put in place to mitigate such risks.

3.1 Defining national security

Though national security is relied upon to impose restrictions on international investment, it is not a well-defined concept.[30] At its most basic (and traditional) conceptualization, national security means 'protecting and ultimately securing the physical survival of the nation-state from external threats in the form of military attack'.[31] Such a definition can also have economic implications. As Raymond Vernon points out: 'Policymakers in the security field have always recognized that the economic performance of any country bore some relationship its threat as a military power'.[32] The richer a state is economically, the more it is able to afford the means to protect its sovereignty and its people. This is why Robert Gilpin, in his classic analysis of US MNEs, argues that '[i]n the long run [...] the economic and security interests of nation-states cannot really be separated'.[33] Vernon applies the same logic to technology, which he also sees as a security issue: a country's technological edge can translate into military advantage.[34] As a result, policy-makers want to make sure that technologies with military applications do not fall into the hands of foreign governments, especially ones that are not considered close allies. In fact, it is sufficient for a technology to have a potential military purpose for its access to be restricted by governments.

Anything that can undermine a country's military capabilities and the productive capacity of its economy can be considered a threat to national security. Clodfelter and Guerrero identify the following national security threats:

---

30 David A Baldwin, 'The concept of security' (1997) 23 *Review of International Studies* 5; Brian C Schmidt, 'The primacy of national security', in Steve Smith, Amelia Hadfield, and Tim Dunne (eds) *Foreign Policy: Theories, Actors, Cases* (Oxford University Press 2008).

31 ibid Schmidt 156.

32 Raymond Vernon, *In the Hurricane's Eye: The Troubled Prospects of Multinational Enterprises* (Harvard University Press 1998) 46.

33 Robert Gilpin, *U.S. Power and the Multinational Corporation: The Political Economy of Foreign Direct Investment* (Basic Books 1975) 103.

34 Vernon (n 32) 47.

military intelligence, espionage, sabotage of critical facilities, infiltration by organized crime or terrorist groups, and unauthorized access to sensitive data and information.[35] Another important national security threat mentioned by the authors is the possible denial of access to resources deemed critical for a country's economic performance and military capability (e.g. food, energy, minerals, technology, infrastructure, and data). Finally, in line with Vernon, Clodfelter and Guerrero note that governments worry about unauthorized transfers of technology to foreign firms and governments. This is why, according to the authors, national security concerns 'are more pronounced when FDI comes from entities controlled by foreign governments'.[36]

3.2 International investment policies to address national security concerns

To address the above-mentioned threats to national security arising from international investment, governments rely on a number of policy instruments. Clodfelter and Guerrero group these instruments into four non-mutually-exclusive approaches: land restrictions, industry-specific restrictions, national security-focused review, and comprehensive foreign investment review.[37] Land restrictions consist of limits or outright prohibitions on the purchase of real estate by foreign investors near territorial borders or near facilities deemed critical for national security. Industry-specific restrictions either prohibit or require approval by government of foreign investments in designated industrial sectors. Limits on foreign ownership in specific sectors also fall into this category. In the previous section, we identified a number of economic sectors that are often deemed 'strategic' by governments. Another approach to managing national security risks is to target specific transactions rather than industries. In this approach, 'designated governmental agencies review transactions with national security implications and may prohibit problematic transactions'.[38] The fourth and final approach is a comprehensive review process for foreign investment, whereby transactions above certain thresholds – which can vary depending on the industry, the investor's country of origin, or the type of investor (e.g. privately-owned or state-owned) – are subject to review and approval by a designated government agency.

The United States is a prime example of the targeted-transaction approach. The Committee on Foreign Investment in the United States (CFIUS) is an inter-agency body, chaired by the Department of the Treasury, responsible for reviewing foreign investments in US businesses on national security grounds and

---

35 Clodfelter and Guerrero (n 1) 174.
36 ibid.
37 ibid 175. The authors also provide at the end of their chapter an annex that indicates for several countries the policy measures in place to regulate international investment in order to address national security.
38 ibid 178.

192   *Patrick Leblond and Sébastien Labrecque*

advising the president on whether to approve or block (or unwind) the transaction.[39] Congress, through the Exon-Florio Amendment to the Defense Production Act of 1950, has granted the President of the United States the 'authority to prohibit or unwind transactions with national security implications where a foreign investor has or would gain control of a U.S. company'.[40] Decisions by the president are not subject to review by the courts. In the case where a transaction presents a national security threat that cannot be mitigated,[41] CFIUS would recommend that it be blocked (or unwound if it has already taken place).[42] In order to avoid a comprehensive international investment review regime (see below), the CFIUS process is based on voluntary filings by foreign investors contemplating a transaction; it is not mandatory.[43] The president has the authority to unwind a transaction not reviewed by CFIUS at any time on the grounds of national security; there is no statute of limitations.[44] All transactions are analysed on a case-by-case basis. Government ownership or control of the foreign investor is only one of the factors that CFIUS considers in its analysis.[45] CFIUS legislation and regulation define 'control' in a broad manner: as 'the ability of a foreign person to determine, direct, cause, reach, or decide "important matters" of U.S. businesses'.[46]

Australia, Canada, and China are good examples of a comprehensive approval regime for international investment.[47] China, for instance, requires that the government – under the aegis of the Ministry of Commerce and the National Development and Reform Commission – approves all inward FDI.[48] If assets owned by the state are involved, then the State-owned Assets Supervision and Administration Commission also needs to give its assent for a transaction to go

---

39 Alan P Larson and David M Marchick, 'Foreign Investment and National Security: Getting the Balance Right' (2006) Council on Foreign Relations CSR No 18 <https://cfrd8-files.cfr.org/sites/default/files/pdf/2006/07/cfiusreport.pdf> accessed 21 June 2019; Alan P Larson, David N Fagan, Alexander A Berengaut, and Mark E Plotkin, 'Lessons from CFIUS for National Security Reviews on Foreign Investment' in Karl P Sauvant, Lisa E Sachs, and Wouter P F Schmit Jongbloed (eds), *Sovereign Investment: Concerns and Policy Reactions Sovereign Investment: Concerns and Policy Reactions* (Oxford University Press 2012).

40 Clodfelter and Guerrero (n 1) 178.

41 National Security Agreements between the foreign investor and CFIUS agencies serve to mitigate national security concerns associated with a particular transaction. In such agreements, the foreign investor undertakes specific security commitments, including penalties for non-compliance. See Larson and Marchick (n 39) 12.

42 According to Larson and Marchick (n 39) 9, the law does not define the term 'national security'; it leaves it to the president to define what it is.

43 ibid 11.

44 ibid 9.

45 Larson, Fagan, Berengaut, and Plotkin (n 39) 427.

46 ibid 430.

47 For details on the Australian regime, see Matthew Durban, 'FDI policy advocacy and investor targeting', Chapter 7 in this volume.

48 Clodfelter and Guerrero (n 1) 179.

National security and investment **193**

forward. In order to provide potential foreign investors with information on the government's intent, the Foreign Investment Industrial Guidelines divide industrial sectors into three categories: sectors where investment is encouraged, sectors where investment is restricted, and sectors where investment is prohibited.[49] The Chinese government revises these guidelines on a regular basis.

Under Canada's regime, all international investments above certain value thresholds are subject to review by the federal government under the Investment Canada Act. The decision for an investment to be approved or blocked rests ultimately with the Minister of Innovation, Science and Economic Development (former Minister of Industry) based on the test of 'net benefit to Canada'. In March 2009, the federal government modified the Act to officially include a special review process for foreign investments (of any value [so no thresholds apply]) that might threaten Canada's national security, with the ultimate decision resting with the cabinet rather than the minister.[50] One year before, the Minister of Industry rejected the sale of MacDonald, Dettwiler and Associates' space division to US-based Alliant Techsystems Inc. on the grounds that he was not satisfied that the transaction represented a net benefit for Canada.[51] It was the first time since the investment review process was introduced in 1985 that the government blocked the acquisition of a Canadian business by a foreign investor. As a result of the debate surrounding this proposed transaction and the federal government's decision,

> [t]here was a clear and pressing need to define and delimit, as fully as possible, what is meant by 'national security' and how any regulations will be interpreted and implemented, otherwise it would become too easy for the concept of national security to trump everything else.[52]

For this reason, the Government of Canada developed guidelines for 'assessing proposed or implemented investments under the national security provisions of

---

49 ibid.

50 For details on this process, see J Anthony VanDuzer, 'Mixed Signals: What Recent Developments Tell Us about Canadian Foreign Investment Policy' (2010) 10 *Asper Review of International Business and Trade Law* 247, at 259.

51 The division was the maker of a high-tech satellite known as the Radarsat 2, which had recently been launched. The Government of Canada had contributed more than C$400 million to Radarsat 2's development. In exchange, it had access to its images for surveillance over the Arctic. The fear was that the US government could instruct Alliant to block the transmission of images to Canadian authorities. David Ljunggren, 'Canada blocks sale of MDA satellite unit to U.S.' *Reuters* (10 April 2008) <https://ca.reuters.com/article/businessnews/idcan1038419320080410> accessed 9 June 2019.

52 A Edward Safarian, 'The Canadian Policy Response to Sovereign Direct Investment' in Karl P Sauvant, Lisa E Sachs, and Wouter P F Schmit Jongbloed (eds), *Sovereign Investment: Concerns and Policy Reactions Sovereign Investment: Concerns and Policy Reactions* (Oxford University Press 2012) 445.

194   *Patrick Leblond and Sébastien Labrecque*

the Act'.[53] The factors that may be considered in the review are the potential effects of the investment: on Canada's defence capabilities and interests; on the transfer of sensitive technology or know-how outside of Canada; on the security of Canada's critical infrastructure; on the supply of critical goods and services to Canadians or the Government of Canada; to enable foreign surveillance or espionage; to hinder current or future intelligence or law enforcement operations; on Canada's international interests, including foreign relationships; to involve or facilitate the activities of illicit actors, such as terrorists, terrorist organizations or organized crime. On these bases, in addition to refusing the investment, the cabinet can authorize the investment on the condition that the foreign investor 'give any written undertakings considered necessary' or 'implement specified terms and conditions' such as requiring 'the investor to divest control of the Canadian business or its investments in an entity'.[54] Even if the goal with these guidelines is to provide foreign investors with some degree of transparency and predictability when it comes to the special national security review process and its outcome, '[n]ational security assessments do not lend themselves to mechanical solutions'; '[u]ncertainty is built into the very concept of national security which is, by its very nature, shrouded in secrecy'.[55]

The danger with using national security as a reason for blocking foreign investment or for imposing other restrictions, such as limits on foreign ownership, is that it can be abused. The main concern is that national security can be used as a justification for what is in reality protectionism in pursuit of economic nationalism. For example, domestic firms can pressure the government to limit competition from abroad on the basis that foreign firms could undermine the country's national security. As a result, they may be able to obtain or maintain a dominant position (through oligopoly or even monopoly) in their domestic market. As indicated above, this type of abuse was a clear concern in the Canadian context.[56]

To try to minimize such risk of abuse, Theodore Moran proposes an analytical framework for differentiating between genuine national security threats and implausible ones.[57] He identifies three types of national security threat from international investment. The first type ('Threat I') is

> that the proposed acquisition would make the country where the acquired firm is located dependent upon a foreign-controlled supplier of goods or

---

53 Government of Canada, 'Guidelines on the National Security Review of Investments' <www.ic.gc.ca/eic/site/ica-lic.nsf/eng/lk81190.html> accessed 10 June 2019.
54 ibid.
55 Clodfelter and Guerrero (n 1) 186.
56 For more details, see Safarian (n 52) 446.
57 Theodore H Moran, 'Foreign Acquisitions and National Security: What Are Genuine Threats? What Are Implausible Worries?' in Zdenek Drabek and Petros C Mavroidis (eds), *Regulation of Foreign Investment: Challenges to International Harmonization* (World Scientific Publishing 2013).

services crucial to the functioning of that economy (including, but not exclusively, the functioning of that country's defence industrial base) who [sic] might delay, deny, or place conditions upon provision of those goods or services.[58]

The second category of threat ('Threat II') concerns the transfer of technology or expertise to a foreign-controlled investor or its home-state government that could be used to harm the host state. The third and final type of national security threat ('Threat III') resulting from a foreign investment relates to the 'insertion of some potential capability for infiltration, surveillance, or sabotage – via human agent, or non-human agent – into the provision of goods or services crucial to the functioning of that economy'.[59] According to Moran, international investments that raise national security concerns should be assessed for all three types of threat.

3.3 What is driving the rise in national security concerns for international investment policies?

Originally, national security concerns associated with international investment were mostly focused on the foreign ownership of land near borders and manufacturing capabilities in the defence industry.[60] Following the 9/11 attacks in the United States, authorities became particularly concerned with protecting critical infrastructure (e.g. telecommunications network, electricity generation and distribution, transportation networks, water supply).[61] Such national security concerns also resulted from the liberalization of industrial sectors related to critical infrastructure in many countries in the 1990s, including the privatization of state-owned companies operating in them, which made international investment possible.

According to Larson and Marchick, a shift in public perceptions towards foreign investment took place in the United States after 9/11:

> Unease about foreign acquisitions today undoubtedly stems in part from the fact that some companies now considering acquisitions in the United States come from China, the Middle East, and other countries [...] [that] the public may perceive [...] as unsympathetic to U.S. interests.[62]

Kang argues that the response of elected officials in Congress to such shifts in public perception as a result of surges in FDI helps explain the change 'from

---

58 ibid 372.
59 ibid 373.
60 Pohl (n 1) 16; Larson and Marchick (n 39) 19.
61 ibid.
62 Larson and Marchick (n 39) 20.

196　*Patrick Leblond and Sébastien Labrecque*

one of benign neglect to one of discretionary restriction in some sectors of the economy' in the United States between the 1970s and 1990s.[63]

In addition, international investments from these countries often come from state-owned enterprises or sovereign wealth funds, which raises national security concerns if home-government influence over the foreign investor leads to decisions made for that government's foreign or defence policy purposes rather than commercial considerations.[64] As a result, in the last decade or so, many governments have introduced specific provisions to deal with SOEs and SWFs in their international investment screening mechanisms.[65] However, in line with Moran's above-mentioned decision framework, Larson and Marchick point out that 'it is important to separate ownership from control, and equally important to determine, on a case-by-case basis, whether government ownership of [...] assets will create real national security issues'.[66] This is because privately-owned firms can also be influenced by the government and SOEs may operate like commercial enterprises.[67]

In more recent years, robotic and digital technologies, which often have potential dual-use purposes (i.e. civilian and military), as well as data-driven network platforms have raised national security concerns.[68] For example, the acquisition of German robotics firm Kuka by China's Midea in 2016 sent alarm bells ringing in Germany and Europe about foreign investors in high-technology sectors, especially firms from countries such as China where there is no such reciprocity in terms of openness to international investment.[69] As

---

63 C S Eliot Kang, 'U.S. politics and greater regulation of inward foreign direct investment' (1997) 51 *International Organization* 301; for more recent analyses of FDI dynamics in the United States and public perceptions of Chinese investment, see Dustin Tingley, Christopher Xu, Adam S Chilton, and Helen V Milner, 'The Political Economy of Inward FDI: Opposition to Chinese Mergers and Acquisitions' (2015) 8 *The Chinese Journal of International Politics* 27; Adam S Chilton, Helen V Milner, and Dustin Tingley, 'Reciprocity and Public Opposition to Foreign Direct Investment' (2017) *British Journal of Political Science* 1.

64 For a discussion of the international investment concerns presented by SOEs and SWFs, see Steven Globerman, Phillip Hensyel, and Daniel Shapiro, 'State-owned enterprises and sovereign wealth funds: An economic assessment', Chapter 4 in this volume.

65 Frédéric Wherlé and Hans Christiansen, 'State-owned enterprises, international investment and national security: The way forward' (2017) Directorate for Financial and Enterprises Affairs, Organisation for Economic Cooperation and Development <https://oecdonthelevel.com/2017/10/04/state-owned-enterprises-international-investment-and-national-security-the-way-forward/> accessed 13 June 2019.

66 Larson and Marchick (n 39) 21.

67 Globerman, Hensyel, and Shapiro (n 64).

68 Pohl (n 1) 16.

69 Investments by Chinese firms in the EU were already causing controversy but had not yet led to any new policies on the part of the EU or Member State governments. See Françoise Nicolas, 'China's direct investment in the European Union: challenges and policy responses' (2014) 7 *China Economic Journal* 103; Sophie Meunier, 'A Faustian bargain or just a good bargain? Chinese foreign direct investment and politics in Europe' (2014) 12 *Asia Europe Journal* 143.

a result, the German government adopted more restrictive policies on international investment.[70] Following pressure from France, Germany, and Italy, the EU adopted in March 2019 a supranational framework for screening international investment with a particular focus on threats to national security and public order.[71] Another example of new digital technologies affecting national security concerns for international investment is CFIUS's recent requirement that the Chinese owner of Grindr, a popular dating application for homosexuals, relinquish its ownership of the app by 30 June 2020, in addition to prohibiting the transmission of sensitive information on US citizens to entities located in China.[72]

Given that advanced digital technologies and data-driven applications are often developed and produced by small firms[73] and early-stage investment has become much more international in the last decade,[74] CFIUS rules were modified in late 2018 to reflect such changes and give the authorities extended powers to scrutinize venture capital transactions for national security risks. As a result, high technology-related investments from China decreased dramatically in 2019, following rapid growth since 2014.[75]

3.4 Finding the right balance

National security risks represent a dilemma for policy-makers when it comes to international investment policies. On the one hand, they want the economic benefits associated with international investment. This means removing restrictions on inward foreign direct investment. This is why there has been significant liberalization of FDI regimes since the late 1980s. On the other hand, policy-makers want to mitigate national security risks. In order to do so, they must adopt policy measures that limit international investment, thereby losing the potential economic benefits associated with such investment.

---

70 Guy Chazan, 'Germany expands powers to block takeovers' *Financial Times* (12 July 2017) <www.ft.com/content/5087c106-66fc-11e7-9a66-93fb352ba1fe> accessed 17 June 2019.

71 Regulation (EU) 2019/452 of the European Parliament and of the Council of 19 March 2018 establishing a framework for the screening of foreign direct investment into the Union [2019] OJ L71 I/1.

72 David McLaughlin and Linly Lin, 'Grindr's Chinese Owner to Sell App by 2020' *Bloomberg* (13 May 2019) <www.bloomberg.com/news/articles/2019-05-13/grindr-s-chinese-owner-to-sell-app-by-2020-on-u-s-concerns> accessed 13 June 2019.

73 Pohl (n 1) 17.

74 Richard T Harrison, 'The internationalisation of business angel investment activity: a review and research agenda' (2016) 19 *Venture Capital: An International Journal of Entrepreneurial Finance* 119; David Devigne, Sophie Manigart, Tom Vanaker, and Klaus Mulier, 'Venture Capital Internationalization: Synthesis and Future Research Directions' (2018) 32 *Journal of Economic Surveys* 1414.

75 Heather Somerville, 'Chinese tech investors flee Silicon Valley as Trump tightens scrutiny' *Reuters* (7 January 2019) <www.reuters.com/article/us-venture-china-regulation-insight/chinese-tech-investors-flee-silicon-valley-as-trump-tightens-scrutiny-iduskcn1p10cb> accessed 13 June 2019.

198   *Patrick Leblond and Sébastien Labrecque*

According to Moran, there is no way to resolve this dilemma. The challenge is to find the right balance, depending on a country's priorities. He argues, however, that it is easier to achieve this balance between openness to international investment and restrictions to protect national security if the screening process allows governments to assess the plausibility of threats in a systematic way by focusing on particular transactions rather than sectors or other broad categories.[76]

As mentioned in the introduction to this chapter, there appears to be a polarization between countries when it comes to putting in place mechanisms to screen international investment for national security risks. However, there is no obvious explanation for this divergence. According to Joachim Pohl:

> Neither the size of the economy, level of development, ratio of FDI to GDP, FDI in total foreign assets, or imitation effects offer a stringent explanation for why countries make such different assessment of whether acquisition- or ownership-related policies are warranted to manage essential security risks.[77]

In some instances, it appears that international investment policies related to national security have been introduced following particular events or transactions,[78] like in the cases of Canada and Germany discussed above. In some countries, fiscal stress and the resulting desire to attract international investment to acquire privatized firms as well as boost economic growth explain governments' reticence to introduce such policies.[79] For instance, as a result of the euro-area sovereign debt crisis, several EU member-state governments whose economies and public finances were suffering encouraged Chinese investments by adopting supportive international investment policies.[80] In poorer, less-developed countries, the egregious need for infrastructure built by foreign capital and expertise is often deemed more important than national security concerns about foreign control over critical infrastructure.[81] The same logic also applies to access to new technologies.[82] As a result, governments in

---

76 Moran (n 57).

77 Pohl (n 1) 13.

78 ibid 14.

79 ibid.

80 Meunier (n 25).

81 A good example is China's Belt and Road Initiative, which has nevertheless begun to raise national security concerns in some recipient countries. See Henrik Hallgren and Richard Ghiasy, 'Security and Economy on the Belt and Road; Three Case Studies' (2017) SIPRI Insights on Peace and Security No 2017/4 <www.sipri.org/sites/default/files/2017-12/sipriinsights1712.pdf> accessed 11 July 2019;
Daniel Kliman, Rush Doshi, Kristine Lee, and Zack Cooper, 'Grading China's Belt and Road' (2019) Centre for New American Security <https://s3.amazonaws.com/files.cnas.org/cnas+report_china+belt+and+road_final.pdf> accessed 11 July 2019.

82 e.g. W Gyude Moore, 'African countries should stay loyal to China's troubled Huawei – regardless of Trump' *Quartz* (27 May 2019) <https://qz.com/africa/1629078/africa-will-stay-loyal-to-chinas-huawei-regardless-of-trump/> accessed 19 June 2019.

National security and investment 199

these countries may overlook national security risks in their international investment policies so as to attract more foreign investment to support their country's economic development. However, more research is required to determine where, when, and for what reasons it happens.

4. Conclusion

Governments throughout the world have become increasingly preoccupied with the impact that international investment may have on their country's national security. This chapter examines such a trend and tries to identify some of the key factors driving it by adopting a political economy perspective, hoping to build on the existing political economy literature analysing the international investment policy-making process. It is a small, first step in the exploration of the political economy of national security and international investment policy, a topic that political economy and international security scholars have neglected.

Unlike more general policies dealing with openness to international investment, which are mainly influenced by domestic organized business and labour interests, it appears that governments, elected officials, and the national security apparatus are responding to the larger public interest (often based in popular concerns) when it comes to national security preoccupations about international investment as they relate to critical infrastructure and advanced digital and robotic technologies. Firms and investors are generally more supportive of fewer restrictions on international investment, so it is unlikely that they would favour greater restrictions on international investment for national security reasons; if they push for protectionism, it will be with respect to particular transactions, not generally-applicable national security policies.

From the limited analysis conducted in this chapter, it is fair to say that we cannot come to any firm conclusion with regards to the political economy dynamics driving international investment policy with respect to national security concerns; doing so is beyond this chapter's scope. As a result, we need more research on the issue of national security and international investment policy. There is a fertile ground for future research. In particular, scholars should take a look at individual country cases to open up the black box of the state with the goal of more clearly understanding the combination of political and economic factors that determine not only national security concerns but also the actual international investment policies that result.

10 International investment agreements

Lukas Vanhonnaeker

1. Introduction

International investment law is constantly evolving. Its constitutive texts, international investment agreements (IIAs), change to adapt to new economic realities and to take into account the concerns that are voiced about the regime. International investment law, whose 'modern' origins are generally traced back to the conclusion of the first bilateral investment treaty (BIT) in 1959 between Germany and Pakistan, is currently constituted by a web of BITs and investment chapters in free trade agreements (FTAs).[1] These agreements are intended to satisfy the needs of developing and developed countries, which seek to encourage foreign direct investment (FDI) by offering international investors more certainty and predictability that their investments would be protected.

The substantive provisions found in IIAs generally include definitions of 'investor' and 'investment' that delimit the scope of application of these agreements. With respect to standards of protection provisions, protection against non-discrimination through national treatment, and most-favoured-nation clauses is a key element of investment agreements, together with the guarantees of fair and equitable treatment and full protection and security. In addition, IIAs generally provide for the protection of foreign investors and investments against unlawful expropriation, ensure that foreign investors are able to transfer funds into and out of the host state, and, in some instances, prohibit imposing performance requirements on investors.

The international investment regime has become the target of stringent criticisms for the imbalances IIAs create. Traditionally, IIAs only create state obligations to protect foreign investors. Experience with investor–state dispute settlement (ISDS) has shown that focusing exclusively on the protection of investors leads to the disregard of states' interests.[2] Especially

---

1 By the end of 2017, there were a total of 3,322 IIAs: 2,946 bilateral investment treaties and 376 other treaties with investment provisions (UNCTAD, *World Investment Report 2018: Investment and New Industrial Policies* (United Nations 2018) 88). Not all of these are in force.
2 For a discussion of ISDS, see J Anthony VanDuzer and Patrick Dumberry, 'Investor–state dispute settlement', Chapter 11 in this volume.

as developed countries increasingly appeared on the receiving end of investment claims based on IIAs, a change in the drafting of IIAs became apparent. Standards of protection that embodied enhanced precision and new elements such as exceptions to preserve host-state policy-making flexibility began to appear.

This chapter provides an overview of IIAs' substantive content and its evolution. It also provides an overview of recent trends in investment treaty-making by analysing how some of the concerns about the regime are taken into account by policy-makers and treaty-drafters through the inclusion of new provisions in IIAs.

2. The twofold objective of international investment agreements

International investment law finds its roots in customary international law and refers to the legal framework that regulates FDI.[3] IIAs were concluded to provide a more comprehensive framework for the protection of investors in light of the 'uncertainties and inadequacies of the customary international law of state responsibility for injuries to aliens and their property'.[4] Accordingly, although IIAs 'treatified' international investment law and strengthened customary rules of international law in this regard, they did not create it.

A generalized process of globalization was triggered by, among other factors, the end of the Napoleonic War in 1815 resulting in a period of peace within Europe, the industrial revolution, and the rise of liberal economic theory.[5] This process led to a substantial increase in FDI flows, which were partly 'stimulated by the need for capital to build infrastructure in the New World'.[6] The need to regulate such operations in order to provide legal certainty to investors increasingly became dire, which led first to Freedom of Commerce and Navigation (FCN) treaties and, later on, to IIAs.

Capital-exporting states started concluding IIAs in order to protect their investors operating abroad. Capital-importing states agreed to enter into such agreements on the 'assumption that they promote investment from investor countries to investor-receiving countries'[7] and with the view, which is often explicitly expressed in IIAs' title or preamble, that the protection of foreign investors in these instruments would

---

3 For a discussion of this legal framework, see Krista Nadakavukaren Schefer, 'Actors, institutions, and policy in host countries', Chapter 3 in this volume.

4 Andrew Newcombe and Lluís Paradell, *Law and Practice of Investment Treaties: Standards of Treatment* (Kluwer Law International 2009) 41.

5 Kenneth J Vandevelde, *Bilateral Investment Treaties: History, Policy, and Interpretation* (Oxford University Press 2010) 20.

6 ibid 26.

7 Surya P Subedi, *International Investment Law: Reconciling Policy and Principle* (3rd edn, Hart Publishing 2016) 110.

202 *Lukas Vanhonnaeker*

lead to 'the promotion of foreign investment, on the one hand, and economic growth and development, on the other'.[8]

Accordingly, IIAs' main goal, especially for capital-exporting countries, is to provide a safe and stable investment climate characterized by a strengthening of the rule of law, which is understood as a 'concept of channelling and restricting public power'.[9] In particular, IIAs provide standards of protection for foreign investors that mitigate political and legal risks. One such risk is known as the 'obsolescing bargain': host-country governments are increasingly likely to interfere in foreign-owned investment over time because the investor's power vis-à-vis the government decreases as it accumulates fixed assets in the country (i.e. it becomes costlier to leave with time).[10] Standards of protection in IIAs enhance certainty and predictability and ultimately 'shape the incentives of key economic actors in society; in particular, they influence investments in physical and human capital and technology, and the organization of production'.[11] However, the twofold objective of protecting investors and generating inward investment is complemented by the objective of economic development for host states. More recently, investment treaty practice has added a new emphasis: investments must also contribute to the sustainable development of the host state. This new focus is explored in Section 5.

Another guarantee provided to foreign investors in IIAs is a dispute-settlement mechanism: investor–state arbitration.[12] This mechanism guarantees to foreign investors that not only do they benefit from the substantive standards of protection provided in IIAs but, in case of a breach of obligation(s) by a host state, they will be able to enforce those protections. This is especially important when the investment operation at issue takes place in a host state whose legal regime is characterized by weak enforcement of the rule of law and where domestic courts are not considered to be reliable in terms of independence and impartiality, particularly in disputes opposing a foreign investor to the host state. Competence and capacity of host-country institutions to provide timely and effective relief may also be concerns.

The following sections take a closer look at IIAs' scope of application and traditional standards of protection.

---

8 Marc Jacob and Stephan W Schill, 'Fair and Equitable Treatment: Content, Practice, Method' in Marc Bungenberg, Jörn Griebel, Stephan Hobe, and August Reinisch (eds), *International Investment Law* (C.H. BECK – Hart – Nomos 2015) 754, para 146. For a discussion of the relation between IIAs, FDI flows, and economic growth, see Eugene Beaulieu and Kelly O'Neill, 'The economics of foreign direct investment and international investment agreements', Chapter 5 in this volume.

9 ibid 754, para 147.

10 Noah Rubins and N Stephan Kinsella, *International Investment, Political Risk and Dispute Resolution: A Practitioner's Guide* (Oceana Publications 2005) 5.

11 Daron Acemoglu, Simon Johnson, and James Robinson, 'Institutions as the Fundamental Cause of Long-Run Growth' in Philippe Aghion and Steven N Durlauf (eds), *Handbook of Economic Growth* (Vol IA, North-Holland 2005) 389.

12 VanDuzer and Dumberry (n 2).

3. The scope of protection of international investment agreements

The protections in an IIA are only available to foreign 'investors' that are undertaking commercial operations that qualify as 'investments', as defined in the IIA. Accordingly, the structure of most IIAs is largely similar and includes, following the preamble, a definitions provision that delimits their scope of application. Other more specific provisions that aim at delimiting IIAs' scope of application are pre-establishment clauses, which address the temporal scope of application of such agreements, and so-called 'umbrella clauses', which extend the material scope of IIAs.

3.1 Definitions of 'investor' and 'investment'

Definitions provisions define, among other terms, who qualifies as an 'investor' and what is an 'investment'.

3.1.1 Definitions of 'investor'

Investors generally qualify as such under an IIA when they are a legal or physical person of one of the contracting states to the IIA who has made, or is making, an investment in the territory of the other (or one of the other) contracting state(s). Definitions of 'investor' are generally drafted broadly. The US Model BIT, for example, defines 'investor of a Party' as a

> Party or state enterprise thereof, or a national or an enterprise of a Party, that attempts to make, is making, or has made an investment in the territory of the other Party; provided, however, that a natural person who is a dual national shall be deemed to be exclusively a national of the State of his or her dominant and effective nationality.[13]

Investors are eligible for protection if they have the nationality of a state party to the IIA. The way in which the investor's nationality is determined thus has important policy implications for host states and critical impacts on the scope of application of the IIA.

Physical – or natural – persons are generally deemed to have the nationality of a state party if the law of that state so provides. Some IIAs extend their scope of application to investors who are not only nationals (citizens) of a state but also residents of that state. The most controversial question that arises with respect to the nationality of natural persons consists in assessing, for the IIA's purpose, the nationality of people who are citizens of both the home and host states. This

---

13 Treaty between the Government of the United States of America and the Government of [Country] concerning the encouragement and reciprocal protection of investment, 2012, art 1.

204   *Lukas Vanhonnaeker*

question, which is generally not addressed by IIAs, has been analysed in investment arbitration cases with tribunals generally finding that dual nationality is not a bar to the application of an investment treaty if no explicit provision excludes dual nationals from the IIA's scope.

The question of nationality is more important and controversial with respect to legal entities. Three main approaches exist to determine the nationality of legal persons; a legal person has the nationality of the country (i) where it is organized or incorporated, (ii) where it has its headquarters, or (iii) in which the nationals who own or control it are located. These three approaches have a varying degree of certainty when it comes to the determination of the legal person's nationality. It is easier to identify the nationality of a legal person on the basis of the incorporation criterion compared to the country-of-ownership criterion, especially for companies whose shares are traded on stock exchanges.

Via corporate restructuring (or 'nationality planning'), it is possible to change the nationality of the investor, especially in corporate groups with subsidiaries, by channelling the investment through a company incorporated in a country that has an IIA with the host state. This practice, known as 'treaty shopping', is not necessarily illegitimate but can be abusive if undertaken after a dispute has arisen or if a dispute is foreseeable. In addition, definitions of 'investor' that use permissive language solely referring to the investor's country of incorporation can create uncertainty for the host state, which is unable to foresee who can qualify as an investor for a given investment.

Accordingly, although broad and flexible definitions of 'investor' can benefit commercial actors, giving them more leeway to structure their investment operation in order to benefit from the most protective IIA, more precise language in IIAs increases certainty and limits treaty shopping. This is sometimes done through more precise definitions of 'investor' and through so-called 'denial of benefits' provisions, which allow host states to deny investors the benefits of the treaty when they do not have substantial business activities in the other state-party's territory or other strong links to the other state-party.[14]

3.1.2 Definitions of 'investment'

Definitions of 'investment' are also broadly drafted. Indeed, a substantial number of IIAs include 'every kind of asset'[15] or, circularly, provide for open-ended coverage of 'every kind of investment'.[16] Such definitions are often

---

14 Denial of benefits can also take place under some treaties when the country in which the investment's ultimate controller resides does not have normal economic relations with the host country, perhaps because the host country imposes economic sanctions on that country.

15 e.g. Agreement between the Government of the United Kingdom of Great Britain and Northern Ireland and the Government of the Republic of Ecuador for the promotion and protection of investments, signed 10 May 1994, entered into force 24 August 1995, art 1.

16 e.g. Agreement on encouragement and reciprocal protection of investments between the Kingdom of the Netherlands and the Federative Republic of Brazil, signed 25 November 1998, not yet entered into force, art 1(a).

International investment agreements 205

followed by a non-exhaustive list of assets in order to illustrate the flexible definition of 'investment'. An example of such an open-ended definition can be found in the 2012 US Model BIT:

> 'investment' means every asset that an investor owns or controls, directly or indirectly, that has the characteristics of an investment, including such characteristics as the commitment of capital or other resources, the expectation of gain or profit, or the assumption of risk. *Forms that an investment may take include*:
>
> (a) an enterprise;
> (b) shares, stock, and other forms of equity participation in an enterprise;
> (c) bonds, debentures, other debt instruments, and loans;
> (d) futures, options, and other derivatives;
> (e) turnkey, construction, management, production, concession, revenue-sharing, and other similar contracts;
> (f) intellectual property rights;
> (g) licences, authorizations, permits, and similar rights conferred pursuant to domestic law; and
> (h) other tangible or intangible, movable or immovable property, and related property rights, such as leases, mortgages, liens, and pledges.[17]

The dominant approach to the definition of 'investment' consists of an 'asset-based' approach that includes everything of economic value, as illustrated by the 2012 US Model BIT above. Some IIAs, however, provide an exhaustive list of assets or interests in enterprises that qualify as 'investments'.[18] Nevertheless, even those IIAs that provide a closed-list definition of 'investment' generally include 'every conceivable form of investment as those included in the open-ended list definitions'.[19]

The breadth of investment definitions illustrates the policy pursued by states and treaty-makers. By encompassing under the scope of their treaties as many economic operations as possible and extending the protections of such instruments to a wide range of commercial actors, host states signal a welcoming climate for FDI. This is especially the case when IIAs include 'indirectly controlled investments' under the definition of 'investment', thus extending treaty protections to all sorts of shareholders such as parent companies, as well as intermediate, and holding companies. For investors, such definitions have the advantage of providing a broad scope of protection.

---

17 2012 US Model BIT (n 13) art 1 [footnotes omitted, emphasis added].
18 e.g. the definition of 'investment' provided in the 2004 Canadian Model Foreign Investment Promotion and Protection Agreement (FIPA) (Agreement between Canada and _____ for the promotion and protection of investments, 2004, art 1).
19 Subedi (n 7) 82.

206 Lukas Vanhonnaeker

To increase certainty and limit IIAs' scope to the protection of investments that states actually seek to attract, mechanisms exist to narrow the definition of the term 'investment' and include the use of exclusions. Portfolio investments as well as certain loans and debt securities, for example, are frequently excluded from the definition of investment.[20] Some definitions limit the notion of 'investment' to operations made 'in accordance with the law of the host state'. Another mechanism is to explicitly require that an 'investment' have 'the characteristics of an investment' in order to qualify as such. This is the approach adopted in Article 1 of the 2012 US Model BIT, set out above, which further provides that an investment includes 'such characteristics as the commitment of capital or other resources, the expectation of gain or profit, or the assumption of risk'. This provision holds some potential to enhance legal certainty and to limit what can consist of an investment. However, the use of 'or' in the provision illustrates the exemplative nature of the criteria. In order to truly enhance legal certainty, such provisions should be more precise about the characteristics that an investment must have.

The ICSID Convention provides the procedure that applies to most investor–state arbitration cases.[21] The interpretation of 'investment' under Article 25 of the Convention illustrates how uncertainty can arise where states fail to specify what the term means. Although some tribunals adopted a deferential approach by relying on the definition of 'investment' in the applicable BIT for the purpose of defining 'investment' in the ICSID Convention, others, such as the *Salini* tribunal,[22] established a set of cumulative objective requirements (the '*Salini* test') that must be met in order for a commercial operation to qualify as an 'investment' pursuant to the Convention's Article 25: an 'investment' requires (1) a contribution, (2) a certain duration of performance, (3) a risk component, and (4) a contribution to the economic development of the host state of the investment.[23] Uncertainties surround this definition of 'investment'. In particular, the *Salini* test omits the criteria of 'a certain regularity of profit and return', which has sometimes been included in the definition of 'investment' under Article 25 of the ICSID Convention.[24] As well, investment tribunals have not been consistent in how they interpret 'contribution to the economic development of the host state'.[25]

---

20 e.g. Agreement between the Slovak Republic and the Islamic Republic of Iran for the promotion and reciprocal protection of investments, signed 19 January 2016, entered into force 30 August 2017, art 1(2).

21 Convention on the Settlement of Investment Disputes Between States and Nationals of Other States, concluded 18 March 1965, entered into force 14 October 1966, 575 UNTS 159. The ICSID Convention is discussed in VanDuzer and Dumberry (n 2).

22 *Salini Costruttori SpA and Italstrade Spa v Kingdom of Morocco*, ICSID Case No ARB/00/4, Decision on Jurisdiction, 23 July 2001.

23 ibid para 52.

24 *Fedax NV v The Republic of Venezuela*, ICSID Case No ARB/96/3, Decision of the Tribunal on Objections to Jurisdiction (11 July 1997) para 43.

25 Campbell McLachlan, Laurence Shore, and Matthew Weiniger, *International Investment Arbitration: Substantive Principles* (2nd edn Oxford University Press 2017) 218–225, paras 6.04–6.30.

3.2 Pre-establishment protections and umbrella clauses

3.2.1 Pre-establishment protections

Modern IIAs generally protect foreign investors and investments only once the commercial operation is established in the host state. However, IIAs increasingly provide for pre-establishment rights, which 'extend certain treaty protections to the stage when an investor is attempting to make or is making its investment in the host country'.[26] Although there is no generalized inclusion of such provisions in IIAs, they are becoming more common in recent IIAs, such as Canadian and US BITs as well as FTAs.[27]

The extension of a treaty's protections to the pre-establishment phase is generally provided for through the use of words such as 'establishment' or 'entry'.[28] Pre-establishment protection can also be inferred from broadly-drafted definitions provisions that define 'investor' as any foreign national or enterprise that 'attempts to make' or that 'seeks to make' an investment.[29] Because the extension of IIAs' scope of application to the pre-establishment phase is often drafted in broad terms, it is not always clear what exactly is covered and foreign investors will have to prove that what they seek to protect qualifies as an investment or is directly linked with the establishment of the investment. Pre-establishment protection is an important expansion of investor rights but constrains host states in their ability to exercise one of their most important tools for regulating investors: controlling entry into the country.

3.2.2 Umbrella clauses

Another way in which the scope of investment treaties can be expanded is through the inclusion of so-called 'umbrella clauses', which extend IIAs' scope of application to obligations of states in contracts or other arrangements entered into between foreign investors and host states. By bringing such obligations under the 'umbrella' of an IIAs' protection, their breach amounts to a breach of the IIA and can lead to a claim in ISDS.[30] A typical umbrella clause can be found in Article 10(1) of the Energy Charter Treaty, which provides that 'Each Contracting Party shall observe any obligations it has entered into with an

---

26 UNCTAD, *Investor–State Disputes Arising from Investment Treaties: A Review* (UNCTAD Series on International Investment Policies for Development, United Nations 2005) 31.

27 e.g. art 139(1) of the China-New Zealand FTA (Free Trade Agreement between the Government of New Zealand and the Government of the People's Republic of China, signed 7 April 2008, entered into force 1 October 2008) and arts 8.4, 8.6(1) and 8.7(1) of the CETA (Comprehensive Trade and Economic Agreement between Canada and the European Union, signed 30 October 2016, provisionally entered into force on 21 September 2017).

28 e.g. art 3(1) of the 2012 US Model BIT (n 13).

29 e.g. art 1 of the 2004 Canadian Model BIT (n 18).

30 *Société Générale de Surveillance SA v Republic of the Philippines*, ICSID Case No ARB/02/6, Decision of the Tribunal on Objections to Jurisdiction (29 January 2004) para 128.

208 Lukas Vanhonnaeker

Investor or an Investment of an Investor of any other Contracting Party'.[31] Umbrella clauses are, however, becoming less common in recent treaty-making practice.

4. Substantive elements: the traditional standards of investor protection

The substantive standards of protection for foreign investors and investments constitute the core elements of IIAs. The key standards of protection include protection against discrimination, which is ensured through national treatment (NT) and most-favoured-nation (MFN) provisions, requirements for fair and equitable treatment (FET) and full protection and security (FPS), protection against unlawful expropriation and, finally, prohibitions on transfer of funds restrictions and the imposition of certain performance requirements on investors.

4.1 The protection against non-discrimination: the national treatment and the most-favoured-nation principles

One of IIAs' main protections consists of meeting investors' expectations that they will not be subject to discriminatory treatment by the host state through NT and MFN provisions.

4.1.1 National treatment provisions

National Treatment ensures that foreign investors and investments are not treated less favourably than domestic investors. The purpose of NT provisions is to 'oblige a host state to make no negative differentiation between foreign and national investors when enacting and applying its rules and regulations and thus to promote the position of the foreign investor to the level accorded to nationals'.[32] NT prohibits both *de jure* and *de facto* discrimination.[33] It entails a comparison between the treatment received by domestic investors and that provided to foreign investors in 'like circumstances', including the effects of a measure on foreign investors that might appear non-discriminatory, but that results in discriminatory treatment. Tribunals have said that discrimination against an investor that is incidental to a measure that achieves a *bona fide* non-discriminatory public policy goal, like environmental protection, is not contrary to NT.[34]

---

31 Energy Charter Treaty, signed 17 December 1994, entered into force 16 April 1998, 2080 UNTS 95, 34 ILM 360 (1995), art 10(1).
32 Rudolf Dolzer and Christoph Schreuer, *Principles of International Investment Law* (Oxford University Press 2008) 178.
33 e.g. *SD Myers, Inc v Government of Canada*, UNCITRAL, Partial Award, 13 November 2000, para 252 and *Marvin Feldman v Mexico*, ICSID Case No ARB(AF)/99/1, Award (16 December 2002) para 181.
34 e.g. *SD Myers v Canada*, ibid para 248–251.

International investment agreements 209

An example of a NT provision can be found in Article 3 of the Canadian Model Foreign Investment Promotion and Protection Agreement (FIPA), which provides that:

> 1. Each Party shall accord to investors of the other Party treatment no less favourable than that it accords, in like circumstances, to its own investors with respect to the establishment, acquisition, expansion, management, conduct, operation and sale or other disposition of investments in its territory.[35]

This provision, through the use of the terms 'establishment, acquisition, expansion, management, conduct, operation and sale or other disposition of investments', has a broad scope of application and extends the standard's application to the pre-establishment phase by referring to 'establishment [and] acquisition'. Accordingly, pursuant to this provision, although states can impose conditions on the admission and establishment of new investments, these restrictions cannot discriminate on the basis of nationality. Pre-establishment NT does not provide unfettered market access to foreign investors but shields investors against entry conditions sometimes found in domestic investment legislation such as the obligations of foreign investors to penetrate the host-state market through a joint venture with a local partner or restrictions imposed on foreign investors to protect domestic firms from competition that do not apply to domestic investors. The only avenue for host states to favour sectors or activities by limiting foreign investors' access to them is to use reservations and exceptions clauses. Frequently, exceptions apply to procurement by the host state as well as host-state subsidies and grants.[36] Reservations may list excluded sectors and activities in schedules or annexes.

NT provisions provide important protections to foreign investors and curtail the regulatory power of host states. States can be held in breach of their obligation to provide NT if a given measure creates a benefit for nationals over foreigners, regardless of whether or not the host state has a protectionist motive or intent.[37] Investment tribunals that have held states in breach of their NT obligations have mostly dealt with provisions extending the application of NT to the pre-establishment phase and with host-state measures dealing with quantitative restrictions on the importation of foreign-produced goods or imposing discriminatory tax treatment.[38]

---

35 Article 3.2 creates an identical obligation in relation to investments.
36 e.g. art 9 of the Canadian Model FIPA (n 18).
37 *SD Myers v Canada* (n 33) paras 252 et seq.
38 Jonathan Bonnitcha, Lauge N Skovgaard Poulsen, and Michael Waibel, *The Political Economy of the Investment Treaty Regime* (Oxford University Press 2017) 101.

210 Lukas Vanhonnaeker

4.1.2 Most-favoured-nation provisions

NT provisions are generally accompanied by MFN clauses. MFN ensures 'equality of treatment and conditions between foreign investors'.[39] In contrast with NT, under MFN the treatment of foreign investors is not compared to the treatment received by domestic investors but with the treatment received by other foreign investors that are in similar circumstances.

An example of an MFN provision can be found in Article 4 of the Canadian Model FIPA which provides that:

> 1. Each Party shall accord to investors of the other Party treatment no less favourable than that it accords, in like circumstances, to investors of a non-Party with respect to the establishment, acquisition, expansion, management, conduct, operation and sale or other disposition of investments in its territory.[40]

MFN is one of the most important standards of protection with key systemic impacts on the international investment law regime. Foreign investors have invoked MFN to 'borrow' different types of more favourable treatment found in other IIAs.[41] Most successful MFN claims have involved invoking more favourable dispute-settlement procedures and more favourable substantive provisions provided in another IIA. MFN claims that were generally unsuccessful include attempts to broaden the subject matter scope of IIAs through the operation of MFN.[42]

Disagreements as to the appropriate scope of application of MFN have led to an evolution in the drafting of this key standard of protection in recent agreements. In particular, some treaties explicitly exclude from the standard's scope of application the importation of procedural provisions,[43] while others explicitly allow the importation of such provisions.[44] The Comprehensive Economic and Trade Agreement (CETA) between Canada and the EU prohibits the importation of both procedural *and* substantive treaty provisions through MFN.[45]

---

39 UNCTAD, *Most-Favoured-Nation Treatment* (UNCTAD Series on Issues in International Investment Agreements II, United Nations 2010) 14.

40 Article 4.2 creates an identical obligation in relation to investments.

41 Stephan W Schill, *The Multilateralization of International Investment Law* (Cambridge University Press 2009) Chapter IV.

42 Bonnitcha, Poulsen, and Waibel (n 38) 99.

43 Comprehensive and Progressive Agreement for Trans-Pacific Partnership (CPTPP), signed 8 March 2018, entered into force on 30 December 2018, art 9.5(3).

44 Agreement for the Promotion and Reciprocal Protection of Investment between the Government of the Republic of Austria and the Government of the Republic of Kazakhstan, signed 1 December 2010, entered into force 21 December 2012, art 3(3).

45 CETA (n 27) art 8.7(4).

International investment agreements 211

MFN's scope of application is of critical importance for both investors and host states. Broad application entitles foreign investors to the level of protection provided by the most protective IIA binding on the host state. At the same time, the prospect of having to offer every investor protected under a treaty with an MFN clause the best protection it has granted to investors under any treaty can make it hard for host states to understand what their obligations require and comply with them.

4.2 Fair and equitable treatment and full protection and security

In contrast to protections against discrimination that are relative, the fair and equitable (FET) and full protection and security standards of protection are 'absolute' because they bestow a guaranteed minimum standard of treatment.

4.2.1 Fair and equitable treatment provisions

The FET obligation has gradually become the 'bedrock of the modern protection of investors operating abroad'[46] and is the most frequently invoked standard of protection in international investment disputes.[47] It can be expressed in a variety of ways such as 'equitable and reasonable treatment and protection'[48] and it can appear in a separate provision or it can be combined with other standards of protection such as FPS.[49] In addition, FET can either be unqualified by any other terms or qualified by making an explicit reference to the 'customary international law minimum standard of treatment of aliens', for example.[50] A traditional unqualified FET provision can be found in Article 3(1) of the 1991 Czech Republic–Netherlands BIT:

1) Each Contracting Party shall ensure fair and equitable treatment to the investments of investors of the other Contracting Party and shall not impair, by unreasonable or discriminatory measures, the operation, management, maintenance, use, enjoyment or disposal thereof by those investors.

---

46 Jacob and Schill (n 8) 702.
47 UNCTAD, *Fair and Equitable Treatment: A Sequel* (UNCTAD Series on Issues in International Investment Agreements II, United Nations 2012) 1.
48 Agreement between the Government of the Kingdom of Norway and the Government of the Republic of Lithuania on the Promotion and Mutual Protection of Investments, signed 16 June 1992, entered into force 20 December 1992, art III.
49 FET is sometimes combined with the FPS standard, such as in Article 5(1) of the Canadian Model FIPA (n 18) or Article 1105(1) of the NAFTA (North American Free Trade Agreement, signed 17 December 1992, entered into force 1 January 1994, 32 ILM 289, 605 (1993)).
50 e.g. art 5(1) of the Canadian Model FIPA (n 18). For a much more detailed FET provision see e.g. article 8.10 of the CETA (n 27).

212   *Lukas Vanhonnaeker*

Despite having been invoked in most investment arbitrations and analysed by many investment tribunals and scholars alike, FET remains one of the most controversial standards of protection whose contours are not clearly delimited. It has been observed that the FET's normative content is 'maddeningly vague, frustratingly general, and treacherously elastic'.[51] Indeed,

> fair and equitable treatment is a broad, overarching standard, that contains various elements of protection, including those elements commonly associated with the minimum standard of treatment, the protection of legitimate expectations, non-discrimination, transparency and protection against bad faith, coercion, threats and harassment.[52]

The obligation of due process and the prohibition of arbitrary conduct and denial of justice have also been identified as being included under the scope of FET. For instance, CETA's Article 8.10(2) explicitly provides that:

> 2. A Party breaches the obligation of fair and equitable treatment referenced in paragraph 1 if a measure or series of measures constitutes:
>
> (a) denial of justice in criminal, civil or administrative proceedings;
> (b) fundamental breach of due process, including a fundamental breach of transparency, in judicial and administrative proceedings;
> (c) manifest arbitrariness;
> (d) targeted discrimination on manifestly wrongful grounds, such as gender, race or religious belief;
> (e) abusive treatment of investors, such as coercion, duress and harassment; or
> (f) a breach of any further elements of the fair and equitable treatment obligation adopted by the Parties in accordance with paragraph 3 of this Article.

One of FET's most contentious issues is its link with the protection of investors' legitimate expectations and the protean and undefined content of this concept,[53] which has been developed through cases and has only recently been explicitly mentioned in FET provisions. The protection of investors' 'legitimate expectations' is the 'dominant' element of the FET standard.[54] Investment

---

51 Jeswald Salacuse, *The Law of Investment Treaties* (2nd ed, Oxford University Press 2015) 244.

52 Newcombe and Paradell (n 4) 278.

53 Alexandra Diehl, *The Core Standard of International Investment Protection: Fair and Equitable Treatment* (Wolters Kluwer 2012) 338–431, para 6.3.1; Newcombe and Paradell (n 4) 279–289, para 6.26.

54 *Saluka Investment BV v The Czech Republic*, UNCITRAL, Partial Award (17 March 2006) para 302.

International investment agreements 213

tribunals have used this concept in at least three different ways. First, legitimate expectations can refer to the investor's expectations arising from specific host-state conduct, such as representations or commitments made by the latter with respect to an investment. Second, legitimate expectations can refer to the expectation of a stable and predictable legal regime that meets certain minimum standards such as transparency and consistency in the creation and application of legal rules. Finally, legitimate expectations can refer in a general manner to the expectation that the conduct of the host state towards the investment will be fair and equitable. Generally speaking, an alleged violation of the investor's legitimate expectations can be argued whenever it is suffering losses as a consequence of changes brought about by some state measures. This concept, and consequently the FET standard of protection, can thus have a very broad scope of application, which is to foreign investors' advantage.

From the perspective of host states, however, a broadly-drafted FET provision protecting legitimate expectations can act as a deterrent to continue regulating, even where regulation is in the public interest, because any change in the business environment that has a negative impact on foreign investors could lead to a claim of breach of FET by the host state. Accordingly, treaty-drafters are increasingly limiting the scope of FET clauses by 'qualifying' them. This is done by explicitly linking the FET standard of protection to the minimum standard of treatment under customary international law, to international law or general principles of international law or by identifying the content of the FET standard of protection by listing specific substantive obligations, as has been done in CETA's Article 8.10(2) (see above). Such approaches provide more clarity as to what FET and the notion of 'legitimate expectations' actually refer to, and thus increase legal certainty for the host state by avoiding overly broad interpretations of that standard.

4.2.2 Full protection and security provisions

The FPS standard is another common guarantee provided in IIAs, although it has been invoked less often in the context of investment disputes. A standard FPS clause provides that '[i]nvestment [...] shall enjoy full protection and security and shall in no case be accorded treatment less than that required by international law'.[55] This standard's precise content, whose wording varies in treaty practice, is not altogether clear, although there is a broad consensus that FPS does not ensure an *absolute* protection against physical or legal harm.[56] FPS

---

55 Treaty between United States of America and the Argentine Republic concerning the reciprocal encouragement and protection of investment, signed 14 November 1991, entered into force 20 October 1994, art II(2)(a).

56 *Elettronica Sicula SpA (ELSI) (US v Italy)*, ICJ Rep (1989) 15, para 108 ('The reference ... to the provision of "constant protection and security" cannot be construed as the giving of a warranty that property shall never in any circumstances be occupied or disturbed'.).

214   *Lukas Vanhonnaeker*

imposes a duty on host states to exercise due diligence when protecting foreign investments against interference.[57]

The standard's uncontested core is the protection against physical harm:[58] '[t]raditionally, the primary ratio of the standard was the need to protect the investor against various types of physical violence including the invasion of premises of the investment'.[59] However, an extension of the scope of FPS has taken place in some cases with the inclusion of the protection 'against infringements of the investor's rights by the operation of laws and regulations of the host state'.[60] Controversy persists with respect to whether FPS extends beyond physical harm and whether its real purpose is in fact to guarantee a stable legal environment.[61] In order to increase legal certainty and to avoid seeing tribunals interpreting FPS too broadly, host states are beginning to define this standard's contours by explicitly referring to the type of protection that it provides to investors.

4.3 The protection against unlawful expropriation

Another standard provided in the vast majority of IIAs is the protection against unlawful expropriation, including measures that have an equivalent effect and measures tantamount to expropriation. Expropriation was governed for a long time by customary international law, which, undisputedly, allows expropriation if certain conditions are met. With the treatification of international investment law, the customary international law protection against unlawful expropriation was incorporated into FCN treaties and then, with gradually enhanced precision, into IIAs. Investment agreements often provide for a general reference to the prohibition of direct[62] and indirect[63] expropriation in order to include an important range of *de jure* and *de facto* expropriatory measures as well as creeping expropriations[64] under the scope of the prohibition. For instance, Article 4(2) of the 2008 German Model BIT provides that:

---

57 *Técnicas Medioambientales Tecmed, SA v The United Mexican States*, ICSID Case No (AF)/00/2, Award (29 May 2003) para 177.
58 Questions subsist with respect to damages caused by state organs and private harm. See Alexander Lorz, 'Protection and Security (Including the NAFTA Approach)' in Bungenberg, Griebel, Hobe, and Reinisch (eds) (n 8) paras 30–45.
59 Dolzer and Schreuer (n 32) 149.
60 ibid.
61 Lorz (n 58) 781–785, paras 46–59.
62 Direct expropriation refers to the 'forcible appropriation by the State of the tangible or intangible property of individuals by means of administrative or legislative action' (*LG&E Energy Corp, LG&E Capital Corp and LG&E International Inc v Argentina*, ICSID Case No ARB/02/1, Decision on Liability (3 October 2010) para 387).
63 'In the case of an indirect expropriation the investor retains ownership of the investment but loses the ability to exercise the economic benefits arising therefrom' (Ursula Kriebaum, 'Expropriation' in Bungenberg, Griebel, Hobe, and Reinisch (eds) (n 8) 971, para 32).
64 UNCTAD defines 'creeping expropriation' as: 'The slow and incremental encroachment on one or more of the ownership rights of a foreign investor that diminishes the value of its

International investment agreements 215

> Investments by investors of either Contracting State may not directly or indirectly be expropriated, nationalized or subjected to any other measure the effects of which would be tantamount to expropriation or nationalization in the territory of the other Contracting State except for the public benefit and against compensation [...].[65]

A direct expropriation occurs when the state takes the investor's property, but such an expropriation is lawful so long as the state acted for a public purpose, followed due process, did not discriminate against the investor, and compensated the investor. On the other hand, establishing an indirect expropriation requires also looking at the impact of the measure at issue, including its interference with the investor's expectations regarding the use of its investment, as well as the measure's nature, character, and purpose.

One of the most contentious issues with respect to this standard of protection resides in the fact that many regulatory measures can have a negative impact on a given investment despite being enacted by state authorities in the legitimate exercise of their public-order functions.[66] It is thus important for host states to clearly distinguish between what can amount to an unlawful expropriation and what consists of a non-compensable regulation. The latter category of measures refers to acts of states that are enacted pursuant to the state's police powers. Although no universally-accepted definition of the 'police powers doctrine' exists, it is generally accepted that it encompasses acts such as the taking of enemy property as payment of reparation for the consequences of an illegal war, the destruction of property of neutrals as a consequence of military operations, measures restricting the use of property for environment, health and safety purposes, and measures enacted to punish or suppress a crime.

Some more recent treaties include an annex specifying how to determine the existence of an indirect expropriation requiring compensation. Annex B.13(1) of the Canadian Model investment treaty provides that:

The Parties confirm their shared understanding that:

a) Indirect expropriation results from a measure or series of measures of a Party that have an effect equivalent to direct expropriation without formal transfer of title or outright seizure;

b) The determination of whether a measure or series of measures of a Party constitute an indirect expropriation requires a case-by-case, fact-based inquiry that considers, among other factors:

---

investment. The legal title to the property remains vested in the foreign investor but the investor's rights of use of the property are diminished as a result of the interference by the State' (UNCTAD, *Taking of Property* (Series on Issues in International Investment Agreements, United Nations 2000) 11–12).

65 Treaty between the Federal Republic of Germany and ... concerning the Encouragement and Reciprocal Protection of Investments, 2008, art 4(2).

66 Kriebaum (n 63) 1000–1006, paras 149–173.

216 *Lukas Vanhonnacker*

i)   the economic impact of the measure or series of measures, although the sole fact that a measure or series of measures of a Party has an adverse effect on the economic value of an investment does not establish that an indirect expropriation has occurred;

ii) the extent to which the measure or series of measures interfere with distinct, reasonable investment-backed expectations; and

iii) the character of the measure or series of measures;

c)   Except in rare circumstances, such as when a measure or series of measures are so severe in the light of their purpose that they cannot be reasonably viewed as having been adopted and applied in good faith, non-discriminatory measures of a Party that are designed and applied to protect legitimate public welfare objectives, such as health, safety and the environment, do not constitute indirect expropriation.

As with other standards of protection generally found in IIAs, in order to avoid an overly broad interpretation of 'indirect expropriation' that unduly restricts host states' ability to regulate in the public interest, it is in the interest of states to draft precise unlawful expropriation provisions, clearly establishing the conditions that must be met to find unlawful expropriation, instead of leaving that task to arbitral tribunals. This entails clearly delimiting the scope of expropriation, providing for the rules applicable to compensation in case of expropriation, as well as defining the assets and interests capable of expropriation. In addition, states should affirm their police powers by explicitly asserting their right to regulate in the public interest. This approach was adopted in the 2004 Canadian Model FIPA which, in its Annex B.13(1), provides a clear definition of 'indirect expropriation' but also describes the test that must be applied to determine whether a finding of indirect expropriation is appropriate and includes a paragraph on police powers and the preservation of states' sovereign regulatory power to 'protect legitimate public welfare objectives'.

4.4 Transfer of funds provisions and prohibitions of performance requirements

The last set of provisions commonly found in IIAs consists of transfer of funds clauses and prohibitions on imposing performance requirements on investors. These provisions, although typically less invoked in ISDS disputes, remain of critical importance for investors.

4.4.1 Transfer of funds provisions

Transfer of funds provisions aim to ensure the ability of foreign investors to transfer funds into and out of the host state. Being able to freely transfer funds is a fundamental concern of investors whose decisions to invest are motivated by the generation of profit. The ability to transfer funds into the host state

International investment agreements 217

(such provisions are typically only included in IIAs that provide for pre-establishment obligations) is often essential in order to establish, maintain, and expand a given investment. The ability to transfer funds out of the host state allows foreign investors to repatriate the profits generated by their investment but also to engage in other investment activities or pay for business expenses. Accordingly, the ability to freely transfer funds can be seen as part of the economic value of a given investment.

Transfer of funds provisions can be distinguished on the basis of their scope of application and of the types of transfer that they cover. While some such provisions allow for the transfer of funds into and out of the host state,[67] other clauses only guarantee the free transfer of funds out of the host state and do not provide for the right to transfer funds into the host state.[68] In addition, transfer of funds provisions can have a broad scope of application by covering all transfers related to an investment (often including an illustrative list of transfers that fall under the scope of the provision)[69] while others provide for an exhaustive list of specific types of transfers that may be freely made.[70] A key component of transfer of funds provisions consists of requiring that transfers be made in a 'convertible' or 'freely convertible' currency and specifying the exchange rate applicable to the transfer. These elements are critical because transfers made in a non-convertible currency would essentially render such clauses useless. Transfer of funds provisions also ensure that such transfers are allowed without restrictions, such as time constraints.[71] However, some IIAs require that the funds must remain in the host state for a certain amount of time before they can be transferred out of its territory.[72]

As important as transfer of funds clauses are for foreign investors, from a policy perspective legitimate reasons exist to justify the restriction of such transfers by host states. For instance, in the event of a financial crisis, which

---

67 e.g. Agreement between Japan and the Socialist Republic of Viet Nam for the Liberalization, Promotion and Protection of Investment, signed 14 November 2003, entered into force 19 December 2004, art 12(1).

68 e.g. Agreement between the Government of the Republic of India and the Government of the Republic of Ghana for the Reciprocal Promotion and Protection of Investments, signed 5 August 2002, not yet entered into force, art 7(1).

69 e.g. Agreement on encouragement and reciprocal protection of investments between the Kingdom of the Netherlands and the Czech and Slovak Federal Republic, signed 29 April 1991, entered into force 1 October 1992, art 4.

70 e.g. Agreement between the Government of the Republic of Cuba and the Government of the Kingdom of Denmark concerning the Promotion and Reciprocal Protection of Investments, signed 19 February 2001, not yet entered into force, art 8.

71 e.g. Agreement on the Encouragement and Protection of Investments between the Government of Hong Kong and the Government of the Kingdom of the Netherlands, signed 19 November 1992, entered into force 1 September 1993, art 6(1).

72 e.g. Agreement between the Government of the Republic of Chile and the Government of the People's Republic of China concerning the Encouragement and the Reciprocal Protection of Investment, signed 23 March 1994, entered into force 1 August 1995, art 6(5).

218 Lukas Vanhonnaeker

entails large amounts of capital leaving the country, a state might need to restrict transfers of funds. Most treaties provide explicit exceptions to transfer of funds obligations, including for the purpose of (i) tax collection; (ii) reporting transfers of currency and other monetary instruments; (iii) satisfying judgements; (iv) enforcing criminal or penal offences; (v) regulating the issuance, trading, and dealing of securities; and (vi) protecting creditors' rights in case of bankruptcy and insolvency.[73] Absent such exceptions, host states lose a considerable amount of leeway to regulate.

4.4.2 Provisions prohibiting performance requirements

Some treaties prohibit states from imposing performance requirements on investors in order to achieve specific economic and social objectives. Host states attach some importance to such requirements and to the objectives that they seek to achieve, such as increasing employment levels, enhancing transfers of technology, or protecting domestic industries by promoting or imposing the use of domestic products and/or services. The legitimate policy objectives pursued by performance requirements can, however, have negative impacts on foreign investors since they impede the efficient allocation of resources (e.g. imposing the use of more expensive domestic products). These negative implications for foreign investors explain the prohibition of performance requirements in some IIAs. Because performance requirements can be imposed by states as conditions of permitting investors to enter their market, their prohibition typically extends to the pre-establishment phase (where that phase is within the scope of the treaty).

In IIAs that prohibit performance requirements, exceptions are generally provided to establish a balance between these requirements' positive and negative impacts. In particular, prohibition of performance requirements clauses generally do not apply to government procurement, export promotion and foreign aid programmes, or to qualification requirements for preferential tariffs and quotas.[74] In addition, some IIAs provide for exceptions with respect to transfers of technology requirements.[75]

5. New IIA issues and developments: recalibrating the balance between investor protection and host states' right to regulate

With the IIA network's expansion, and the increasing number of controversial and mediatized investment disputes, there have been growing concerns about

---

73 e.g. Agreement between the Government of Canada and the Government of the Republic of Venezuela for the Promotion and Protection of Investments, signed 1 July 1996, entered into force 28 January 1998, art VIII(4).

74 e.g. art 7 of the Canadian Model FIPA (n 18).

75 e.g. art 1106.2 of NAFTA (n 49).

the far-reaching consequences of the international investment law regime. One is so-called 'regulatory chill', which refers to the constraining effect of international investment law on host states' exercise of their legitimate regulatory power. According to the regulatory chill argument, the broad and often vague protections provided in IIAs, their inconsistent interpretation, and the threat of ISDS proceedings reduce states' willingness to regulate; not being able to assess whether a given measure could amount to a breach of their international obligations, states prefer not regulating at all rather than face the risk of arbitration procedures and eventual liability. Smaller and less wealthy states are more exposed to regulatory chill because they do not have the financial means to face costly investment arbitration(s).[76] The serious prospect of regulatory chill has led negotiators and treaty-drafters to insert new language and provisions in recent IIAs.

Indeed, the concerns over IIAs' negative and constraining impacts on domestic governance and policy-making have led to a global rethinking of the international investment law regime and of IIAs' content. In this regard, although the traditional standards of protection analysed above remain the core of IIAs, they are increasingly drafted in more precise terms and completed by annexes clarifying how they must be understood, interpreted, and applied by investment tribunals. Traditional standards of protection are also increasingly accompanied by new types of provisions that aim at recalibrating the balance between investor protection and host states' right to regulate.

To preserve host states' right to regulate, some IIAs now include exception clauses that aim to ensure foreign investors cannot invoke the IIA's protections with respect to measures pursuing specific goals.[77] Specific exception clauses may apply to an agreement's individual provisions. For instance, Article 7(2) of the Canadian Model FIPA provides such an exception clause with respect to its provision on the prohibition of performance requirements.[78] General exception clauses, on the other hand, apply to the entire agreement. These clauses are generally modelled on the General Agreement on Tariffs and Trade Article XX and seek to ensure that host states can regulate in the public interest and enact, for example, health, safety, or environment-related measures.[79]

Although the broader inclusion of exception clauses undeniably reflects the will of states to preserve their right to regulate in the public interest, the concrete impact of such provisions remains to be proven in practice. To date,

---

76 VanDuzer and Dumberry (n 2).
77 Armand de Mestral and Lukas Vanhonnaeker, 'Exception Clauses in Mega-Regionals (International Investment Protection and Trade Agreements)' in Thilo Rensmann (ed), *Mega Regional Trade Agreements* (Springer 2017) 75.
78 Canadian Model FIPA (n 18).
79 e.g. art 10 of the Canadian Model FIPA (ibid).

220 Lukas Vanhonnaeker

there are few cases where tribunals have interpreted and applied such provisions;[80] therefore, their effectiveness is yet to be confirmed.

General exception clauses may have little practical impact because tribunals have, when appropriate, taken into account the policy objectives of contested host-state measures in determining whether substantive standards of investor protection have been breached.[81] Indeed, the inclusion of general exception provisions can have negative and counterintuitive impacts. While they force a tribunal to consider whether the host state's measure falls within the specified categories of public policy listed in the exception, the tribunal might interpret the exception as exhaustively prescribing the policy flexibility the states intended to preserve. This approach might, therefore, make it more difficult to balance standards of investor protection and public policy objectives.[82] Accordingly, host states may be better off clarifying existing standards of protection, including the way in which they should be interpreted by investment tribunals, rather than providing for general exception clauses.

Another way in which host states have sought to affirm their right to regulate in IIAs is through the inclusion of 'right to regulate provisions'.[83] Such provisions recall the widely-accepted principle that states are sovereign and have the right to regulate, especially to pursue public policy objectives. However, right to regulate provisions typically neither impose any specific obligation nor create enforceable rights. Similar to general exception clauses, the practical impact of the explicit inclusion of right to regulate provisions in IIAs remains to be proven but it is unlikely that it will drastically change the approach adopted by investment tribunals.

The other category of new provisions found in IIAs are those that aim at ensuring that IIAs attract investments that contribute to sustainable development. States emphasize this goal through the inclusion of provisions that recognize the importance of protecting the environment and/or respecting international labour norms[84] as well as corporate social responsibility standards.[85] The utility of such

---

80 *Copper Mesa Mining Corporation v The Republic of Ecuador*, PCA Case No 2012–2, Award (15 March 2016) and *Bear Creek Mining Corporation v Republic of Perú*, ICSID Case No ARB/14/21, Award (30 November 2017).

81 e.g. *Philip Morris Brand Sàrl, Philip Morris Products SA and Abal Hermanos SA v Oriental Republic of Uruguay*, ICSID Case No ARB/10/7, Award (8 July 2016).

82 Andrew Newcombe, 'General Exceptions in International Investment Agreements', Draft Discussion Paper prepared for BIICL Eight Annual WTO Conference, 13 and 14 May 2008, London, 8–9.

83 e.g. art 8.9(1) – (2) of the CETA (n 27) and art 12 of the 2015 Norway Draft Model BIT (Agreement between the Kingdom of Norway and ... for the Promotion and Protection of Investments, 2015)

84 e.g. arts 12 ('Investment and Environment') and 13 ('Investment and Labor') of the 2012 US Model BIT (n 13), and art 11 ('Health, Safety and Environmental Measures') of the Canadian Model FIPA (n 18).

85 e.g. art 8.16 ('Corporate Social Responsibility') of the Canada-Republic of Korea FTA (Free Trade Agreement between Canada and the Republic of Korea, signed 22 September 2014, entered into force 1 January 2015).

provisions has not, however, been tested in practice and it is unlikely that they could be used in any other way than to encourage the interpretation by investment tribunals of investor protection obligations in a manner that would be consistent with them.

These provisions contrast with another set of more recent provisions included in IIAs that also aim at ensuring that these agreements attract investments that contribute to sustainable development: investor obligations. These provisions ensure that foreign investors do not hamper or disregard sustainable development objectives by imposing positive obligations on investors. Such obligations respond to criticisms that international investment law and its IIAs are one-sided by only imposing obligations on host states. Examples of such provisions can be found in the 2012 SADC Model BIT,[86] the 2015 Indian Model BIT,[87] and the 2016 Morocco–Nigeria BIT.[88] Investor obligations can include (i) prohibiting fraudulent activities; (ii) requiring compliance with host-state laws;[89] (iii) conducting environmental and social impact assessments for proposed investments;[90] and (iv) respecting the environment[91] and/or human rights.[92] Some treaties also impose transparency obligations on investors.[93]

It is too early to assess the effectiveness of investor obligations with respect to recalibrating the balance between the rights and obligations of states and investors and their potential to ensure that IIAs attract investments that contribute to sustainable development. So far, these provisions are mainly provided in Model agreements and IIAs that have not yet entered into force.

From a policy perspective, while this new approach and novel provisions will likely not find favour with investors, host states should contemplate the far-reaching consequences of including such provisions in IIAs. In particular, including investor obligations in IIAs entails the possibility that these provisions will be litigated before an ISDS tribunal. This raises the question of whether such tribunals are the proper forum to address, for example, human rights issues or claims. In an era where ISDS is criticized for its lack of legitimacy, the inclusion of investor obligations in IIAs, as well-intended as it might be, risks opening a Pandora's box and even aggravating the concerns expressed about

---

86 SADC Model Bilateral Investment Template, 2012.

87 Bilateral Investment Treaty between the Government of the Republic of India and............, 2015.

88 Reciprocal Investment Promotion and Protection Agreement between the Government of the Kingdom of Morocco and the Government of the Republic of Nigeria, signed 3 December 2016, not yet entered into force.

89 e.g. art 11 of the 2015 Indian Model BIT (n 87).

90 e.g. art 13 of the SADC Model BIT (n 86).

91 e.g. arts 14(3) and 18(1) and (4) of the Morocco-Nigeria BIT (n 88).

92 e.g. art 15(1) of the SADC Model BIT (n 86) and arts 18(2) and 20 of the Morocco-Nigeria BIT ibid.

93 e.g. art 18 of the SADC Model BIT ibid art 14.7(2) of the Australia-Japan EPA (Agreement between Australia and Japan for an Economic Partnership, signed 8 July 2014, entered into force 15 January 2015).

222 Lukas Vanhonnaeker

ISDS.[94] Nevertheless, the inclusion of the above-mentioned provisions in recent IIAs illustrates states' desire to reform the IIA system. Other states, however, have taken a more extreme stand, and answered criticisms by withdrawing from their IIAs, thus signalling hostility towards the regime.[95] In such instances, foreign investors have no choice but to rely on the protections provided by domestic legislation.

6. Conclusion

IIAs crystallize and strengthen customary international law rules on the protection of foreign investors. They seek both to protect and promote foreign investment. In order to fulfil these objectives, IIAs contain standards of protection that have been relatively constant in investment treaty-making: the protection of foreign investors and investments against discrimination (NT and MFN clauses), fair and equitable treatment and full protection and security, protection against unlawful expropriation, and, finally, transfer of funds provisions and clauses prohibiting states from imposing performance requirements on investors.

More than mere legal instruments, IIAs can provide important insights into host-state policies. IIAs also have consequences on domestic policy and decision-making. One negative impact of IIAs consists of constraining host states in the exercise of their legitimate regulatory power.

States are constantly adapting IIAs to improve their effectiveness and to address concerns about their effects. Traditional standards of protection are increasingly drafted in precise terms. New provisions are being included, such as exceptions and obligations on investors, in an attempt to rebalance IIAs that have traditionally only protected foreign investors and investments as well as to ensure that foreign investments contribute to sustainable development in the host state. How effective these new provisions are in practice remains to be seen, however.

---

94 For a more detailed discussion of this issue, see VanDuzer and Dumberry (n 2).
95 e.g. Ecuador and South Africa are engaged in the process of withdrawing from several of their IIAs.

11 Investor–state dispute settlement

J Anthony VanDuzer and Patrick Dumberry

1. Introduction

The 1990s marked a new era of globalization in which private foreign investment became (almost) universally accepted by states as an essential tool for economic development.[1] There was no consensus as to what kind of protection from host-state action foreign investors were afforded under customary international law.[2] As a result, states increasingly relied on treaties to regulate the treatment of foreign investments. It is now estimated that over 2,946 bilateral investment treaties for the protection and promotion of investments ('BITs') have been concluded worldwide.[3] In addition, more than 376 international agreements (such as free trade agreements) also include provisions on investment.[4] The substantive rules for the protection of foreign investments are mostly found in these treaties (collectively referred to as international investment agreements [IIAs]).[5] Most IIAs provide foreign investors with significant procedural rights. They typically allow an investor of one party to a treaty to bring a direct claim alleging breach of an investment protection obligation in an IIA against another party to the treaty that is the host state for the investment. The claim can be submitted to an international arbitral tribunal, which renders a final and binding award.

The inclusion of investor–state dispute settlement mechanisms in IIAs has been described by Schwebel as 'one of the most important progressive developments in the procedure of international law of the 20th century'.[6] Without this extraordinary procedure any dispute between a foreign investor and the host state would normally have to be settled before that state's

---

1 World Bank, *Guidelines on the Treatment of Foreign Direct Investment* (World Bank 1992).
2 See Lukas Vanhonnaecker, 'International investment agreements', Chapter 10 in this volume.
3 UNCTAD, *Recent Developments in the International Investment Regime*, IIA Issues Note No 1 2018 (United Nations 2018) 2. Only about 2,400 BITs are in force.
4 ibid.
5 Protection is also often found in contracts entered into directly between foreign investors and states (or state-owned entities) or in the legislation of the host state of the investment.
6 Stephen M Schwebel, 'The United States 2004 Model Bilateral Investment Treaty: An Exercise in the Regressive Development of International Law' (2006) 3 *Transnational Dispute Management* 2.

224   *J Anthony VanDuzer and Patrick Dumberry*

domestic courts or through diplomatic protection. As discussed below, in most circumstances, neither of these options is as attractive to investors as ISDS.

As the number of IIAs containing ISDS clauses rapidly increased in parallel with substantial growth in international investment from the 1980s to the early 2000s, the number of arbitration cases between investors and states also grew dramatically.[7] By the end of 2017, 855 claims had been initiated by investors against states and 542 final awards had been issued. Experience with ISDS has caused a variety of concerns about the process, especially in Europe.[8] Because investor–state cases can involve challenges to public acts by governments, many argue that investor–state arbitration needs to meet high standards for democratic accountability, including guarantees of transparency and participation rights for all affected interests.[9] Traditionally, ISDS procedures, which largely follow a private commercial arbitration model, have offered few guarantees of this kind.[10] Critics also argue that ISDS procedures need to incorporate the same guarantees of independence for decision-makers that characterize domestic judicial systems. Their concern is that the usual approach of having the parties appoint arbitrators on an *ad hoc* basis for each dispute does not guarantee a sufficient level of independence from the parties. For example, arbitrators may be tempted to favour the party that appoints them because of their interest in future appointments. Other concerns relate to the outcome of arbitration awards. Some awards, interpreting the broad investor-protection standards in IIAs, have found that host-state actions in pursuit of legitimate public policy goals have breached IIA requirements. There are also many examples of inconsistent awards considering claims with the same or similar facts under the same treaty standards, undermining predictability. The problem of inconsistency is exacerbated by the absence of an appeal right. As a result of all these concerns, ISDS is experiencing a legitimacy crisis.[11]

---

7 A number of empirical studies have been conducted in recent years, e.g. Susan D Franck, 'Empirically Evaluating Claims about Investment Treaty Arbitration' (2007) 86 *North Carolina Law Review* 1.

8 The first few ISDS cases against Germany and other European countries, the adoption of ISDS in the Canada–Europe Comprehensive Economic and Trade Agreement, and its potential incorporation in a trade agreement between the European Union and the United States caused such concern in Europe that the European Commission conducted a public consultation on ISDS in the summer of 2014. The EU's report on the results found 'widespread opposition to ISDS' (European Commission, Commission Staff Working Document, *Report: Online public consultation on investment protection and investor-to-state dispute settlement (ISDS) in the Transatlantic Trade and Investment Partnership (TTIP)*, Brussels 13 January 2015 SWD (2015) 3 final, 14).

9 e.g. Gus van Harten, 'The European Commission and UNCTAD Reform Agendas: Do They Ensure Independence, Openness, and Fairness in Investor–State Arbitration?' in Steffen Hindelang and Markus Krajewski (eds), *Shifting Paradigms in International Investment Law: More Balanced, Less Isolated, Increasingly Diversified* (Oxford University Press 2016) 128.

10 ibid.

11 e.g. Susan D Franck, 'The Legitimacy Crisis in International Treaty Arbitration: Privatizing Public International Law Through Inconsistent Decisions' (2005) 73 *Fordham Law Review* 1521.

We begin the chapter with an overview of the evolution and current state of ISDS practice. Next, we describe the basic features of ISDS procedures. This is followed by a discussion of the arbitration system's systemic deficiencies, which have become apparent in the past two decades. Finally, we discuss paths to reform.

2. Context

2.1 Traditional rationale

The right for investors to bring claims for IIA breaches through ISDS distinguishes investment treaties from almost all other international instruments, which do not permit private parties to claim relief directly. When ISDS began to become a common feature of BITs in the 1960s, the main goal was to ensure that investors from developed, capital-exporting states making investments in developing countries could seek relief from actions of local governments without having to resort to domestic administrative and judicial institutions,[12] which were typically regarded as corrupt, incompetent, not sufficiently independent of the state, or incapable of providing timely and effective relief. As well, domestic institutions in many countries had no jurisdiction to enforce IIA commitments in favour of foreign investors and domestic laws often provided no comparable protection. Investors from developed countries also wanted a process that they could initiate and manage themselves rather than the more politically and practically complex alternative of having to rely on their home states to espouse their claims.[13] Whether an investor's home state espouses an investor's claim is a matter of that state's discretion; the investor does not have the 'right' to receive such protection. A wide range of political, economic, and other considerations may dissuade an investor's home state from espousing its claim. Even if a home-state takes up an investor's claim, the state, not the investor, decides how to pursue it, when to settle, and for what relief. In contrast, ISDS makes investment protection commitments in IIAs more credible and readily realizable for investors.

Enhancing the credibility of their IIA commitments can benefit host states. By agreeing to ISDS in a treaty, they signal their commitment to the treaty's substantive investor-protection obligations with the hope of attracting investment. Empirical evidence of actual investment-inducing effects, however, is mixed at best.[14] Another

---

12 UNCTAD, *World Investment Report 2003: FDI Policies for Development: National and International Perspectives* (United Nations 2003) 114–118.

13 ibid.

14 Karl Sauvant and Lisa Sachs (eds), *The Effect of Treaties on Foreign Direct Investment: Bilateral Investment Treaties, Double Taxation Treaties and Investment Flows* (Oxford University Press 2009); Eugene Beaulieu and Kelly O'Neill, 'The economics of foreign direct investment and international investment agreements', Chapter 5 in this volume.

226   *J Anthony VanDuzer and Patrick Dumberry*

host-state benefit commonly attributed to ISDS commitments is the depoliticization of foreign investment disputes. Disputes are adjudicated by arbitral tribunals on the basis of the application of law rather than determined by contests of political, economic, or military power, which characterize state-to-state diplomatic negotiations.[15]

2.2 Statistics on *investor–state* arbitration cases

Even though investor–state arbitration provisions have been included in IIAs since the 1960s, investors only began to bring claims in the late 1980s. By the end of 2017, however, 113 different states had been respondents in a total of 855 known ISDS cases.[16] In most cases, the respondents have been developing states.[17] In contrast, in more than 75 per cent of cases, the claimants were investors from developed states.[18]

By the end of 2017, 542 ISDS proceedings had been concluded. About one-third of cases were decided in favour of the state.[19] In about half of these cases, tribunals found they did not have jurisdiction to hear the investor's claim, perhaps because the investor was not eligible for protection under the treaty. In the other cases decided in favour of the state, the tribunals rejected the investor's claim that the host state had breached its IIA investor-protection obligations. About one-quarter of all ISDS cases have been decided in favour of the investor and monetary compensation awarded. Another quarter of all cases were resolved by an agreed settlement between the investor and the state. In most cases, settlement terms have not been made public.

Awards in ISDS cases can be very large. In three cases related to the Yukos company against the Russian Federation, the investors claimed $US114 billion and were awarded $50 billion.[20] These awards were the largest by far in the history of ISDS but were subsequently set aside by The

---

15 Mavluda Sattorova, 'Return to the Local Remedies Rule in European BITs: Power (Inequalities), Dispute Settlement, and Change in Investment Treaty Law' (2012) 39 *Legal Issues of Economic Integration* 223. Sattrorova argues that inequalities continue because treaty-making and dispute settlement remain politicized.

16 UNCTAD, *World Investment Report, 2018: Investment and New Industrial Policies* (United Nations 2018) 91–93. As some arbitrations can be kept fully confidential, the actual number of disputes filed in 2017 and previous years is likely to be higher.

17 ibid; UNCTAD (n 3) 30–2.

18 UNCTAD (n 3) 30–2; UNCTAD (n 16) notes that the most frequent home states of claimant investors were the United States (156 cases), the Netherlands (102), United Kingdom (74), Germany (59), Canada (45), France (44), Spain (44), Luxembourg (39), and Italy (35).

19 All of these statistics are set out in UNCTAD (n 3) 5.

20 *Yukos Universal Limited (Isle of Man) v The Russian Federation*, UNCITRAL, PCA Case No AA 227, Final Award (18 July 2014); *Hulley Enterprises Ltd (Cyprus) v The Russian Federation*, UNCITRAL, PCA Case No 2005-03/AA226, Final Award, (18 July 2014); *Veteran Petroleum Ltd. (Cyprus) v The Russian Federation*, UNCITRAL, PCA Case No 2005-05/AA228 Final Award (18 July 2014).

Hague District Court.[21] An appeal of the court's judgement is currently pending. Even excluding these extraordinary awards, the amounts at stake in ISDS are substantial. The average amount claimed is $454 million and the average amount awarded is $125 million, approximately 28 per cent of the amount claimed.[22] These amounts do not include interest or legal costs, which can be significant.

3. Basic features of ISDS

3.1 Introduction

IIAs typically provide for two types of dispute settlement: state-to-state arbitration and investor–state arbitration. State-to-state arbitration has rarely been used in investment disputes. Investor–state arbitration clauses are found in the overwhelming majority of IIAs. According to an OECD study that examined 1,660 BITs, only 4 per cent did not provide for some form of ISDS.[23]

Treaty-based investment arbitration always involves investors as claimants and states as respondents. This is because IIAs are asymmetrical (and imbalanced) as investors are accorded substantive rights, without being subject to any specific obligations, while states only have obligations.[24]

IIAs show a great deal of variation in ISDS language: 'there are probably more than 1,200 different ISDS clauses in the roughly 1,500 treaties that provide for ISDS through international arbitration'.[25] One noteworthy difference in ISDS language can be found between the single ISDS clause approach adopted by European countries and the much more detailed approach followed by Canada, the United States, and some other countries. In spite of

---

21 Judgment of the District Court of The Hague [*Rechtbank's-Gravenhage*] was rendered on 20 April 2016.

22 All of these statistics are set out in UNCTAD (n 3) 5.

23 Joachim Pohl, Kekeletso Mashigo, and Alexis Nohen, 'Dispute Settlement Provisions in International Investment Agreements: A Large Sample Survey', (2012) OECD Working Papers on International Investment No 2012/2 <www.oecd.org/daf/inv/investment-policy/wp-2012_2.pdf> accessed 14 July 2019.

24 See the discussion in Mehmet Toral and Thomas Schultz, 'The State, a Perpetual Respondent in Investment Arbitration? Some Unorthodox Considerations', in Michael Waibel, Asha Kaushal, Kyo-Hwa Liz Chung, and Claire Balchin (eds), *The Backlash Against Investment Arbitration: Perceptions and Reality* (Kluwer Law International 2010) 577.

25 Pohl, Mashigo, and Nohen (n 23) 43, adding that 'Such variation in the treaty language is likely to both motivate and complicate possible harmonisation of international investment law. It may also affect the apparent consistency of arbitral awards, and increase the costs of arbitration and other dispute settlement, since each difference in language opens an angle for difference in interpretation and consequently different decisions on similar matters. Differences in treaty provisions, even slight differences, invite legal counsel to argue for different treatment, which in turn, requires arbitrators to respond to such legal reasoning, thereby driving up fees for legal counsel and arbitrators alike'.

228   *J Anthony VanDuzer and Patrick Dumberry*

such diversity, several basic features can be identified: the parties' consent to arbitration, provisions defining the scope of ISDS (meaning what claims can be made), and rules governing the dispute settlement process.[26] A number of additional features found in some ISDS procedures are discussed below.

3.2 Consent

In IIA arbitration, a tribunal's jurisdiction over a dispute is based on the consent to arbitration given by both the claimant investor and the respondent state. The investor's consent is assumed from the fact that it commenced the arbitration proceedings, though in some agreements, the investor must file a document expressing its consent when it makes its arbitration claim.[27] The state's consent is found in the IIA. Each state consents to arbitration for claims submitted by any investor of the other state party that satisfies the requirements under the agreement.[28]

Because a state's consent to arbitrate in an IIA extends to all investors claiming a breach of rights protected under that agreement, states are exposed to claims from a broadly defined, indeterminate class of businesses that invest while the agreement is in force.[29] By comparison, a state's consent to arbitrate in a contract with a particular investor exposes the state only to claims by that investor with respect to the specific obligations in the contract undertaken by the state. Liability risks in relation to contracts are more limited and predictable. As well, arbitration is available to the state in relation to the obligations of the investor. The second significant implication of the state's consent being given in advance in an IIA is that in many investor–state arbitration cases there is an issue as to whether the investor is entitled to make its claim in relation to its investment. Dealing with these types of jurisdictional issues often significantly extends the time needed to conclude ISDS proceedings.

IIAs increasingly include procedural requirements that must be satisfied before an investor can proceed with an investor–state claim; these requirements are designed to limit state exposure to claims and facilitate early resolution of

---

26 UNCTAD, 'Investor–State Dispute Settlement: A Sequel', UNCTAD Series on Issues in International Investment Agreements II (United Nations 2014) 20.

27 e.g. Comprehensive Economic and Trade Agreement between Canada and the European Union, signed 30 October 2016, entered into force 21 September 2017 (CETA), art 8.22. The parties' consent is in art 8.25.

28 Jan Paulsson, 'Arbitration without Privity' (1995) 10 *ICSID Review – Foreign Investment Law Journal* 232. It should be added, however, that other IIAs contain different forms of 'diluted' consent to arbitration. Some treaties, for instance, provide that a state 'shall agree' to give its consent *in the future*. Others indicate that an investor cannot initiate arbitral proceedings on the basis of the treaty alone but must first obtain the consent of the host state in relation to the specific dispute concerned. See, UNCTAD (n 26) 31 ff.

29 Sometimes agreements extend protection to investments made before the agreement is in force (e.g. CETA (n 27) art 8.1).

Investor–state dispute settlement 229

claims. In some agreements, a state's consent to arbitration is subject to the claimant investor fulfilling one or more of these requirements.[30]

- A waiting (or 'cooling-off') period (typically 6 months) must elapse before the arbitration procedure can begin.[31]
- An attempt to resolve the dispute 'amicably' through negotiations and consultations must be made by the disputing parties for a certain period of time (typically from 3 to 12 months) before the arbitration procedure can start.[32] Requirements for consultations and cooling-off periods are intended to ensure that states will have early information about investor claims and a minimum time period to consult with investors with a view to settling or otherwise disposing of claims expeditiously and before significant costs are incurred and positions entrenched.
- An investor must have unsuccessfully pursued local remedies before the courts of the host state for a certain period of time (typically 18 months) before being allowed to seek relief in arbitration. These exhaustion-of-local-remedies requirements are intended to ensure that there is an opportunity for local courts to resolve the investor's concern before an ISDS claim is made.[33]
- As an alternative to an exhaustion-of-local-remedies requirement, an investor can only seek relief in one forum, typically domestic courts in the host state or ISDS (a so-called 'fork-in-the-road' provision) or in one forum at a time.[34] The former type of provision is intended to ensure that states do not have to deal with an investor's claim more than once, while the latter ensures that states do not have to deal with multiple claims arising out of the same facts at the same time.
- An investor must bring a claim within a specific period of time (typically ranging from 2 to 5 years) after having acquired knowledge of the alleged breach.[35] These provisions are intended to limit state exposure to investor claims by cutting off the risk of an investor–state claim after the time has expired.[36]

---

30 e.g. Agreement between the Government of Canada and the Government of the Peoples' Republic of China for the Promotion and Protection of Investments, signed 9 September 2012, entered into force 1 October 2014, *Canada Treaty Series* 2014/26, art 21 (Canada-China BIT). Many treaties that impose these kinds of procedures do not specify that compliance with them is a condition of a state's consent and an arbitral tribunal's jurisdiction.

31 This condition was found in 90 percent of the treaties examined in a recent survey by Pohl, Mashigo, and Nohen (n 23) 17.

32 ibid. This condition was found in 81 percent of the treaties surveyed.

33 ibid 13. Only 8 percent of these treaties require an investor to first present its dispute to a domestic court before having access to international arbitration.

34 The second option requires the claimant to waive its right to pursue domestic litigation during the period it is pursuing an international arbitration.

35 This kind of provision was found in only 7 percent of the treaties surveyed by Pohl, Mashigo, and Nohen (n 23) 18.

36 A number of investor–state arbitration tribunals have allowed investors to avoid the application of these kinds of requirements based on a most-favoured nation (MFN) clause found in

230   *J Anthony VanDuzer and Patrick Dumberry*

3.3 Scope of ISDS

As discussed in Chapter 10 in this volume, the definitions of investors and their investments in IIAs determine the class of economic actors protected under an IIA. For the purposes of ISDS, these definitions establish to whom states may be held liable when they fail to provide protection. Arbitral tribunals do not have jurisdiction over an investor's claim if the investor has not made an investment within the definition of that term in the IIA.[37] In negotiating definitions of investor and investment, then, a state should consider, on the one hand, the kinds of investments that treaty commitments backed up by ISDS will attract, and, on the other hand, its exposure to investor–state arbitration.

IIAs may also contain provisions that define the types of dispute that both states have agreed to submit to arbitration. There are ISDS clauses that only allow an investor to submit a claim to arbitration in cases where it alleges a breach of the treaty itself (such as the obligation to accord a fair and equitable treatment).[38] Some treaties, however, contain very broad language whereby 'all' or 'any' disputes that are 'in connection with an investment' (or disputes 'arising out', 'with respect to' or 'concerning' an investment) can be submitted to arbitration. Such broad language may allow a tribunal to have jurisdiction over disputes that do not involve any alleged violation of the treaty, such as contractual claims.[39] Some IIAs contain clauses that extend jurisdiction not only to 'any dispute relating to investments' but also require the host state to 'observe any obligation it may have entered to' in relation to an investor. These kinds of provisions are often referred to as 'umbrella clauses'. According to one estimate, 40 per cent of BITs contain some form of umbrella clause.[40] Arbitral tribunals have offered different interpretations regarding the circumstances in which investors can rely on them.[41] Because umbrella clauses expose

---

the IIA under which the proceedings were commenced where the host state had agreed to provide access to ISDS without meeting them: UNCTAD, 'Most-Favoured-Nation Treatment: A Sequel', UNCTAD Series on Issues in International Investment Agreements II (United Nations 2010) 12. MFN clauses are discussed by Vanhonnaeker (n 2).

37 Some treaties include 'denial of benefits' clauses that permit a host state to deny treaty protection to investors that are 'shell' (or 'mailbox') companies that have no substantial business activities in the other state or are controlled by nationals of third states.

38 Canada-China BIT (n 30).

39 UNCTAD (n 26) 38.

40 Judith Gill, Matthew Gearing, and Gemma Birt, 'Contractual Claims and Bilateral Investment Treaties: A Comparative Review of the SGS Cases' (2004) 21 *Journal of International Arbitration* 31.

41 e.g. different interpretations were given by these two tribunals: *SGS Société Générale de Surveillance SA v Philippines*, ICSID Case No ARB/02/6, Award on Jurisdiction (29 January 2004); *SGS Société Générale de Surveillance SA v Pakistan*, ICSID Case No ARB/01/13, Award on Jurisdiction (6 August 2003).

Investor–state dispute settlement   231

states to a wide and unpredictable range of claims and create the prospect of parallel proceedings, they are less and less common in recent IIAs.[42]

States may also agree to exclude from ISDS certain subject matters (e.g. taxation and public procurement).[43] Where IIA obligations extend to protect investors in the 'pre-establishment' phase, that is before they have entered the host-state market, such exceptions are especially common. Even states that have agreed to provide some protection to foreign investors in connection with entry into their market may not want to be subject to ISDS claims in relation to such investments, perhaps because at the pre-establishment stage investors have not made any contribution to the host country's economy.[44]

3.4 Applicable arbitration rules

Treaty provisions on ISDS are complemented by arbitration rules referred to in the agreement. These rules govern many of the most important issues arising in arbitration proceedings, including the appointment and composition of the arbitral tribunal, the place of arbitration, and the applicable law, because most IIAs do not include provisions dealing with these issues. In the event of any conflict between the arbitration rules and the agreement, the latter prevails. Modern IIAs typically offer two or more possible sets of arbitration rules that the investor can choose from to govern ISDS proceedings.[45] Only a few require the parties to agree on a specific forum.[46] The ICSID Convention[47] (and its arbitration rules) and the Arbitration Rules of the United Nations Commission on International Trade Law (UNCITRAL)[48] are by far the most-often referred to options in IIAs.[49]

---

42 UNCTAD, *UNCTAD's Reform Package for the International Investment Regime* (United Nations 2018) 46.

43 Under CETA (n 27), certain claims in relation to government debt restructuring are excluded from dispute settlement (Annex 8-B).

44 As discussed in Vanhonnaeker (n 2), most IIA obligations do not apply to the pre-establishment stage. Even countries that do routinely enter into IIAs that have pre-establishment commitments, like Canada, have some exclusions from ISDS in relation to those commitments. For example, Canada excludes its review of foreign investment from ISDS in its IIAs (e.g. CETA, ibid, art 8.45 and Annex 8-C).

45 According to one estimate, 56 percent of treaties offer investors the possibility to choose from among at least two arbitration rules (Pohl, Mashigo, and Nohen (n 23) 8, 21).

46 ibid.

47 Convention on the Settlement of Investment Disputes between States and Nationals of Other States, 18 March 1965, 575 UNTS 160, 4 ILM 532 (1965). In 1978, the ICSID Additional Facility Rules entered into force. The Additional Facility Rules are designed primarily to offer an arbitral procedure for the settlement of investment disputes where the host state or the state of the investor's nationality, but not both, is a party to the ICSID Convention.

48 The UNCITRAL Arbitration Rules were approved by the United Nations General Assembly on 15 December 1976, UN GAOR, 31st Session, Supp. No. 17, at 46, Ch. V, Sec. C, UN Doc. A/31/17, 1976.

49 Pohl, Mashigo, and Nohen (n 23) 8.

The majority of known investor–state claims have been arbitrated under either the ICSID Convention (or the ICSID Additional Facility Rules) (63 per cent) or the UNCITRAL Arbitration Rules (28 per cent).[50] A limited number of cases have been conducted under the rules of the Stockholm Chamber of Commerce and those of the International Chamber of Commerce.[51] There are undoubtedly a large number of other arbitration cases for which information is not publicly available.

The main difference between the ICSID Convention and other arbitral rules is that an award rendered by a tribunal under the ICSID Convention can only be 'annulled' by an *ad hoc* 'annulment committee' appointed by the Chairman of the ICSID Administrative Council on the following grounds: (i) the tribunal was not properly constituted; (ii) the tribunal has manifestly exceeded its powers; (iii) corruption on the part of a member of the tribunal; (iv) a serious departure from a fundamental rule of procedure; or (v) the award has failed to state the reasons on which it is based. If an award is not annulled, every state party to the ICSID Convention must enforce it as if it were a decision of its domestic courts. By contrast, an award by a tribunal established under the UNCITRAL Arbitration Rules or any other arbitration rules contemplated in an IIA can usually be set aside by the domestic court at the place of arbitration. The grounds for doing so are established under domestic law in the place where the set-aside application is brought. In many countries, however, the grounds are limited to situations where there was some kind of fundamental problem with the arbitration procedure, the tribunal exceeded its jurisdiction, or the award is contrary to public policy in the state where the set-aside application was made. Typically, an award cannot be set aside because the tribunal made a legal or factual error.[52] As well, 159 countries are parties to the United Nations Convention on the Recognition and Enforcement of Foreign Arbitral Awards (called the New York Convention).[53] Under the New York Convention, all party states commit to enforcing foreign arbitral awards just as if they were domestic judgements, unless these same kinds of grounds are made out. Overall, because of the ICSID Convention and the New York Convention, states are legally required to enforce ISDS awards in most circumstances. By contrast, domestic court decisions of one country are often not enforceable in another.

---

50 As of 30 June 2018, ICSID had registered 676 cases under the ICSID Convention and the Additional Facility Rules (ICSID, *The ICSID Caseload-Statistics*, Issue 2018–2 (World Bank 2018) 8). 89 percent of these cases were conducted under the ICSID Convention and another 9 percent under the ICSID Additional Facility Rules (n 47).

51 UNCTAD (n 3) 9.

52 These grounds are provided for in art 34 of the UNCITRAL Model Law on International Commercial Arbitration, which has been adopted in 80 countries world-wide, available at <www.uncitral.org/uncitral/en/uncitral_texts/arbitration/1985Model_arbitration_status. html> accessed 15 March 2019.

53 Convention on the Recognition and Enforcement of Foreign Arbitral Awards, New York, 10 June 1958, 330 UNTS No 4739.

Investor–state dispute settlement 233

3.5 *Additional elements of ISDS procedures*

As noted by UNCTAD, 'many ISDS provisions have grown in sophistication and complexity as States attempt to respond to problems they have encountered when arbitrating investor–state disputes under previously-concluded IIAs'.[54] Not surprisingly, this trend is best reflected in the practice of states that have frequently appeared as respondents in investment disputes (such as Canada and the United States in the context of NAFTA proceedings). An increasing number of treaties are adopting additional requirements that must be satisfied for a claim to be pursued, as discussed above. But a number of other kinds of clauses are appearing with increasing regularity to give states greater control over the process, thereby allowing states to manage their exposure to liability.

Consolidation of ISDS claims: Some treaties, like NAFTA and CETA, provide that a respondent state can ask to have claims by multiple investors consolidated when they have a common question of law or fact and arise out of the same events.[55] Consolidation allows a state to avoid the costs of multiple duplicative proceedings and the risk of inconsistent decisions regarding the same state action.

Early determination of preliminary objections by the state: A concern frequently expressed by states is that they must often go through an entire arbitration process and incur substantial costs in relation to ISDS claims that should have been thrown out early because the tribunal ultimately found that it did not have jurisdiction to decide the matter, but only did so after the case had been fully argued both orally and in writing.[56] A few treaties have sought to address this. Under CETA, when a state makes a preliminary objection to the jurisdiction of the tribunal to hear the investor's claim, the tribunal should, wherever possible, decide the matter before proceeding to the merits.[57] A similar early determination requirement applies to state objections that the investor's claim is 'manifestly without merit'. This kind of expedited process to dispose of weak cases is also provided for under the ICSID Arbitration Rules.[58]

Limitations on remedies: The general practice in ISDS cases is to award only compensatory damages.[59] Some agreements make this explicit. In CETA and

---

54 UNCTAD (n 26) 20.

55 North American Agreement Free Trade Agreement, signed 14 September 1993, entered into force 1 January 1994, *Canada Treaty Series* 1994/2 (NAFTA), art 1126; CETA (n 27) art 8.43.

56 UNCTAD, *Bilateral Investment Treaties 1995–2006: Trends in Investment Rule-making* (United Nations 2007).

57 CETA (n 27) art 8.33. Objections to the admissibility of the claim are also covered by this provision.

58 Preliminary objections relating to jurisdiction and (since 10 April 2006) a manifest absence of legal merit are provided for in the Arbitration Rules of the International Center for the Settlement of Investment Disputes (ICSID Arbitration Rules, art 41).

59 Borzu Sabahi, *Compensation and Restitution in Investor–State Arbitration: Principles and Practice* (Oxford University Press 2011). There have been cases in which tribunals have awarded behavioural relief: e.g. the payment of an energy tariff was ordered to be reinstated in *Nykomb Synergetics Technology Holding AB v The Republic of Latvia*, SCC, Award (6 December 2003).

NAFTA, remedies against the state are limited to financial compensation for losses incurred. No punitive damages are available and states cannot be forced to change their regimes.[60] Also, CETA contains a unique rule that damages must be reduced to take into account any restitution by the state of the investor's property or the repeal or modification of the measure on which the claim is based.[61]

State role in interpretation: An increasing number of agreements, like CETA and NAFTA, permit state parties to adopt interpretations of treaty provisions. This mechanism may be used to correct what the parties consider inappropriate interpretations by ISDS tribunals.[62] Both agreements also permit submissions by the state party that is not the respondent in an ISDS case on issues of treaty interpretation that are at stake in the case.[63]

4. Current issues dealing with ISDS clauses – systemic challenges and proposed solutions

The practice of arbitral tribunals in the past two decades has highlighted a number of systemic deficiencies in ISDS.[64] Several of these are discussed below.

4.1 Arbitrator independence and quality

A concern that goes to the legitimacy of ISDS is whether party-appointed arbitrators are really independent and impartial.[65] The worry is less that there is evidence of actual bias than that ISDS features do not guarantee independence and impartiality. In ISDS, the investor and the respondent state each appoint one arbitrator and they agree to the appointment of the president of the tribunal. Arbitrators are appointed for a particular case and are paid by the parties on an hourly basis. Critics have identified a number of risks related to arbitrator independence from the parties and partiality in relation to the outcome of cases that arise with this arrangement.[66] One obvious risk is that party-appointed

---

60 NAFTA (n 55) art 1135; CETA (n 27) art 8.39. Behavioural orders may be made for the purposes of granting interim relief such as to preserve evidence prior the conclusion of a case (e.g. CETA, ibid, art 8.34).

61 ibid CETA art 8.39.3.

62 ibid CETA art 8.31(3); NAFTA (n 55) art 1131.

63 ibid CETA art 8.38; ibid NAFTA art 1128.

64 UNCTAD, *Reform of Investor–State Dispute Settlement: In Search of a Roadmap*, IIA Issues Note, No 2, June 2013, 2–4: Armand de Mestral, 'Investor–State Arbitration Between Developed Democratic Countries' (2015) Centre for International Governance Innovation Investor–State Arbitration Paper Series No 1 available at <www.cigionline.org/publications/investor-state-arbitration-between-developed-democratic-countries> accessed 14 July 2019.

65 UNCTAD ibid 4. On this question, see David Gaukrodger and Katharine Gordon, 'Investor–State Dispute Settlement: A Scoping Paper for the Investment Policy Community' (2012) OECD Working Papers on International Investment No 2012/3, 45 ff.

66 ibid Gaukrodger and Gordon.

arbitrators might favour the party that appointed them. More generally, since only investors can initiate cases, arbitrators might favour investors to ensure future opportunities for work. Arbitrators might be encouraged not only to make favourable decisions on the merits of ISDS claims but also to reject jurisdictional challenges by states. Rejecting jurisdictional challenges would also prolong proceedings and, as a result, increase arbitrators' fees. Outside work in other cases as arbitrators or as advocates on behalf of investors or expert witnesses creates the risk of additional conflicts of interest. For example, a counsel in one case may appoint someone as an arbitrator in the hope that he or she will be appointed as an arbitrator when that arbitrator is the counsel in a future case. Or, more simply, a person's role as an advocate in one case may affect their actions as an arbitrator in another case. While the seriousness of these concerns is contested,[67] challenges to arbitrators based on conflicts of interests are increasing.[68] Calls to address these concerns are being made by an ever-growing number of academics and governments.[69] Many have argued that the only way to address them is to move to a judicial model with ISDS decision-makers appointed for fixed terms with security of tenure, independently funded, and precluded from engaging in outside activities to avoid conflicts of interest.[70] Such a proposal is discussed below.

Another concern that relates to ISDS legitimacy is that investor–state arbitration disputes sometimes involve an investor challenging a state's public policy, including matters such as environmental protection and public health. It has been argued that an arbitral tribunal, consisting of three arbitrators, who are often private-sector lawyers or legal academics, appointed on an *ad hoc* basis by the investor and the state, is not an appropriate body to assess the validity of states' acts, especially when the dispute involves sensitive public policy issues.[71] The concern is that arbitrators' mandate is limited to adjudicating the investor's claim that the state has breached its investor-protection obligation under the IIA, without regard to the interests of other stakeholders affected by the

---

67 Alexis Mourre, 'Are unilateral appointments defensible? On Jan Paulsson's Moral Hazard in International Arbitration' Kluwer Arbitration Blog (5 October 2010), <http://arbitration blog.kluwerarbitration.com/2010/10/05/are-unilateral-appointments-defensible-on-jan-paulssons-moral-hazard-in-international-arbitration/> accessed 14 July 2019.

68 Georgios Dimitropolous, 'Constructing the Independence of International Investment Arbitrators: Past Present and Future' (2016) 36 *Northwestern Journal of International Law and Business* 371.

69 e.g. Markus Krajewski, *Modell-Investitionsschutzvertrag mit Investor-Staat-Schiedsverfahren für Industriestaaten unter Berücksichtigung der USA* submitted to the Council of Europe by German Vice Chancellor and Minister of Foreign Affairs and Energy Sigmar Gabriel on 7 May 2015.

70 Gus van Harten, 'Investment Treaty Arbitration, Procedural Fairness, and the Rule of Law' in Stephan Schill (ed), *International Investment Law and Comparative Public Law* (Oxford University Press 2010) 627.

71 UNCTAD (n 64) 3; UNCTAD (n 26) 25. To some extent this issue can be addressed by better drafting of the substantive standards of investor protection to ensure states have sufficient freedom to regulate in the public interest as discussed by Vanhonnaeker (n 2).

236   *J Anthony VanDuzer and Patrick Dumberry*

investor's actions or other non-investment concerns that might have motivated the state action that the investor is now challenging. Unlike domestic judges, they do not have a duty to consider these other interests and concerns and little expertise in doing so.

4.2 Transparency and non-disputing party participation

The absence of guarantees of transparency and rights of persons, other than the state and the investor, to participate in investor–state disputes has also been characterized as impairing the legitimacy of ISDS.

While most arbitration proceedings are subject to a degree of transparency in practice and some arbitration rules have adopted stronger transparency requirements over the years,[72] it remains the case that not all awards are made public. As well, with few exceptions (such as, for instance, CETA), most treaties contain no requirements for public disclosure of pleadings or other submissions of the parties or tribunal orders made prior to the final award. In practice, the pleadings of the parties often remain confidential. There is also generally no public access to hearings and non-disputing parties are not allowed to participate as parties or, often, even to submit briefs during the proceedings.[73] Moreover, under many treaties the very existence of proceedings can be kept confidential if both parties wish. As discussed above, investor–state cases can involve challenges to public acts by governments as opposed to commercial disputes. As a result, many argue that investor–state arbitration must meet higher standards for democratic accountability than have traditionally been required in ISDS procedures, including much greater transparency and the participation of affected interests other than the investor and the respondent state.[74]

4.3 Inconsistency and incoherence in tribunal awards

Different tribunals have sometimes rendered inconsistent and incoherent awards in situations where they had to interpret identical or similar treaty provisions or when they were faced with cases involving similar or even identical facts.[75] As noted by UNCTAD, inconsistent interpretations by tribunals 'have led to uncertainty about the meaning of key treaty obligations and lack of

---

72 e.g. the 2006 amendments to the ICSID Arbitration Rules and the UNCITRAL Rules on Transparency in Treaty-based Investor–State Arbitration, GA Res 68/109 adopted on 16 December 2013.

73 Pohl, Mashigo, and Nohen (n 23) 37, indicating that out of the 1,600 treaties surveyed, 8 bilateral treaties contain provisions regarding public access to hearings of arbitral tribunals and that only 25 treaties in the sample contain provisions on the participation of non-disputing parties, experts, *amici curiae* or other interested individuals or entities.

74 Van Harten (n 70).

75 On this question, see Gaukrodger and Gordon (n 65) 58 ff.

predictability of how they will be applied in future cases'.[76] This problem is compounded by the fact that currently no review or appeal mechanism exists under IIAs that could reconcile divergent outcomes or correct erroneous decisions rendered by tribunals. As mentioned above, under the ICSID Convention, an *ad hoc* annulment committee may only annul an award based on a limited number of grounds that do not include errors in assessing the facts or interpreting and applying the treaty. National court review to set aside an award at the place of arbitration for cases under the ICSID Additional Facility Rules and other non-ICSID arbitrations is also possible, but typically the grounds of review are narrow and do not include errors of fact or law.[77]

4.4 Cost of ISDS

Investment arbitration is time-consuming and very expensive. As noted, awards average in excess of US$100 million with some awards many times that. According to one study, '[o]n average, costs, including legal fees and tribunal expenses, have exceeded $8 million per party per case'.[78] High costs are a concern for all states, but especially for developing states. As noted by OECD researchers, 'developing States with little experience in international litigation and with small in-house legal departments may be overwhelmed by the resources available to large investors'.[79] Costs are also a concern for small investors. A report examining about 100 ISDS cases found that 22 per cent of the claimants in these cases were either individuals or very small corporations with limited foreign operations.[80] The authors summarized the effects as follows:

> It has been noted that the high costs of ISDS or the threat of such costs can have a dissuasive effect on States and that investors can use the spectre of high-cost ISDS litigation to bring a recalcitrant State to the negotiating table for purposes of achieving a settlement of the dispute. Similar effects may also exist for investors. It appears that a number of ISDS claims by investors have been discontinued due to the refusal or inability of the investors to pay the costs. High costs will likely generally play to the advantage of financially stronger parties (including third party sources of funding) on either side.[81]

---

76 UNCTAD (n 26) 3.

77 e.g. under the rules of the UNCITRAL Model Law on International Commercial Arbitration (n 52), art 34, an arbitration award can only be set aside on the basis of very limited grounds not including substantive error.

78 Gaukrodger and Gordon (n 65) 19, noting that the fees for legal counsel and experts represents about 82 percent of the total costs, those of arbitrators represent 16 percent and those of institutions 2 percent.

79 Pohl, Mashigo, and Nohen (n 23).

80 ibid 17–18, also noting that medium and large multinational enterprises account for about half of the total sample.

81 ibid.

238 *J Anthony VanDuzer and Patrick Dumberry*

It should be added that there exists no uniform rule with respect to the final allocation of costs by tribunals.[82] Even if the respondent state ends up winning the case, a tribunal may decide not to order the claimant investor to pay the respondent's costs.[83] In fact, most investment tribunals have ordered parties to share the costs of the proceedings equally and to bear their own legal fees.[84] Yet, there has been a trend in recent cases to shift at least some costs to the losing party.[85]

4.5 *Treaty shopping*

A final area of concern is the problem of so-called 'nationality planning' or 'treaty shopping'. This occurs where investors channel an investment through a company established in an intermediary country with the sole purpose of benefiting from an IIA concluded by that country with the host state, including by gaining access to ISDS procedures against the host state.[86] Treaty shopping is facilitated by IIA provisions requiring only that investors be incorporated under the laws of a country in order to be eligible to be protected under treaties entered into by that country. This common type of IIA provision was famously abused by US cigarette producer Philip Morris, which brought a case against Australia through its Hong Kong subsidiary because there was no ISDS in the Australia–United States Free Trade Agreement.[87]

5. Paths to reform

Widespread dissatisfaction with the existing ISDS system has encouraged a rethinking of the system. A very wide range of reform options have been proposed.[88]

States could simply abandon ISDS as a means of dispute resolution and return to state-to-state arbitration proceedings.[89] This solution is favoured by

---

82 UNCTAD (n 26) 148, referring to Richard Kreindler, 'Final Rulings on Costs: Loser Pays All?' (2010) 7 *Transnational Dispute Management*.

83 UNCTAD ibid 28, 147. It should be noted that while the ICSID Arbitration Rules contain no presumption about the allocation of costs, Article 42(1) of the UNCITRAL Arbitration Rules (n 48) (as amended in 2010) provides that 'The costs of the arbitration shall in principle be borne by the unsuccessful party or parties. However, the arbitral tribunal may apportion each of such costs between the parties if it determines that apportionment is reasonable, taking into account the circumstances of the case'.

84 ibid 149, referring to Susan Franck, 'Rationalizing Costs in Investment Treaty Arbitration' (2011) 88 *Washington University Law Review* 769.

85 Gaukrodger and Gordon (n 65).

86 ibid 51 ff; UNCTAD (n 64) 3.

87 *Philip Morris Asia Limited v The Commonwealth of Australia*, UNCITRAL, PCA Case No 2012–12, Award on Jurisdiction and Admissibility (7 December 2015). The tribunal found the claim inadmissible as an abuse of rights.

88 UNCTAD (n 64) 4; UNCTAD, *Investment Policy Framework for Sustainable Development* (United Nations 2015).

89 UNCTAD (n 26).

a number of scholars,[90] and has been adopted by several states in recent IIAs.[91] For instance, in 2011, Australia issued a policy statement to the effect that it would no longer include an ISDS clause in its investment treaties.[92] Some states have terminated existing IIAs. South Africa and Indonesia among others have terminated some BITS and publicly stated an intention to terminate others. It should be noted, however, that, typically, such a dramatic step will have a limited impact for a number of years post-termination. This is because most IIAs include so-called 'survival' clauses, whereby IIA protections, including ISDS, remain in effect for many years (5 to 20 years) post-termination for investments in place prior to termination. A number of states (such as Ecuador, Venezuela, and Bolivia) have denounced the ICSID Convention and thus terminated its application to them. But so long as there are other arbitration rules available under their IIAs, these countries will continue to be exposed to ISDS claims.

A number of other less drastic options are available to states. By tailoring the existing system, states could preserve the main features of investment arbitration while at the same time addressing deficiencies in the ISDS system. Changes can be implemented in the context of new IIAs or through amendments to existing ones. An estimated 1,185 BITs are presently eligible for renegotiation or termination under their terms and, of course, parties can always renegotiate their treaties if they both agree.[93] The highly fragmented nature of the international investment regime, however, makes coordinated reform extremely difficult. In this section some of the main options to respond to the systemic deficiencies outlined above are discussed.

5.1 Arbitrator quality and independence

A range of proposals have been made to address concerns about arbitrator quality and independence, some of which have been incorporated in recent treaties. Some seek to improve the existing *ad hoc* arbitration model. For

---

90 See, *Open Letter from Lawyers to the Negotiators of the Trans-Pacific Partnership Urging the Rejection of Investor–State Dispute Settlement* (8 May 2012), available at <http://tpplegal. wordpress.com/open-letter/> accessed 10 June 2019.

91 See UNCTAD (n 64), referring to Japan-Philippines Economic Partnership Agreement (2006), Australia–United States Free Trade Agreement (2004), Australia-Malaysia Free Trade Agreement (2012).

92 Gillard Government Trade Policy Statement: *Trading Our Way to More Jobs and Prosperity*, April 2011, available at <www.dfat.gov.au/publications/trade/trading-our-way-to-more-jobs-and-prosperity.pdf> accessed 10 June 2019. Australia has, however, since then apparently abandoned that policy and signed a FTA with South Korea (2013), which includes an ISDS mechanism (available at <www.dfat.gov.au/fta/kafta/downloads/fact-sheet-isds.pdf> accessed 10 June 2019). The more recent Australia–Japan Free Trade Agreement, however, does not include an ISDS mechanism.

93 UNCTAD, *Phase 2 of IIA Reform: Modernizing the Existing Stock of Old-Generation Treaties*, IIA Issues Note No 2, 2017 (United Nations 2017); UNCTAD, *International Investment Policymaking in Transition: Challenges and Opportunities of Treaty Renewal*, IIA Issues Note No 4 2013 (United Nations 2013).

240 *J Anthony VanDuzer and Patrick Dumberry*

example, several treaties set out standards for arbitrator competence, though for the most part, these are quite general.[94] Many of the same treaties contemplate codes of conduct for arbitrators that specifically define and require disclosure regarding possible conflicts of interest.[95] One approach is to incorporate by reference the International Bar Association's Guidelines on Conflicts of Interest,[96] as in CETA.[97]

CETA also adopts far more fundamental changes to the traditional ISDS model, though these aspects of the agreement are not yet in force. Instead of having arbitrators appointed by the parties for a particular case, CETA will establish a standing tribunal whose members are chosen by the state parties for fixed terms. The tribunal is to be composed of 15 members; 5 Canadians, 5 EU nationals, and 5 who are not nationals of the EU or Canada. Each case is to be decided by a three-person 'division' of the tribunal chosen by the president of the tribunal who is not a Canadian or EU national and is chosen by lot from the members of the tribunal every year. The President is to ensure that appointments are random and unpredictable, though the modalities for how this is to occur are not specified. Once appointed, the ability of members of the tribunal to engage in outside work is constrained in ways intended to limit the prospects for conflicts of interest. Tribunal members are to be paid a retainer that is still to be fixed, have a general obligation to be available to perform their functions, and cannot work as counsel or expert witnesses in other investor–state disputes. Tribunal members are not, however, prohibited from taking appointments as arbitrators in other cases.[98] The proposed CETA Tribunal is not fully a court. Unlike a court, tribunal members are not full time or permanent and are not paid a fixed, secure salary regardless of whether cases are brought or how long they last. They are compensated on the same *per diem* basis as arbitrators in ICSID arbitrations. Outside CETA's context, the EU and Canada have proposed the creation of a permanent multilateral investment court to replace the present system of *ad hoc* tribunals that would have jurisdiction to hear all investor–state disputes under IIAs between countries that agreed to submit to it.[99] Establishing such a court raises

---

94 e.g. Canada's model bilateral investment treaty requires 'expertise or experience in public international law, international trade or international investment rules, or the resolution of disputes arising under international trade or international investment agreements' (art 27).

95 e.g. CETA (n 27) art 8.44(2). At this point, however, the code is still to be developed by the Committee on Services and Investment established under CETA.

96 The Guidelines have been relied on previously in ISDS cases.

97 A very similar structure, however, was included in the EU–Vietnam Investment Protection Agreement in arts 3.38 and 3.39. An agreed text of this agreement was released in January 2016 for information purposes. It has not been ratified.

98 CETA (n 27) art 8.30(1).

99 European Commission, 'SPEECH: Commissioner Malmström lays out EU plans for a multilateral investment court' (Dispute Settlement, Brussels, 22 November 2018) <http://trade.ec.europa.eu/doclib/press/index.cfm?id=1943> accessed 15 January 2019.

Investor–state dispute settlement 241

a host of complex issues that are still to be resolved.[100] There are institutional issues such as how states will transfer jurisdiction over investor–state disputes to the court from investor–state arbitration tribunals contemplated in their thousands of IIAs. Questions exist as to the ways in which enforcement of the court's decisions can be guaranteed, because the treaties that virtually guarantee enforcement of investor–state arbitration awards (the ICSID Convention and the New York Convention) will not automatically apply. There are also more specific concerns, including the question of how judicial appointments will be made in a way that ensures improved quality, independence, and diversity compared to the existing ISDS system. Funding for the court will also be challenging, at least until a number of states agree to have the court adjudicate their investor–state disputes. At the moment, many countries, including the United States and leading developing countries like Argentina, Brazil, and India, remain opposed.

5.2 Transparency and non-disputing party participation

Only a few countries include transparency guarantees in their IIAs, though some transparency is provided in practice, especially with respect to tribunal awards, despite the absence of legal requirements.[101] A significant step forward regarding transparency was taken on 1 April 2014, when the UNCITRAL Rules on Transparency in Treaty-based Investor–State Arbitration (UNCITRAL Transparency Rules) came into force.[102] These rules require a high degree of transparency and apply to all ISDS disputes that are governed by the UNCITRAL Arbitration Rules and initiated under IIAs concluded on or after 1 April 2014. For ISDS disputes governed by the UNCITRAL Arbitration Rules under earlier treaties, the new rules apply only if the state parties (or the parties to the dispute) agree.[103] The UNCITRAL Transparency Rules provide that all documents submitted to and issued by an ISDS tribunal must be made public and all hearings must be open the public, subject to any restrictions

---

100 Robert Howse, 'Designing a Multilateral Investment Court: Issues and Options' (2017) 36 *Yearbook of European Law* 209.

101 e.g. though such disclosure is not required in NAFTA, it has been the practice of Canada, the US and Mexico to seek the disclosure of those documents and hold public hearings in any case, and typically all these documents have been made public (J Anthony VanDuzer, 'Enhancing the Procedural Legitimacy of Investor–State Arbitration through Transparency and *Amicus Curiae* Participation' (2007) 52 *McGill Law Journal* 681).

102 ibid.

103 States can commit to having the UNCITRAL Rules on Transparency in Treaty-based Investor–State Arbitration (n 72) apply to ISDS disputes under their IIAs concluded before 1 April 2014 under the United Nations Convention on Transparency in Treaty-based Investor–State Arbitration (adopted 10 December 2014, in force 18 October 2017). Only five states have ratified this treaty at the date of writing. CETA was the first treaty to incorporate the UNCITRAL Transparency Rules (CETA (n 27) art 8.36).

242   *J Anthony VanDuzer and Patrick Dumberry*

necessary to protect confidential information. The UNCITRAL Transparency Rules also provide that persons with an interest in an ISDS case may seek leave to make submissions to the ISDS tribunal as friends of the court or *amicus curiae*. Under this procedure, it is up to the tribunal to decide whether an *amicus curiae* submission will be accepted on the basis of whether it would 'assist the arbitral tribunal in the determination of a factual or legal issue related to the arbitral proceedings by bringing a perspective, particular knowledge or insight that is different from that of the disputing parties'.[104] There is no right for interested parties to participate and they have no standing as parties to an ISDS case even if they will be directly affected by the outcome of the case.

5.3 Inconsistency and incoherence

As discussed above, IIA provisions allowing parties to issue interpretations of treaty provisions that are binding on arbitral tribunals are one way for states to address inconsistent or incorrect decisions. A number of other reform proposals go much farther. More than a decade ago, UNCTAD suggested that to deal effectively with the main concerns regarding systemic deficiencies in the ISDS regime states should consider setting up an appeals mechanism.[105] This mechanism could take the form of a 'standing body with a competence to undertake a substantive review of awards rendered by arbitral tribunals' as a means 'to improve consistency among arbitral awards, correct erroneous decisions of first-level tribunals and enhance predictability of the law'.[106]

CETA provides for the establishment of an appeal tribunal with jurisdiction to review awards of the first instance tribunal described above for errors of law and manifest errors in the assessment of facts as well as for the procedural and jurisdictional grounds for annulments under the ICSID Convention. Like the first instance tribunal, this aspect of the agreement is not yet in effect.[107] Appellate review has the potential to improve both the quality and consistency of arbitration awards. Yet, while an 'appeals facility would add direction and order to the existing decentralized, non-hierarchical and *ad hoc* regime', 'absolute consistency and certainty would not be achievable in a legal system that consists of more than 3,000 legal texts'.[108]

---

104 ibid UNCITRAL Transparency Rules, art 4.
105 See ICSID, 'Possible Improvements of the Framework for ICSID Arbitration', Discussion Paper, 22 October 2004, Part VI and Annex (Possible Features of an ICSID Appeals Facility).
106 UNCTAD (n 26).
107 It will not be in force until the treaty is ratified by all member states of the EU.
108 UNCTAD (n 26).

Investor–state dispute settlement 243

5.4 Reducing the cost and burden of ISDS and avoiding treaty shopping

To reduce the cost and burden of ISDS procedures and address the problem of treaty shopping by investors, the following kinds of provisions could be adopted, some of which are already found in recent treaties as discussed above.[109]

- Limit the range of disputes that can be settled by arbitration, such as, for instance, permitting only claims alleging violation of the treaty itself, or by excluding disputes in a particular sector or industry (e.g. financial services and energy), or certain subject matters (e.g. environment and national security), or those concerning certain provisions, such those relating to the admission and acquisition of an investment.[110]
- Require that an investor wait for a specific period of time before initiating a claim to provide an opportunity for an agreed resolution through consultations.[111]
- Require an investor to exhaust local remedies in the domestic courts of the host state before having access to ISDS to ensure that, if possible, the investor's concern is resolved by the courts.[112]
- Require an investor to bring its claim within a specific period of time after having acquired knowledge of the alleged breach to put a time limit of state exposure.
- Establish a mechanism for the consolidation of related claims to avoid the risk that states will face multiple claims by investors arising out of the same facts.[113]
- Provide for the early discharge of frivolous claims and jurisdictional challenges to quickly address claims that have no substantive merit or are outside the consent of the state and avoid the delay and costs associated with these issues only being dealt with in the final award.[114]
- Limit the categories of people and firms who can make investor–state claims by adopting a narrower definition for the types of 'investment' and 'investor' covered under the treaty such as by excluding 'mailbox' investors with no substantial activities in the home state or that are ultimately owned

---

109 These different options are discussed in ibid 173 ff; for a number of examples, see UNCTAD (n 64) 7; J Anthony VanDuzer, Penelope Simons, and Graham Mayeda, *Integrating Sustainable Development into International Investment Agreements: A Guide for Developing Country Negotiators* (Commonwealth 2013) 408–492.

110 See, for example, the US–Mexico–Canada Agreement (USMCA), signed 30 November 2018, not yet in force, Annex 14-D.2; CETA (n 27) Annex 8-C – Exclusions from Dispute Settlement.

111 Canada-China BIT (n 30).

112 n 41; e.g. USCMA (n 110) art 14.D.5.

113 Pohl, Mashigo, and Nohen (n 23).

114 e.g. USCMA (n 110) art 14.D.7.

by people who are not nationals of a treaty state or providing that the benefits of the treaty including access to ISDS could be denied to such investors by the host state.[115]

Other kinds of provisions that depart more fundamentally from the traditional model could also be adopted. For example, a state, instead of giving consent in *advance* to arbitration by any investor of the other state party to the treaty, could reserve its right to give such consent on a case-by-case basis to a particular investor.[116] Of course, this would significantly reduce the role of ISDS as a guarantor of IIA investor-protection obligations. Indeed, a state might never consent. Another proposal is to expand the scope for states to bring counterclaims against investors. Under current IIAs and applicable arbitration rules, the scope for states to bring counterclaims is limited and few have been brought successfully. A counterclaim provision could allow a state to submit a counterclaim for injuries suffered by the state or others from the investor's conduct in breach of its obligations under domestic law or any investor obligations included in the treaty.[117]

6. Conclusions and policy implications

The inclusion of an ISDS mechanism in an IIA, at least in theory, can be beneficial for capital-exporting and capital-importing states. From the perspective of capital-exporting states, an ISDS mechanism has been described as 'a cornerstone of investment protection' because 'it serves as a procedural enforcement mechanism for the core substantive provisions of the treaty'.[118] The very fact that a foreign investor can at any time commence arbitration proceedings creates a powerful incentive for the host state to respect its treaty commitments to investors.[119] ISDS is especially appealing as a way to address claims against host states in which the rule of law is weak and the prospects of obtaining relief for investors' claims in domestic procedures is poor. ISDS is also popular among investors because it gives them control over the initiation and conduct of claims and a direct entitlement to relief. The commitment to respect IIA obligations signalled by host-state agreement to ISDS can have benefits for host states too. Drafters of IIAs assume that a foreign investor is more likely to invest in a country where its investment is protected under an international treaty wherein its rights can be enforced directly against the host state before an international arbitral tribunal. The evidence, however, regarding whether the

---

115 e.g. USCMA ibid art 14.14.
116 UNCTAD (n 88).
117 Options for imposing standards on investors in IIAs is discussed by Vanhonnaecker (n 2); See also VanDuzer, Simons, and Mayeda (n 109) 267–407; ibid UNCTAD 75–76, 109–111.
118 UNCTAD (n 26) 20.
119 Gaukrodger and Gordon (n 65) 10.

existence of an ISDS clause truly has this effect on investment flows in practice is not consistent.[120]

Experience with ISDS has raised a variety of concerns, which have led states to reconsider the costs and benefits of ISDS. These include: (i) the ease of gaining access to treaty protections and ISDS for a very wide range of sophisticated multinational businesses; (ii) the legitimacy of a process that operates, in most cases, without much transparency or the effective participation of people and groups affected by investment activity other than the investor and the state and where the decision-makers are appointed by the parties with few institutional guarantees regarding their independence, impartiality, and quality; and (iii) inconsistent and unpredictable decision-making by arbitrators with no prospect for appeal on errors of law or fact. As well, while awards of billions of US dollars in favour of investors are exceptional, awards can be large and the costs of arbitration proceedings are very high for states and investors. The combination of these concerns and weak evidence of positive investment-inducing effects resulting from IIAs have caused some countries to opt-out of ISDS, while others are considering, and in some cases adopting, a wide range of reforms.

One of the key considerations for capital-exporting states contemplating an IIA with another country in which their investors are operating or will do so in the future is whether they trust the domestic court systems of that country to apply the rule of law and provide effective relief against state action for their investors.[121] Where trust in domestic systems exists, states may decide to sign an IIA without an ISDS clause. The actual effectiveness of host-state law and institutions, however, is not typically reflected in the negotiation of IIAs. Most BITs and investment chapters in free trade agreements are based on pre-established models that are not modified in the negotiations to reflect the relative effectiveness of the rule of law and domestic law institutions in the negotiating countries states.

There are signs, however, that this one-size-fits-all approach may be changing. Australia decided not to include an ISDS mechanism in its recent FTAs with the United States and Japan but did agree to it in its FTA with China. The question as to whether ISDS is needed in the context of the negotiation of a free trade agreement between the EU and the United States has been hotly debated.[122] Both parties have effective domestic court systems and a strong

---

120 See Vanhonnaeker (n 3) and Beaulieu and O'Neill (n 14).

121 de Mestral (n 64) 14.

122 See Lauge Poulsen, Jonathan Bonnitcha, and Jason Yackee, 'Transatlantic Investment Treaty Protection', Paper No 3 in the CEPS-CTR Project on TTIP in the Balance and CEPS Special Report No 102/March 2015; Freya Baetens, 'Transatlantic Investment Treaty Protection – A Response to *Poulsen, Bonnitcha and Yackee*', Paper No 4; ibid. The same discussion took place during the negotiation of the USMCA (n 110), which provides that ISDS will be phased out between Canada and the United States.

commitment to the rule of law.[123] In contexts like these, the traditional rationale for ISDS has limited relevance.

In short, the right approach to ISDS for a country in a negotiation should depend on (i) the magnitude and direction of the current and likely future investment relationship between it and the other state(s) at the negotiation table and (ii) the robustness of the rule of law and domestic legal institutions in each state. Each state must assess the need for ISDS as an alternative to domestic remedies to protect their investors in their activities in the other state as well as the need to complement their own investment protection commitments with ISDS in order to attract investment from the other state. Where there are or might be investors from the other state, all this must be balanced against the risks associated with being subject to ISDS claims by incoming investors from the other party state. Such a calculation is complex and there will not be an ISDS arrangement that is optimal for all states in all circumstances.

Acknowledgement

Patrick Dumberry wishes to thank Jonathan Nadler for his assistance and suggestions.

123 de Mestral (n 64) 22.

12 Social and environmental issues in foreign direct investment

A legal and policy perspective

Lorenzo Cotula

1. Introduction

In a capitalist economy, financial return drives private sector-led foreign direct investment (FDI). For public authorities, however, promoting FDI is not an end in itself but a means to pursue certain public goals. Depending on policy approaches, the goals may involve, for example, promoting national development, reducing poverty, or facilitating uptake of cleaner technologies. Yet evidence shows that FDI can produce both positive and negative social, economic, and environmental outcomes in recipient countries – for example, generating public revenues and creating employment,[1] while also dispossessing people of their land and natural resources.[2] The quality of investments, not just their volume, matters a great deal in ensuring that FDI contributes to stated policy goals.[3] This situation raises questions about how to assess quality in investment processes, and how to translate those assessments into the design and implementation of investment policy and law.

This chapter reviews normative standards of quality in FDI, discussing key concepts and international instruments. It then examines experience in three policy areas, focusing on the social and environmental dimensions of FDI: impact assessments, land rights, and labour rights. These policy areas are not representative of the full spectrum of social and environmental issues at stake but they reflect diverse and important sites of public action. Furthermore, all

---

1 See Eugene Beaulieu and Kelly O'Neill, 'The economics of foreign direct investment and international investment agreements', Chapter 5 in this volume.
2 e.g. Lorenzo Cotula, '"Land Grabbing" and International Investment Law: Toward a Global Reconfiguration of Property?' (2016) *Yearbook on International Investment Law & Policy 2014–2015* 177.
3 UNDP and UNEP, *Managing Private Investment in Natural Resources: A handbook for pro-poor growth and environmental sustainability* (United Nations Development Programme and United Nations Environment Programme 2011) available at <http://tinyurl.com/zdeg9dz> accessed 16 June 2019.

248　*Lorenzo Cotula*

three policy areas highlight the multi-actor nature of contemporary FDI: while traditionally framed around the bilateral relationship between the investor and the state, investment processes can in fact involve or affect a much wider range of actors – including local landholders, workers, and people who experience environmental impacts.[4] While each policy area presents specificities, multi-actor dimensions raise cross-cutting questions for national and international policy. A brief conclusion develops a few general insights. Throughout the chapter, the legal dimensions underpin much of the analysis, but they are embedded in a discussion of the theoretical constructs and the practical challenges relating to social and environmental issues in investment policy.

2. Quality investment: key concepts and instruments

2.1 The business entry: corporate social responsibility

A vast literature has articulated the case for businesses to consider factors other than financial return. For a long time, the concept of 'corporate social responsibility' (CSR) catalyzed public debates on how to frame societal expectations for businesses to uphold ethical standards of conduct. CSR approaches emerged during the Cold War,[5] often as a possible alternative to increased state control over the economy, and boomed from the early 1990s. Prominent approaches include:

- The 'stakeholder approach', which emphasizes the need for companies to consider the interests not only of shareholders but of a wider range of stakeholders;[6]
- The 'triple bottom line', whereby companies should consider not only profit but also 'people and planet';[7]
- The 'bottom of the pyramid', which highlights the role of businesses in servicing the markets of low-income groups;[8]

---

4 Lorenzo Cotula, *Human Rights, Natural Resource and Investment Law in a Globalised World: Shades of Grey in the Shadow of the Law* (Routledge 2012); Nicolás M Perrone, 'The International Investment Regime and Local Populations: Are the Weakest Voices Unheard?' (2016) 7 *Transnational Legal Theory* 383.

5 e.g. Howard R Bowen, *The Social Responsibilities of the Businessman* (Harper & Row 1953); Archie B Carroll, 'A Three-Dimensional Conceptual Model of Corporate Performance' (1979) 4 *Academy of Management Review* 497.

6 R Edward Freeman, 'The Stakeholder Approach Revisited' (2004) *Zeitschrift fur Wirtschafts- und Unternehmensethik* 5, 228.

7 John Elkington, 'Partnerships from Cannibals with Forks: The Triple Bottom Line of 21st-Century Business' (1998) *Environmental Quality Management (Autumn)* 37.

8 CK Prahalad, *The Fortune at the Bottom of the Pyramid: Eradicating Poverty through Profits* (Wharton School Publishing 2004).

- 'Shared value', whereby mutually beneficial actions in value chains can create or improve business opportunities and increase financial returns;[9]
- 'Inclusive business', whereby firms should rethink the way they make money to both improve financial returns and benefit low-income groups.[10]

These concepts have proved influential in corporate thinking and practice, but they have also been subjected to critique.[11] In different ways, all the concepts reflect an attempt to go beyond corporate philanthropy and entrench social and environmental considerations within an enterprise's core business. In emphasizing the 'win–wins', however, these approaches can gloss over important tensions and trade-offs. In addition, the concepts tend to take the viewpoint of the individual business and to downplay the structural factors affecting business conduct. As such, they largely emphasize what a firm can do within the parameters of existing economic ordering, and they have often failed to deliver genuinely transformational change.[12]

2.2 Sustainable development

Public policy requires using a broader societal lens. This shift in perspective has major implications. For example, there is an important distinction between the financial returns generated by an investment (the 'profit' element of the 'triple bottom line') and the economic outcomes of that investment (such as its effects on economic growth, balance of payments, and livelihood opportunities), even though the two are connected (a financially unviable investment is less likely to generate positive economic outcomes in the longer term).

One societal approach to connecting social, environmental, and economic considerations is the notion of sustainable development. Unlike CSR concepts, this notion has been articulated in a range of international instruments adopted over the past three decades. The 1992 United Nations Conference on Environment and Development played a key role in shaping the normative foundations of sustainable development,[13] and it was followed up by several

---

9 Michael E Porter and Mark R Kramer, 'Creating Shared Value' (2011) 89 *Harvard Business Review* 62.

10 World Business Council for Sustainable Development and Netherlands Development Organization, *Inclusive Business: Profitable Business for Successful Development* (World Business Council for Sustainable Development 2008).

11 e.g. Aneel G Karnami, 'Mirage at the Bottom of the Pyramid' (2006) *William Davidson Institute Working Paper No 835*, available at doi: 10.2139/ssrn.924616 accessed 16 June 2019; Thomas Beschorner and Thomas Hajduk, 'Creating Shared Value: A Fundamental Critique', In Joseph Wieland (ed) *Creating Shared Value – Concepts, Experience, Criticism* (Springer 2017).

12 e.g. Priyan Senevirathna, 'Critical Review: Creating Shared Value through Partnerships in Agricultural Production in Sri Lanka' (2018) 90 *Geoforum* 219.

13 Rio Declaration on Environment and Development, Annex I to the Report of the United Nations Conference on Environment and Development (UNCED), Rio de Janeiro, 3–14 June 1992, UN Doc A/CONF.151/26 (Vol I).

250 *Lorenzo Cotula*

multilateral conferences and instruments.[14] In 2015, the United Nations General Assembly adopted a set of Sustainable Development Goals (SDGs) that are fuelling new shifts in the way sustainable development is conceptualized and operationalized.[15]

The concept of sustainable development has made its way into the rulings of international courts. These pronouncements have variously framed sustainable development as a 'concept',[16] a 'principle',[17] or a tool affecting the interpretation of other norms.[18] And while these rulings have thus far described sustainable development primarily in terms of integration between environmental protection and economic development,[19] conceptual advances through international declarations and plans of action over the years have brought out more strongly the social dimensions as well.[20]

In the context of foreign investment, sustainable development raises two sets of issues. The first flows from Principle 1 of the 1992 Rio Declaration on Environment and Development, which places human beings 'at the centre of concerns for sustainable development'.[21] Giving real meaning to this concept entails a shift away from just managing the social and environmental risks of prevailing investment patterns, and from treating people as passive beneficiaries or victims of investment projects.

Rather, it entails ensuring that public policies and decisions on what types of investment to promote respond to a bottom-up, strategic vision of sustainable development based on local and national aspirations. This is reflected in 'the sovereign right [of states] to exploit their own resources pursuant to their own environmental and developmental policies',[22] but also in rules on how governments should exercise that right and manage resources on behalf of their

---

14 Plan of Implementation of the World Summit on Sustainable Development, World Summit on Sustainable Development ('Rio+10'), Johannesburg, 4 September 2002, UN Doc A/CONF.199/20; and The Future We Want: Outcome Document, adopted at Rio+20, United Nations Conference on Sustainable Development ('Rio+20'), Rio de Janeiro, June 2012.

15 Transforming Our World: The 2030 Agenda for Sustainable Development, adopted by the United Nations General Assembly on 25 September 2015, UN Doc A/RES/70/1.

16 *Case Concerning the Gabčikovo–Nagymaros Dam (Hungary v Slovakia)* ICJ 25 September 1997, para 140.

17 *Pulp Mills on the River Uruguay (Argentina v Uruguay)*, ICJ 20 April 2010, para 177.

18 *United States – Import Prohibition of Certain Shrimp and Shrimp Products*, Report of the Appellate Body, 6 November 1998, WT/DS58/AB/R, para 153; Virginie Barral, 'Sustainable Development in International Law: Nature and Operation of an Evolutive Legal Norm' (2012) *European Journal of International Law* 377.

19 *Gabčikovo–Nagymaros* (n 16), para. 140; *Award in the Arbitration regarding the Iron Rhine ('Ijzeren Rijn') Railway between the Kingdom of Belgium and the Kingdom of the Netherlands*, 24 May 2005, XXVI RIAA 35–125, paras 59–60; *Pulp Mills* (n 17) para 177.

20 For example, the Plan of Implementation (n 15) contains language on poverty, hunger, health, energy, water and sanitation, and corporate social accountability. Social issues are also central throughout the SDGs (Transforming Our World (n 15)).

21 Principle 1 of the Rio Declaration (n 13).

22 ibid Principle 2 of the Rio Declaration.

Social and environmental issues in FDI   251

citizens – for example, enabling people to access information, participate in decision-making, and obtain legal redress.[23]

The second set of investment-related issues flowing from the notion of sustainable development concerns the holistic consideration of the social, environmental, and economic issues at stake in any investment process. Principle 3 of the Rio Declaration refers to the right to development, and several international instruments refer to the role of private investment in realizing this right,[24] though maximizing the economic benefits from that investment would also be a relevant aspect – for example, via public revenues, employment creation, supply chain opportunities, technical know-how, technology transfer, and infrastructure development.

With regard to environmental considerations, Principle 4 of the Rio Declaration states that 'environmental protection shall constitute an integral part of the development process', while Principle 3 affirms the principle of intergenerational equity. In an investment context, addressing environmental issues may involve minimizing negative impacts on the environment, clearly allocating responsibility for environmental damage and remediation, and actively promoting environmental benefits, for instance through investment in low-carbon technologies.

When it comes to social considerations, the Rio Declaration makes poverty eradication 'an indispensable requirement for sustainable development',[25] and calls on states to support the interests of Indigenous peoples and local communities.[26] As discussed, subsequent international instruments have more fully recognized the importance of social issues in sustainable development, and social issues are central throughout the SDGs. From this perspective, even an investment that is economically beneficial to the country as a whole (for instance in terms of gross domestic product) may be incompatible with sustainable development if, for example, affected people are arbitrarily dispossessed of the land they depend on for their livelihoods and social identity.

In practice, real-life FDI processes can raise difficult trade-offs between multiple social, economic, and environmental considerations. Different groups often put forward competing visions of what constitutes sustainable development, and how to balance multiple considerations. Much depends on how these differences and trade-offs are understood and addressed, which links back to the procedural dimensions of placing people 'at the centre of concerns for sustainable development' (e.g. access to information, public participation, access to justice).

---

23 ibid Principle 10 of the Rio Declaration.
24 e.g. Plan of Implementation (n 14) para 84; The Future We Want (n 14) paras 46 and 56–74; and Transforming Our World (n 15) para 67.
25 Principle 5 of the Rio Declaration (n 13).
26 ibid Principle 22 of the Rio Declaration.

252 *Lorenzo Cotula*

2.3 Human rights

Investments can affect enjoyment of human rights. They can contribute public revenues to fund the provision of public services necessary to realize economic, social, and cultural rights such as the rights to health, housing, and education. But, in polluting waterways or taking land for project implementation, they can also undermine Indigenous peoples' rights to their ancestral territories, or the right to an adequate standard of living. Abuses may also involve violations of labour rights and repression of environmental and human rights defenders.

While human rights and sustainable development have historically emerged as distinct policy agendas, the two concepts intersect. The Plan of Implementation of the 2002 World Summit on Sustainable Development affirms that 'respect for human rights [is] essential for achieving sustainable development'.[27]

The investment context raises distinctive issues about the human rights responsibilities of businesses. Under international human rights law, states have a legal obligation to respect human rights and to protect those rights against interference by private parties, including businesses. In addition, the United Nations Guiding Principles on Business and Human Rights affirm that businesses have the responsibility to act with due diligence in order to avoid infringing on human rights and address adverse impacts that may arise from their activities.[28]

This responsibility requires that enterprises: '(a) Avoid causing or contributing to adverse human rights impacts through their own activities, and address such impacts when they occur'; and '(b) Seek to prevent or mitigate adverse human rights impacts that are directly linked to their operations, products or services by their business relationships, even if they have not contributed to those impacts'. The Guiding Principles also call for effective remedies including courts and non-judicial grievance mechanisms. The ongoing negotiation of a proposed binding treaty on business and human rights, if successful, could entail significant conceptual as well as legal reconfigurations in this area of law.

2.4 From concepts to policy

As societal expectations evolve, so do approaches to setting standards of conduct, and the operational instruments to ensure the standards are complied with. Multiple approaches to standard-setting are possible. At one end of the spectrum, individual businesses can and often do set their own standards through corporate policies. This voluntary, company-level approach chimes with CSR thinking that emphasizes the agency of individual firms in processes of change. However, there is also growing experience with contractualized forms

---

27 Plan of Implementation (n 14) para 5.
28 Guiding Principles on Business and Human Rights: Implementing the United Nations 'protect, respect and remedy' framework. Report of the Special Representative of the Secretary-General on the Issue of Human Rights and Transnational Corporations and Other Business Enterprises (John Ruggie), 21 March 2011, UN Doc A/HRC/17/31.

of CSR, including via agreements between the business and the people who stand to be affected by the investment.[29] In some jurisdictions, national legislation promotes or even requires forms of contractualized CSR.

Company-level voluntary approaches are not particularly well-suited to address systemic issues, or to tackle the structural factors that businesses must come to terms with in their operations (e.g. unequal negotiating power in value chains, pressures from competitors). If left unaddressed, these factors could ultimately undermine corporate resolve to uphold their own standards, particularly in times of crisis.

Setting social and environmental standards applicable to all firms is more conducive to creating a level playing field and addressing the challenges in systemic terms. This method may involve diverse approaches to public policy, in terms of both process (e.g. from 'top-down' regulation to diverse forms of consultative processes) and output (e.g. 'soft' to 'hard' law). It also encompasses public action at multiple levels – from local to global. While national law and policy typically provide a key normative and institutional reference in investment processes, sub-national agencies (depending on the jurisdiction) may have relevant responsibilities, which can enhance opportunities for public participation in decision-making but also create policy incoherence.

In addition, the transnational nature of FDI flows has made international law an important site of public regulation.[30] Discussions about investment-related issues in international law date back to the nineteenth century. However, public reflection on ways to address social and environmental issues in investment processes became more prominent from the 1970s, when states started negotiating a proposed Code of Conduct on Transnational Corporations at the United Nations. Originally, these negotiations covered both standards of corporate behaviour for investors to uphold, and standards of investment protection directed at states.[31] Ultimately, however, separate bilateral and regional negotiations came to entrench investment protection standards into hundreds of investment treaties worldwide, while the negotiation of a multilateral Code of Conduct setting standards of investor conduct was abandoned in the early 1990s.

The expansion of international investment agreements (IIAs) and the abandonment of efforts to develop a multilateral Code of Conduct reflected changes in the prevailing economic thinking, and weakening of developing country cohesiveness and negotiating power after the end of the Cold War.[32]

---

29 e.g. Dominic M Ayine, *Social Responsibility Agreements in Ghana's Forest Sector* (International Institute for Environment and Development 2007).

30 Krista Nadakavukaren Schefer, 'Actors, institutions, and policy in host countries', Chapter 3 in this volume.

31 Karl P Sauvant, 'The Negotiations of the United Nations Code of Conduct on Transnational Corporations: Experience and Lessons Learned' (2015) 16 *Journal of World Investment & Trade* 11.

32 ibid.

254   *Lorenzo Cotula*

The resulting international legal frameworks created far-reaching rights and remedies, but not obligations, for foreign investors.[33]

International instruments do provide guidance for businesses on how to address social and environmental issues, but they are primarily of a non-binding nature. Examples include the Guidelines on Multinational Enterprises of the Organisation for Economic Co-operation and Development (OECD);[34] and commodity-specific multi-stakeholder certification schemes such as the Roundtable on Sustainable Palm Oil (RSPO), which has developed principles and criteria that businesses must comply with in order to obtain certification.[35]

While these instruments do not create legal obligations, they are sometimes cross-referenced in contractual arrangements that do create obligations. This fluid nature of hard and soft law is evident, for example, in the social and environmental standards applied by development finance institutions (DFIs) such as the International Finance Corporation (IFC) and its bilateral equivalents. While the IFC Performance Standards per se do not create legal obligations, they are typically embedded in the financing agreements the DFIs conclude with their clients.[36] As a result, businesses have a contractual obligation to adhere to those standards.

Recent developments have fostered shifts towards rebalancing rights and obligations in investment processes. Although the Guiding Principles on Business and Human Rights have received widespread support, dissatisfaction remains in connection with their non-binding nature,[37] and a process to develop a binding treaty is currently underway.[38]

Meanwhile, some recent investment treaties feature more explicit provisions on responsible investment, including obligations for states (e.g. not to lower labour and environmental standards) and – more rarely, and often in hortatory language – provisions that affirm investor responsibilities or obligations in areas such as CSR, human rights, the environment, and labour rights.[39]

---

33 Lukas Vanhonnaeker, 'International investment agreements', Chapter 10 in this volume.

34 OECD, *Guidelines for Multinational Enterprises* (OECD 2011).

35 Roundtable on Sustainable Palm Oil, 'RSPO Principles and Criteria Certification' Roundtable on Sustainable Palm Oil.

36 IFC Performance Standards on Environmental and Social Sustainability (January 2012 version).

37 Robert C Blitt, 'Beyond Ruggie's Guiding Principles on Business and Human Rights: Charting an Embracive Approach to Corporate Human Rights Compliance' (2012) 48 *Texas International Law Journal* 33.

38 United Nations Human Rights Council, 'Open-ended intergovernmental working group on transnational corporations and other business enterprises with respect to human rights' *Resolution 26/9* (United Nations Human Rights Council 2014).

39 Jesse Coleman, Lise Johnson, Lisa Sachs, and Kanika Gupta, 'International Investment Agreements, 2015–2016: A Review of Trends and New Approaches', *Yearbook on International Investment Law and Policy 2015–2016* (Oxford Univesity Press 2017) paras 2.81–2.88; Lorenzo Cotula, *Raising the Bar on Responsible Investment: What Role for Investment Treaties?*

Social and environmental issues in FDI 255

3. Selected themes

Having mapped a few key concepts and policy approaches, the remainder of the chapter explores in greater detail evolutions concerning three areas of public policy: environmental and social impact assessments, land rights, and labour rights. The aim is to illustrate trends and issues rather than provide a comprehensive discussion. For each theme, the text outlines key features of international law and guidance, trends in national law, and practical experiences in national and international law.

3.1 Environmental and social impact assessments

Environmental and social impact assessments (ESIAs) assess the likely or potential impacts of a proposed project. They also identify alternatives to the option proposed and consider preventative or mitigating actions to minimize any impact identified. Impact assessments are typically carried out in the early stages of the project cycle and are part of the process whereby proposed investments are approved.

Under many national systems, ESIA findings inform the formulation of the social and environmental management plans to be applied during the project. Management plans identify how particular risks, such as an oil spill, would be dealt with. Where government authorities approve an ESIA and management plan, they typically issue the environmental permits or licences that are legally required for the investor to implement the project.

3.1.1 International law and guidance

Several international treaties contain provisions on environmental impact assessments. Article 14 of the Convention on Biological Diversity (CBD) commits states to introduce, 'as far as possible and as appropriate', 'procedures requiring environmental impact assessment of [...] proposed projects that are likely to have significant adverse effects on biological diversity'.[40] Some treaties specifically require or regulate impact assessments for projects that are likely to have transboundary environmental impacts – that is, impacts on the environment in other states or in areas beyond national jurisdiction.[41]

Even where such treaties do not apply, general international law still requires all states to conduct an environmental impact assessment for activities

---

(International Institute for Environment and Development 2018); IISD, *Integrating Investor Obligations and Corporate Accountability Provisions in Trade and Investment Agreements* (International Institute for Sustainable Development 2018); Vanhonnaecker (n 34).

40 Convention on Biological Diversity, adopted 5 June 1992, entered into force 29 December 1993, 1760 UNTS 382.

41 e.g. Espoo Convention on Environmental Impact Assessment in a Transboundary Context, signed at Espoo on 25 February 1991, in force 10 September 1997, 1089 UNTS 309.

256 *Lorenzo Cotula*

within their jurisdiction that are likely to cause environmental harm to other states.[42] Impact assessments have also been found to be required under international human rights norms. In *Saramaka People v Suriname*, for example, the Inter-American Court of Human Rights held that respecting the right to collective property of a tribal people required the government to ensure that an ESIA is conducted before awarding commercial concessions.[43]

International environmental law tends to focus on environmental impact, while human rights law has implications for both social and environmental impact assessments. But requirements in some environmental treaties have been interpreted broadly to also include social dimensions. For example, the Conference of the Parties of the CBD issued guidelines on how to conduct impact assessments where proposed projects affect Indigenous peoples; the guidelines cover social and cultural as well as environmental impacts.[44] Practical guidance on how to conduct ESIAs is also available in the standards developed by DFIs,[45] and, depending on the economic sector, by multi-stakeholder certification bodies such as the RSPO.[46]

Most IIAs do not explicitly address issues concerning environmental impact assessments. However, explicit or implied requirements for investments to be made in compliance with applicable national law could mean that a project developed without a required environmental licence is excluded from the protection of an investment agreement.[47] IIA clauses that explicitly address environmental issues are relatively rare but are making their way into treaty practice. For example, several IIAs contain 'non-lowering of standards' clauses to discourage states from deviating from national environmental laws to attract FDI.[48]

The effectiveness of these clauses partly depends on the content of applicable national law; if national law sets the bar low, investments that adhere to it could still cause environmental harm. Creating effective enforcement mechanisms for non-lowering of standards clauses is also problematic. These provisions are not

---

42 *Pulp Mills* (n 17) para 204; *Certain Activities Carried out by Nicaragua in the Border Area (Costa Rica v Nicaragua)/Construction of a Road in Costa Rica along the San Juan River (Nicaragua v Costa Rica)*, ICJ, 16 December 2015, para 104.

43 *Saramaka People v Suriname*, (ser C) No 172, Judgment, Inter-American Court of Human Rights (28 November 2007) para 134.

44 CBD Decision VII/16F Annex, 'Akwé: Kon Voluntary Guidelines for the Conduct of Cultural, Environmental and Social Impact Assessment regarding Developments Proposed to Take Place on, or which are Likely to Impact on, Sacred Sites and on Lands and Waters Traditionally Occupied or Used by Indigenous and Local Communities, in art 8(j) and related provisions' (13 April 2004) UN Doc UNEP/CBD/COP/7/21.

45 See particularly IFC Performance Standards on Environmental and Social Sustainability (n 37), Performance Standard No 1 ('Assessment and Management of Environmental and Social Risks and Impacts').

46 RSPO Principles and Criteria (n 36).

47 *Cortec Mining Kenya Limited, Cortec (Pty) Limited and Stirling Capital Limited v Republic of Kenya*, ICSID Case No ARB/15/29, Award (22 October 2018).

48 J Anthony VanDuzer and Patrick Dumberry, 'Investor–state dispute settlement', Chapter 11 in this volume.

Social and environmental issues in FDI 257

primarily designed to benefit foreign investors,[49] and so are unlikely to be enforced through the investor–state arbitration.

Some recent IIAs contain more specific requirements for investors to conduct ESIAs according to certain standards. Unlike non-lowering of standards clauses, these provisions purport to create investor, rather than state, obligations. For example, the Morocco–Nigeria BIT of 2016 requires investors to comply with environmental assessment processes 'as required by the laws of the host state [...] or the laws of the home state [...] whichever is more rigorous in relation to the investment in question'.[50]

Effectively drafted investor obligations clauses could help the state to have an investor–state dispute thrown out due to inadmissibility or lack of jurisdiction, influence the tribunal's decision on the merits of the case, or reduce the amount of compensation due to the investor where those obligations have been breached. They could also allow states to make counterclaims – that is, to respond to an investor's arbitration claim by seeking damages for harm caused by the investor.[51]

3.1.2 Trends in national law

Since the early 1990s, many low and middle-income states have adopted national legislation that requires an environmental impact assessment for proposed projects that may have significant effects on the environment. National requirements frequently also include identification and mitigation of social impacts. Many sector-specific laws, including mining and petroleum codes, also require impact assessments for activities carried out under their provisions.

The quality of impact assessment legislation varies greatly. The Environmental Law Alliance Worldwide (ELAW) website contains a global database and comparative analysis of many impact assessment laws.[52] Key parameters include:

- The types of projects that require an ESIA;
- The mandated content and scope of ESIAs, including the extent to which assessments must tackle social impacts;
- Whether legislation, regulations, or guidelines provide clear guidance on the ESIA process;
- Transparency and disclosure requirements, including whether draft and/or final ESIA documentation must be disclosed;

---

49 However, a situation could arise where selective non-enforcement of regulations might place some investors at a disadvantage.

50 Reciprocal Investment Promotion and Protection Agreement between the Government of the Kingdom of Morocco and the Government of the Federal Republic of Nigeria, signed 3 December 2016; not yet in force, [Morocco–Nigeria BIT of 2016], art 14.

51 Coleman, Johnson, Sachs, and Gupta (n 40) paras 2.81–2.88; and Cotula (n 40) 142.

52 Available at <www.elaw.org> accessed 16 June 2019.

258   *Lorenzo Cotula*

- Scope for local consultation and public participation, including public hearings and opportunities to comment on draft and final ESIAs;
- The extent to which the law deals with any conflicts of interest that may arise in ESIA processes;
- Scope for citizens to seek administrative and/or judicial review of government decisions to approve ESIAs; and
- Nature and enforceability of environmental permits issued on the basis of ESIAs, and arrangements to monitor compliance.

3.1.3 Making impact assessments work

In practice, the implementation of ESIA requirements is often marred by difficulties. Recurring problems include inadequate company systems and expertise, perverse incentives, and lack of institutional capacity in the government agencies that scrutinize impact studies and subsequently monitor compliance with management plans. Impact studies are often financed by the investor, creating potential conflicts of interest. Government authorities can push for rigour by demanding use of recognized experts and scrutinizing drafts submitted by companies.

Best-practice environmental permits include detailed conditions (for instance, to safeguard groundwater resources or regulate waste management), either directly or through reference to the management plans. For these conditions to be effective, government authorities need to have the power to monitor compliance and withdraw or suspend permits in case of non-compliance. This requires agencies to be properly resourced, equipped with the full range of skills needed (including to deal with social impacts), and backed up by strong political support at the highest level of government.

Meaningful participation of affected people and concerned citizens in the ESIA process can help ensure that the assessment identifies and addresses all relevant issues. Some national laws explicitly require local consultation and public participation in ESIA exercises and public disclosure of ESIA documentation. While government agencies have primary institutional responsibility for overseeing ESIAs, activists often play an important role in supporting affected people to participate in ESIA processes, scrutinizing impact studies and monitoring compliance with social and environmental management plans.[53]

Tensions can arise between environmental impact assessment and licensing processes on the one hand, and the investment protection provisions of IIAs on the other. Use of particularly rigorous assessment procedures, refusal to issue environmental permits following the conduct of an assessment, and non-renewal of existing environmental permits have all resulted in investor–state

---

53 e.g. ELAW, *Guidebook for Evaluating Mining Project EIAs* (Environmental Law Alliance Worldwide 2010).

arbitrations.[54] In some cases, arbitral tribunals have awarded damages to investors in connection with environmental approval processes, and concerns have been raised about a possible chilling effect on impact assessment processes.[55] States keen to minimize this 'regulatory chill' risk would need to give careful consideration to the investment protection standards and the dispute-settlement mechanisms they agree to. They would also need to ensure their conduct complies with applicable standards if they are to minimize the risk of arbitration claims.[56]

3.2 Land rights

Land acquisition is a major source of conflict in many large-scale FDI projects, particularly in sectors such as mining, petroleum, agriculture, and infrastructure. Acquiring land to enable project implementation can have a devastating impact on people, particularly where they depend on land for their livelihoods. In many countries, land also embodies significant and sometimes all-encompassing cultural and spiritual values, and provides the basis for social identity.

Land issues can create significant tenure risks for companies as well, for example where affected people or concerned groups contest the legality or legitimacy of land allocation, or where public mobilization causes reputational or operational costs. Issues concerning land acquisition tend to arise in the early stages of project implementation, at the land clearance and construction stages. But new land issues may arise later, for example if the project area is extended.[57]

3.2.1 International law and guidance

International human rights instruments have a bearing on land rights issues in investment processes. Close connections exist between land and human rights, not least because access to and use of land may provide the basis for realizing human rights. For example, human rights bodies have consistently held that the internationally-recognized human right to property[58] protects collective,

---

54 Stefanie Schacherer with Nathalie Bernasconi-Osterwalder and Martin Dietrich Brauch, *International Investment Law and Sustainable Development: Key Cases from the 2010s* (International Institute for Sustainable Development 2018).

55 *William Ralph Clayton, William Richard Clayton, Douglas Clayton, Daniel Clayton and Bilcon of Delaware, Inc v Government of Canada*, PCA Case No 2009–2004, Dissenting opinion of Professor Donald McRae (10 March 2015) paras 48 and 51.

56 See Vanhonnaecker (n 34); VanDuzer and Dumberry (n 49).

57 e.g. Lorenzo Cotula, Thierry Berger, Rachael Knight, Thomas F McInerney, Margret Vidar, and Peter Deupmann, *Responsible Governance of Tenure and the Law: A Guide for Lawyers and Other Legal Service Providers* (Food and Agriculture Organization of the United Nations 2016).

58 GA Res 217 (III) A, art 17, Universal Declaration of Human Rights (10 December 1948); Protocol to the European Convention for the Protection of Human Rights and Fundamental Freedoms, art 1 (adopted 20 March 1952); American Convention on Human Rights, art 21 (adopted 22 November 1969); African Charter on Human and Peoples' Rights, art. 14 (adopted 27 June 1981).

260   *Lorenzo Cotula*

customary land rights, including those of Indigenous and tribal peoples, even in the absence of formal titles or legal recognition under national law.[59]

Other directly relevant human rights include the rights to housing,[60] to food (where people depend on natural resources for their food security),[61] to enjoy one's own culture (where traditional culture is connected to land and resources),[62] to freely dispose of natural resources,[63] and to self-determination,[64] as well as Indigenous peoples' rights to their ancestral territories.[65] All human rights are interdependent and interrelated, and the interface between resource rights and human rights encompasses all internationally-recognized human rights.[66]

The normative content of these human rights has implications for handling land acquisition for investment projects. For example, human rights bodies have clarified that, in the context of large-scale development projects affecting Indigenous and tribal peoples, the protection of the right to collective property requires prior ESIAs, benefit-sharing arrangements that enable affected people to participate in the benefits generated by the investments, as well as free, prior, and informed consent (FPIC).[67] International treaties, declarations, and jurisprudence have established FPIC as an essential condition for protecting the human rights of Indigenous and tribal peoples in an investment context.[68]

---

59 e.g. *Mayagna (Sumo) Awas Tingni Community v Nicaragua*, (ser C) No 79, Judgment, Inter-American Court of Human Rights (31 August 2001), paras 146, 148–149, 153; *Sawhoyamaxa Indigenous Community v Paraguay*, (ser C) No 146, Judgment, Inter-American Court of Human Rights (29 March 2006) para 91.

60 UDHR (n 59) art 25, and International Covenant on Economic, Social and Cultural Rights (16 December 1966), 993 UNTS 3, art 11 [ICESCR].

61 ibid; Olivier De Schutter (Special Rapporteur on the Right to Food), *Large-Scale Land Acquisitions and Leases: A Set of Minimum Principles and Measures to Address the Human Rights Challenge*, UN Doc A/HRC/13/32/Add.2 (28 December 2009).

62 International Covenant on Civil and Political Rights (16 December 1966), 999 UNTS 171, art 27 [ICCPR]. See also UN Human Rights Commission, CCPR General Comment No 23, art 27 (Rights of Minorities), UN Doc CCPR/C/21/Rev.1/Add.5 (8 April 1994); UN Human Rights Commission, *Ivan Kitok v Sweden*, Commission No 197/1985, UN Doc CCPR/C/33/D/197/1985 (1988); and UN Human Rights Commission, *Lubicon Lake Band v Canada*, Commission No 167/1984, UN Doc Supp No 40 (A/45/40) (26 March 1990).

63 ibid ICCPR, art 1(1)-(2); ICESCR (n 61), art 1(1)-(2).

64 ibid ICCPR; ibid ICESCR art 1.

65 International Labour Organisation, Convention Concerning Indigenous and Tribal Peoples in Independent Countries (27 June 1989), 1650 UNTS 383 [ILO Convention No 169]; and United Nations Declaration on the Rights of Indigenous Peoples (13 September 2007) [UNDRIP].

66 Voluntary Guidelines on the Responsible Governance of Tenure of Land, Fisheries and Forests in the Context of National Food Security (Committee on World Food Security 11 May 2012) [VGGT], paras 4–8.

67 *Saramaka People* (n 44), para 134.

68 ILO Convention No 169 (n 66), art 6; UNDRIP (n 66), arts 10 and 32. See also *Ángela Poma Poma v Peru*, UN Human Rights Committee, Views, Communication No 1457/2006, 24 April 2009, CCPR/C/95/D/1457/2006, available at <www.uio.no/studier/emner/jus/jus/JUS5710/h13/undervisningsmateriale/angela_poma_poma-v-peru.pdf> accessed 16 June 2019; *Saramaka People* (n 44), para 134.

Social and environmental issues in FDI 261

International soft law instruments also provide authoritative guidance on how to address land issues in FDI processes. In 2012, the Committee on World Food Security (the top United Nations body in food security matters) endorsed the Voluntary Guidelines on the Responsible Governance of Tenure of Land, Fisheries and Forests in the Context of National Food Security (VGGT).[69] The VGGT call on states and investors to respect all 'legitimate tenure rights', including Indigenous and customary tenure rights, and including socially legitimate rights that are 'not currently protected by law'.[70] The VGGT provide guidance on handling resource rights issues in investment processes, including through local consultation, FPIC (where relevant), and community-investor partnerships.[71] Additional international guidance is embodied in instruments that are more explicitly oriented towards businesses, such as the IFC Performance Standards.[72]

3.2.2 Trends in national law

Land laws are extremely diverse, influenced by history, politics, and the place of land in the local economy and society. In relation to foreign investment, particularly difficult issues can arise in jurisdictions where national law provides no or limited legal recognition and protection of land rights that are perceived to be socially legitimate by their holders or the population at large. These contexts can exacerbate the risk that affected people are dispossessed, and that foreign investors are faced with land disputes and contestation.

In several countries, particularly low and middle-income states, many people access land through 'customary' or other local systems of land tenure. Depending on the jurisdiction, legal and practical factors may undermine the protection of these rights. Legal protection may be subject to evidence that the land is being used productively. This requirement can undermine local claims to rangelands, hunting-gathering grounds or sacred sites, for example, or the farming rights of shifting cultivators, often affecting a large share of local landholdings.[73]

Several countries have revised their legislation to strengthen the protection of rural land rights. For example, some law reforms have:

- Legally recognized customary land rights where relevant, protected customary rights even if they are not formally registered, and provided these rights with the same legal protection available to land rights allocated by the state;

---

69 VGGT (n 67).
70 e.g. ibid VGGT paras 3.1, 3.2, 4.4, 5.3, 7.1 and s 12.
71 ibid VGGT paras 9.9, 12.6, 12.7 and 12.9.
72 IFC Performance Standards on Environmental and Social Sustainability (n 37), Performance Standards No 5 ('Involuntary Resettlement') and 7 ('Indigenous Peoples').
73 Cotula, *Human Rights, Natural Resource and Investment Law in a Globalised World* (n 4).

262 *Lorenzo Cotula*

- Protected collective as well as individual landholdings, and recognized rights associated with diverse land uses including pastoralism and hunting-gathering;
- Promoted gender equality in land relations, for example through prohibiting discrimination, requiring joint titling for couples, and promoting women's representation in land institutions; and
- Established geographically, economically and culturally-accessible systems to record land rights, building on local practice.[74]

Safeguards in relation to the compulsory acquisition by the state of land ownership and/or use rights for the purposes of allocating resources to commercial projects are a particularly important issue in FDI processes. Many national laws present gaps, because, for example, they exclude widely-held rights from legal protection or provide inadequate standards of compensation in the case of appropriation.[75]

At a deeper level, there is a difference between compensating for lost assets and restoring livelihoods to pre-project levels.[76] The application of conventional legislative approaches centred on payment of cash compensation at market value may achieve the former, but not necessarily the latter, because compulsory acquisition may have impacts beyond the lost value of the asset taken.

Where land is held communally, additional issues arise regarding how compensation is distributed within the group, considering social differentiation based on gender, generation, status, income, and socio-economic activity. Recognizing these challenges, some laws require authorities to minimize compulsory acquisition and link cash payments or in-kind compensation (such as the provision of alternative land) to what is needed to restore the livelihoods of affected people to a position that is better than or equal to their position pre-acquisition.[77]

Many states have enacted legislation that makes local consultation or consent a legal requirement as part of investment approval processes. For

---

74 e.g. Rachael S Knight, *Statutory Recognition of Customary Land Rights in Africa: An Investigation into Best Practices for Law Making and Implementation* (Food and Agriculture Organization of the United Nations 2010); Rights and Resources Initiative, *Legislative Best Practices for Securing Women's Rights to Community Lands* (Rights and Resources Initiative 2018).

75 Nicolas K Tagliarino, 'The Status of National Legal Frameworks for Valuing Compensation for Expropriated Land: An Analysis of Whether National Laws in 50 Countries/Regions across Asia, Africa, and Latin America Comply with International Standards on Compensation Valuation' (2017) 6 *Land* 37.

76 Michael M Cernea, *African Involuntary Population Resettlement in a Global Context* (World Bank 1997).

77 Brendan Schwartz, Lorenzo Cotula, Samuel Nguiffo, Jaff Bamenjo, Sandrine Kouba, and Teclaire Same, *Towards Fair and Effective Legislation on Compulsory Land Acquisition in Cameroon* (International Institute for Environment and Development 2018).

Social and environmental issues in FDI **263**

example, Mozambique's Land Act of 1997 requires the consultation of legally defined 'local communities' before a land lease can be allocated to an investor, while legislation in the Philippines requires free, prior, and informed consent for developments affecting the ancestral lands of Indigenous peoples.[78]

3.2.3 Making land rights real

Implementation of land legislation often falls short of expectations, particularly in the rural areas of many low and middle-income countries. Government agencies may lack financial resources and institutional capacity. Rural people may lack legal awareness. Official rules and institutions may not be perceived as legitimate. Furthermore, asymmetries in information, capacity, and negotiating power often characterize relations between businesses, governments, and affected people.

Implementation requires legislators to carefully consider budget implications at the law reform stage – for example, avoiding reform approaches that would require the establishment of overly expensive administrative structures, and making adequate budget allocations to cover the costs of implementation. Non-governmental organizations (NGOs) have helped people to defend land rights in the context of large-scale investments through means such as:

- Awareness raising via radio broadcasting;[79]
- Support to community paralegals;[80]
- Participatory land-use mapping to document community land claims;[81]
- Community-based monitoring of land acquisition;[82]
- Legal literacy training to strengthen grassroots capacity to claim rights;[83]

---

78 Mozambique, Land Act of 1997: Lei No 19/97 of 1 October 1997 (Lei de Terras); and Philippines, Indigenous Peoples' Rights Act No 8371 of 29 October 1997.

79 e.g. Mamadou Goïta and Mohamed Coulibaly, *Listen, Think and Act: Radio Broadcasting to Promote Farmers' Participation in Mali's Land Policy* (International Institute for Environment and Development 2012).

80 e.g. Chris Tanner and Marianna Bicchieri, *When the Law is Not Enough: Paralegals and Natural Resources Governance in Mozambique* (Food and Agriculture Organization of the UN 2014).

81 e.g. Samuel Nguiffo and Robinson Djeukam, 'Using the Law as a Tool for Securing Communities' Land Rights in Southern Cameroon', in Lorenzo Cotula and Paul Mathieu (eds), *Legal Empowerment in Practice: Using Legal Tools to Secure Land Rights in Africa* (Food and Agriculture Organization and International Institute for Environment and Development 2008).

82 e.g. Godfray Massay, *Pillars of the Community: How Trained Volunteers Defend Land Rights in Tanzania* (International Institute for Environment and Development 2016).

83 Amadou Keita, Moussa Djiré and Lorenzo Cotula, *From Legal Caravans to Revising Mali's Mining Code: Lessons from Experience with Legal Empowerment in Communities Affected by Mining* (International Institute for Environment and Development 2014).

264   *Lorenzo Cotula*

- Public interest litigation to challenge resettlement or compensation packages;[84] and
- Support for affected people in using grievance mechanisms to protect their land rights.[85]

3.3 Labour rights

Jobs are often one of the most prominent benefits that companies and governments promise when they conclude investment contracts. But employment creation has often fallen short of expectations. In addition, employment can only be beneficial if labour standards are upheld to protect human dignity, creating the need for legal instruments to set standards and for institutional arrangements to promote and monitor compliance.

3.3.1 International law and guidance

International human rights instruments affirm labour rights. The Universal Declaration of Human Rights (UDHR) and the International Covenant on Economic, Social and Cultural Rights (ICESCR) affirm the right to freely choose an occupation, to enjoy a just and favourable remuneration, to work in safe and healthy conditions, and to form and join a trade union.[86]

Under the Convention on the Elimination of All Forms of Discrimination Against Women (CEDAW), women have a right to employment opportunities and treatment equal to men, including equal remuneration for work of equal value, the right to enjoy special protection during pregnancy and paid maternity leave, and the right not to be dismissed on grounds of pregnancy or maternity leave.[87]

In addition, the International Labour Organisation (ILO) has developed many international treaties that cover a wide range of issues – from freedom of association and collective bargaining to child labour or discrimination, through to health and safety, working time, and social security. The 1998 ILO Declaration on Fundamental Principles and Rights at Work affirms the core principles and rights that all ILO member states must observe by virtue of their membership – irrespective of whether they have ratified the relevant conventions.[88] These core principles and rights include:

---

84 e.g. Mutuso Dhliwayo, *Public Interest Litigation as an Empowerment Tool: The Case of the Chiadzwa Community Development Trust and Diamond Mining in Zimbabwe* (International Institute for Environment and Development 2013).

85 e.g. Tom Lomax, *Asserting Community Land Rights Using RSPO Complaint Procedures in Indonesia and Liberia* (International Institute for Environment and Development 2015).

86 UDHR (n 59), arts 23 and 24; ICESCR (n 61) arts 7 and 8.

87 Convention on the Elimination of All Forms of Discrimination Against Women (CEDAW), adopted 18 December 1979, entered into force 3 September 1981, art 11.

88 ILO Declaration on Fundamental Principles and Rights at Work and its Follow-up, adopted by the International Labour Conference (Geneva, 18 June 1998; Annex revised 15 June 2010).

Social and environmental issues in FDI   265

- Freedom of association and the effective recognition of the right to collective bargaining;[89]
- Elimination of all forms of forced or compulsory labour;[90]
- The effective abolition of child labour;[91] and
- The elimination of discrimination in respect of employment and occupation.[92]

Soft law instruments also provide guidance on labour rights, including the OECD Guidelines for Multinational Enterprises[93] and the IFC Performance Standards.[94]

A further issue is whether trade and investment agreements can promote the protection of labour rights. As with environmental provisions, clauses on labour rights are making their way into treaty practice. Several agreements contain non-lowering of standards clauses in relation to labour rights, while others go beyond national law standards – for instance, reaffirming the obligations of the parties under ILO conventions.[95] Some contain more extensive provisions. For example, the Dominican Republic–Central America–United States Free Trade Agreement (CAFTA) includes a labour chapter that, in addition to the above, also contains requirements for workers' access to national law remedies for alleged violations of labour rights.[96]

As with environmental provisions, the effectiveness of non-lowering of standards clauses partly depends on the content of applicable national law, and creating effective enforcement mechanisms is often problematic. However, CAFTA's more

---

89 ILO Conventions No 87 concerning Freedom of Association and Protection of the Right to Organise, adopted 9 July 1948, in force 4 July 1950, and No 98 Concerning the Application of the Principles of the Right to Organise and to Bargain Collectively, adopted 1 July 1949, in force 18 July 1951.

90 ILO Conventions No 29 Concerning Forced or Compulsory Labour, adopted 28 June 1930, in force 1 May 1932, and 105 Concerning the Abolition of Forced Labour, adopted 25 June 1957, in force 17 January 1959.

91 See ILO Conventions No 138 Concerning Minimum Age for Admission to Employment, adopted 26 June 1973, in force 19 June 1976, and No 182 Concerning the Prohibition and Immediate Action for the Elimination of the Worst Forms of Child Labour, adopted 17 June 1999, in force 19 November 2000.

92 ILO Conventions No 100 (Equal Remuneration Convention, adopted 29 June 1951, in force 23 May 1953, and No 111 Concerning Discrimination in Respect of Employment and Occupation, adopted 25 June 1958, in force 15 June 1960.

93 OECD (n 39).

94 IFC Performance Standards on Environmental and Social Sustainability (n 37), Performance Standard No 2 ('Labor and Working Conditions').

95 e.g. the US Model Bilateral Investment Treaty of 2012 and the Morocco–Nigeria BIT of 2016 (n 51).

96 Dominican Republic–Central America–United States Free Trade Agreement (CAFTA), signed 5 August 2004, into force 1 March 2006 for El Salvador and the United States, 1 April 2006 for Honduras and Nicaragua, 1 July 2006 for Guatemala, 1 March 2007 for the Dominican Republic, and 1 January 2009 for Costa Rica.

266 *Lorenzo Cotula*

extensive provisions have given rise to state-state dispute settlement in relation to labour standards that could be used to enhance compliance.[97]

A few recent trade and investment agreements also clarify certain responsibilities of investors by encouraging investors to apply international CSR standards, though these clauses are not typically formulated in mandatory language or backed by effective enforcement mechanisms. An illustrative exception is the Morocco–Nigeria BIT 2016, which uses mandatory language when requiring investors to respect human rights and act in accordance with ILO Declaration on Fundamental Principles and Rights at Work.[98]

3.3.2 Trends in national law

Many national constitutions affirm the human right to work, the principle of non-discrimination in labour relations, and fundamental rights concerning employment conditions. Many also protect the right of freedom of association, and some make explicit reference to the right of workers to form or join a trade union of their choosing.

In addition, well-formulated labour laws guarantee freedom of association and the right to collective bargaining, and they tackle forced and child labour as well as discrimination in the workplace. National legislation can also set parameters for employment conditions, including minimum wage, working hours, health and safety, social benefits, and unfair dismissal as well as ensure that people not in formal employment enjoy adequate protections.

Widespread concerns have been raised about the adequacy of labour legislation and its enforcement, particularly in low and middle-income countries. In some cases, the concerns have sustained law reforms to tighten up standards. One particular set of concerns involves labour rights in special economic zones (SEZs), which are demarcated geographic areas where special business rules apply. In some jurisdictions, different rules govern labour relations in the SEZs.[99]

Prioritizing certain geographic areas for their potential to generate positive ripple effects in the national economy is a legitimate policy goal. These efforts might justify, for example, public choices on budget allocations for the development of public infrastructure. However, exempting SEZs from the application of labour rights is likely to breach international labour conventions and, possibly, human rights treaties.

---

97 ICTSD, 'Trade Dispute Panel Issues Ruling in US–Guatemala Labour Law Case' (2017) 41 *Bridges Weekly* 9.

98 Morocco–Nigeria BIT of 2016 (n 51), arts 15 and 18. See also Vanhonnaecker (n 34); Van-Duzer and Dumberry (n 49).

99 Benjamin Richardson, James Harrison and Liam Campling, *Labour Rights in Export Processing Zones with a Focus on GSP+ Beneficiary Countries* (European Parliament 2017); Lorenzo Cotula and Liliane Mouan, *Special Economic Zones: Engines of Development or Sites of Exploitation?* (International Institute for Environment and Development 2018).

Social and environmental issues in FDI 267

3.3.3 *Labour rights in practice*

Independent and accessible systems for settling labour disputes, and robust government agencies to monitor and enforce compliance with labour legislation, are an important part of effective institutional frameworks to ensure respect for labour law. Besides the role of government, trade unions and organized labour have played a crucially important role in improving wages and labour conditions both in law and in practice.

In recent years, the transnational nature of FDI, and/or of supply chains linked to companies incorporated or operating in capital exporting or export-market countries, has created opportunities for activists to advance labour rights through recourse mechanisms that transcend national boundaries.

This trend is illustrated by the role played by the National Contact Points (NCPs), which are the national institutions that oversee compliance with the OECD Guidelines for Multinational Enterprises. On several occasions, trade unions and NGOs have taken alleged violations of OECD Guidelines that deal with labour standards to NCPs, including those located in the investor's or the buyer's home country. In several cases, the complaint led to conciliation between company and complainants. Where conciliation failed, NCPs investigated the merits of the allegations and – in case of documented breaches – made recommendations on ways to address the problem.[100]

4. Conclusion

This chapter examined trends in legal and policy instruments relevant to social and environmental issues in foreign direct investment. It briefly reviewed key concepts and international instruments concerning CSR, sustainable development, and human rights as they relate to FDI. It then discussed experience in three policy areas – namely, impact assessments, land rights, and labour rights. For each of these themes, the analysis outlined key features of international law and guidance, main trends in national law, and a few insights from practical experiences.

The discussion highlighted the multi-actor dimensions of investment processes, exploring how those processes can affect the land rights of affected landholders, workers' labour rights, and environmental resources that may have socio-cultural as well as ecological value. The multi-actor nature of FDI processes raises questions not only for national and international instruments devoted to social and environmental matters but also for investment policy. Further, the discussion pointed to the diversity and interconnectedness of relevant policy arenas – from national law reform to different types of both hard

---

100 'National Contact Points for the OECD Guidelines for Multinational Enterprises' (Organisation for Economic Co-operation and Development) available at <http://oecd.org/daf/inv/mne/ncps.htm> accessed 25 July 2019.

268 *Lorenzo Cotula*

and soft law international instruments, transnational avenues for recourse, and practical approaches for advancing implementation at the local level.

Some of the issues discussed are not restricted or specific to FDI. Impact assessment, land rights, and labour rights challenges can arise in relation to economic activities irrespective of whether FDI is involved. However, the presence of FDI does have implications for applicable legal frameworks, such as international instruments specifically devoted to FDI (e.g. IIAs). The past few years have witnessed timid but significant evolutions towards integrating social and environmental considerations in those instruments. In addition, transnational value chains (with or without FDI) have created opportunities to advance enforcement of rights and/or adherence to international standards (e.g. OECD NCPs in connection with labour rights disputes).

Holistically considering the diverse social and environmental issues at play in FDI projects creates opportunities for cross-fertilization in the policy approaches pursued. For example, the development of labour clauses or chapters in some recent trade and investment agreements raises questions about the relevance of also integrating provisions on respect for land rights and on advancing implementation of the Voluntary Guidelines on the Responsible Governance of Tenure in an investment context.

In practice, it is often difficult to translate 'progressive' norms into real change, particularly because investment relations tend to involve substantial vested interests and power imbalances. The nature and scale of the challenges call for a key role not just for public authorities, which have the primary institutional mandate for developing and enforcing applicable rules, but also for activists such as trade union representatives, land rights defenders, and environmental advocates to both influence the rules and sustain their full implementation.

Part IV

Conclusion

13 Moving beyond disciplinary silos

Towards an integrated approach to international investment policy

J Anthony VanDuzer, Patrick Leblond, and Stephen Gelb

1. Introduction

The chapters in this book discuss issues and questions regarding international investment activity and policy from a range of disciplinary perspectives. To begin with economics, Van Assche presents both the traditional economic analysis of trade and investment as well as newer economic thinking that responds to growth in the organization of international production in global value chains, a structure implicating both trade and investment.[1] Beaulieu and O'Neill also address the economics of foreign investment and its relationship with trade, emphasizing the need for a more integrated approach, as well as providing a survey of the evidence of the economic effects of foreign investment and international investment agreements (IIAs) on host states.[2] Globerman, Hensyel, and Shapiro engage in an economic analysis of an increasingly important category of international investor, state-owned enterprises, and sovereign wealth funds, examining the assumption that they behave differently than private investors.[3] All three chapters, to varying degrees, address the investment policy implications of their analysis for host states.

The chapters by Durban and Hamzaoui-Essoussi, Papadopoulos, and El Banna address particular strategies to attract investment in light of the international business research on how investors choose locations. Hamzaoui-Essoussi, Papadopoulos, and El Banna focus on explaining the role of place branding in investor choice and suggest considerations relevant to developing a place branding strategy.[4] Durban uses case studies of investment promotion

---

1 Ari Van Assche, 'Trade and foreign direct investment in the 21st century', Chapter 2 in this volume.

2 Eugene Beaulieu and Kelly O'Neill, 'The economics of foreign direct investment and international investment agreements', Chapter 5 in this volume.

3 Steven Globerman, Phillip Hensyel, and Daniel Shapiro, 'State-owned enterprises and sovereign wealth funds: An economic assessment', Chapter 4 in this volume.

4 Leila Hamzaoui-Essoussi, Nicolas Papadopoulos, and Alia El Banna, 'Attracting foreign investment: Location branding and marketing', Chapter 6 in this volume.

272   *J Anthony VanDuzer et al.*

agencies in Australia and Indonesia to explain the nature and purpose of such agencies and analyse the determinants of their success.[5]

Turning to legal research, Vanhonnaeker and VanDuzer and Dumberry provide a conventional account of international investment law focussing on the substantive protections guaranteed to foreign investors under IIAs and the investor–state dispute settlement (ISDS) process in IIAs that allows investors to seek compensation where states violate those standards. Both describe current concerns about the impact of this regime on host states and recent reform efforts.[6] Nadakavukaren Schefer develops a broader conception of law related to investment that includes other international rules (hard and soft), domestic law, and how international and domestic law interact. She also addresses the relationship between these sources of law and explains the institutional process by which laws are created.[7] Cotula adopts a similarly broad conception of law related to investment, highlighting the way in which particular domestic laws influence how foreign investment affects social interests and the environment in the host state and the corresponding need to ensure that those affected are involved in the process of developing and implementing such laws.[8] Christians and Garofalo explain the use of tax policy by states as part of a competitive strategy to attract investment as well as the prospect for supra-national rules in the European Union and the WTO to address states' abuse of these strategies.[9]

Finally, Leblond and Labrecque provide an overview of political science research on investment policy and develop an analysis of how security considerations play into investment policy-making.[10]

Taken together, these chapters lay the foundation for developing a more complete analysis of international investment than is found in any single discipline. In this concluding chapter, we build on these contributions and the profiles of economics, international business, law, and political science presented in Chapter 1 to identify some of the areas in which combining disciplinary approaches can provide a richer understanding of international investment activity as it relates to policy-making by states. We also point out some of the gaps in our current understanding of international investment policy that

---

5 Matthew Durban, 'FDI policy advocacy and investor targeting', Chapter 7 in this volume.

6 Lukas Vanhonnaeker, 'International investment agreements', Chapter 10 in this volume; J Anthony VanDuzer and Patrick Dumberry, 'Investor–state dispute settlement', Chapter 11 in this volume.

7 Krista Nadakavukaren Schefer, 'Actors, institutions, and policy in host countries', Chapter 3 in this volume.

8 Lorenzo Cotula, 'Social and environmental issues in foreign direct investment: A legal and policy perspective', Chapter 12 in this volume.

9 Allison Christians and Marco Garofalo, 'Tax competition as an investment promotion tool', Chapter 8 in this volume.

10 Patrick Leblond and Sébastien Labrecque, 'National security and the political economy of international investment policy', Chapter 9 in this volume.

Moving beyond disciplinary silos 273

a comparison of disciplinary approaches reveals. We offer a variety of suggestions for interdisciplinary research that scholars should undertake.

We use disciplinary labels in this chapter in order to more clearly point to the merit of a particular approach. In doing so, however, we do not mean to suggest that the research and analytical methods most closely associated with a particular discipline can be employed uniquely by people with credentials in that discipline.

2. The need for firm-specific approaches to understanding international investment

One of the distinctive strengths of international business scholarship is its sophisticated and nuanced understanding of the multiple, complex, intersecting, and dynamic factors that affect MNE decision-making in relation to investment. Recent work in economics has moved toward a more firm-specific understanding of trade but it is not as well developed in relation to investment and does not encompass the breadth of firm-specific considerations captured in the international business literature. Political science's study of international investment is still relatively shallow and limited in scope and has not gone very far to address variations across firms. International investment law, with its narrow focus on investment treaties, essentially treats all firms as identical in terms of the need for treaty protection.

Blinkered perspectives regarding firm differences have so far limited the development of a deep understating of a range of issues related to international investment. For example, most studies in all four disciplines on the investment-inducing effects of IIAs have focussed on aggregate investment flows into host states.[11] Only recently, and in a still limited way, have scholars begun to investigate whether the investment-inducing impact of IIAs varies with different kinds of investors, such as whether they are large, small, state- or privately-owned, or operating in different sectors. More firm-specific research of this kind would enable a much richer understanding of how IIAs actually work on the ground, how they should be drafted to be most effective and whether they are needed at all.

Limited recognition of firm differences also explains, in part, why there has been no effort to customize IIAs to the needs of particular investors that the home state wants to protect or the host state wants to attract. Though a few IIAs have carve-outs for particular sectors that host states want to protect, none have provisions positively targeted at particular categories of investors. A deeper understanding of differences in firm-specific decision-making from international business would allow policy-makers to better understand how IIAs work and, as a result, make them more effective instruments to achieve a state's objective of

---

11 This research is reviewed in Beaulieu and O'Neill (n 2).

274 *J Anthony VanDuzer et al.*

attracting particular kinds of investors (or investments) compatible with its development priorities.[12]

More generally, existing and further work by economists and international business scholars on the local effects of international investment in host states, informed by firm-specific research, could be the basis of a treasure trove of new hypotheses about the drivers of international investment policy that political scientists and legal scholars, as well as economists and international business scholars, could analyse. To do so, scholars in the various disciplines might usefully combine qualitative and quantitative methodological approaches: case studies, surveys, and interviews, on the one hand, and multivariate regression analysis and formal modelling, like game theory, on the other.

3. The need for country-specific international investment policy

Following from the previous point, it is essential for governments designing their policies on international investment to understand a wide variety of factors related to particular foreign investors and their investment decisions. That way, they can determine what investors to attract and what investors to keep away as well as how best to do so. This requires assessing how particular investor activities align (or not) with local advantages, the likely (positive and negative) effects of investment from certain kinds of foreign investors in particular sectors, and the state's capacity to regulate investors both before and after the investment takes place.[13] As illustrated in the chapters by Cotula, Leblond and Labrecque, and Globerman, Hensyel, and Shapiro in this volume, non-economic considerations, especially national security but also investments' social and environmental impacts, are relevant factors for governments to consider.[14]

Once particular investors or categories of investors have been identified as a domestic priority, governments need to know what kinds of policies are likely to be attractive to those investors. Detailed and specific information on prospective investors is required to make optimal policy in this way. It is increasingly accepted that international investment policy should not follow a 'one-size-fits-all' approach but be tailored to a country's economic and political realities.[15] International business scholars' insights into MNEs would

---

12 For example, Globerman, Hensyel, and Shapiro (n 3) examine the extent to which SOEs are more likely to take non-economic considerations into account in management decision-making.

13 This point is also made by Durban (n 5).

14 Cotula (n 8); Leblond and Labrecque (n 10), and Globerman, Hensyel, and Shapiro (n 3). The need to take into account non-economic impacts is further discussed in Section 5 below.

15 UNCTAD, *Investment Policy Framework for Sustainable Development* (United Nations 2015); OECD, *FDI Qualities Toolkit: Investment for Inclusive and Sustainable Growth. Progress Report III* (OECD 2019); World Bank, *Maximizing Potential Benefits of FDI for Competitiveness and Sustainable Development: World Bank Group Report on Investment Policy & Promotion Diagnostics and Tools* (World Bank Group 2017).

allow the incorporation of more firm-specific information into the policy-making process.[16]

Political science work on investment policy-making could also be better informed by the work of international business scholars, as it has so far been limited to high-level policy questions regarding whether a country is open to international investment based on the impacts of foreign investment on host-state economic interests like business and labour.[17] Policy-makers need more research on the political impact of sector- and firm-level investment. As well, complementary work is needed on the political economy of particular international investment policy options, building on the limited work that has been done on the political economy of financial incentives to investors, such as tax breaks and subsidies.[18]

As noted in the previous section, one area in which abandoning a 'one-size-fits-all' approach would be valuable is IIAs. As discussed by Vanhonnaeker and VanDuzer and Dumberry, IIA negotiators have, in large measure, focussed on universal standards of investor protection rather than tailoring them to the development objectives of the parties and the policies needed to achieve them.[19] In order to determine what kinds of agreements to negotiate, if any, governments should take into account the likely impact of IIAs on the particular kinds of firms they are seeking to attract. These impacts will be determined not only by investor characteristics but also by host-state characteristics. For example, the relative utility of host-state IIA commitments will vary depending on the effectiveness and reliability of local property rights protection and the rule of law.[20] IIA protections may not be needed where other local features, such as economic policy stability provided by domestic political institutions, are sufficiently attractive to investors.[21] Seeking to limit IIA protections to investments that a state decides to target is an important policy consideration given the constraining effect of IIAs backed up by investor–state arbitration on the state's ability to achieve its policy goals.

It may be that there are some forms of basic investment protection that are both universally useful to attract investment and compatible with good governance in host states. Economic research shows, for example, that virtually all investors view property rights protection as important.[22] Some investment

---

16 See J Anthony VanDuzer, Patrick Leblond and Stephen Gelb, 'Introduction to international investment policy and rationale for an interdisciplinary approach', Chapter 1 in this volume.

17 ibid VanDuzer and Leblond; Leblond and Labrecque (n 10). International business scholars are increasingly focused on the policy relevance of their work.

18 e.g. Nathan M Jensen and Edmund J Malevsky, *Incentives to Pander: How Politicians Use Corporate Welfare for Political Gain* (Cambridge University Press 2018); Stephanie J Rickard, *Spending to Win: Political Institutions, Economic Geography, and Government Subsidies* (Cambridge University Press 2018).

19 Vanhonnaeker (n 6) and VanDuzer and Dumberry (n 6).

20 See ibid VanDuzer and Dumberry.

21 Beaulieu and O'Neill (n 2).

22 World Bank Group, 'Global Investment Competitiveness Report 2017/2018 Foreign Investor Perspectives and Policy Implications' (25 October 2017), 25, available at <http://documents. worldbank.org/curated/en/169,531,510,741,671,962/Global-investment-competitiveness-report-2017-2018-foreign-investor-perspectives-and-policy-implications> accessed 27 June 2019.

276   *J Anthony VanDuzer et al.*

law scholars argue that most IIA protections represent generally-accepted good governance standards that are compatible with appropriate regulatory freedom, though this benign view of IIAs is highly contested.[23] Nevertheless, the interest of investors in property rights is not a sufficiently compelling argument for securing these rights in IIAs in all cases regardless of the domestic regime. At the very least, decisions to secure rights need to be balanced with state freedom to act to achieve policy objectives and prevent, mitigate, and remedy potential negative effects associated with international investment.

Overall, more work needs to be done to understand how IIA protections work in order to assess the need for such agreements and what they should include. Concepts like good governance and property rights need to be unpacked and given specific content by lawyers and then the constituent elements analysed by international business scholars in terms of how they affect investors' decision-making. Political scientists could explain the political economy of the process to create these specific institutional characteristics and the determinants of particular institutional outcomes.[24]

Finally, the chapters by Hamzaoui-Essoussi, Papadopoulos, and El Banna, Nadakavukaren Schefer, and Durban all make clear that the discussion of policies related to international investment cannot be limited to legal instruments, a point that is not reflected in most legal scholarship on investment. Hamzaoui-Essoussi, Papadopoulos, and El Banna discuss the complex psychology of location branding and its role in investment attraction.[25] Nadakavukaren Schefer identifies the role of soft law instruments, like non-binding corporate social responsibility codes, as relevant to investor behaviour.[26] Durban describes the role of investment promotion agencies (IPAs) in communicating information about investment opportunities, facilitating investment, and advocating for policy change.[27] IPAs' effectiveness depends on their understanding of investor interests as well as the changing global marketplace, such as the role of SOEs,[28] the nature and importance of GVCs,[29] and investor decision-making criteria.[30] In discussing IPAs, Durban's work raises questions for lawyers, economists, international business scholars, and political scientists. For example, to what extent can the IPA activities substitute

---

23 e.g. Benedict Kingsbury and Stephan Schill, 'Investor-State Arbitration as Governance: Fair and Equitable Treatment, Proportionality and the Emerging Global Administrative Law', In Albert Jan van den Berg (ed), *50 Years of the New York Convention, ICAA Congress Series* 5 (Kluwer Law International 2009); Vanhonnaeker (n 6); VanDuzer and Dumberry (n 6).

24 Durban (n 5) summarizes some of what is known about the effectiveness of particular invest-ment-attraction policies, including investment promotion authorities.

25 Hamzaoui-Essoussi, Papadopoulos, and El Banna (n 4).

26 Nadakavukaren Schefer (n 7). The role of soft law instruments is also discussed in Cotula (n 8).

27 Durban (n 5).

28 See Globerman, Hensyel, and Shapiro (n 3).

29 See Van Assche (n 1).

30 See Beaulieu and O'Neill (n 2).

for hard legal reforms to address corruption, weak governance, and red tape? What is the risk that international investors will capture IPAs?

International business scholars and political scientists, to a lesser degree, have paid some attention to state actions that are not implemented through legal rules; however, economists and investment law scholars have not investigated state actions outside the hard law context. Overall, much more needs to be done in the four disciplinary approaches to understand soft law and non-law country-specific policy activity.

4. Investment and other economic activity by foreign investors

As described in the chapters by Van Assche and Beaulieu and O'Neill, MNEs increasingly organize their activities in the form of GVCs.[31] While this is not a new trend, the trade and investment implications have only recently become a major focus for policy-makers. Contributions from multiple disciplines are needed to respond to the policy-making challenges. However, not all disciplines have put GVCs at the core of their analyses when it comes to researching international investment and related activities. Economics and international business have made the most progress in understanding GVCs and their implications for interactions between trade and investment activities. By contrast, legal analysis of national and international regulatory instrument reform to take account of GVCs has not progressed very far. For example, while the definitions of investors and investments typically found in IIAs are broad, they need to be re-examined to determine if they can accommodate the increasingly diverse array of equity and non-equity relations involved in GVCs. Also, GVCs' significant role in the global economy means that there is a greater need to coordinate trade and investment policies and to pay more attention in both contexts to trade in services in addition to resource extraction and industrial production, as well as to re-examine the existing scope and categories of treaty commitments. So far, legal analysis of trade and investment has tended to be siloed. This is also true for political science research, where scholars have analysed international trade and investment separately. Political science research on international trade has been paying more and more attention to GVCs in recent years but work on international investment has yet to do so.[32] The insights of economists and international business scholars regarding the structure and organization of MNEs is needed if legal scholars are to successfully develop a more integrated understanding of trade and investment rules. Finally, as Van Assche demonstrates in his chapter, looking at investment as an element of GVC behaviour shifts the politics of trade and investment, which is something that political scientists should pay more attention to as they analyse

---

31 Van Assche (n 1); Beaulieu and O'Neill (n 2).

32 e.g. Jappe Eckhardt and Arlo Poletti, 'The politics of global value chains: import-dependent firms and EU–Asia trade agreements' (2016) 23 *Journal of European Public Policy* 1543; Frederick W Mayer and Nicola Phillips, 'Outsourcing governance: states and the politics of a "global value chain world"' (2017) 22 *New Political Economy* 134.

278   *J Anthony VanDuzer et al.*

international investment policy-making.[33] Combining these distinct disciplinary contributions would better inform governments about what investments to seek and how best to do so in light of competing policy objectives and political constraints.

All disciplines need to more fully address investment in services. Services represent more than 60 per cent of global investment. Services investment as well as trade in services are essential elements of most GVCs. Until recently, however, services have not attracted the same attention from economists and international business scholars as investment in goods manufacturing. Opening up domestic services sectors to global competition, especially through investment, also raises distinct political economy and legal issues that have received insufficient attention.[34] Important services sectors, like finance and telecommunications, are highly regulated in each country to achieve important public policy goals unrelated to international trade or investment. These systems of regulation are more heterogeneous than rules dealing with trade or investment, generally making it more difficult to use international treaties as a mechanism to dismantle barriers.[35] Liberalizing market access for services requires broad reform of these regulatory systems. The nature of services trade regulation means that there are many vested domestic interests with substantial stakes in the status quo that would be affected by any liberalizing reform, including services regulators, responsible government departments, and services businesses.[36] Partly as a consequence of these challenging distinct features of services trade and investment, lawyers have made little progress in developing effective rules for services liberalization. The prospect for gains on this front could be enhanced by international business research on different services suppliers. More research into the political economy of individual sector reforms to enhance participation in GVCs by host-state businesses would also be helpful to policy-makers.

5. Investment, non-economic impacts, and the policy process

Foreign investment can have significant positive impacts both directly and through spillover effects in the host country;[37] however, negative impacts also occur.[38] Sustainable development requires using host-state policy not only to attract investment, but also to capture its positive effects and mitigate its negative impacts.

---

33 Van Assche (n 1).

34 Joseph Francois and Bernard Hoekman, 'Services trade and policy' (2010) 48 *Journal of Economic Literature* 642; Magnus Lodefalk, 'Servicification of firms and trade policy implications' (2017) 16 *World Trade Review* 59.

35 e.g. Bernard Hoekman, Aaditya Mattoo, and André Sapir, 'The political economy of services trade liberalization: a case for international regulatory cooperation?' (2007) 23 *Oxford Review of Economic Policy* 367.

36 J Anthony VanDuzer, 'A critical look at the prospects for robust rules for services in preferential trading agreements' (2012) 38 *Legal Issues of Economic Integration* 29.

37 Beaulieu and O'Neill (n 2).

38 Cotula (n 8).

Moving beyond disciplinary silos 279

None of the disciplines discussed has much to say about how to achieve sustainable development.

Economists' work on host-state impact of FDI has been on a limited range of factors: productivity of local firms, wages and employment, product variety, technology transfer, exports, and integration of local firms into GVCs. Non-economic factors have generally been regarded as outside the discipline.[39]

Some international business scholarship has focussed on the role of non-economic factors. Dunning recognized the importance of non-economic effects, including 'political, legal, cultural, organizational, managerial and other elements' as significant contributors to transactions costs and so relevant to MNEs' investment decisions. In part, this was what motivated his call for an interdisciplinary approach.[40] Because these are the kinds of issues international business people deal with in practice on a regular basis, the study of MNEs had to adopt an interdisciplinary approach to be relevant. Apart from a few recent studies, however, international business research has typically not considered the impact of MNE activity in the host state.[41] As noted, however, this is changing with the 'policy turn' advocated by some international business scholars.

Political science has investigated the impact of international investment on labour, though the focus has been on how their economic interests are affected and how this shapes their political preferences. Some political scientists have studied FDI's effects on domestic political conditions other than investment policy, such as democratization, governance, human rights and income equality, but much more could be done on such non-economic conditions.[42]

Investment law has focussed on the relationship of the host state to foreign investors once the investors have entered their territory, but, until recently, only from the perspective of how investors can be protected from state action. No attention is paid in traditional treaties to promoting sustainable development through investment. More recently, there have been modest reforms to prevent investor protections from impeding state regulation to achieve sustainable

---

39 Roberto Echandi, Jana Krajcovicova, and Christine Qian, 'The Impact of Investment Policy in a Changing Economy: A Review of the Literature'; (2015) World Bank Policy Research Working Paper No 7437 <http://documents.worldbank.org/curated/en/664491467994693599/pdf/wps7437.pdf> accessed 27 June 2019.

40 John H Dunning, 'The Study of International Business: A Plea for a More Interdisciplinary Approach' (1989) 20 *Journal of International Business Studies* 411, 429, 433.

41 Ans Kolk, 'The social responsibility of international business: From ethics and the environment to CSR and sustainable development' (2016) 51 *Journal of World Business* 23.

42 Sonal Pandya, 'Political Economy of Foreign Direct Investment: Globalized Production in the 21st Century' (2016) 19 *Annual Review of Political Science* 455, 457; Olivier De Schutter, Johan Swinnen, and Jan Wouters (eds), *Foreign Direct Investment and Human Development: The Law and Economics of International Investment Agreements* (Routledge 2013).

280　*J Anthony VanDuzer et al.*

development but no clear positive agenda to transform treaties into instruments to promote sustainable development has emerged in state practice.[43]

In sum, there is not much work in any discipline that looks rigorously at the non-economic impacts of investment in host states. Particular non-economic effects are studied by academics who consider international investment as just one factor among many that influence their primary focus on issues like human and labour rights, environmental protection, and sustainable development.

Better research on non-economic effects is needed because it is increasingly recognized that international investment has what Cotula calls a multi-actor nature. Investment policy-making must move beyond a binary model limited to the interests of states and investors.[44] Investment policy-making should involve a complex iterative process. Because different kinds of FDI may have different economic, social, and environmental impacts, the process of policy-making must permit affected interests to participate in an effective way in choosing targets of investment, and crafting policies to attract the investment, and regulations to ensure that benefits are received, risks of harm mitigated, and actual harms compensated.[45] But since the identity of affected interests depends upon the nature of the investment and its expected impact, the policy process must be recursive. Investment policy must be coordinated with areas of domestic policy that implicate domestic interests affected by foreign investment. In his chapter, Cotula argues that domestic rules regarding areas like environmental assessment as well as land and labour rights may not be conceived of as investment policy but play a role in the way in which foreign investment affects domestic interests. He also points out that MNEs' accountability for their activities in host states may be achieved through actions taken by their home states, though existing rules and arrangements impede them from playing such a role.[46]

The prospects for interdisciplinary collaboration to assist investment policy formation that is responsive to affected interests are easy to identify. Economists and international business scholars can explain distributional and other local effects of international investment. Political scientists can deduce policy preferences from those effects. Lawyers can work on the institutional arrangements for the policy development process as well as the legal arrangements to achieve desired policy outcomes.

43　Vanhonnaeker (n 6); VanDuzer and Dumberry (n 6). A recent exception is Emma Aisbett, Bernali Choudhury, Olivier de Schutter, Frank Garcia, James Harrison, Song Hong, Lise Johnson, Mouhamadou Kane, Santiago Peña, Matthew Porterfield, Susan Sell, Stephen E Shay, and Louis T Wells, 'Rethinking International Investment Governance: Principles for the 21st Century' (2018) <http://ccsi.columbia.edu/files/2018/09/rethinking-invest ment-governance-september-2018.pdf> accessed 19 June 2019.

44　Cotula (n 8).

45　Nadakavukaren Schefer (n 4) characterizes such a process as contributing to the 'legitimacy' of the policy outcome.

46　Cotula (n 8).

6. Conclusions

It is certainly true that rigorously employing an interdisciplinary approach drawing on the theoretical insights and empirical evidence developed in law, economics, international business, and political science would be extremely challenging in the everyday practice of international investment policy-making. It would be impossible for even the most sophisticated government to apply an interdisciplinary approach in a comprehensive way on an ongoing basis. As well, the value of complementary contributions and useful background knowledge from multiple disciplines may be outweighed by the loss of a 'sharpness of analytical focus'.[47] As suggested in a recent guide to investment policy-making from the World Bank, there is a risk that '[c]ountries get lost'.[48]

On the other hand, the relative importance of even universally-desirable factors, like property rights and strong institutions and the viability of dealing with them through state policy, will vary with an investor's business strategy and organizational characteristics, as well as the characteristics of home and host states. Understanding these variables requires an interdisciplinary approach. An interdisciplinary approach would permit researchers to address more complex questions and be more practically relevant.[49]

In this concluding chapter, we sought to build on the previous chapters to suggest ways in which the insights, approaches, and research methods of four disciplines could be used to address gaps and limitations regarding our understanding of investors and their decisions as well as the roles played by governments, other state actors, non-state actors, and domestic and international institutions. To be sure, this chapter's goals were limited. We sought only to illuminate some of the right questions to ask, both for researchers and policy-makers, as well as some of the assumptions made and efforts to test them. We argued that pushing law, economics, and political science to more fully incorporate firm-specific characteristics building on insights of international business would enrich our understanding of firm behaviour and how states should think about their policy choices with respect to attracting and managing international investment, including whether a country should sign IIAs and, if so, what their content should be, all in light of their distinctive circumstances. We also identified two particular challenges in understanding firm behaviour and the related policy implications: (1) how firms engage in GVCs, especially in relation to investment in services and trade; (2) what

---

47 John Cantwell and Mary Y Brannen, 'Positioning JIBS as an interdisciplinary journal' (2011) 42 *Journal of International Business Studies* 1.

48 World Bank Group, *Maximizing Potential Benefits of FDI for Competitiveness and Sustainable Development: World Bank Group Report on Investment Policy & Promotion Diagnostics and Tools* (World Bank Group 2017) 9.

49 Cantwell and Brannen (n 47); Stephen D Cohen, *Multinational Corporations and Foreign Direct Investment: Avoiding Simplicity, Embracing Complexity* (Oxford University Press 2007).

policies are needed to attract GVC investment and promote local firm participation in GVCs. Finally, we argued that all disciplines need to do more to understand the social, environmental, and other non-economic effects of international investment on host states as well as their implications for the process and outcomes of host-state policy-making to ensure that investment policy contributes to sustainable development.

Index

Locators in **bold** refer to tables and those in *italics* to figures, though where interspersed with related text these are not distinguished from principal locators. The acronym FDI is used throughout for 'foreign direct investment', and MNCs for 'multinational corporations'.

4Ps (marketing) 128
9/11 195–196

administrative agencies 66–67
advertising places *see* location choice for MNCs
advocacy: definition 145; policy advocacy 145–148
anti-bribery legislation 157
approval regimes for international investment 192–194
arbitration: cases 223–224, 226–227; independence of arbitrators 234–236, 239–241; law scholarship 18; rules 231–232; types 230–231
Austrade 141, 143–145, 158
Australia: Export Finance and Insurance Corporation 155; investment promotion agency 141–142, 143–145, 151, 152, 158; investor-state dispute settlement mechanisms 245–246; regulatory context 156, 157

banking networks 157–158
bilateral investment treaties (BITs) 105; fair and equitable treatment 211–212; inclusion of investor-state dispute settlement mechanisms 227; investment definition 205–206; law scholarship 14; origins 200; political science scholarship 23; unlawful expropriation protection 214–215; worldwide use of

223; *see also* international investment agreements
biological diversity 255–256
BKPM (Indonesia's Badan Koordinasi Peranaman Modal) 142–143, 147, 151–152, 158
'bottom of the pyramid' 248
branding *see* place marketing
bribery 156–157

Canada: approval regime for international investment 193–194; international investment agreements 107–108; legal system 68; non-discrimination protection 209, 210; unlawful expropriation protection 215–216
certification schemes 254
China: approval regime for international investment 192–193; investor-state dispute settlement mechanisms 245–246; privatization effects 93; state-owned enterprises 80, 83
Committee on Foreign Investment in the United States (CFIUS) 191–192
Communication, globalization of production 42–43
comparative advantage 8, 37, 40, 129, 141
competition: for foreign direct investment 117; investment policy 139; state aid 172–173; tax strategy as an investment promotion tool 160–161, 164–168, 178–179

284   *Index*

Comprehensive Economic and Trade Agreement (CETA): fair and equitable treatment 212; investor-state dispute settlement 233–234, 240, 242; Most-Favoured-Nation 210

consumers: competition 106; globalization of production 36, 46; place marketing 128–129; trade and the national production paradigm 33; trade liberalization 34–35, 48

Convention on Biological Diversity (CBD) 255

Convention on the Elimination of All Forms of Discrimination Against Women (CEDAW) 264

corporate restructuring 204

corporate social responsibility (CSR) 248–249, 252–255; *see also* environmental issues in FDI; social issues in FDI

corruption 156–157

courts: domestic legal systems 67; EU Court of Justice 171–172; relationship between domestic and international law 70; *see also* investor-state dispute settlement (ISDS)

cultural distance 123–124

customary law 61

Czech Republic, fair and equitable (FET) treatment 211–212

data sector, national security concerns 196–197

de facto discrimination 208

de facto expropriatory measures 214

de facto selectivity 170

de facto specific subsidies 175

debt, economic crises 188–189

Defense Production Act 192

development finance institutions (DFIs) 254

disciplinary approaches: interdisciplinary approach 2–4, 280, 281–282; investment, non-economic impacts, and the policy process 278–280; investment and other economic activity by foreign investors 277–278; moving beyond disciplinary silos 26–28, 271–273; need for country-specific international investment policy 274–277; need for firm-specific approaches to understanding international investment 273–274; *see also* economics scholarship; international business; law scholarship; political science

discrimination 208–209

dispute settlement mechanisms 200–201, 202, 219, 221–222

domestic investment policy *see* international investment policy

domestic law: disciplinary approaches 271; environmental and social issues 257–258; foreign direct investment 63–68; international business scholarship 12; in international dispute resolution 62–63; labour rights 266; land rights 261–263; relationship to international law 68–70

domestic legal systems: executive offices 65–67; interactions between parts of 52; legislatures 64–65; political parties 65; role of 63–64

Dominican Republic-Central America-United States Free Trade Agreement (CAFTA) 265–266

double taxation 161–164

dualist system of law 68

Dunning's 'OLI paradigm' 9–10, 36, 120

'eclectic paradigm' 10

economic crises 188–189

economics scholarship: characterization of investors 7; disciplinary silos 26–28, 271; foreign direct investment 4–6, 8–9, 99–100, 101–103; global value chains 100–101; host-state characteristics 8; impact of foreign investment in host state 8–9; international investment agreements 99–100; scope 4–6; values 6–7

efficiency: economic scholarship 6–7; foreign direct investment 47–48; global value chains 41

emotions, location choice decision process 124–126

employees *see* labour rights in FDI; workers

environmental and social impact assessments 255–259

environmental issues in FDI 247–248; corporate social responsibility 248–249, 252–255; quality investment 248–254; sustainable development 249–251

Environmental Law Alliance Worldwide (ELAW) 257–258

environmental protection principle 251

European Union (EU): implications for tax competition 176–178; investor-state dispute settlement mechanisms

245–246; state aid 169–173, 174–175, 179
executive branch of government 65–66
Exon-Florio Amendment 192
expropriation protection 214–216

factor prices 47
fair and equitable (FET) treatment 211–213
financial crises 188–189
firms (privately owned): FDI politics implications 48–49; global value chains 40–41, 281–282; national production paradigm 32–38; need for firm-specific approaches to understanding international investment 273–274; private vs. state ownership 81–83; *see also* multinational enterprises; state-owned enterprises
flexibility: global value chains 41–42; international investment agreements 14; investor protection 21
foreign direct investment (FDI): in the 21st century 31–32; attracting FDI by location branding 132–136; attracting using international investment agreements 104–109; attracting using tax incentives 156, 161–168; attractiveness of locations 117–118; competition for 117; domestic law 63–68; economics of 4–6, 8–9, 99–100, 101–103; effectiveness of international investment agreements 110–116; evolving scholarship 49–50; globalization of production 46–48; international business 9–10; investment promotion, place marketing, nation branding 126–131; location choice decision process 118–126, 136–137; national production paradigm 32–38; national security concerns 183; political science scholarship 22–23, 24–25; sources of investment law 70–73; traditional FDI politics 37–38; traditional FDI theory 35–37; *see also* environmental issues in FDI; international investment policy; social issues in FDI
foreign direct investment policy *see* international investment policy; investment promotion agencies
foreign investment's impact in host state: economic scholarship 8–9; international business scholarship 13–14; investment,

non-economic impacts, and the policy process 278–280; investment and other economic activity by foreign investors 277–278; law scholarship 20–21; political science scholarship 26
foreign investors *see* investor protection
Foreign Sales Company (FSC) regime 177
free, prior, and informed consent (FPIC) 260
free trade agreements (FTAs) 105, 200, 265–266; *see also* international investment agreements; North American Free Trade Agreement
free trade, economic scholarship 6–7
Freedom of Commerce and Navigation (FCN) treaties 201
full protection and security (FPS) provisions 213–214

gender, equal labour rights 264
General Agreement on Tariffs and Trade (GATT) 16, 59–60, 173, 176
geographic distribution of activities, state-owned enterprises 86
Germany: national security concerns 196–197; unlawful expropriation protection 214–215
Global Investment Promotion Best Practices project 148–149
global value chains (GVCs) 6; in the 21st century 31–32; FDI implications 46–47; firm behaviours 40–41, 281–282; investment and other economic activity by foreign investors 277–278; multinational enterprises 100–104; trade implications 39–45; trade politics implications 45–46
globalization: foreign direct investment impacts 46–48; liberalization of FDI 201; multinational enterprises 100–104; of production 38–49; three periods of 32, 39, 40, 43, 49; trade implications 39–45; trade politics implications 45–46
government policy *see* domestic law; domestic legal systems; state-owned enterprises
Grindr 197
Guidelines on Multinational Enterprises 254
GVC *see* global value chains

'hard law' 58
Heckscher-Ohlin model 33, 34, 36
horizontal FDI 5, 47, 103

286 *Index*

host-state characteristics: actors, institutions, and policy 51–52; approval regime for international investment 192–194; attracting FDI by location branding 132–136; attracting using international investment agreements 104–109; attracting using tax incentives 156, 161–168; attractiveness of locations 117–118; disciplinary silos 27; economic scholarship 8; international business scholarship 12–13; investor protection and host states' right to regulate 200–201, 218–222; law scholarship 19–20; need for country-specific international investment policy 274–277; political science scholarship 26; *see also* foreign investment's impact in host state; investor-state dispute settlement

human rights 252, 259–260

IBM 147, 151

import tariffs 34–35, 42, 45, 46

'inclusive business', corporate social responsibility 249

income tax 161–164

India, international investment policy 188

Indonesian investment promotion 142–143, 147, 151–152; *see also* BKPM

industry policy 158–159

information and communication technology (ICT): in the 21st century 31; online transactions 158

informed consent 260

infrastructure, investment promotion 153–154

institutions *see* public institutions

intellectual property rights 17

interdisciplinary approach 2–4, 280, 281–282

internalization: Dunning's framework 10, 36, 120; location choice decision process 120

international business: characterization of investors 12; disciplinary silos 26–28; host-state characteristics 12–13; impact of foreign investment in host state 13–14; scope 9–11; values 11–12

international business scholarship: foreign investment's impact in host state 279; need for firm-specific approaches to understanding international investment 273–274

International Centre for the Settlement of Investment Disputes (ICSID) Convention 206, 231–232, 237, 239, 242

International Court of Justice (ICJ) 54, 57

International Covenant on Economic, Social and Cultural Rights (ICESCR) 264

International Covenant on Civil and Political Rights (ICCPR) 260

International Finance Corporation (IFC) 254

international investment agreements (IIAs): attracting foreign investment 104–109; basic provisions 200–201; contemporary developments and the balance between investor protection and host states' right to regulate 218–222; disciplinary approaches 27, 273–274; economics of 99–100; effectiveness in promoting FDI 110–116; inclusion of investor-state dispute settlement mechanisms 223–224, 225, 227–228, 244–246; investor protection 208–218; law scholarship 14–17, 19–21; legitimacy crisis 115, 224; need for country-specific policy 275–276; objectives 201–202; origins 200; political science scholarship 23–25, 26; scope of protection 203–208; source of law 59–62; worldwide use of 223

international investment policy *see also* investment promotion agencies: approval regimes 192–194; content of investment policies 139–145; corporate social responsibility 252–255; international investment agreements 106–109, 111–115; investment, non-economic impacts, and the policy process 278–280; legal context 51–52; liberalization 186–187, 189; location choice decision process 121–122; national security concerns 183–184, 191–195; need for country-specific policy 274–277; political economy 185–190; political science scholarship 21–22; sources of investment law 56–63, 70–73

international joint ventures (IJVs) 123

International Labour Organisation (ILO) 264–266

international law: basic tenets 53–56; definition 53; environmental and social impact assessments 255–256; hierarchy of laws 55; labour rights 264–266; land rights 259–260; relationship to domestic law 68–70; rules of behaviour 54–55; sources of 56–63; state actions 51–52; state responsibility 55–56; state sovereignty 53–54

international trade law 15–17, 231

International Trade Organization 16

Internet, online transactions 158

investment: definition 204–206; need for firm-specific approaches to understanding international investment 273–274; non-economic impacts, and the policy process 278–280; *see also* foreign direct investment; international investment policy

investment promotion: place marketing 126–131; tax strategy 160–168, 178–179; *see also* international investment policy

investment promotion agencies: content of investment policy 139–145; disciplinary approaches 276–277; environmental and social protection 253–254; FDI policy and advocacy 138, 158–159; future directions for investment promotion 154–158; investor targeting 148–154; place marketing 127, 133; policy advocacy 145–148

investor characteristics: economic scholarship 7; international business scholarship 12; law scholarship 18–19; political science scholarship 25

investor decision-making 1

investor nationality 123–124

investor obligations 221–222, 257

investor protection: balancing with host states' right to regulate 200–201, 218–222; dispute settlement mechanism 202; international investment agreements' scope 203–208; 'obsolescing bargain' 202; traditional international investment agreements 208–218

investor targeting 148–154

investors, definition of 203–204

investor-state dispute settlement (ISDS) 223–225; arbitration cases 226–227; basic features 227–234; current issues dealing with ISDS clauses 234–238; international investment agreements 200–201, 216, 219, 221–222; policy implications 244–246; rationale 225–226; reform options 238–244

Japan, investor-state dispute settlement mechanisms 245–246

judges: domestic legal systems 67; relationship between domestic and international law 70

knowledge-seeking: foreign direct investment 47–48; global value chains 42

labour rights in FDI 264–267

land rights 259–264

language barriers 124–125

law scholarship: actors, institutions, and policy 51–52; characterization of investors 18–19; disciplinary silos 26–28; host-state characteristics 19–20; impact of foreign investment in host state 20–21; scope 14–16; values 16–18; *see also* domestic law; international law

legal instruments 57–59, 62–63

legal systems *see* domestic legal systems; international law

legislatures 64–65

liberalization: consumer benefits 34–35, 48; context of globalization 201; international investment policy 186–187, 189; services sector 278

location choice for MNCs: attractiveness of 117–118; competition between 117; decision process 118–126, 136–137; Dunning's framework 10, 36, 120; effectiveness of investment promotion agencies 149–152; location branding 132–136; nation branding and place marketing 118, 126–131; tax 156

Malaysia, SME development boards 154–155

marketing mix 128

markets: economics of 7; foreign direct investment 47; investment policy 139

merger and acquisitions (M&As) 123

monist system of law 68

Morocco-Nigeria BIT 266

Most-Favoured-Nation (MFN): investor protection 208, 210–211; tax 173

movements *see* social movements

Mozambique's Land Act 263

multidisciplinary approach 4; *see also* inter-disciplinary approach

multinational enterprises (MNEs): attractiveness of locations 117–118; economic scholarship 4–5; globalization and global value chains 100–104;

288 *Index*

international business scholarship 9–12;
international dispersal and IIAs 104–109;
investment and other economic activity
by foreign investors 277–278; location
choice decision process 118–126,
136–137; national security 190; political
science scholarship 22, 23–24; state-
owned enterprises 78–80, 79; variations
in FDI behaviour by investor, investment
and location characteristics 122–123; *see
also* state-owned multinational enterprises
(SOMNEs)

nation branding 118, 130–131, 133,
134–135, 136–137; *see also* location
choice for MNCs; place marketing
nation states *see* domestic law; international
investment policy; state sovereignty
National Contact Points (NCPs) 267
national law *see* domestic law
national production paradigm 4, 32–38
national security 183–184; definition
190–191; international investment policy
183–184, 191–199; rise in concern
about 195–197
National Treatment (NT): investor
protection 208–211; tax 173
nationality 203–204
nationality planning 204, 238, 243–244
the Netherlands, fair and equitable (FET)
treatment 211–212
new trade theory models 33
non-discrimination protection 208–209
non-governmental organisations (NGOs):
land rights 263–264; as source of law
67–68
non-interference principle 54
North American Free Trade Agreement
(NAFTA) 44–45, 233–234

'obsolescing bargain' 202
'OLI paradigm' 9–10, 36, 120
online transactions 158
Organisation for Economic Cooperation
and Development (OECD):
Guidelines on Multinational
Enterprises 254; labour rights
267; tax treaties 163
ownership: Dunning's framework
10, 36, 120; extent of ownership
in SOEs 83–84; forms of SOEs
84–85; location choice decision
process 120; privatization 92–94

performance requirement prohibitions 218
place brand equity 129–130
place marketing 118, 122–123, 126–131,
134–137; *see also* location choice for
MNCs
policy *see* government policy; international
investment policy
policy advocacy 145–148
political economy of international
investment policy 185–190
political parties 65, 70–71
political risk insurance 155
political science: characterization of
investors 25; disciplinary silos 26–28;
foreign investment's impact in host state
279; host-state characteristics 26; impact
of foreign investment in host state 26;
investment policy 275; scope 21–24;
values 24–25
Porter's Value Chain 39, *40*
precedent in law 67
pre-establishment protections, IIAs 207
pre-globalization period 32
privatization, state-owned enterprises
92–94
profit maximization: economics of 7;
state-owned enterprises 90
property rights: disciplinary silos 2; host-
state characteristics 27, 106, 275–276;
law scholarship 17; political science 24
protection *see* investor protection
public institutions: international business
scholarship 12–13; international
investment policy 188; law scholarship
15, 19–20
public movements *see* social movements
public opinion, national security 195–196
public safety *see* national security

rational choice, location choice decision
process 124–126
regulatory context: international investment
agreements' role 202; investor protection
and host states' right to regulate
200–201, 218–222; investor protection
provisions 208–218; location choice for
MNCs 156–157; national security
192–194
resource-extracting companies (RECs)
165–168
resource-seeking FDI 36
return-on-assets (ROA) 90
return-on-equity (ROE) 90

return-on-sales (ROS) 90
Rio Declaration on Environment and Development 250, 251
risk: disciplinary silos 2; international investment agreements 106–107; political risk insurance 155
Roundtable on Sustainable Palm Oil (RSPO) 254

'selectivity' as a fiscal issue 170–171, 174–175
services sector 278
'shared value', corporate social responsibility 249
Singapore: regulatory context 156; SME development boards 154–155
small and medium enterprises (SMEs): development boards 154–155; political risk insurance 155; regulatory context 156–157; use of banks 157–158
social issues in FDI 247–248; corporate social responsibility (CSR) 248–249, 252–255; environmental and social impact assessments 255–259; human rights 252; labour rights 264–267; land rights 259–264; quality investment 248–254; sustainable development 249–251
social movements: private and state-owned enterprises 82; as source of law 67–68
'soft law' 57–58
source of law 70–73
Sovereign Wealth Fund Institute 76
sovereign wealth funds (SWFs) 75; conclusions about 94–95; heterogeneity 75; importance to international economy 74; largest examples of 76, 77, **78**; overview 76–77; performance of 87–89
sovereignty, international law 53–54
special economic zones (SEZs) 266
stakeholder approach, corporate social responsibility 248
stare decisis 67
state aid 169–173, 174–175, 179
state responsibility, international law 55–56
state sovereignty, international law 53–54
state-owned enterprises (SOEs) 74–76; conclusions about 94–95; extent of ownership 83–84; geographic distribution of activities 86; heterogeneity 75; importance to international economy 74; influence of government ownership assumptions

74–75; influence of government ownership in practice 87–94; influence of government ownership in theory 80–87; largest firms 79; national security 196; overview 78–80; ownership forms 84–85; performance of 90–92; privatization effects 92–94
state-owned multinational enterprises (SOMNEs) 86
states *see* foreign investment's impact in host state; host-state characteristics
subsidies, tax as 173–178
Subsidies and Countervailing Measures Agreement (SCM) 173–174, 177
supply chains: in the 21st century 31–32; globalization of production 38–41
sustainable development 221, 249–251, 252
Sustainable Development Goals (SDGs) 250

tax: competition as an investment promotion tool 160–161, 164–168, 178–179; declining to tax 169–173; disciplinary approaches 271; EU state-aid law on tax competition 169–173; income tax and double taxation 161–164; law scholarship 15; location choice for MNCs 156; strategies to promote investment 161–168; as subsidy in the WTO 173–178
technology sector, national security concerns 196–197
terrorism 195–196; *see also* national security
trade: in the 21st century 31–32; evolving scholarship 49–50; free trade economics 6–7; globalization of production 38–49; investment promotion agencies 148; national production paradigm 32–38; traditional theory 33; traditional trade politics 33–35, **35**; *see also* free trade; international trade law
trade agreements, law scholarship 14; *see also* free trade agreements; international investment agreements
Trade in Value Added (TiVA) dataset 44
trade unions 188, 264, 266–267, 268
Trade-Related Investment Measures Agreement (TRIMs Agreement) 60–61, 173
transaction-cost analysis 5
transfer of funds provisions, IIAs 216–218
treaty instruments 57, 59–60, 68, 70

290 *Index*

'treaty shopping' 238, 243–244
'triple bottom line' 248

umbrella clauses, IIAs 62, 207–208, 230–231
United Nations Commission on International Trade Law (UNCITRAL) 231–232, 241–242
United Nations Conference on Environment and Development (UNCED) 249–250
United States: Foreign Sales Company (FSC) regime 177; international investment agreements 112–113; international investment policy 188; investor-state dispute settlement mechanisms 245–246; national security 191–192; place marketing 122–123
Universal Declaration of Human Rights (UDHR) 264
unlawful expropriation protection against 214–216

value chains: in the 21st century 31–32; corporate social responsibility 249; defining 39, *40*; globalization of production 38–41, *39–45*; investment promotion 154; *see also* global value chains
values: economic scholarship 6–7; international business scholarship 11–12; law scholarship 16–18; political science scholarship 24–25
vertical FDI 5–6, 47, 103

women, equal labour rights 264
workers: FDI liberalization 186–187; foreign direct investment impacts 45–46, 48–49; labour rights in FDI 264–267; national production paradigm 34–38
World Summit on Sustainable Development 252
World Trade Organization (WTO): implications for tax competition 176–178; legal agreements 60–61; tax as subsidy approach 173–178